"Mark Rooker and Ken Keathley have produced a [...] students and lay people, alike. Science-faith discussi[...] [...] for the uninitiated. Rooker and Keathley bring much needed clarity to the conversation. *40 Questions about Creation and Evolution* provides the reader with an excellent introduction to the key issues in the science-faith dialogue and helps the reader appreciate the varying perspectives held by Christians. The question and answer format allows the reader to engage the topic in manageable, "bit-sized chunks." I whole-heartedly recommend *40 Questions about Creation and Evolution*. In fact, I plan to keep a copy on my bookshelf."

—Fazale (Fuz) R. Rana
Vice President of Research and Apologetics, Reasons To Believe

"No one interested in exploring this issue can ignore this book. It is superb in it' breadth and the depth explored in each question is surprising substantial. This work will serve a valuable purpose for many years to come. My two colleagues have rendered an extremely valuable service to the Body of Christ!"

—Daniel L. Akin
President, Southeastern Baptist Theological Seminary

"Rooker and Keathley have produced a book that is accessible and brief enough for use in Bible and doctrinal studies in the local church, but dense and comprehensive enough to serve as a textbook in a seminary classroom. It will surely become an invaluable resource on the doctrine of creation and related topics for seminarians, pastors, and scholars alike, and deserves a spot on the office bookshelves of each."

—John D. Laing
Associate Professor of Systematic Theology & Philosophy, J. Dalton Havard
School for Theological Studies, Southwestern Baptist Theological Seminary

"*40 Questions about Creation and Evolution* is the best one-stop introduction to questions about creation and evolution. Ken Keathley is an accomplished theologian and Mark Rooker is an accomplished Old Testament scholar, and together they have produced a fine book."

—Bruce Riley Ashford
Provost and Associate Professor of Theology & Culture, Southeastern Baptist Theological Seminary

"The Bible is God's book–true and trustworthy–from Genesis to Revelation. Though many question the historicity of Genesis and the creation account, God's story from the earliest verses of Scripture is without error. But an accurate creation account matters more than to fulfill man's curiosities about human origins. It is germane to the full narrative of Scripture and essential to the gospel message itself. In *40 Questions About Creation and Evolution*, Mark F. Rooker and Kenneth D. Keathley helpfully set forth key issues pertaining to creationism, the Genesis account, and how these issues intersect throughout God's written revelation of himself. I am grateful to God for this fine work by Rooker and Keathley, and I wish I could place a copy of it in the hand of every church member."

—Dr. Jason Allen
President, Midwestern Baptist Theological Seminary & College

"40 Questions About Creation and Evolution is the most helpful reference volume available for the student attempting to distill the essence of the debate into critical questions and cogent answers. While I do not agree with all the conclusions, I recognize commendable fairness and succinct and thorough coverage of the subject on the part of two of my favorite authors. I guarantee the reader of this book a fabulous experience."

—Paige Patterson
President, Southwestern Baptist Theological Seminary

"As a pastor, I am always scouting for books for our people—especially on difficult and controversial subjects. The relationship between the doctrine of creation and the science of evolution is one of those subjects. So, in this case, I need a book I can be comfortable handing to a PhD in microbiology, a homeschool mom, and my own 17-year-old son. This is that book. It is scholarly, compelling, and accessible. The thing I appreciate most is that its authors trust the Word of God more than a particular doctrinal expression. Christian scholarship should always be open to the most accurate and refined expressions of truth."

—Pete Schemm
Pastor, Cave Spring Baptist Church, Roanoke, VA

"We discover in the book, *40 Questions About Creation and Evolution,* a well-researched doctrinal treatise engaging a topic of on-going interest and critical importance: the origins of our world. Ken Keathley and Mark Rooker offer us an in-depth, Christian exploration of the most pertinent matters on this much discussed yet often misunderstood doctrine. Given that the authors disclose their personal perspectives early in the book, Keathley and Rooker still represent all the major sides of this issue fairly and accurately. Each position is examined regarding its faithfulness to the teachings of Scripture and how each interprets the evidences of science. The presentation and structure of the book is itself a model for proper theological method: sound biblical exegesis that is historically informed, development of coherent doctrinal beliefs, and relevant, apologetic engagement. Keathley and Rooker have interjected into the contemporary debate a significant work that must surely be considered by all who desire to participate seriously in the discussion of Christian perspectives on this doctrine. These two authors have provided the evangelical world, if not all of Christendom, a convictional and charitable treatment on creation and evolution that for years to come will most certainly be a classical text on this central tenet of the Christian faith."

—R. Stanton Norman
Provost and Executive Vice President for Campus Life,
Professor of Theology, Oklahoma Baptist University

"Mark Rooker and Ken Keathley are nationally known scholars who bring together their respective areas of expertise (Old Testament and Theology) to provide cogent evangelical Christian responses to the most interesting questions about creation and evolution. Pastors, well-informed laypersons, and college and seminary students will find this book immensely helpful in framing the key issues on this crucial topic."

—Steve Lemke
Provost and Professor of Philosophy and Ethics, New Orleans Baptist Theological Seminary

"Kenneth Keathley and Mark Rooker have written one of those books that belongs on every Christian's bookshelf. It treats a very controversial topic in a very fair, irenic yet bold fashion that gives light and not heat in every chapter. The chapter dealing with belief in theistic evolution is a case in point. After reading this chapter, one comes away with a clear understanding of the various shades and nuances of this perspective and its inherent strengths and weaknesses. Scientists, theologians, pastors, and lay people would all be wise to get this book, read it, and keep it for future reference."

—James Merritt
Pastor, Cross Pointe Church, Duluth, GA

"Ken Keathley and Mark Rooker provide a map through the tangled 'creation and evolution' forest. More than that, they offer the reader skills to read the map intelligently. You will not encounter partisan rancor in this volume, which is one of its great strengths. You will discover solid, reflective, Christian thought on crucial questions related to this contentious topic. This is a helpful and needed resource for the church and the classroom."

—Heath A. Thomas
Director of Ph.D. Studies and Associate Professor of Old Testament & Hebrew,
Southeastern Baptist Theological Seminary

"Kenneth Keathley and Mark Rooker have given careful attention to the issues surrounding man and his origins. This book deals with the biblical witness, the scientific questions, and the apologetic application. Christians disagree on many points regarding these issues, but this book is a valuable tool regardless of where one comes down on the age of the earth or the finer questions of the relationship between science and exegesis."

—Russell D. Moore
President, Southern Baptist Ethics & Religious Liberty Commission

"There are many fine features in this valuable contribution to the ongoing debate on this profoundly important topic. First is the breadth of views presented. They give calm and judicious consideration of views that often produce attacks that give off more heat than light. They acknowledge that all views have some difficulties and themselves model that on some questions, different interpretations may be viable for evangelicals. At the same time, they recognize and identify essential elements in any evangelical view of creation. A second notable feature is the breadth of topics. A host of biblical, theological, scientific, and philosophical topics related to creation and evolution are addressed. The flood, the image of God in humans, the fall, and Darwinism as an ideology are just some of the forty questions the authors include in their study. Another aspect that deserves mention is the 40 questions format. While reading the entire book is valuable, readers may easily locate the topics of most pressing interest to them in the table of contents. I congratulate my colleagues on this fine piece of work."

—John S. Hammett
John L. Dagg Senior Professor of Systematic Theology and Associate Dean for Theological Studies,
Southeastern Baptist Theological Seminary

40 QUESTIONS ABOUT
Creation and Evolution

Kenneth D. Keathley and Mark F. Rooker

Benjamin L. Merkle, Series Editor

40 Questions About Creation and Evolution
© 2014 by Kenneth D. Keathley and Mark F. Rooker

Published by Kregel Academic, an imprint of Kregel Publications, 2450 Oak Industrial Dr. NE, Grand Rapids, MI 49505-6020.

This book is a title in the 40 Questions Series edited by Benjamin L. Merkle.

Library of Congress Cataloging-in-Publication Data

Rooker, Mark F., author.
    40 questions about creation & evolution / Mark F. Rooker, Kenneth D. Keathley.
      pages cm
    Includes bibliographical references and index.
    1. Creation—Miscellanea. 2. Evolution—Miscellanea. 3. Bible and evolution--Miscellanea. I. Keathley, Kenneth, 1958– author. II. Title. III. Title: 40 questions about creation and evolution. IV. Title: Forty questions about creation & evolution.
    BS651.R753 2014
    231.7'652—dc23

                                          2014007377

ISBN 978-0-8254-2941-5

Printed in the United States of America
18 19 20 21 22 23 24 25 / 6 5 4 3 2

Dedicated to Ava Dell Rooker,
my second granddaughter,
whose very life has caused me to reflect
on the beauty and wonder of God's creation.
—Mark F. Rooker

For my grandchildren—Elliott,
Grant, and those yet to come.
I pray that you will grow up
confident that the God who created
the heavens and the earth has revealed
himself and redeemed us through
his Son, Jesus Christ.
—Kenneth K. Keathley

Contents

Abbreviations / 11

Part 1: Questions about the Doctrine of Creation

1. What Are the Major Issues and Concepts Concerning Creation and Evolution? / 15
2. What Are the Distinctive Elements to the Doctrine of Creation? / 25
3. Why Is the Doctrine of Creation Important? / 35
4. What Is Creation's Role in the Grand Narrative of the Bible? / 45

Part 2: Questions about Creation and Genesis 1–2

5. What Is the Relationship of Genesis 1-2 to Other Creation Accounts? / 57
6. How Did God Create Everything? / 65
7. What Is the Connection of Genesis 1:1 to Genesis 1? / 73
8. What Is the Relationship of Genesis 1 to Genesis 2? / 83
9. What Is the Meaning of the Seventh Day? / 91
10. What Does Genesis Teach About the Purpose of Man's Creation? / 101

Part 3: Questions about the Days of Creation

11. What Is the Gap Theory? / 111
12. What Is the Day-Age Theory? / 119
13. What Is the Framework Theory? / 127
14. What Is the Temple Inauguration Theory? / 137
15. What Is the Historical Creationism Theory? / 147
16. What Is the Twenty-Four Hour Theory? / 157

Part 4: Questions about the Age of the Earth

17. Are There Gaps in the Biblical Genealogies? / 169
18. What Have Been the Attempts to Determine the Age of the Earth? / 179
19. What Are the Evidences that the Universe Is Young? / 189
20. What Are the Evidences that the Universe Is Old? / 201
21. If the Universe Is Young, How Can We See Stars So Far Away? / 211
22. What Is the Mature Creation Argument? / 217

Part 5: Questions about the Fall and the Flood

23. What Does It Mean that Man Is Made in God's Image? / 227
24. Were Adam and Eve Historical Persons? / 237
25. What Was the Nature of the Original Sin? / 245
26. Was There Animal Death Before the Fall? / 255
27. What Effect Did the Fall Have on Creation? / 263
28. What Does Genesis 3:15 Say About God's Plan for Creation? / 271
29. Does the Flood Depict a Re-Creation? / 279
30. What Was the Extent of Noah's Flood? (Part 1: The Biblical Evidence) / 285
31. What Was the Extent of Noah's Flood? (Part 2: The Geological Evidence) / 295

Part 6: Questions about Evolution and Intelligent Design

32. What Is the Theory of Evolution? / 313
33. What Is Darwinism? / 329
34. How Is Darwinism an Ideology? / 335
35. Why Are Some Evolutionists Opposed to Darwinism? / 345
36. What Are the Arguments for Evolution? / 357
37. What Are the Arguments Against Evolution? / 363
38. Can a Christian Hold to Theistic Evolution? / 377
39. What Is Intelligent Design? / 387
40. What Is the Fine-Tuning Argument? / 397

Select Bibliography / 409
Scripture Index / 415
Ancient Sources Index / 429

Abbreviations

AB	Anchor Bible
ABD	*Anchor Bible Dictionary*. Edited by D. N. Freedman. 6 vols. New York, 1992
ANET	*Ancient Near Eastern Text Related to the Old Testament*. Edited by J. B. Pritchard. 3rd ed. Princeton, 1969
AUSS	*Andrews University Seminary Studies*
BDB	Brown, F., S. R. Driver, and C. A. Briggs. *A Hebrew and English Lexicon of the Old Testament*. Oxford, 1907
BT	*The Bible Translator*
BJRL	*Bulletin of the John Rylands University Library of Manchester*
BSac	*Bibliotheca Sacra*
CBQ	*Catholic Biblical Quarterly*
CJ	*Concordia Journal*
CTJ	*Calvin Theological Seminary*
DNTB	*Dictionary of New Testament Background*. Edited by C. A. Evans and S. E. Porter. Downers Grove, IL, 2000
DOTP	*Dictionary of the Old Testament: Pentateuch*. Edited by T. D. Alexander and D. W. Baker. Downers Grove, IL, 2003
EBC	Expositor's Bible Commentary
EDBT	*Evangelical Dictionary of Biblical Theology*. Edited by Walter A. Elwell. Grand Rapids, 1996
EDT	*Evangelical Dictionary of Theology*
EvQ	*Evangelical Quarterly*
ExAud	*Ex Audito*
GKC	*Gesenius' Hebrew Grammar*. Edited by E. Kautzsch. Translated by A. E. Cowley. 2nd ed. Oxford, 1910
HALOT	Koehler, L., Baumgartner, and J. J. Stamm. *The Hebrew and Aramaic Lexicon of the Old Testament*. Translated and edited under the supervision of M. E. J. Richardson. 4 vols. Leiden, 1994–1999
HTR	*Harvard Theological Review*
IBHS	*An Introduction to Biblical Hebrew Syntax*. B. K. Waltke and M. O'Connor. Winona Lake, IN, 1990
ICC	International Critical Commentary

IDBSup	*Interpreter's Dictionary of the Bible: Supplementary* Volume. Edited by K. Crim. Nashville, 1976
JBL	*Journal of Biblical Literature*
JETS	*Journal of the Evangelical Theological Society*
JPSTC	Jewish Publication Society Torah Commentary
JR	*Journal of Religion*
JSOTSupp	Journal for the Study of the New Testament: Supplement Series
JSJ	*Journal for the Study of Judaism Journal*
JTS	*Journal of Theological Studies*
MSJ	*The Master's Seminary Journal*
NAC	New American Commentary
NACSBT	NAC Studies in Bible and Theology
NICOT	New International Commentary on the Old Testament
NIDOTTE	*New International Dictionary of Old Testament Theology and Exegesis.* Edited by W. A. VanGemeren. 5 vols. Grand Rapids, 1997
NIGTC	New International Greek Testament Commentary
NIVAC	NIV Application Commentary
NSBT	New Studies in Biblical Theology
OTL	Old Testament Library
PAAJR	*Proceedings of the American Academy of Jewish Research*
PRSt	*Perspectives in Religious Studies*
Presb	*Presbyterion*
SBJT	*Southern Baptist Journal of Theology*
SBLDS	Society of Biblical Literature Dissertation Series
TDOT	*Theological Dictionary of the Old Testament.* Edited by G. J. Botterweck and H. Ringgren. Translated by J. T. Willis, G. W. Bromily, and D. E. Green. 8 vols. Grand Rapids, 1974–
TLOT	*Theological Lexicon of the Old Testament.* Edited by E. Jenni, with assistance from C. Westermann. Translated by M. E. Biddle. 3 vols. Peabody, MA, 1997
TrinJ	*Trinity Journal*
TynBul	*Tyndale Bulletin*
VT	*Vetus Testamentum*
WBC	Word Biblical Commentary
WTJ	*Westminster Theological Journal*
ZAW	*Zeitschrift für die alttestamentliche Wissenschaft*

PART 1

QUESTIONS ABOUT THE DOCTRINE OF CREATION

What Are the Major Issues and Concepts Concerning Creation and Evolution?

Type the word "evolution" in the Amazon.com search line, and it will offer over 61,000 books. A similar search for books on "creation" will yield over 31,000 results. The creation/evolution controversy is an overwhelmingly large subject, and the debate shows no signs of diminishing. This book attempts to distill the conversation to the 40 most significant questions and, in so doing, provide the reader with an adequate overview of the main issues.

The creation/evolution controversy has been ongoing for over 200 years (the debate actually predates Darwin's publication of *On the Origin of Species*, 1859). Certain issues, concepts, and views are recurring while other significant notions have recently come to the forefront, and anyone hoping to have a grasp of the debate must be familiar with them. This chapter briefly discusses the four major approaches to creationism, the distinction between creation and creationism, the role that presuppositions play in evaluating scientific data, and the various concordist and nonconcordist interpretations of Genesis 1–3.

The Major Approaches to Creationism
Young-Earth Creationism (YEC)

YEC proponents argue for a literal, six-day creation that occurred approximately 6,000 years ago. They contend that the proper interpretation of Genesis 1–3 requires this position. Death, disease, and predation (i.e., the predator/prey relationship) entered the world through the fall of Adam. For the most part, geological evidences of an ancient earth are attributed to the flood of Noah. YEC advocates find the astronomical evidences of an ancient universe (such as light from distant stars) much more difficult to explain. A variety of theories are offered, but the predominant one is still the mature creation view, otherwise known as the "appearance of age" hypothesis. We address questions about the age of the earth in Questions 17 through 22. The leading representative group today for the YEC position is the organization Answers in Genesis, headquartered in Petersburg, Kentucky.[1]

Old-Earth Creationism (OEC)

Old earth creationism is sometimes called progressive creationism. OEC proponents argue that God created in successive stages over a period of millions or billions of years. In other words, OEC advocates accept the scientific evidence for an ancient universe (and the big bang theory), but they do not accept the predominant biological theory of origins, which of course is Darwinian evolution. OEC theorizes that God miraculously created Adam and Eve about 60 to 100 thousand years ago. The strongest objection YEC proponents have to OEC is its acceptance of animal death and disease prior to Adam's fall. We address questions about death and the fall in Questions 25–27. The leading representative group today for the OEC position is the organization Reasons to Believe, based in Glendora, California.[2]

Evolutionary Creationism (EC)

Proponents of evolutionary creationism (also called "theistic evolution") accept the current scientific theories both of the origin of the universe and of the human race. That is, EC accepts the Darwinian hypothesis that all life, including humans, descended from a common ancestor (generally understood to be a single-cell life form). EC advocates believe that God endued creation with the principles and laws that caused the essential components of life to self-organize. Random mutation provided the immense variety we observe in the fossil record and in living things today, and natural selection determined which species survived and which went extinct. Some EC proponents do not understand Adam and Eve to be literal persons (though, as we will see, there are significant exceptions to this point). We address questions pertaining to this model in Question 24 and Question 38. The leading representative group today for the EC position is the BioLogos Foundation, located in Grand Rapids, Michigan.[3]

Intelligent Design (ID)

The Intelligent Design movement began as a group of scholars and scientists who were unconvinced by the Darwinian hypothesis and were disturbed by the philosophical naturalism that seems to underlie it. ID proponents argue that an objective examination of the scientific evidence alone (without appealing to the Genesis account) will lead an unbiased inquirer to the

---

1. http://www.answersingenesis.org.
2. http://www.reasons.org.
3. http://www.biologos.org.

conclusion that design by an Intelligent Being (i.e., God) makes an inference to the best explanation. ID contends that arguing over the age of the earth distracts from the bigger adversary—Darwinism and the philosophical atheism underlying it. As a result, one can find both YEC and OEC proponents within the ID movement, and in fact a handful of ID advocates hold to certain non-Darwinian versions of evolution (Michael Behe, author of *Darwin's Black Box*, is a prime example). We address questions pertaining specifically to ID in Questions 39 through 40. The leading representative group today for the ID position is the Discovery Institute, headquartered in Seattle, Washington.[4]

The Distinction between Creation and Creationism

We often forget to make the distinction between creation and creationism. One is a doctrine while the other is an apologetic approach. On the one hand, creation is a foundational doctrine of the Christian faith. The essential features of the doctrine of creation are unchangeable tenets. The Bible teaches that those features include the truths that God, without compulsion or necessity, freely created the universe out of nothing according to his own will and for his own good purposes. Though marred by the arrival of evil and sin, creation reflects the nature of its Creator. So creation is both great and good.

On the other hand, creationism is an apologetic approach which attempts to integrate the doctrine of creation with the current understandings of the natural sciences. In particular, creationism seeks to relate the first 11 chapters of Genesis to the latest findings of science. For example, how does the biblical account of God creating the sun, moon, and stars square with what we understand through astronomy? Or the creation of plants and animals with research in biology and genetics? Or the account of Noah's flood with geology? Or the account of the dispersing of nations after the Tower of Babel with anthropology? Creationism deals with issues such as the age of the universe, the origin of the first humans, and the nature of the world prior to the fall of the original couple.

So creation is an unchanging and unchangeable doctrine while creationism, by its very nature, must constantly change and be amended. The doctrine of creation is derived from Scripture and is as old as the biblical witness itself. Creationism is relatively new, because it arose alongside the scientific revolution in the seventeenth century. As science developed, so did creationism, especially after Darwin published *On the Origin of Species* in 1859. We must keep the distinction between creation and creationism in mind as we explore the important issues highlighted by this book. We must know what to hold firmly and what must be open to revision. Our commitment to doctrine must be strong, but we hold to any particular apologetic approach much more loosely. We address the essential features of the doctrine

---

4. http://www.discovery.org.

of creation in the next three questions. The remainder of the book focuses primarily (but not exclusively) on issues relating to creationism.

The Role of Presuppositions when Interpreting Empirical Data

Everyone approaches the empirical evidence with presuppositions. It is generally recognized that facts are not self-interpreting. No facts "just speak for themselves." *Presuppositionalism* recognizes that all approaches to truth begin with certain presuppositions, assumptions, or postulates, and these assumptions are taken on faith.[5] This is true of all human studies, whether the field of study is mathematics, geology, or theology. A study of the universe must start with one of two presuppositions: *supernaturalism* or *naturalism*.[6] Christian theists start with the presupposition of supernaturalism. Supernaturalism is the view that reality is greater than nature. God transcends the universe and is its Creator. Atheists start with the presupposition of naturalism (or more precisely, philosophical naturalism). The astrophysicist Carl Sagan famously began his discussion of the universe by declaring, "The Cosmos is all that is or ever was or ever will be."[7] Sagan is not making an empirical observation; he is giving his presuppositional starting point.

The question is how, when, and how much the empirical evidence should cause us to adjust or change our presuppositions. What should we do when the scientific data seems to clash strongly with our presuppositions? If that happens, should we consider completely jettisoning our presuppositions? In this book we will examine the views of Darwinian evolutionists and theistic evolutionists, old-earth creationists and young-earth creationists. Perhaps it should not be surprising, but the positions at the ends of the spectrum— Darwinian evolutionists and young-earth creationists—are the positions that hold the most adamantly to their respective presuppositions. Both refuse to let the empirical data cause them to step away from their original philosophical commitments. Theistic evolutionists and old-earth creationists, by contrast, more readily allow the scientific data to affect their respective interpretative models.

In the writings of Darwinists and young-earth creationists, the controlling influence of presuppositions is striking. As noted previously, the two positions are at opposite ends of the spectrum of positions. Yet, they have some features in common. Significantly, both recognize two things about the universe: first, the universe appears to be ancient and, second, it appears to be

---

5. See R. C. Sproul, John Gerstner, and Arthur Lindsley, *Classical Apologetics: A Rational Defense of the Christian Faith and a Critique of Presuppositional Apologetics* (Grand Rapids: Baker, 1984), 304–9; John Frame, *The Doctrine of the Knowledge of God* (Phillipsburg, N.J.: P&R, 1987), 348–54.

6. See Phillip Johnson, *Reason in the Balance: The Case against Naturalism in Science, Law, and Education* (Downers Grove, Ill.: InterVarsity Press, 1995).

7. Carl Sagan, *Cosmos* (New York: Random House, 1980), 1.

very well designed. But they both believe these appearances are an illusion. What they disagree on is what part is the illusion. Darwinists believe the earth is old and the inference of design is a misconception. Young earth creationists argue that the truth is the other way around: the world is designed but its origin is very recent.

What is going on here? Controlling presuppositions are at work. Atheists presuppose naturalism while theists presuppose supernaturalism. A precommitment to naturalism can be seen in the writings of the well-known atheist Richard Dawkins. He admits that the world certainly appears designed and that, at first blush, the Darwinian explanation seems absurd.[8] However, Dawkins believes that Darwinism allows him to dismiss the evidences of design. In a well-known passage, Dawkins declares,

> An atheist before Darwin could have said, following Hume: 'I have no explanation for complex biological design. All I know is that God isn't a good explanation, so we must wait and hope that somebody comes up with a better one.' I can't help feeling that such a position, though logically sound, would have left one feeling pretty unsatisfied, and that although atheism might have been *logically* tenable before Darwin, Darwin made it possible to be an intellectually fulfilled atheist.[9]

A presupposition to philosophical naturalism (i.e., materialism or atheism) predisposes Dawkins to embrace Darwinism over the evidences of design. Evolutionary biologist Richard Lewontin is even more explicit:

> Our willingness to accept scientific claims that are against common sense is the key to an understanding of the real struggle between science and the supernatural. We take the side of science *in spite* of its failure to fulfill many of its extravagant promises of health and life, *in spite* of the tolerance of the scientific community of unsubstantiated just-so-stories, because we have a prior commitment to materialism. It is not that the methods and institutions of science somehow compel us to accept a material explanation of the phenomenal world, but on the contrary, that we are forced by our *a priori* adherence to material causes to create an apparatus of investigation and a set of concepts that produce material explanations, no matter how counterintuitive, no matter how mystifying to

---

8. Richard Dawkins, *The Blind Watchmaker: Why the Evidence of Evolution Reveals a Universe without Design* (New York: W. W. Norton, 1987), 3.
9. Ibid., 6.

> the uninitiated. Moreover, that materialism is absolute, for we cannot allow a Divine Foot in the door. The eminent Kant scholar Lewis Beck used to say that anyone who could believe in God could believe in anything. To appeal to an omnipotent deity is to allow that at any moment the regularities of nature may be ruptured, that miracles may happen.[10]

In the above quote, Lewontin admits two things. First, the scientific enterprise itself does not require an acceptance of materialism. And second, his absolute allegiance to materialism causes him to reject the inference of design, no matter how compelling the evidence. With these words Lewontin reveals that he is not operating as a dispassionate scientist, but as a devotee to his presuppositions.

Presuppositionalism or Fideism?

There are a number of approaches to the relationship between faith and reason, and at this point it is helpful to note the distinction between presuppositionalism and *fideism*.[11] As we noted before, presuppositionalism recognizes that all approaches to truth begin with certain assumptions that are taken on faith. However, there is one important caveat at this point. The presuppositionalist believes that the validity of one's presuppositions must eventually be tested by using the laws of logic and be demonstrated by a consistency with the evidential findings. Fideism, by contrast, does not believe one's presuppositions can be tested. Like the presuppositionalist, the fideist believes that one starts with certain presuppositions. But unlike the presuppositionalist, the fideist does not subject his starting assumptions to any type of feedback or check. The fideist operates by "blind faith."

Most YEC proponents identify themselves as presuppositionalists.[12] They start with the presupposition of the Bible's inspiration and authority (as do all conservative evangelicals). YEC advocates, however, add another crucial presupposition. Namely, they seem to hold that the YEC reading of Genesis 1–11 is the only interpretation available to the Bible-believing Christian.[13] The approach of many YEC adherents seems to veer perilously

---

10. Richard Lewontin, "Billions and Billions of Demons," *New York Review of Books* 44, no. 1 (January 9, 1997): 28–31 (emphasis original).
11. See Norman Geisler, *Christian Apologetics* (Grand Rapids: Baker, 1976), 47–65.
12. Ronald Numbers, *The Creationists: The Evolution of Scientific Creationism* (New York: Alfred Knopf, 1992), 207.
13. "Since the Bible undisputedly teaches a young earth, when someone claims that scientific evidence proves otherwise, we can be certain that they are mistaken" (Tim Chaffey and Jason Lisle, *Old-Earth Creationism on Trial: The Verdict Is In* [Green Forest, Ark.: Master, 2008], 153). See also John MacArthur, "Creation Believe It or Not," *MSJ* 13, no. 1 (Spring 2002): 17.

close to fideism. Consider the testimony of Kurt Wise about his attitude toward empirical evidence:

> As I shared with my professors years ago when I was in college, if all the evidence in the universe turned against creationism, I would be the first to admit it, but I would still be a creationist because that is what the Word of God seems to indicate. Here I must stand.[14]

As the context makes clear, when Wise spoke of creationism, he meant the young-earth position. His courage, candor, and fidelity to the Scriptures must be commended. But if one's presuppositions are unassailable, then his approach has shifted from presuppositionalism to fideism.

In contrast, old-earth creationists and evolutionary creationists concede that they allow the finding of science to influence the way they approach the creation account in Genesis. Philosophically, they follow more closely in the tradition known as *empiricism*. Empiricism allows experience and evidence to have a significant role in the formation of one's position. Young-earth creationists are strongly critical of this feature and often characterize OEC and EC in very harsh terms.[15]

Integrating the Bible and Science: Concordist and Non-concordist Approaches

So how should Christians go about the task of reconciling what they understand the Bible to teach about origins with the consensus understandings within the scientific community? Or is such an attempt misguided from the start? Interpretive models that attempt to harmonize Scripture and science are called *concordist* approaches (*concord* means "harmony" or "agreement"). Other models understand the Bible and science to be speaking in such different ways that they are non-overlapping. Not surprisingly, these models are called *non-concordist* approaches.

Concordists contend that God has revealed himself through two books—the book of nature and the Bible.[16] They argue that creation gives us general revelation about the Creator (Ps. 19:1–6) while Scripture gives

---

14. Kurt Wise, *In Six Days: Why Fifty Scientists Chose to Believe in Creation*, ed. John F. Ashton (Green Forest, Ark.: Master, 2001), 355.

15. See, e.g., Jonathan Sarfarti, *Refuting Compromise: A Biblical and Scientific Refutation of "Progressive Creationism" (Billions of Years), as Popularized by Astronomer Hugh Ross* (Green Forest, Ark.: Master, 2004).

16. Hugh Ross, *A Matter of Days: Resolving a Creation Controversy* (Colorado Springs: NavPress, 2004), 87–90. Some attempt to narrowly define concordism to include only progressive creationism. In this book we define concordism as any attempt to legitimately integrate the findings of science with Scripture.

us special revelation that reveals who the God of creation is (Ps. 19:7–11). Therefore, Christians have the ability and responsibility to adopt an interpretive model that constructively integrates Genesis 1–3 with modern science. Often this is accomplished by a significant reinterpretation of either the natural or biblical data.

Concordist Approaches
Concordists interpret the creation account of Genesis 1–2 with a number of different theories. The major concordist theories are these:

- *The 24-hour theory*: This theory holds that the days of Genesis 1 are literal 24-hour days, and that the universe was created in six days.
- *The gap theory*: Proponents of this view posit that an indeterminate period of time—a gap—exists between the first two verses of the Genesis account. This view allows for the earth to be ancient while still interpreting the six days of creation as literal 24-hour days.
- *The day-age theory*: Day-age theorists argue that each day of creation in Genesis one is an era of time. This view understands the six days to extend over millions or billions of years.
- *The promised land theory*: This theory holds that the Hebrew expression for "In the beginning" denotes an unspecified length of time—perhaps billions of years. The six days of Genesis 1 speak of the preparation of the promised land and do not refer to the creation of the earth or universe as a whole.

Each of these theories has a chapter devoted to it in Part 3 of this book.

Non-concordist Approaches
Proponents of non-concordism view concordism as misguided. They believe that attempts to harmonize the Bible and science fail to take Scripture on its own terms. Therefore, concordism is doomed to failure and, as an apologetic endeavor, does more damage than good. The major non-concordist approaches are as follows:

- *Genesis as myth*: Many neo-Orthodox and liberal theologians view Genesis in mythical terms. They believe that the author of Genesis borrowed many of the details of the creation account from prior Canaanite and Mesopotamian myths.
- *Genesis as allegory*: Some evangelicals consider Genesis 1–3 to be a nonliteral description of the general human condition. Rather than providing actual history, Genesis presents the theological truths that God is the sovereign Creator and that humanity is estranged from him due to our sinfulness.

- *Genesis as literary device*: This position views Genesis 1–3 as a polemic against the polytheistic idolatry of the surrounding culture. The six days of creation are understood to be a literary structure rather than literal 24-hour days. The first three days describe the forming of creation, while the second three days describe the filling of creation. The framework theory and the temple inauguration theory are examples of evangelical versions of non-concordist interpretations. Though they view the six days of creation as a literary device, they reject the low view of Scripture as expressed by the myth and allegory positions.

Separate chapters are devoted to the framework theory and the temple inauguration theory in Part 3. We address the question of whether or not the mythological and allegorical approaches to Genesis are viable options to evangelicals in Questions 24 ("Were Adam and Eve Historical Persons?") and 38 ("Can a Christian Hold to Theistic Evolution?").

A Word as We Move Forward

No issue has less unanimity among evangelicals than the matter of discerning the best way to relate the doctrine of creation to the scientific theory of evolution. Therefore, we devote much of the book simply to surveying the options proposed by various camps. The arena for the debate is rapidly changing, and the number of scientific discoveries, especially in the field of genetics, is accelerating. By necessity some of the positions set forth in these pages are done so tentatively.

None of the four views—young-earth creationism, old-earth creationism, evolutionary creationism, and intelligent design—are without serious problems. We, the authors, have differing opinions with one leaning to young-earth creationism (Rooker) and the other to old-earth creationism (Keathley). At times our differences show up in the answers we provide to the upcoming questions. But our fellowship in Christ is strong. We both affirm the inspiration and inerrancy of Scripture, and we both believe that the God Who gave us the Bible is the God Who created heaven and earth.

These are exciting days to be involved in the task of developing a theology of science. Evangelicals are a missional people. As such we cannot shy away from the difficult issues presented by origins science. We must engage the natural sciences with confidence and integrity. We must endeavor that the Lord Jesus Christ will have worshippers in every vocation, and we must advance the kingdom of God into every arena of life—including the natural sciences.

REFLECTION QUESTIONS

1. What are the differences between creation and creationism?

2. What is the primary disagreement that young-earth creationists have with the old-earth creationist position?

3. What role do presuppositions play in our interpretation of the evidences?

4. What are the distinguishing characteristics between concordist and non-concordist approaches?

5. Why have young-earth creationists, old-earth creationists, and some evolutionary creationists joined together in the intelligent design movement?

What Are the Distinctive Elements to the Doctrine of Creation?

Controversy concerning the biblical teaching about creation is nothing new. For the most part, the opening declaration of the Bible—"In the beginning, God created the heavens and the earth"—has always been countercultural. During Old Testament times the Babylonians believed that the world was fashioned out of the carcass of a defeated goddess, while the Egyptians taught that a primordial chaos was prior to the emergence of the gods. By the time of the New Testament, the Greeks held that the world is eternal and that there was no initial moment of creation. This view, which came to be called *eternalism*, will make a comeback during the Enlightenment of the seventeenth and eighteenth centuries. The modern and postmodern views of nature are highlighted by a loss of confidence in the purpose and goodness of creation. In contrast, the scriptural understanding of creation stands against both ancient and modern views. God, without opposition or equal, called the world into existence out of nothing for his own good purposes.

The biblical doctrine of creation is unique. Even other monotheistic religions do not understand creation in the Trinitarian terms that Christianity does. We should not be surprised or discouraged by the controversies and debates about creation. Nor should we expect them to go away.

God is the Author of creation. Augustus Strong provides a definition of creation that we will use here: "By creation we mean that free act of the triune God by which in the beginning for his own glory he made, without the use of preexisting materials, the whole visible and invisible universe."[1] We will briefly note eight distinctive elements of the Christian doctrine of creation.

---

1. Augustus H. Strong, *Systematic Theology* (Valley Forge: Judson, 1907), 371.

God Created the World out of Nothing

The Bible teaches *creatio ex nihilo*—"creation out of nothing." The Apostle Paul declares that God "calls into existence the things that do not exist" (Rom. 4:17) while the author of Hebrews rejects any notion that the world was created out of pre-existing materials: "By faith we understand that the universe was created by the word of God, so that what is seen was not made out of things that are visible" (Heb. 11:3).

The ancient philosophers rejected any notion that something could be created out of nothing. Instead of *creatio ex nihilo*, they argued that *ex nihilo nihil fit* ("Out of nothing comes nothing").[2] When considering creation we have only three options: (1) God made the world out of himself; (2) God made the world out of something other than himself; or (3) God made the world out of nothing. All three options have been championed by various adherents, but the Bible clearly teaches option three: creation out of nothing.[3] The first option—that God made the world out of himself—leads to the notion that the world is divine or that it is at least a part of God. We will look at these views (called *pantheism* and *panentheism*, respectively) further in the next chapter.

The second option—that God created out of something other than himself—is called *dualism*. In the *Timaeus*, Plato taught that a deity (called the demiurge) created the world using pre-existing, formless matter.[4] Scripture, however, disallows any type of dualism. It teaches that God is the ultimate reality and that there is no room for any other: "I am the LORD, and there is no other, besides me there is no God" (Isa. 45:5). God worked with no pre-existing materials. If he had, then those materials would also have to be eternal and would in some way also have to be divine.

The third option—that God created out of nothing—is the position called *theism*. The Bible clearly teaches that God was before all things and created all things.[5] The early church prayed to the "Sovereign Lord, who made the heaven and the earth and the sea and everything in them" (Acts 4:24). Christians have always admitted that *creatio ex nihilo* is a difficult concept to grasp. J. I. Packer observes, "The act of creation is mystery to us; there is more in it than we can

---

2. Aristotle made this claim: "We ourselves are in agreement with them in holding that nothing can be said without qualification to come from what is not" (Aristotle, *Physics* 1.8 in *The Complete Works of Aristotle* vol. 1 (Princeton: Princeton Univ. Press, 1984), 327.

3. Theologians such as Karl Barth and Paul Tillich viewed "nothing" as a kind of substance (perhaps reflecting the influence of the existential philosophy of Martin Heidegger). They turned nonbeing into a virtual metaphysical reality of its own. For this reason, several theologians prefer the expression "without the use of preexisting materials."

4. Plato, *Timaeus*, 30–37 in *Plato: Complete Works*, trans. Donald Zeyl (Indianapolis: Hackett, 1997), 1236–42.

5. See, e.g., 1 Samuel 2:6–8; Nehemiah 9:6; Psalm 96:5; 115:15; Isaiah 42:5; 45: 7–8, 18–19; Jeremiah 51:15.

understand. We cannot create by fiat, and we do not know how God could. To say that he created 'out of nothing' is to confess the mystery, not explain it."[6]

God's act of creating is unique. Human creativity always requires the use of pre-existing materials. Only God can create out of nothing. The Genesis account, however, makes clear that though God created directly, immediately *ex nihilo*, he also created using existing "raw materials." For example, the text says that God made Adam out of dust from the ground (Gen. 2:7) and that he used the earth to bring forth vegetation (Gen. 1:11–12). The Bible teaches that God employed both methods—at times creating out of nothing and at other times creating with materials he had earlier called into existence.[7]

God Alone Is Eternal; Creation Began in Time

> *Before the mountains were brought forth,*
> *or ever you had formed the earth and the world,*
> *from everlasting to everlasting you are God. (Ps. 90:2)*

Space and time are elements of creation. "God is not 'in' either; nor is he bound by either as we are."[8] Whether or not time existed before the creation of the universe is a matter of ongoing discussion among Christian scholars, but the majority position has been that time is an element of creation and came into being at the initial moment of creation. Augustine jokingly replied to the question as to what God was doing before he created the world: "He was preparing hell for those who pry into such mysteries."[9] Augustine argued that the question had no meaning—if time is an element of creation then there was no "before" the events of Genesis 1:1.

In the ancient world, the debate was over whether or not the earth was eternal. Aristotle, and most of the Hellenistic philosophers after him, argued that the universe had no beginning and would have no end.[10] The advent of

---

6. J. I. Packer, *Concise Theology: A Guide to Historic Christian Beliefs* (Carol Stream, IL: Tyndale, 1993), 21. Bartholomew and Goheen observe, "This is truly one of the points through which logic can barely wade, whereas faith can swim" (Craig Bartholomew and Michael Goheen, *The Drama of Scripture: Finding Our Place in the Biblical Story* [Grand Rapids: Baker, 2004], 34).

7. "In 1769 before the rise of modern science John Gill's *Body of Divinity* distinguished the mediate creations of Adam out of dust and of Eve out of Adam from the earlier immediate creation out of nothing. The source of the distinction was Scripture, not scientific theory" (Gordon Lewis and Bruce Demarest, *Integrative Theology*, vol. 2 [Grand Rapids: Zondervan, 1996], 36).

8. Packer, *Concise Theology*, 21; cf. Wayne Grudem, *Systematic Theology* (Grand Rapids: Zondervan, 1994), 266.

9. Augustine, *Confessions* 11.12.14., Philip Burton, trans. (New York: Alfred A Knopf, 2001), 269.

10. Aristotle, *Physics* 8.1, 418–21.

the scientific revolution would see a resurgence of eternalism. Copernican astronomy and the Newtonian worldview seemed to imply an infinite, thus everlasting, universe. In the eighteenth and nineteenth centuries, cosmologists saw the cosmos as not merely potentially but actually infinite. Not until the latter half of the twentieth century, with the acceptance of the big bang theory, will the notion of a beginning to the universe become universally embraced (but not without a great deal of resistance within the scientific community).[11]

By contrast, the Church consistently has testified to creation's beginning. Against the prevailing views of their day, the church fathers—from the Patristic through the Medieval theologians—uniformly rejected the eternality of nature.[12] Whether the world is young or old, the fact that it had a beginning is an important point because whatever is eternal is divine. Even if the universe is nearly 14 billion years old, it is finite. Only God is self-sufficient and eternal; therefore only God is worthy of worship. All other worship is idolatry because everything else has had a beginning and has existed only for a finite period of time.

God Is Distinct from Creation

> *Of old You laid the foundation of the earth,*
> *And the heavens are the work of Your hands.*
> *They will perish, but You will endure;*
> *Yes, they will all grow old like a garment;*
> *Like a cloak You will change them,*
> *And they will be changed.*
> *But You are the same,*
> *And Your years will have no end. (Ps. 102:25–27 NKJV)*

This point—that God is distinct from creation—correlates to the previous two points. Since God alone is eternal and he called the universe into existence out of nothing, then there is a fundamental difference between the Creator and that which he created. This again is in contrast to any version of pantheism or panentheism. God and the world are not on a continuum, nor is the world an extension of the essence of God. Prior to creation, God was the sum total of reality. To allow that which is not-God to exist was in itself an act of condescension.

If God is "wholly other," then how can we intelligently speak about him? It is important to remember that God is completely distinct from the world, not completely different. God created the world in such a way that it reflects

---

11. See Robert Jastrow, *God and the Astronomers* (New York: Warner, 1978); Stanley Jaki, *God and the Cosmologists* (Washington, DC: Gateway, 1989).

12. Some examples are Tertullian, *Against Hermogenes* (New York: Newman, 1956); Basil of Caesarea, *The Hexaemeron*, Homily 1 (Leuven, Belgium: Peeters, 1995); Augustine, *The City of God*, 11.4–6 (Cambridge: Cambridge Univ. Press, 1998); Thomas Aquinas, *Summa Theologica*, 1.46.1–3 (Lander, Wyo.: The Aquinas Institute, 2012).

his nature and character.[13] He created humans in a particular way to reflect his image. Because of this we are able to speak of God by analogy. This is different from the view of Islam about Allah. Muslims believe that Allah is so different from creation that there is no point in common between the two. The nature of Allah is therefore lost, and humans cannot know anything about his true nature. By contrast, the Bible teaches that we can have some genuine knowledge of God, even though it is limited, and we can speak about him in an analogous way. Christians generally distinguish between God's communicable and incommunicable attributes. Those attributes that in a reflected way can be seen here on earth are said to be communicable (God's love, justice, etc.), and those that have no earthly corollary are said to be incommunicable (God's omniscience, omnipresence, etc.). God is distinct from creation, yet he continues to relate to what he created.

God Did Not Create out of Necessity

> To him who by understanding made the heavens,
>   for his steadfast love endures forever;
> to him who spread out the earth above the waters,
>   for his steadfast love endures forever;
> to him who made the great lights,
>   for his steadfast love endures forever;
> the sun to rule over the day,
>   for his steadfast love endures forever;
> the moon and stars to rule over the night,
>   for his steadfast love endures forever. (Ps. 136:5–9)

Did God have to create anything at all? The answer to this question is no, and it speaks of the *aseity* of God. When we speak of God's, aseity we mean that God is complete within himself, dependent on nothing, and that creation adds nothing to him. God did not create out of any necessity or out of any sense of lack. From all eternity God has been and continues to be a perfect fellowship of Father, Son, and Holy Spirit. He has always and perfectly possessed all excellencies, and if God had chosen never to create it would not have detracted from his glory. This means nothing internal or external necessitated creation. Garrett observes, "God did not create in order to bring himself to completion. Nor did he create because he was driven to do so by external compulsion."[14]

---

13. See "God Created a World That Is Consistent with His Nature and Character" on page 31 in this chapter.
14. James Leo Garrett, *Systematic Theology: Biblical, Historical, and Evangelical*, vol. 1 (Grand Rapids: Eerdmans, 1990), 298–99.

So why did he create? The answer to this question is that the creation of the world is a completely gratuitous act on the part of God. We exist by God's grace and his good pleasure. Creation is an expression of "his steadfast love," which endures forever. This contrasts with the god of the ancient Greek philosophers. Aristotle believed in the "unmoved mover"—a god who was the source of the world but who was completely unaware of its existence. The universes' relationship to this god is like a microbe on the skin of a person's elbow—completely dependent on the host and just as unimportant. This god meditated only on himself.[15] Aristotle saw no need to worship such a deity, and if his portrait of the divine being were correct, then we would have to agree with him. However, the biblical God deliberately created the world and remains carefully and lovingly involved in every aspect of it (Acts 17:24–26).

God Did Not Have to Create This Particular World; This World Exists Purely by the Will of God

> *Worthy are you, our Lord and God,*
>   *to receive glory and honor and power,*
> *for you created all things,*
>   *and by your will they existed and were created. (Rev. 4:11)*

Could God have created a different type of world? Yes, he could have. While the previous point affirms the aseity of God, this point highlights God's *freedom*. Not only could God have refrained from creating, he also could have created a world very different from this one. This naturally brings a follow-up question: Why did he create a world in which evil was possible? The Bible gives no clear answer to this question. In Genesis 3 the serpent appears, but no back story is supplied. Among all Scripture the book of Job provides the most instruction concerning the nature and origin of evil. But in the end, instead of getting an answer, Job is told that this is an area where he must trust God. As D. A. Carson points out, Job does not say, "Ah, at last I understand!" but rather, "I repent."[16] Concerning this question we, too, must live by faith. Whatever answers we put forth must be tentative. And the leading answer advocated by theologians is that, in order to create beings with free will (i.e., angels and humans), there had to be a real possibility of evil.

We have difficulty understanding how it is possible that angels and humans are completely dependent upon God while at the same time they are not

---

15. Edward Grant, "Aristotle and Aristotelianism," in *Science and Religion: A Historical Introduction,* ed. Gary B. Ferngren (Baltimore: John Hopkins, 2002), 35–36.
16. D. A. Carson, *How Long, O Lord? Reflections on Suffering and Evil* (Grand Rapids: Baker, 1990), 174.

mere puppets. Yet God's freedom establishes the possibility of our freedom.[17] While human freedom may be a difficult concept to understand in a theistic worldview, it is impossible in an atheist one. If this material world were all that there is, then there could be no real human freedom. Our decisions and actions would simply be the product of physical and biochemical processes. The fact that God is free shows that freedom is a logical possibility.[18] Scripture teaches that God has indeed endowed humans with the ability to make choices and that he also holds us morally responsible for those choices.

God's freedom means he is free, not just to create, but also to intrude. God freely acts in creation. He acts through miracles, signs, and wonders, by regenerating hearts, by establishing his kingdom on earth, and ultimately by his Son becoming man in Jesus Christ.

God Created a World That Is Consistent with His Nature and Character

What type of world did God create? God is both great and good. Correspondingly, he has created a world that is consistent with his great nature and his good character. So creation is also both great and good. Scripture teaches that the heavens and the earth manifest at least three aspects of God's greatness. First, the world displays his glory. The psalmist states, "The heavens declare the glory of God, and the sky above proclaims his handiwork" (Ps. 19:1). Calvin called the universe "the theater of God's glory."[19] Creation displays God's glory by obeying his will. In this way, humans have the potential to bring the greatest glory to God because, as Erickson points out, "Only humans are capable of obeying God consciously and willingly and thus glorifying God most fully."[20]

Second, the world displays his power. God created the heavens and the earth by his word (*creatio per verbum*). Words, by themselves, have no power. Words are as powerful as the one who speaks them.

> *By the word of the* LORD *the heavens were made,*
> *And all the host of them by the breath of His mouth...*
> *For He spoke, and it was done;*
> *He commanded, and it stood fast. (Ps. 33:6, 9 NKJV)*

---

17. Packer, *Concise Theology*, 21.
18. "There is such a thing as free will, and free will does not, like the deterministic will, run in a groove. If there be free will in man, then much more is there free will in God, and God's will does not run in a groove" (Strong, *Systematic Theology*, 390).
19. John Calvin, *Institutes of the Christian Religion* (1559; reprint, Philadelphia: Westminster, 1960), 1.5.8; 1.6.2; 1.14.20; 2.6.1; cf. Michael Horton, *The Christian Faith* (Grand Rapids: Zondervan, 2011), 327.
20. Millard Erickson, *Christian Theology* (Grand Rapids: Baker, 1998), 399.

No less than eight times Genesis 1 states, "And God said, 'Let there be . . .'" and then the account observes that it was so. Because of his irresistible power, for God to speak is for God to act.

Third, the world manifests God's greatness by displaying his majesty. Psalm 8 begins and ends with a declaration of God's majesty: "O LORD, our Lord, how majestic is your name in all the earth!" In between, this brief psalm describes the heavens as the work of God's fingers and marvels that he condescends to humans (Ps. 8).

In addition to having the world display his greatness, God created the heavens and the earth in such a way that they are consistent with his character. In other words, the universe also displays the goodness of God. The universe is good because a good God created it. This means that there is nothing intrinsically evil about creation. The creation account repeatedly reports that God looked upon what he had made and "saw that it was good" (Gen. 1:4, 10, 12, 18, 21, 25, 31). Even with the effects of the fall, the Bible still describes the material creation as "good" (Num. 14:7; 1 Tim. 4:4–5). This is an important point. Recognizing that creation reflects God's goodness will help to safeguard us from any tendency to asceticism.[21] As Wolfhart Pannenberg points out, "The very existence of the world is an expression of the goodness of God."[22]

Creation manifests a second good quality of God, namely his wisdom. Scripture repeatedly states that God created by means of his wisdom, especially in the Proverbs (Prov. 3:19–20; 8:22–36). Proverbs 8:30–31 likens God to a master craftsman, delighting in what he had created. The prophets continue the theme:

> It is he who made the earth by his power,
> who established the world by his wisdom,
>   and by his understanding stretched out the heavens. (Jer.
> 10:12; cf. Jer. 51:15)

Psalm 148 declares that the world exists for the purpose of praising God. This brief psalm divides easily into two parts: God is praised from the heavens (vv. 1–6) and he is praised by the earth (vv. 7–14). Creation displays God's wisdom, knowledge, and genius.

God Is Sovereign over the World

> Sovereign Lord, who made the heaven and the earth and the
> sea and everything in them. (Acts 4:24)

---

21. Erickson, *Christian Theology,* 402; Grudem, *Systematic Theology,* 272; Garrett, *Systematic Theology,* 300.
22. Wolfhart Pannenberg, *Systematic Theology,* vol. 2 (Grand Rapids: Eerdmans, 1994), 21.

If there was one thing the ancient world understood, it was the notion of an absolute ruler.[23] Even tribal leaders were the unquestioned authority over their subjects. Moses presents God as the unrivaled, unopposed monarch over all creation. He wanted the Hebrews to know that their God, who delivered them in the Exodus, is not one god among many, but rather the one and only God who created all things and is lord over all things.

The all-inclusive nature of creation entails God's control and rule over all of it. Moses opens Genesis with "In the beginning God created the heavens and the earth." He intends the expression "heavens and the earth" to communicate that the Lord created everything "from A to Z." In the other ancient near-eastern accounts, certain entities were presented as adversaries and competitors of the creator deity. Moses presents all such elements—the deep and darkness, the celestial bodies, the fearsome beasts—as subjects created by and obedient to God.

God's sovereignty includes everything in the spiritual realm. Nehemiah prayed, "You are the LORD you alone. You have made heaven, the heaven of heavens, with all their host, the earth and all that is on it, the seas and all that is in them; and you preserve all of them; and the host of heaven worships you" (Neh. 9:6). His reference to the "heaven of heavens" and the "host of heaven" seems clearly to refer to the angelic beings and their habitation. Paul declares that Christ created all things "visible and invisible" (Col. 1:16).[24] It must be noted that the Genesis creation account gives no specific information about the creation of the angels. However, the Bible seems to indicate that the angels already existed by the time God began to create the world. Job tells us that when God laid the foundation of the earth "the morning stars sang together and all the sons of God shouted for joy" (Job 38:7). Since Scripture speaks so little on the matter, little more can be said.

God Continues to Be Actively Involved with the World

> *Your faithfulness endures to all generations;*
> *You established the earth, and it abides. (Ps. 119:90 NKJV)*

As we noted earlier, Aristotle taught that whatever deity created the world was apathetic toward it. Similarly, during the Enlightenment many embraced *deism.* Deism holds that God relates to the world like an absentee landlord: though he created the universe he no longer interacts with it. By contrast, the Bible teaches that at every level God constantly involves himself with creation.

God is simultaneously transcendently above and immanently within creation. When we speak of God's *transcendence,* we mean that God is distinct from and greater than creation. Yet, at the same time, the Bible affirms God's

---

23. Bartholomew and Goheen, *The Drama of Scripture*, 34.
24. Cf. Grudem, *Systematic Theology*, 265.

immanence within creation. By that we mean he is omnipresent and he is thoroughly and meticulously involved in every aspect of the universe (Acts 17:25–28). God is transcendently above the world, so he is able to save it. Since he is immanently within the world, he cares enough to save it.

God's involvement with the world speaks of his providence. He provides for the world in at least three ways: through his sustenance, his governance, and his concurrence. By his sustenance we mean that the world is not self-sustaining. It continues to exist because God continues to uphold it. The world came from nothing. If God stopped sustaining the world, then it would return to nothing. (Col. 1:17; Heb. 1:3). The created order depends on God for its existence. The world is real, but it is a *"conferred* reality."[25] God displays his involvement by his governance of the heavens and the earth. The psalmist declares that God controls the land and sea, and the lives of all who live and work on them (Ps. 107). He works directly and indirectly, unilaterally and concurrently, in and with the cosmos.

God's involvement with the world speaks of his purpose. The heavens and the earth exist for a reason, and that reason is God's glory (Rom. 11:36; 1 Cor. 15:28). Culver observes, "The goal of God for himself, in creation, is the manifestation of his perfections."[26] God created according to his plan, and he is fulfilling his purposes. The chief end of the universe is God himself.

REFLECTION QUESTIONS

1. What are the ways that eternalism is opposed to the doctrine of creation?

2. How does our understanding of creation affect our understanding of God?

3. In what ways does creation reveal the nature and character of God?

4. If God did not create the world out of necessity or to meet a need, then why did he create?

5. What are the ways that God providentially engages with the world?

---

25. Garrett, *Systematic Theology*, 299.
26. Robert Duncan Culver, *Systematic Theology: Biblical and Historical* (Fearn, Scotland: Mentor, 2005), 160–1. "[God's purpose in creating] may be summed up in four statements. God finds his end (a) in himself; (b) in his own will and pleasure; (c) in his own glory; (d) in the making known of his power, his wisdom, his holy name" (Strong, *Systematic Theology*, 397).

Why Is the Doctrine of Creation Important?

Why should we give careful attention to the doctrine of creation? Millard Erickson lists five reasons.[1] First, the Bible places great significance on creation. Second, the doctrine plays a significant role in the church's faith. The Apostle's Creed begins with "I believe in God the Father Almighty, Maker of heaven and earth." Third, as we will see, the doctrine of creation is important because of its effect on our understanding of other doctrines. Fourth, Christianity's understanding of creation is different from that of all other religions, including the other monotheistic religions. And fifth, the doctrine of creation is where Christianity most interacts with the natural sciences. Any one of these five reasons warrant giving consideration to creation; taken together, they make a compelling case for paying close attention to the doctrine.

The doctrine of creation affirms that the realm of nature was created by the God who reveals himself in Jesus Christ. A proper view of creation weds salvation history with natural history. As Wolfhart Pannenberg notes, "A failure to claim that the world that the sciences describe is God's world is a conceptual failure to confess the deity of the God of the Bible."[2] Several modern approaches to theology—such as neo-orthodoxy, existentialism, and linguistic analysis—are in many ways simply attempts to avoid this fact. However, we must understand that the world the scientist explores (of quarks, genetics, and the geological column) was created by the triune God of Scripture. A biblical understanding of creation gives us a proper view of four important realities, which we will briefly survey.

---

1. Millard Erickson, *Christian Theology*, 2nd ed. (Grand Rapids: Baker, 1998), 392–93.
2. Wolfhart Pannenberg, *Systematic Theology*, vol. 2 (Grand Rapids: Eerdmans, 1994), 60.

The Doctrine of Creation Gives Us a Proper Understanding of God's Relationship to the Universe

Augustine observed that one's understanding of creation profoundly influences his view of God.[3] The biblical doctrine of creation refutes a number of erroneous views that have been embraced by various proponents from the ancient world until now.

Polytheism

Ancient pagan cultures generally held to belief in a pantheon of gods. These deities were believed to oversee various geographical regions or vocations. It was not assumed that whichever deity created the world was the most powerful or the most benevolent. Shintoism and other religions that practice ancestor worship are modern examples of polytheism.

Materialism

Materialism argues that matter is the sum of reality and that all other things (such as soul, spirit, and mind) either do not exist or can be reduced down to matter. Materialism holds to a monistic view of reality (monism is the idea that all of reality is made of one substance). Materialism entails (i.e., logically necessitates) atheism. Ironically, matter has turned out to be very difficult, if not impossible, to define. Modern physics has rendered materialism untenable, since it has demonstrated that matter is interchangeable with energy and that information cannot be reduced to mere matter.[4]

Dualism

Gnosticism was a second century heretical movement that plagued the early church. The gnostics taught there were two self-existent realities—God and matter. Though matter consisted of a much inferior substance than God, it also was eternal. The Manichees (another heretical group that arose in the third century) also taught a form of dualism in that they believed there existed two eternal spirits—one who was a good spirit and the other evil. They taught that the material universe was an instrument in the hands of the evil spirit.[5] Dualism excludes any notion that God is almighty. Mormonism is a modern day proponent of metaphysical dualism in that they hold to the eternality of matter.[6]

---

3. Augustine, *City of God*, 11.4–5 (Alfred A Knopf: New York, 2001), 264–65.
4. Philip Clayton, "Unsolved Dilemmas: The Concept of Matter in the History of Philosophy and in Contemporary Physics," in *Information and the Nature of Reality*, ed. Paul Davies and Niels Henrik Gregersen (Cambridge: Cambridge University Press, 2010), 38–62.
5. Augustus H. Strong, *Systematic Theology* (Valley Forge: Judson, 1907), 378–82.
6. James Leo Garrett, *Systematic Theology: Biblical, Historical, and Evangelical*, vol. 1 (Grand Rapids: Eerdmans, 1990), 306 (cf. *Doctrine and Covenants* 93:33; *Book of Abraham* 4:1).

Pantheism

Pantheism teaches that the universe is made of the same substance as God and is thus divine. Oddly enough, the tendency to deify nature generally has had the effect of denigrating individual humans.[7] Like materialism, pantheism is monistic. But pantheism argues that spirit (or mind) is all and rejects the reality of matter. Hinduism holds to pantheism and thus teaches that the universe is an illusion. The early Enlightenment philosopher Baruch Spinoza (1632–1677) was a leading proponent of monistic pantheism.[8]

Panentheism

Process theism argues that God contains the world or that the universe is part of the divine being. Process theologians often use the metaphor of the world constituting God's body. This understanding of God's relationship to the world is called panentheism (i.e., "the world in God").[9] In process thought, God needs creation; the universe completes him. He is just as dependent on the world as the world is on him. God can desire that the world go in a certain direction, and he can attempt to persuade it to do so, but he cannot command the universe to obey. His plans can be and generally are thwarted. Because of this, process theism offers no hope that God will eventually overcome evil.[10] A number of theists in the scientific community, such as Philip Clayton and Arthur Peacocke, have advocated panentheism.[11]

Apathetic Monotheism

As we saw in the previous chapter, Hellenistic philosophers and deists of the Enlightenment affirmed an ultimate being (e.g., Aristotle's "unmoved mover"). But they were convinced he had no interest in the world and subsequently no involvement. Such a god merely plays the role of an intellectual placeholder and, as a practical matter, is no different from no god at all.

---

7. Erickson, *Christian Theology,* 403.
8. Matthew Stewart, *The Courtier and the Heretic: Leibniz, Spinoza, and the Fate of God in the Modern World* (New York: Norton, 2006), 308–9.
9. "Process theologians diametrically oppose the biblical doctrine of creation. Nor is this denial some peripheral element in the system: their panentheism—the doctrine that the world is not ontologically distinct from God but rather constitutes a part of the divine being—entails that God did not at any time create the universe *ex nihilo* nor does He conserve it in being" (William Lane Craig, "*Creatio ex nihilo,*" in *Process Theology,* ed. Ronald Nash [Grand Rapids: Baker, 1987], 145).
10. Pannenberg, *Systematic Theology,* 2:16.
11. See Philip Clayton and Arthur Peacocke, *In Whom We Live and Move and Have Our Being: Panentheistic Reflections in a Scientific World* (Grand Rapids: Eerdmans, 2004). For an evangelical critique see John W. Cooper, *Panentheism: The Other God of the Philosophers: From Plato to the Present* (Grand Rapids: Baker, 2006).

Trinitarian Monotheism

By contrast, the Bible teaches Trinitarian monotheism. By monotheism we mean the one almighty God created the world. He is not just the first cause but the divine Creator who willed the universe into existence with freedom and integrity.[12] By *Trinitarian* we mean that God, who is eternally Father, Son, and Holy Spirit, engages with the world by means of his triune relationships.[13] A proper view of the Trinity safeguards against any tendency towards dualism, pantheism, and the other errors listed above. The New Testament teaches that the entire triune Godhead was involved in creation (John 1:3; 1 Cor. 8:6; Heb. 1:1–3), yet the apostles also differentiate between the roles each Person played. Irenaeus described the Son and the Holy Spirit as the Father's "two hands" in creation, thereby emphasizing how God relates to creation through his Word and his Spirit.[14] As Colin Gunton pointed out, too often the doctrine of creation is "merely monotheistically or unitarianly construed."

> Rather, it should be said that creation, reconciliation and re-demption are all to be attributed to the Father, all realized through the work of his two hands, the Son and the Spirit, who are themselves substantially God. There is mediation, but it is through God, not ontological intermediates. This tends to be lost when any other mediator conceived inde-pendently of the 'two hands'—Platonic forms, Aristotelian causes, Lockean or Newtonian substance, Berkeleyan arche-types—becomes the central focus of attention.[15]

A Trinitarian understanding of creation emphasizes that God is deeply in-volved with this world. A triune view of mediation successfully describes the relationship between God and creation while Aristotelianism, Gnosticism, Islam, and deism all fail. Rather than positing God's relationship (or lack thereof) in terms of ideal forms or causality, this view holds that God's in-teraction with the world is personal.

---

12. Michael Horton, *The Christian Faith: A Systematic Theology for Pilgrims on the Way* (Grand Rapids: Zondervan, 2011), 335.
13. "The work was not divided among the three persons, but the whole work, though from different aspects, is ascribed to each one of the persons. All things are at once *out of* the Father, *through* the Son, and *in* the Holy Spirit. In general it may be said that *being* is out of the Father, *thought* or the *idea* out of the Son, and *life* out of the Holy Spirit. Since the Father takes the initiative in the work of creation, it is often ascribed to Him economically" (Louis Berkof, *Systematic Theology,* new edition, vol. 2 [Grand Rapids: Eerdmans, 1996], 129, emphasis original).
14. Irenaeus, *Against the Heresies*, 4.20.1.
15. Colin Gunton, *The Triune Creator: A Historical and Systematic Study* (Grand Rapids: Eerdmans,1998), 154.

The Doctrine of Creation Gives Us a Proper Understanding of Humanity's Place in the Universe

Lewis and Demarest make the point that the proper view of creation protects us from both idolatry and despair.[16] The Bible tells us that we are related to the animals, but we are not merely animals. Like other creatures, we were made out of the dust from the ground (Gen. 2:7). Scripture declares that humans were made in the image of God, but goes on to make clear that we are not divine (Gen. 1:26–27). Having a proper knowledge of the relationship between the Creator and creation makes it possible for one to know his proper place in the world. In terms of status and authority, God placed humans between the animals and the angels (Ps. 8:5–8).[17]

Jonah claimed to have the correct understanding of God and creation when he told the pagans who were on the ship with him, "I am a Hebrew, and I fear the LORD, the God of heaven, who made the sea and the dry land" (Jonah 1:9). The pagan sailors did not know the Creator, and therefore they lived in darkness and ignorance. Jonah, as a Hebrew, knew the true relationship between God, creation, and humans. The biblical doctrine of creation safeguards against idolatry and self-worship.[18] In the garden, God assigned humans with a creational mandate. We were given a stewardship over the earth, and we were to function as God's vice-regents over creation. More attention will be given to this theme in the next chapter.

The Doctrine of Creation Gives Us the Proper Understanding of the Nature of Creation

A proper understanding of the nature of creation was necessary for the advent of science. Historians of science have noted that it was Christian Europe of the Renaissance and the Reformation that birthed the scientific revolution.[19]Other cultures of the time—Chinese, Arabic, and even Aztec—had better technology, superior economic resources, and greater social stability. Yet none of these cultures were able to bring about what today we call

---

16. Gordon R. Lewis and Bruce A. Demarest, *Integrative Theology*, vol. 2 (Grand Rapids: Zondervan, 1996), 17.
17. "Yet you have made him a little lower than the heavenly beings" (Ps. 8:5). Whether the psalmist has God or angels in mind is a matter of ongoing debate.
18. Charles R. Swindoll and Roy B. Zuck, eds. *Understanding Christian Theology* (Nashville: Thomas Nelson, 2003), 650–52.
19. A number of historians of science make this point. See Nancy R. Pearcey and Charles B. Thaxton, *The Soul of Science: Christian Faith and Natural Philosophy* (Wheaton, Ill.: Crossway, 1994). See also Rodney Stark, *For the Glory of God: How Monotheism Led to Reformations, Science, Witch-hunts, and the End of Slavery* (Princeton: Princeton University Press, 2003); Gary B. Fergern, *Science and Religion: A Historical Introduction* (Baltimore: John Hopkins University Press, 2002); R. Hooykaas, *Religion and the Rise of Modern Science* (Vancouver: Regent, 1972). The "warfare metaphor" propagated in the nineteenth century by Andrew White and John William Draper has been thoroughly refuted.

the scientific method. This is because Europe enjoyed something that the rest of the world did not: a Christian view of the universe. The Christian doctrine of creation contains unique elements that are crucial to the scientific outlook. Pearcey and Thaxton list six special beliefs that the Christian worldview provides.[20]

Nature Is Real

The Genesis account of creation makes clear that the world is not an illusion. The eastern religions lack this conviction. Pearcey and Thaxton point out that confidence in the reality of creation gave European Christians confidence that the world is "a realm of definable structures and real relations, and so is a possible object both for scientific and for philosophical study."[21]

Nature Has Value

The ancient Greeks lacked this conviction. The gnostics reflected the ancient worldview that saw the material world as intrinsically evil.[22] The world was considered a prison from which one could only hope to flee. The doctrine of creation, along with the Incarnation and the coming kingdom of God, demonstrates that the universe has great significance.

Nature Is Not God

Scripture, with its prohibition against idolatry, discouraged the tendency to deify nature. By contrast, the pagan "lives in an enchanted forest." The biblical doctrine of creation rules out all this. "The de-deification of nature was a crucial precondition for science. As long as nature commands religious worship, dissecting her is judged impious."[23] One cannot experiment with what one worships.

Nature Has Order

The pagan polytheist believed in many gods, so he had no reason to believe that the universe was controlled by one set of laws. By contrast, the Bible presents a single transcendent Creator, whose handiwork is a unified, coherent universe. Belief in a universal set of natural laws that are repeatable and dependable was essential for the birth of science. Isaac Newton postulated that the law of gravity that makes an apple fall to the ground is the same law that directs the course of the moon. How could he make such an imaginative

20. Pearcey and Thaxton, *The Soul of Science*, 17–56.
21. Ibid.
22. Colin Gunton, *The Triune Creator*, 48–49. See also Gerhard May, *The Doctrine of "Creation Out of Nothing" in Early Christian Thought* (Edinburgh: T&T Clark, 1994), 39–45.
23. Pearcey and Thaxton, *The Soul of Science*, 23.

leap in his thinking? It is because he believed in one great Lawgiver, whose laws governed both heaven and earth.[24] Physicist Richard Feynman observed,

> Incidentally, the fact that there are rules at all to be checked is a kind of miracle; that it is possible to find a rule, like the inverse square law of gravitation, is some sort of miracle. It is not understood at all, but it leads to the possibility of prediction—that means it tells you what you would expect to happen in an experiment you have not yet done.[25]

Since Genesis teaches that we are created in the image of the Creator, then we could expect that it is possible to think his thoughts after him. Even though the ancient Chinese were technologically superior to Medieval Europe, they had no concept of natural law. "There was no confidence that the code of Nature's laws could be unveiled and read, because there was no assurance that a divine being, even more rational than ourselves, had ever formulated such a code capable of being read."[26]

Nature Is Subservient

God created the universe *ex nihilo* and hence has absolute control over it. This idea was alien to the ancient world. In all other religions, the creation of the world begins with some kind of pre-existing substance with its own inherent nature. As a result, in the pagan religions the creator is not absolute and does not have the freedom to mold the world exactly as he wills.

Nature Has Purpose.

The other ancient cultures saw history in cyclic, fatalistic, or deterministic terms. They had no reason to expect improvement or progress. But the biblical doctrine of creation is the beginning of a grand narrative that is linear and open to divine activity. In the course of time, God can create something genuinely new.[27] So can human beings, who are made in his image.

Lewis and Demarest argue that, in addition to the necessity of the Christian view of creation for the birth of science, the Christian worldview is

---

24. "It is not hard to discover where this picture of physical laws comes from: it is inherited directly from monotheism, which asserts that a rational being designed the universe according to a set of perfect laws. And the asymmetry between immutable laws and contingent states mirrors the asymmetry between God and nature: the universe depends utterly on God for its existence, whereas God's existence does not depend on the universe" (Paul Davies, "Universe from Bit," in *Information and the Nature of Reality*, ed. Paul Davies and Niels Henrik Gregersen [Cambridge: Cambridge University Press, 2010], 70).
25. Richard Feynman, quoted in Horton, *The Christian Faith*, 340.
26. Joseph Needham, quoted in Pearcey and Thaxton, *The Soul of Science*, 26.
27. Pearcey and Thaxton, *The Soul of Science*, 36.

necessary for science to continue to flourish. Without a transcendent norm for ethics and morals, the intellectual honesty essential to science will not be maintained. Nor can science be sustained long term in milieus of materialism, pantheism, and other idolatrous environments.

The Doctrine of Creation Gives Us the Proper Understanding of Salvation and Redemption

As we noted earlier in the chapter, the heretical teachings of the gnostics presented the early church with one of its greatest challenges. The errors of Gnosticism demonstrate how vitally interrelated the doctrines of creation, Christology, and salvation really are. The various gnostic teachers, such as Cerinthus, Marcion, and Valentinus, attempted to merge Hellenistic speculation with Christian theology. Because they rejected the goodness of the material world, they refused to believe that the God of the Old Testament is the heavenly Father of Jesus Christ. They understood Jehovah to be uncouth and ignorant, and they ascribed to him satanic qualities. The gnostics taught that God related to the world through a descending cascade of intermediate beings (that they called "aeons"). The lowest aeon, Jehovah, was a capricious, malevolent being who created the world. Consider the following from the Nag Hammadi corpus, a body of early gnostic works:

> The world came about by a mistake. For he who created it wanted to create it imperishable and immortal. He fell short of attaining his desire. For the world never was imperishable, nor, for that matter, was he who made the world. (The Gospel of Philip 75:2)

According to the Gospel of Philip, the world is simply a very big "mistake."

The gnostics also taught that Christ, as the highest of the aeons, could not possibly have been incarnated. To them it was unthinkable that the Logos of God would take on something as filthy and reprehensible as a human body. Rather, they contended for *docetism*, the view that Jesus was a phantom who merely appeared to be human.

According to the gnostics, the world is without worth and beyond saving. They understood salvation to be deliverance *from* creation. By contrast, the Bible teaches that salvation is the deliverance *of* creation. Several of the early church fathers refuted the gnostic errors, but none so effectively or thoroughly as Irenaeus (AD 130–202), the bishop of Lyon.[28] He demonstrated that the Father of Jesus Christ and the God of the Old Testament are one and the same. Irenaeus showed that the Bible clearly affirms the bodily incarnation of Jesus and that Scripture teaches God's love for and lordship over creation.

---

28. Irenaeus, *Against Heresies* (New York: Paulist Press, 2012).

The account in Genesis 1–2 teaches the goodness of creation. The incarnation of the Son of God in the person of Jesus Christ, along with his bodily resurrection after his death on the cross, subsequently affirm this teaching. In addition, the Bible connects creation with the world to come. The narrative of this great drama is the topic of our next question.

REFLECTION QUESTIONS

1. In what ways is the Christian doctrine of creation different from other monotheistic religions?

2. Why do many historians believe that the Christian doctrine of creation played a crucial role in the scientific revolution?

3. How does the doctrine of creation protect humans from having either an idolatrous attitude toward ourselves or a disparaging view of ourselves?

4. In what ways do the errors of the gnostics show how our understanding of creation affects our understanding of salvation?

What Is Creation's Role in the Grand Narrative of the Bible?

Michael Horton points out that the Bible does not present the doctrine of creation as a scientific explanation or as a philosophical solution.[1] Rather, Scripture teaches that God is the sovereign Creator of all, and this fact has "ethical and religious significance." We are morally responsible to the one who created us in his image.

Creation is literally the foundational truth of Scripture. The Bible begins with the declaration, "In the beginning, God created the heavens and the earth" (Gen. 1:1). This truth is then repeated throughout the Bible. The doctrine of creation provides the bedrock for all the other doctrines of the Christian faith. Consider, for example, how creation informs our understanding of the Sabbath (Heb. 4:3), traditional marriage (Matt. 19:4), and the unity of humanity (Acts 17:26).[2]

There is an arc to the biblical narrative. The storyline begins with the Tree of Life in the garden (Gen. 1–3) and ends with that same Tree in the New Jerusalem (Rev. 22). In this chapter we will see that creation begins the story of redemption and then provides the framework for understanding the age to come. Last, the New Testament lets us know that a truly biblical doctrine of creation will not merely be theistic. Above all else our view of creation must be Christocentric.

Creation Is the Beginning of the Story of Redemption

The first eleven chapters of Genesis provide the background for God's work of saving humanity. Moses lets his people know that the God who

---

1. Michael Horton, *The Christian Faith: A Systematic Theology for Pilgrims on the Way* (Grand Rapids: Zondervan, 2011), 325.
2. Carl F. H. Henry, *God, Revelation and Authority*, vol. 6 (Wheaton, Ill: Crossway, 1999), 119.

redeemed Israel is not just a parochial deity, nor is he just a member of a polytheistic collage. Israel's God created the entire cosmos. "When the names *Yahweh* (LORD) and *Elohim* (God) are joined as in Genesis 2:4, it makes the powerful point that the same God who rescues Israel from slavery is the God who has made all things, the Creator of heaven and earth."[3]

The Garden of Eden

Genesis 2 presents the surprising picture of the majestic Creator condescending to earth to plant a garden. But this is not just any garden. The garden of Eden was the world as God designed it to be. The description provided in Genesis 2:8–14 portrays Eden much more like a national park than a backyard flower plot.[4] In fact, Genesis 1–2 makes clear that God intended Eden to function as a temple and that Adam was to serve in it as his priest.[5]

The biblical narrative introduces Adam and Eve as the pinnacle of creation. They were God's representatives on earth—not as tyrants, but as stewards *coram deo*. Their life in the garden was a pattern of the kingdom of God. They were under God's rule and enjoyed his unfettered presence and blessing.[6] Adam and Eve's assignment was to make the rest of the world look like Eden (Gen. 1:28; 2:19). To grasp the scope of this assignment, Craig Bartholomew and Michael Goheen ask us to imagine receiving a request from Michelangelo to complete a work of art that he has begun.[7] The original couple received an immensely greater task—one of great privilege and responsibility.

The Fall

Adam and Eve tragically fail their assignment. They commit the inexcusable sin of idolatry when they determine to live life independent of God. They join Satan in his rebellion and place themselves under condemnation. They leave the garden cursed. But in the midst of tragedy, the narrative presents hope. God does not abandon his creation, but rather promises to reclaim and redeem what is rightfully his (Gen. 3:15).

---

3. Craig G. Bartholomew and Michael Goheen, *The Drama of Scripture: Finding Our Place in the Biblical Story* (Grand Rapids: Baker, 2004), 30.

4. Ibid., 38.

5. J. V. Fesko, *Last Things First: Unlocking Genesis 1–3 with the Christ of Eschatology* (Fearn, Scotland, UK: Mentor, 2007), 57–77; G. K. Beale, *The Temple and the Church's Mission: A Biblical Theology of the Dwelling Place of God* (Downers Grove: InterVarsity Press, 2004), 81–95; G. K. Beale, *A New Testament Biblical Theology: The Unfolding of the Old Testament in the New* (Grand Rapids: Baker, 2011), 29–58.

6. Bartholomew and Goheen, *The Drama of Scripture*, 38; Vaughn Roberts, *God's Big Picture: Tracing the Storyline of the Bible* (Downers Grove: InterVarsity Press, 2002), 32–33.

7. Bartholomew and Goheen, *The Drama of Scripture*, 37.

Israel's Call

God initiates the task of redemption by calling Abraham (Gen. 12:1–3). He gives Abraham the promise of a kingdom and a universal blessing. Abraham becomes the father of a mighty people, the nation of Israel. Israel's story is one of partial victory but ultimate failure. God's deliverance of the Hebrew people from Egypt marks the high point of the Old Testament, but Nebuchadnezzar's destruction of the Temple and Israel's subsequent exile surely marks the low point.

The exile brought a crisis to the people of Israel. They struggled to understand how the God who had chosen Israel was also the God who rules over the natural world (with its regularity of seasons and tides) and who governs history (with its rising and falling of nations). This struggle is seen in the wisdom literature and the prophetic writings of the Old Testament.[8]

As Israel returns to the land, they are promised an eventual triumph. However, this victory requires that a spiritual transformation must take place. Israel's failure to keep the Law demonstrated her inability to measure up to the requirements of the Mosaic covenant.[9] A new covenant was coming, the prophets declared (Isa. 54:1–10; Jer. 31:31–34). This covenant of grace would perform an inward work on the human heart (Ezek. 11:17–21; 36:26–27).

The Good News

The new covenant promised by the prophets arrives in the Gospels in the person of Jesus of Nazareth. Jesus, the incarnate Logos, the living Wisdom who created all things, accomplished redemption by his life, death, and resurrection. The Incarnation was not an afterthought, nor was it merely an emergency measure or fallback plan enacted only to remedy the fall. The Incarnation was the purpose and goal from the beginning. God created the world with the intent of wedding himself to creation through his Son.[10]

When Jesus Christ died on the cross, his atonement provided a penal satisfaction to God for our sins (Rom. 3:25–26; 1 John 2:2) and defeated sin, death, and the cosmic powers which held creation in bondage (Col. 2:14–15; Heb. 2:14–15). Our Lord's death holds ultimate significance for both the individual sinner and the entire universe. God vindicated his Son when he raised him from the dead, and the resurrection of Christ promises that God has accomplished a new thing in the world.

---

8. Wolfhart Pannenberg, *Systematic Theology*, vol. 2 (Grand Rapids: Eerdmans, 1994), 68.
9. John Sailhamer, *The Meaning of the Pentateuch: Revelation, Composition, and Interpretation* (Downers Grove: InterVarsity Press, 2009), 26–28.
10. Pannenberg, *Systematic Theology*, 2:64.

The Present Age

The New Testament teaches that we now live between the times. The church experiences the tension of the "now and not yet" reality of this age. The kingdom of God began to arrive at the first coming of Christ, and the end of the age began with his resurrection. The end has already begun. However, the kingdom is not yet here in its fullness, and we eagerly await the consummation of this age when Jesus Christ returns.

The Restoration

What God did for the Lord Jesus Christ on Easter, he intends to do for the whole cosmos. In this respect, the end of the age could be understood as the final stage of God's work of creation. Horton sees three aspects of the creative work of God—the original work of creation, his continuing work through the church and the kingdom of God, and the eventual new heavens and earth. This expectation is a matter of faith. "The hope for a new creation—that is, a miraculous restoration of the cosmos at Christ's return—does not arise from empirical observations and mathematical probabilities but from God's promise in Scripture."[11]

As we noted in the previous chapter, the restoration of all things affirms the goodness and significance of creation. Like the incarnation, the doctrine of the resurrection powerfully verifies the value of creation. Humanity will spend eternity in resurrected bodies—bodies that had their origin in this present creation. The Bible puts such emphasis on the connection between the present creation and the world to come that we need to look at it further in the next point.

Creation Provides the Framework for Understanding the Age to Come

Theologians diverse as Wolfhart Pannenberg and J. V. Fesko point out that one must look at the world from the perspective of its end in order to properly understand its beginning.[12] This is because the Bible connects creation with the new creation. Speaking through Isaiah, the Lord declares: "For behold, I create (*bara*) new heavens and a new earth, and the former things shall not be remembered or come into mind. But be glad and rejoice forever in that which I create; for behold, I create (*bara*) Jerusalem to be a joy, and her people to be a gladness" (Isa. 65:17–18).

Many of the themes begun in the creation account of Genesis resurface in Revelation 21–22. Consider such things as the Tree of Life and the unencumbered presence of God. The Tree of Life disappears after Genesis 3. Remarkably, the Bible is silent about it until the very last chapter. Then we are told that the tree will stand by the "river of the water of life" and its leaves

---

11. Horton, *The Christian Faith*, 348.
12. Pannenberg, *Systematic Theology*, 2:160; Fesko, *Last Things First*, 29–34.

will provide "healing for the nations" (Rev. 22:1–2). Similarly, in the New Jerusalem we are promised the return of the unimpeded presence of God. Prior to the fall, God walked with the original couple "in the cool of the day" (Gen. 3:8). In the new creation, once again "God will dwell with them" (Rev. 21:3). The Bible relates the present creation with the new creation in at least five additional ways that are worthy of note.

The Bible Teaches That the Present Creation Will One Day End
This world had a beginning and it shall have an end, at least as it exists in its present state or condition (2 Peter 3:1–13; Rev. 22:1–3). The early church encountered strong opposition on this point from the Hellenistic philosophers. As we noted earlier, Aristotle taught that the cosmos was without beginning or end. These ideas resurfaced again during the modern era. James Hutton, the father of modern geology, argued for "geological deep time" with his famous maxim, "In nature we find no vestige of a beginning,—no prospect of an end."[13] Commitment to an eternal universe caused many scientists initially to resist the big bang hypothesis.[14] By contrast, the Bible teaches that the universe is finite in duration. It started at a definite time and it will one day stop.

The Bible Teaches That the End Will Be Catastrophic in Nature
T. S. Eliot famously wrote, "This is the way the world ends; Not with a bang but a whimper." Eliot's vision does not square with that of the biblical prophets. They spoke of the coming "day of the Lord" which will be universally calamitous. It was a familiar theme to Isaiah. He declared that the day is coming when "the LORD will empty the earth and make it desolate, and he will twist its surface and scatter its inhabitants" (Isa. 24:1). Later he states, "All the host of heaven shall rot away, and the skies roll up like a scroll" (34:4). Whether these prophecies should be understood literally or figuratively is a matter of debate, but it is clear that Christ's return will be accompanied by universal events.[15]

The End Will Be a Time of Judgment
The consummation will be marked by vindicating the evil and inequities of the present order. The Bible gives an eschatological answer to the problem of evil.[16] Creation, throughout its existence, has testified of God's power and

---

13. Davis A. Young and Ralph F. Stearley, *The Bible, Rocks, and Time: Geological Evidence for the Age of the Earth* (Downers Grove: InterVarsity Press, 2008) 88; Frank J. Tipler, *The Physics of Immortality: Modern Cosmology, God, and the Resurrection of the Dead* (New York: Doubleday, 1994), 77–85.
14. Robert Jastrow, *God and the Astronomers* (New York: Warner, 1978), 101–6; Stanley Jaki, *God and the Cosmologists* (Washington, DC: Regnery Gateway, 1989), 57–83.
15. For a helpful discussion of this question, see G. K. Beale, *The Book of Revelation*, NIGTC (Grand Rapids: Eerdmans, 1999), 396–99.
16. Pannenberg, *Systematic Theology*, 2:162–67.

nature (Rom. 1:18–21). Yet, because of sin, humanity has deliberately ignored this testimony and embraces evil wholesale (Rom. 1:22–31). The apparent, temporary success of evil creates a stumbling block for many. Presently, this outrageous situation must be seen in the light of Calvary and our Lord's resurrection. Christ's death on the cross is God's answer to evil, sin, and suffering. The eschatological promise of the risen Christ gives hope to an otherwise futile world. Philosophical speculations about the "best of all possible worlds" give little comfort during times of immense or intense suffering and grief. Scripture declares that sin and evil are not the will of God. Rather, the Bible portrays them as "accompanying phenomena."[17] They are "conditions" for realizing his purpose.

The Return of Christ Rescues Creation from Futility
Paul uses the metaphor of childbirth to describe creation's anticipation of the next age when he declares:

> For the creation waits with eager longing for the revealing of the sons of God. For the creation was subjected to futility, not willingly, but because of him who subjected it, in hope that the creation itself will be set free from its bondage to corruption and obtain the freedom of the glory of the children of God. For we know that the whole creation has been groaning together in the pains of childbirth until now. (Rom. 8:19–22)

An eschatological promise ties Christ and creation (Col. 1:20; Eph. 1:10; Rom. 8:19). We are promised that we will have the privilege of participating in the Trinitarian fellowship of the Father, Son, and Holy Spirit. All creation will benefit from this union. Pannenberg observes, "The goal of all creation, not just humanity, is to share in the life of God. Why else should it sigh under the burden of corruptibility (Rom. 8:21f.)?"[18]

Creation Will Be Not Annihilated but Transformed
Taken in isolation, certain passages can give the impression that the universe will be obliterated. John states that at the Great White Throne Judgment "from his presence earth and sky fled away, and no place was found for them" (Rev. 20:11) and then a few verses later says, "Then I saw a new heaven and a new earth, for the first heaven and the first earth had passed away" (21:1). Similarly, Peter declares that "the heavens will be set on fire and dissolved, and the heavenly bodies will melt as they burn" (2 Peter 3:12). However, in each context both apostles make clear that the present creation will give way

---

17. Ibid.
18. Ibid., 2:136.

to a new creation (2 Peter 3:13; Rev. 21:1–2). Wright observes, "Redemption doesn't mean scrapping what's there and starting again from a clean slate but rather liberating what has come to be enslaved."[19] There will be continuity between this world and the next, and as a result there is a surprising amount of similarity.[20] When Christ returns it will not be the end. It will be the end of the beginning.

Creation Is to Be Understood Ultimately in Relationship to Jesus Christ

In the beginning was the Word, and the Word was with God,
and the Word was God. He was in the beginning with God.
All things were made through him, and without him was not
any thing made that was made. (John 1:1–3)

Creation cannot be properly grasped without comprehending it in relation to Jesus Christ. The apostles instruct us that the Son of God is "the origin, the center, and the goal of the universe."[21] In this regard, the New Testament is unique. No similar claims can be found in the Jewish Wisdom literature or other ancient Jewish writings.[22]

We Must Understand That the Son of God Is the Creator of the World
Repeatedly the New Testament declares that God created the world through him (John 1:1–3; Heb. 1:1–3). For example, the apostle Paul states that "there is one God, the Father, from whom are all things and for whom we exist, and one Lord, Jesus Christ, through whom are all things and through whom we exist" (1 Cor. 8:6). The second person of the Trinity operated as the instrumental, active agent in creation.

The Son of God Is the Sustainer of the World
The world does not have the capability to self-sustain, nor are its properties self-perpetuating. In proclaiming the preeminence of Jesus, Paul declares, "And he is before all things, and in him all things hold together" (Col. 1:17). Without Christ's ongoing sustenance, governance, and guidance we would disintegrate. We would literally evaporate into nothingness. The author of Hebrews tells us that Christ "upholds the universe by the word of his power" (Heb. 1:3). The universe continues to be, and continues to behave with law-like regularity, because of our Lord's providential care.

---

19. N. T. Wright, *Surprised by Hope: Rethinking Heaven, the Resurrection, and the Mission of the Church* (New York: Harper One, 2008), 96.
20. Randy Alcorn, *Heaven* (Carol Stream, Ill.: Tyndale, 2004), 159–61.
21. Christoph Schonborn, *Chance or Purpose? Creation, Evolution, and a Rational Faith* (San Francisco: Ignatius Press, 2007), 135.
22. Peter T. O'Brien, *Colossians, Philemon*, WBC 44 (Nashville: Thomas Nelson, 2000), 47.

The Son of God Is the Focus of the World

"All things were created through him and for him . . . that in everything he might be preeminent" (Col. 1:16, 18). John Piper makes the point well:

> All that came into being exists for Christ—that is, every-
> thing exists to display the greatness of Christ. Nothing—
> nothing!—in the universe exists for its own sake.
> Everything—from the bottom of the oceans to the top of
> the mountains, from the smallest particle to the biggest
> star, from the most boring school subject to the most fas-
> cinating science, from the ugliest cockroach to the most
> beautiful human, from the greatest saint to the most wicked
> genocidal dictator—everything that exists, exists to make
> the greatness of Christ more fully known—including you,
> and the person you have the hardest time liking.[23]

The One who created all and sustains all became human in Jesus Christ and then by his death became redeemer of all. Clearly he must be the center of all.

The Son of God Is the Goal of the World

God's ultimate plan is in "the fullness of time to unite all things in him, things in heaven and in earth" (Eph. 1:10). As beautiful as the universe is, apart from Christ no ultimate purpose for its existence can be discerned. Apart from him the cosmos appears futile. Creation makes no sense without the incarnation, especially the actualizing of a world in which the fall was possible. However, once we grasp the significance of who Jesus Christ is and what he has done, then the purpose becomes clear. The uniting of God with creation through his Son is the final goal of all that is transpiring. The accomplishment of the divine plan will be maximally glorious (1 Cor. 15:28).

Considering all the evil the world has seen, is creation worth it? For the Buddhist and the Hindu the answer is no. For both of these the ultimate goal for a human being is to return to nothingness. The answer for the atheist would seem to be similarly negative. Candid atheists, such as Samuel Beckett and Bertrand Russell, have admitted this. For Beckett, life oscillated between "the boredom of living" and "the suffering of being."[24] Russell conceded that an atheistic worldview was a "firm foundation of

---

23. John Piper, *Spectacular Sins and Their Global Purpose in the Glory of Christ* (Wheaton, Ill.: Crossway, 2008), 33; cf. Mark Noll, *Jesus Christ and the Life of the Mind* (Grand Rapids: Eerdmans, 2011), 27–28.

24. Antony Cronin, *Samuel Beckett: The Last Modernist* (New York: HarperCollins, 1997), 143.

unyielding despair."[25] Physicist and Nobel laureate Steven Weinberg concludes, "The more the universe seems comprehensible, the more it also seems pointless."[26] We should not be surprised by their outlook. If one looks to nature—and only to nature—then he will inevitably conclude that all is vain and futile (Eccl. 1; Rom. 8:20). Take Christ out of the picture, and the universe appears all dressed up with nowhere to go.

Christians, however, know that God is infinitely wise and good, and the decision to create was his. Therefore we can be sure that it is better for the world to exist than not to exist. This is true despite the existence of sin and sorrow in the world. Only the Christian doctrine of creation provides an explanation about the things for which no other religion (or atheism) can offer an answer or comfort—the pain and cruelty in nature and the universe's apparent futility (Rom. 8:19–23).[27]

Strong argues that we should be optimists, not pessimists. He gives four reasons why Christ is the remedy for pessimism.[28] First, Christ reveals to us God's transcendence and lets us know that the universe at present is "not fully expressing his power, his holiness, or his love." In this present age God has not yet demonstrated fully who he is. Second, sin has its origin in the free choices of the creature. God is in no way the origin of moral evil. Third, Christ's work on the cross reveals to us God's self-sacrificing love and his perfect plan to deliver us from evil. And fourth, Christ reveals that this age is a time of probation, that there is a coming judgment, and that "the scandal now resting upon divine government" will be answered. The ways of God will be justified to men.

The God of the Bible is the only true God, because he is the God who created the heavens and the earth. This same God is the Father of Jesus Christ, and through his Son he reconciled the world to himself. The doctrine of creation anchors salvation history and unites it with natural history. He who created all that we see is the One who saves us in Jesus Christ. Creation, seen in the light of the Gospel, is glorious.

REFLECTION QUESTIONS

1. How does creation fit in the grand narrative of the Bible?

2. What was the assignment of Adam and Eve in the garden?

25. Bertrand Russell, *A Free Man's Worship*, in *The Collected Papers of Bertrand Russell*, vol. 12 (New York: Routledge, 1988), 62–63.
26. Steven Weinberg, *The First Three Minutes: A Modern View of the Origin of the Universe* (New York: Basic, 1977), 149.
27. John Polkinghorne, *Testing Scripture: A Scientist Explores the Bible* (Grand Rapids: Brazos, 2010), 101–2.
28. Augustus H. Strong, *Systematic Theology* (Valley Forge: Judson, 1907), 405.

3. According to the New Testament, what is the eventual destiny of the world?

4. What is the relationship of the Lord Jesus Christ to creation?

5. Why does the Christian view of creation have an optimism that materialism does not?

PART 2

QUESTIONS ABOUT CREATION AND GENESIS 1–2

QUESTION 5

What Is the Relationship of Genesis 1–2 to Other Creation Accounts?

Former Princeton Theological Seminary professor Bernhard W. Anderson introduces his book *Creation in the Old Testament*, with the observation that the understanding of biblical creation in the twentieth century has been profoundly affected by two major events that occurred in the mid-nineteenth century. The first was the publication of Charles Darwin's *On the Origin of Species* in 1859, a work that has overwhelmingly influenced the discussion of creation almost from its inception. The second major event, that actually occurred six years earlier, was the discovery of the library of Ashurbanipal in ancient Nineveh in 1853.

After the documents from the ancient library of Nineveh began to be deciphered, it became clear that many of these documents addressed ancient primeval history, including creation accounts. It was not long after this discovery that George Smith published *The Chaldean Account of Genesis* in 1876 based upon these findings from Ashurbanipal's library. The publication of this work was like a "shot heard around the world."[1] Since this discovery, documents and tablets from other ancient cultures have been deciphered, exponentially increasing our knowledge of how these ancient cultures understood the beginning of the world and the universe. Particularly relevant are the discoveries of cosmogonic texts, texts that deal with theories of origins, from Egypt and Mesopotamia.

Egyptian Cosmogonies

In Egyptian mythology there were distinctive views regarding creation. For example, in ancient Egypt the creation of the world was linked to the birth and creation of the gods. All matter was thought to be part of the god and

---

1. Bernhard W. Anderson, ed., *Creation in the Old Testament* (Philadelphia: Fortress, 1984), 1.

thus a natural extension of the gods themselves. From other ancient Egyptian texts, we learn of additional information about the involvement of the gods in bringing about creation. In the *Coffin Texts* from Hermopolis, we learn that a dark and watery chaos existed prior to creation. Eight deities or genii from the primeval waters formed a primeval egg that hatched, and the result was the establishment of the created order. In texts from Heliopolis Nun, the preexistent primeval ocean came into being and then the primeval hill emerged out of Nun. The watery chaos thus was pre-existent with no explanation provided for how it came to be. The cosmogony associated with Nun became the dominant Egyptian explanation of creation.

In the Pyramid Texts the god Ptah of Memphis was recognized as the supreme deity. Ptah was associated with thought and speech and was believed to be involved with the creative process. The dominant Egyptian view of the creation of man associated man's creation with the god Khnum. The god Khnum was involved in the creation of man as he formed man like a potter working at the potter's wheel.[2]

Mesopotamian Cosmogonies

By far the most well-known creation account from Mesopotamia was a cuneiform inscription known as the *Enuma Elish* tablets (the words *Enuma Elish* are the actual first two words of this creation document, translated "When on high"). The importance of this epic superseded all others as it became the great national epic of Babylon and established Babylon's social norms and organizational structure.[3] The structure of the introductory verses of *Enuma Elish* is argued to be identical to Genesis 1 where a dependent temporal clause and parenthetic clauses are followed by the main clause. According to this myth, before heaven and earth were formed nothing existed except water. The mingling of the water gods Apsu (sweet-water ocean) and Tiamat (salt-water ocean) resulted in the birth of the gods. Then Tiamat and her followers threatened a group of young gods with destruction. After some of the younger gods withdrew from the conflict with Tiamat, Ea's son Marduk agreed to take on Tiamat on the condition that if he were victorious, he would be declared ruler of the divine government. Marduk was successful and cut the ocean goddess Tiamat into two parts. Marduk constructed the cosmos and the cosmological order from the remains of Tiamat. Half of Tiamat was created into the firmament of heaven and the other half into the foundation of the earth. Because of the

---

2. See John H. Stek, "What Says the Scriptures?" in *Portraits of Creation: Biblical and Scientific Perspectives on the World's Formation*, ed. Howard J. van Til (Grand Rapids: Eerdmans, 1990), 228; Gerhard F. Hasel, "The Polemic Nature of Genesis Cosmology," *EvQ* 46 (1974): 84; John Walton, *Ancient Literature in Its Cultural Context* (Grand Rapids: Zondervan, 1989), 24, 32, 33.

3. See Alexander Heidel, *The Babylonian Genesis* (Chicago: Chicago University Press, 1942), 10.

complaints of the gods about their toil and function in the cosmos, Ea then persuaded Marduk to allow the blood of Kingu, Tiamat's spouse and general, to be used for the creation of humanity. Human beings were thus created to serve the gods and allow the gods to be free from toil.

After Marduk's victory over Tiamat and the subsequent creation of the world, the gods built a mighty temple for Marduk. When all was completed, the gods were able to rest.

While Ptah's creation by creative word has been compared to God's creation by spoken word in Genesis 1, the primary emphasis in the discussions around parallels to the Genesis account has centered on the parallels in *Enuma Elish*. There are several possible parallels between *Enuma Elish* and Genesis 1, but the most substantial is the dividing of Tiamat by Marduk into two distinct spheres of water. This has been compared to God's dividing the firmament on the second day.[4] But perhaps the primary reason for comparing the *Enuma Elish* account with Genesis 1 has been the assertion that the name Tiamat is to be identified with the Hebrew word *tehom* "deep" (Gen. 1:2). It was believed that by using this word the author of Genesis 1 clearly alluded to Tiamat from the Babylonian creation account.[5]

Was Genesis 1 Influenced by the Creation Accounts of the Ancient Near East?

When one observes the similarities between the creation account in Genesis 1 and the ancient Near Eastern creation accounts, it is natural to consider the possibility that they are related and consider that one may have borrowed from the other. Arvid Kapelrud, for example, stated that the time had come to stop the debate over the issue of the relationship of the Genesis creation account and Mesopotamian beliefs. It was time, he insisted, to accept as a fact that the Mesopotamian texts were well known to the Israelites. This consensus has now been overturned.

John Walton argues that the similarities between Genesis and *Enuma Elish* are not nearly strong enough to assert that the author of Genesis was in any way addressing the content of *Enuma Elish*.[6] The purpose of these accounts is vastly different. For example, *Enuma Elish* was written to exalt Marduk in the

---

4. See John H. Walton, *Ancient Literature in Its Cultural Context*, 26.
5. It has been maintained by some that this imitation indicated that the author of Genesis was familiar with the Babylonian creation accounts. See Arvid S. Kapelrud, "The Mythological Features in Genesis Chapter I and the Author's Intentions," *VT* 24 (1974): 181, 183. In the Ugaritic texts from Syria, the gods were rewarded with the building of a temple after great victories.
6. See Walton, *Ancient Literature in Its Cultural Context*, 34; David Toshio Tsumura, "Genesis and Ancient Near Eastern Stories of Creation and Flood: An Introduction" in *I Studied Inscriptions from before the Flood*, ed. Richard S. Hess and David Toshio Tsumura (Winona Lake, Ind.: Eisenbrauns, 1994), 31.

pantheon of Babylon, while Genesis 1 was written to establish the sovereignty of God over all creation. Most biblical scholars agree that there is little basis for assuming that the biblical writer used or had access to any of the ancient Near Eastern creation myths. It is best to affirm that the accounts have no direct relationship.[7]

Differences of Ancient Near Eastern Cosmogonies and Genesis 1–2

In spite of the many interesting parallels between Genesis 1–2 and other ancient Near Eastern creation accounts the differences between these two traditions are far more distinctive. The most basic ideas in the biblical account are fundamentally different from the pagan conceptions. As Herman Gunkel noted,

> The difference between the Babylonian creation account and that of Genesis 1 is great; it could hardly be more pronounced. In the Babylonian account everything is wild and grotesque; it is barbaric, riotous poetry. In Genesis 1 everything is quietly solemn and elevated; it is expansive and occasionally somewhat pedantic prose. There the gods emerged in the course of things; here God is one and the same from the very beginning. In the Babylonian account there is the deity who slays the monster in heated combat and forms the world out of its corpse; in Genesis 1 there is God "who speaks and it is so."[8]

Similarly Thorkild Jacobsen has captured the major distinction between pagan and biblical religion with regard to pagan mythology: "World origins, it holds, are essentially accidental: gods were born out of a mingling of the primeval waters and they engendered other gods."[9] The Bible, by contrast, is totally disinterested in the origin of God. In Egyptian and Mesopotamian creation texts nothing is known of a once-for-all creation that took place at the beginning of time. The focus of these accounts is not really about creation as much as the power and function of the gods. There is no reason to assume that *tehom* ("the deep"; Gen. 1:2) was a depersonification of the Babylonian goddess Tiamat. The etymological connection between these two terms cannot

---

7. See Walton, *Ancient Israelite Literature in Its Cultural Context*, 34–38. This would also apply to the myth of the conflict of Cosmos and Chaos. See Edward J. Young, *Studies in Genesis One* (Philadelphia: P&R, 1964), 82n.80.
8. Herman Gunkel, "The Influence of Babylonian Mythology upon the Biblical Creation Story," in *Creation in the Old Testament*, ed. Bernard W. Anderson (Philadelphia: Fortress, 1984), 47.
9. Thorkild Jacobsen *The Treasures of Darkness* (New Haven: Yale University Press, 1976), 191.

be firmly established.[10] "In Genesis 1, *tehom* is clearly inanimate, a part of the cosmos, not the foe of God, but simply one section of the created world."[11] As Westermann has concluded, the ancient near eastern cosmogonies have no comparable parallel to Genesis 1:1.[12]

The cuneiform literature of the ancient Near East is consistent in asserting that the purpose of the creation of man was to relieve the gods of their work and provide for the needs of the gods. This contrasts with the biblical account where man was created to rule and have dominion and have a relationship with God (see Question 23, "What Does It Mean That Man Is Made in God's Image"). In Genesis 1 man is the pinnacle of creation. He is not an afterthought created only to relieve the gods of their labors. Unlike the Mesopotamian accounts, the Bible shows man created with dignity.[13]

God had no difficulty in his creation; there was no trouble or opposition of any kind. He spoke and the creation took place. Creation by the word is unknown in the Mesopotamian creation texts. Whereas Egyptian literature does reflect this concept, in Memphite theology the utterance does not seek to reflect power as much as it does magic. Saying the right formula or performing the right activities was thought to animate properties inherent in matter. Creation by the word in the biblical text may be a way of confronting the philosophy of magic.[14]

Polemics

One explanation for the similarities that do exist between the biblical creation account and the myths of the ancient Near East is that the Bible alluded to these myths but only in a way to undermine them and assert that the God of Israel is the true God of all. The God of Israel is far superior and beyond comparison when compared to the alleged gods referred to in these pagan myths. This can be seen particularly in possible allusions to pagan creation myths primarily found outside Genesis 1. As Fishbane stated:

---

10. See David Toshio Tsumura, *The Earth and the Waters in Genesis 1 and 2*, JSOTSup 83 (Sheffield: JSOT Press, 1989), 65.
11. Hasel, "The Polemic Nature of Genesis Cosmology," 83–84. There are, however, possible remnants of a conflict as seen in reference to enemies of God who are described as dragonlike creatures, including Rahab (Job 9:13; Ps. 40:5 [4]; Ps. 87:4; Ps. 89:10–15 [9–14]; Isa. 30:7; Isa. 51:9–10); Leviathan (Job 3:8; Job 40:25–41:26 [41:1–34]; Ps. 74:12–19; Ps. 104:25–26; Isa. 27:1); Behemoth (Job 40:15–24); the Dragon in the Sea (Job 7:12; Ps. 44:20 [19]; Ezek. 29:3–6a; 32:2–8; and the Serpent (Amos 9:2–3). See Gunkel "The Influence of Babylonian Mythology," 35–36.
12. See Claus Westermann, *Genesis 1–11*, trans. John J. Scullion S. J. (Minneapolis: Fortress, 1994), 97.
13. See Hasel, "The Polemic Nature of Genesis Cosmology," 90; Walton, *Ancient Literature in Its Cultural Context*, 29.
14. See Hasel, "The Polemic Nature of Genesis Cosmology," 90–91.

In several passages YHWH, the God of Israel, manifests His primordial might by routing antagonistic sea monsters before the creation itself (Psalms 89:9–12). Similar passages can be found in Isaiah 27:1–2; 51:9–11; Habakkuk 3:8–11, 14–15; Ps. 74:13–14. The monsters referred to, Yam and Rahab, also appear elsewhere in the Bible, along with other sea monsters—Nachash, Tanin and Leviathan—names which, like the battle descriptions themselves, bear a striking similarity to ones found in ancient Canaanite myths. Elements also recall the story of the divine creator-hero Marduk in the Mesopotamian creation-epic, *Enuma Elish*. Before the creation of the world, Marduk fought and defeated both the sea-monster Tiamat and her cohorts with winds (IV: 42–48, 96–100) and a net (IV:41, 95, 112). See Job 9:13; 26:12–13 . . . many of the aforementioned texts (and also Psalms 104:25–26) cite the primordial battle of YHWH with a sea monster as prologue to a request for, or prophecy of, a remanifestation of divine power against evildoers and antagonists of the Israelites in history.[15]

The name Tanin (*tannim*; "great sea creatures") in Genesis 1:21, though spelled similarly to the mythological creature, is a generic term rather than a personal name. The special verb *bara* ("create") is used to describe the creation of this creature. Since *bara* was not used in connection with the creation of other land animals (Gen. 1:25), it appears that this verb was used to describe the creation of the *tannim* to stress the fact that the *tannim* were created by God in an effortless act. Hasel states that this allusion to the creation of a pagan god is a deliberate attempt to contradict the view that creation took place as the result of a cosmic struggle.[16] In addition, the ancient view that the sun, moon, and stars were deities is completely debunked in Genesis 1 where they are the results of God's creation fiat, "Let there be light" (Gen. 1:3).[17]

Thus the author of Genesis 1 wrote to break the age-old religious notions that still held many ancient peoples including the Israelites in their thrall. The biblical author's purpose was to proclaim knowledge of the true God as he has manifested himself in his creative works, as well as to proclaim the right understanding of humankind, the world, and history that the correct knowledge of God entails. These assertions were made in the historical context of the false

---

15. Michael Fishbane, *Text and Texture* (New York: Schocken, 1979), 13–14.
16. See Hasel, "The Polemic Nature of Genesis Cosmology," 86–87.
17. The demythologization of the sun goes even further as it is created on the fourth day while light was created on the first day. See Jon D. Levenson, *Creation and the Persistence of Evil* (San Francisco: Harper & Row, 1988), 65. Thus Genesis 1:14–19 appears to have an anti-mythological aim.

religious notions dominant throughout the world of the day. These beliefs included the notion that all the forces of nature were deities; while, in Genesis 1 all the forces of nature are subject to God's word. Notice the distinctiveness of the God of the Bible compared to the pagan gods of the ancient Near East.

FALSE RELIGIONS	TRUE GOD
Gods from watery mass	Watery mass God's creation
Gods from divine procreation	Cosmos order by God's word
Gods from all spheres of existence	God is one and Creator of all
Order from conquering chaos deity or deities	Creator not threatened by powers
Monsters lurk in chaos waters	These are mere creatures like fish
Sun, moon, and stars are deities	Heavenly bodies are mere lights
Procreation involves participation with divine	Procreation is by God's blessing
Humans are pawns and slaves for the gods	Humanity is crown of creation

John Stek commented on the diverse worldviews of pagan mythology when compared to the Bible: "But an attentive reading of the whole against the background of the several myths of the ancient Near East discloses a view of God, humanity, and world that, whatever its more or less incidental affinities with conceptions abroad in Israel's environment, stands in striking opposition to almost all that those religions had in common."[18]

The God of the Bible is without peer. He does not need to establish his power and authority by defeating other gods of a pantheistic pantheon. The outstanding feature of the biblical account is the absence of mythology; there is nothing that hints of the creation of gods. In the biblical account, the clear line between God and his creation was never violated. And most distinctively, creation is never predicated on pagan gods.[19]

Conclusion

It is somewhat ironic that, while many in our culture want to draw a line in the sand to separate scientific endeavors from the biblical faith, it is the distinctiveness of the biblical religion in contrast to the pagan views of the ancient world that have made scientific experimentation a possibility. Were it believed that the world was controlled by a multitude of capricious deities, or

---

18. Stek, "What Says the Scripture?," 231–32. See Gordon J. Wenham, *Genesis 1–15*, WBC 1 (Waco, Tex.: Word, 1987), 37–38; Nahum M. Sarna, *Understanding Genesis* (New York: Schocken, 1966), 9, 11.
19. See Wenham, *Genesis 1–15*, 14.

that the world was subject to mere chance, no consistency could be expected in experimental results and no scientific laws could be discovered. The biblical view that God is not part of nature, that nature is not an extension of God but rather is the result of his creation, provided the ideological basis for the rise of modern science. "Because God is completely benevolent, as well as all-powerful, humanity has nothing to fear from creation."[20]

REFLECTION QUESTIONS

1. Is the biblical account of creation distinct? Explain.

2. What biblical word in Genesis 1:2 has been alleged to be related to the goddess Tiamat?

3. Did the ancient Near Eastern creation accounts influence Genesis 1? Explain.

4. Is there evidence that the Israelites were aware of the creation accounts in other cultures? Explain.

5. How is the biblical worldview different from the pagan ancient Near Eastern perspective?

---

20. Bruce K. Waltke and Cathi J. Fredricks, *Genesis* (Grand Rapids: Zondervan, 2001), 57. See Francis Schaeffer, *How Should We Then Live?* (Old Tappan, NJ: Revell, 1976), 132; Wenham, *Genesis 1–15*, 39; Ken Mathews, *Genesis 1–11:26*, NAC 1A (Nashville: B&H, 1996), 129.

How Did God Create Everything?

The belief in the eternity of matter was a common conception in many of the civilizations of the ancient world. For example, the preeminent Greek philosophers Plato and Aristotle believed that the material universe had no beginning. Many of the creation accounts from the ancient Near East begin with the notion that matter is already in existence when the formative creative events begin. This view is also shared by many contemporary interpreters of Genesis 1:1. According to these interpreters, we can assume that when the events of Genesis 1 begin, matter is already in existence.

Precreation Chaos Theory

One such view held by many evangelicals is the Precreation Chaos Theory. One of the chief advocates of this view is Bruce Waltke. This view understands the chaotic state described in Genesis 1:2 as existing before the creation spoken of in the Bible. Thus, the Genesis creation account is a relative beginning and by necessity there must be a pre-Genesis time and space. Or as Waltke states: "The narrator begins the story with the planet already present, although undifferentiated and unformed."[1]

According to the Precreation Chaos Theory, Genesis 1:1 is an independent clause and functions as a title for the events of Genesis 1:2–2:3. Thus, Genesis 1:1 summarizes the creation account. Genesis 1:2 is viewed as a circumstantial clause subordinate to Genesis 1:3. Genesis 1:2 thus describes the state of the earth and the universe when the account of creation is taken up in Genesis 1:3. It is not the purpose of Genesis to tell how the chaos came about (any more than it is interested in identifying the serpent of chapter 3). The narrative shows how God brought this world from its primitive condition of desolation and waste to its fullness and order. The creation account

---

1. Bruce K. Waltke and Cathi J. Fredricks, *Genesis* (Grand Rapids: Zondervan, 2001), 59.

of Genesis 1 thus does not address the original creation, but refers to a recreation of the earth that somehow came to exist out of this chaotic state.[2]

The Verbs of Creation

Three primary verbs are used in the creation account in Genesis 1–2. The three verbs are *yatsar, asah*, and *bara*.[3] The root *yatsar* has the basic connotation of forming or "fashioning." It is used of a potter's work with clay. The verb occurs for the first time in Genesis 2:7 where God fashions man from the dust of the ground.

The root *asah* is used numerous times in the creation account (Gen. 1:7, 16, 25, 26, 31; 2:2, 3). It is usually rendered "to do" or "to make." In the creation account the verb is used almost synonymously with the third verb of creation, the verb *bara* (Gen. 1:1). For example, the verb *asah* appears virtually equivalent in meaning to *bara* in Genesis 1:7, where God makes the expanse to divide the waters, or makes the heavenly bodies (Gen. 1:16), or makes the animals that live on the land (Gen. 1:25). Like *bara, asah* is used in conjunction with the creation of mankind (Gen. 1:26–27). It is also used in reference to the creation of heaven and earth (Ex. 20:11; Neh. 9:6). The verb is used at the conclusion of the six days of creation to refer to all that God made (Gen. 1:31). The close association between both verbs can be recognized by their occurrence together at the close of the seven day creation week in Genesis 2:3. The verbs *asah* and *bara* thus often appear to be interchangeable.[4]

The Unique Verb of Creation

The first word of creation from Genesis 1:1 is the word *bara* which also occurs in Genesis 1:21, 25, 27; 2:3. It has been the argument of many that it is not proper to assert that *bara* means *creatio ex nihilo*, "creation out of nothing." While this may be a true assertion, it could be noted that perhaps no verb in any language has this precise connotation. And yet, *bara* is distinct in many ways. For example, it is often pointed out that in the Hebrew Bible God is the only subject for *bara*. Nowhere is *bara* associated with human production. This cannot be said of other verbs of creation such as *asah* and *yatsar* in Genesis 1–2. Furthermore, rarely could it be said that when a *bara* creation occurs, preexisting material is merely reworked (as in Ps. 51:10a [12a]; Isa. 57:19). On the contrary, a *bara* creation always refers to the finished product but not to the material from which the product was made. In other words, something entirely new that had never existed before is produced—something

---

2. Proponents of this view are not opposed to creation out of nothing and believe that other biblical passages affirm this view. They just maintain that it is not taught in Genesis 1.

3. Other verbs not in the Genesis creation account that are used in the context of creation are *p'l* "make, work" (Ex. 15:17) and *kwn* "to establish, make firm" (Prov. 8:27).

4. See James Barr, "The Image of God in the Book of Genesis—A Study of Terminology," *BJRL* 51 (1968–69): 25.

that is radically new, unprecedented and unique (Ps. 104:30; Isa. 41:20; 48:6–7; 65:17–18; Jer. 31:32; cf. Ex. 34:10; Num. 16:30; Deut. 4:32).[5] And as should be expected since this type of creativity is reserved for God alone, a *bara* creation is one that is completely effortless and unconditioned. The late Jewish scholar Nahum Sarna eloquently summarized the distinct nature of the verb *bara*:

> The Hebrew stem *b-r-'* is used in the Bible exclusively of divine creativity. It signifies that the product is absolutely novel and unexampled, depends solely on God for its coming into existence, and is beyond the human capacity to reproduce. The verb always refers to the completed product, never to the material of which it is made. . . . Precisely because of the indispensable importance of preexisting matter in the pagan cosmologies, the very absence of such mention here is highly significant. This conclusion is reinforced by the idea of creation by divine fiat without reference to any inert matter being present. Also, the repeated biblical emphasis upon God as the exclusive Creator would seem to rule out the possibility of preexistent matter. Finally, if *bara'* is used only of God's creation, it must be essentially distinct from human creation. The ultimate distinction would be *creatio ex nihilo*, which has no human parallel and is thus utterly beyond all human comprehension.[6]

Ultimately, however, it is true that one could not define the concept of *creatio ex nihilo* from the use of a single term. This idea must emerge from the context as a whole. As Stek has explained,

> Walter Eichrodt is no doubt close to the mark when he observes that the author's strict monotheism, the radical difference between his cosmogony and that of the current myths with their assumption of a primordial substrate from which the first generation of the gods emerges, his opening reference to an "absolute beginning for the creation," his emphasis on creation by divine word, and his choice of the verb *bara'* in the superscript (v.1) all tend toward a concrete depiction of original creation for which anything short of *ex nihilo* in

5. See Bernhard W. Anderson, *Creation Versus Chaos* (New York: Association Press, 1967), 130; John Skinner, *Genesis* ICC, 2nd ed. (Edinburgh: T&T Clark, 1930), 15; John H. Stek, "What Says the Scriptures?" in *Portraits of Creation: Biblical and Scientific Perspectives on the World's Formation* (Grand Rapids: Eerdmans, 1990), 207n.4.
6. Nahum M. Sarna, *Genesis*, JPSTC (Philadelphia: Jewish Publication Society, 1989), 5.

more abstract language would fail to do justice. Nevertheless, although for us *ex nihilo* in its strictest sense certainly qualifies the absolute beginning of the creation, *it does not necessarily apply to all of God's acts that are viewed as "creative" by the Old Testament writers.*[7]

The context is key, but it could also be stated that the verb *bara* expresses better than any other available term the concept of *creatio ex nihilo*. It describes exclusively divine activity—a distinction without parallel in any other language.[8] "If in Genesis 1:1 Moses desired to express the thought of absolute creation there was no more suitable word in the Hebrew language at his disposal."[9]

The verb *bara* occurs a total of six times in the creation account of Genesis 1:1–2:3 (1:1, 21, 27 [3x]; 2:3). The verb is used like a marker that opens and closes the creation week (Gen. 1:1; 2:3). It also is the verb used to describe the creation of the first and last living creatures (1:21, 27).[10] It often occurs in close proximity to the word *barakh*, "bless," a word that is similar in sound in the early chapters of Genesis (1:21–22; 1:27–28; 2:3; 5:1–2).[11] Each new stage of the creation account is marked by the employment of the verb *bara*. It is used with reference to the universe (1:1); the living creatures (1:20–21); and humanity (1:26–27).

We have seen how several terms in the Hebrew Bible could refer to God's act of creation as well as to man's. Of these only *bara* exclusively has God as its subject. But in the context of creation the same could also be said for the verb *amar*, "to speak." Here in the creation account, *amar* is clearly used as well to speak of a divine fiat and creation *ex nihilo*.[12] Creation by the word from the context also indicates *creatio ex nihilo*. The creative act is revealed in the word of creation as the supreme source of power and life. As Michael Fishbane has observed, "God's speaking and creating are one and indissoluble. His words create and order the heaven and the earth; they give a syntax to the formless and the void, they transform the primordial, undifferentiated unity into order and classification. The prosaic, reflective discourse of the human speaker ('there was') counterpoints the commanding tones ('Let there be') of the divine speeches, as well as the force expressed in naming the things of creation ('Day!' 'Heaven!' 'Earth!')."[13]

---

7. Stek, "What Says the Scriptures?" 221. See also Kenneth Mathews, *Genesis 1–11:26*, NAC 1A (Nashville: B&H, 1996), 128–29.
8. See Julius Wellhausen, *Prologomena to the History of Israel* (Cleveland and New York: Meridan, 1957), 304.
9. Edward J. Young, *Studies in Genesis One* (Philadelphia: P&R, 1964), 6–7.
10. See W. Randall Garr, "God's Creation: ברא in the Priestly Source," *HTR* 97 (2004): 84.
11. The first two letters of *bara* and *barakh* are identical.
12. See Shemaryahu Talmon, "The Biblical Understanding of Creation and the Human Commitment," *ExAud* 3 (1987): 111.
13. Michael Fishbane, *Text and Texture* (New York: Schocken, 1979), 7.

When biblical writers referred to God's creation by divine fiat, they most frequently referred to the creation by the word.[14] As von Rad stated, "The idea of creation by the word preserves first of all the most radical essential distinction between Creator and creature. Creation cannot be even remotely considered an emanation from God; it is not somehow an overflow or reflection of his being, i.e., of his divine nature, but is rather a product of his personal will."[15]

Creatio Ex Nihilo in Early Jewish Literature

It is often noted that the notion of *creatio ex nihilo* is explicitly stated for the first time in 2 Maccabees 7:28: "I beg you, my child, to look at the heaven and the earth and see everything that is in them, and recognize that God did not make them out of things that existed" (NRSV). 2 Maccabees 7:28 appears to be directly dependent on the LXX of Genesis 1:1 (see Jub. 2:2).[16] In 2 Baruch 21:4 the term "the beginning" is related to the idea of *creatio ex nihilo*: "O hear me, you who created the earth, the one who fixed the firmament by the word and fastened the height of heaven by the spirit, the one who in the beginning of the world called that which did not yet exist and they obeyed you." In 2 Enoch 24:2 God produces the creatures *ex nihilo*: "Before anything existed at all, from the very beginning, whatever exists I created from the non-existent, and from the invisible the visible" (see 4 Ezra 3:4; 6:38). In the Midrash Genesis Rabbah 1.9.1, Gamaliel II (ca. AD 100) reacted to the notion that God was only an artist who had good preexistent matter to work with: "all of them (material in Gen. 1:2) are explicitly described as having been created by (God)."[17]

---

14. See Psalm 33:6, 9; 148:5–6; Isaiah 48:13; Jeremiah 31:35–36; cf. 33:25; Job 33; Isaiah 45:12; Job 38:8–11; cf. Psalm 104:9; Jeremiah 5:22; Job 36:32; 37:6; Proverbs 8:29; Psalm 147:15–18; Amos 5:8; 9:6. See Stek, "What Says the Scriptures?" 216–18.

15. Gerhard Von Rad, *Genesis*, rev. ed. (Philadelphia: Westminster, 1972), 51–52. "In the language of the Old Testament, it can be said of all that God effects in the world (alike in "nature" and "history") that he does so by his word" (Stek, "What Says the Scriptures?" 219).

16. All the nouns listed in Genesis 1:1–5 of the LXX occur in Jubilees 2:2 indicating its dependence upon the language of the creation account. See S. D. Diere, *A New Glimpse of Day One: Intertextuality, History of Interpretation, and Genesis 1.1–5* (Berlin: Walter de Gruyter, 2009), 243, 278–79. According to Brown, Origen understood 2 Maccabees 7:22–29 as the first unequivocal statement of *creatio ex nihilo*. See William P. Brown, *Structure, Role and Ideology in the Hebrew and Greek Texts of Genesis 1:1–2:3*, SBLDS 132 (Atlanta: Scholars Press, 1993), 32–35.

17. See James H. Charlesworth, *The Old Testament Pseudepigrapha*, 2 vols. (Garden City, New York: Doubleday, 1983, 1985), 1:142, 628; Masanobu Endo, *Creation and Christology* (Tübingen: J. C. B. Mohr [Paul Siebeck], 2002), 206–7; Jacob Neusner, *Genesis Rabbah*, vol. 1 (Atlanta: Scholars Press, 1985), 13. A similar sentiment is found in the text 1QS 3:15 among the Dead Sea Scrolls. See J. C. O'Neill, "How Early Is the Doctrine of Creatio Ex Nihilo? *JTS* 53 (2002): 461.

Creatio Ex Nihilo in the New Testament

The influence of Genesis 1:1, as well as the notion of *creatio ex nihilo*, is reflected in the later biblical writers of the New Testament (see John 1:3; Heb. 11:3). John Sailhamer observed with regard to Hebrews 11:3 that, "the writer of the book of Hebrews, for example, laid it down as a fundamental article of faith that the world was created out of nothing (*ex nihilo*)."[18] To this should be added Paul's statement to the Romans: "as it is written, 'I have made you the father of many nations'—in the presence of the God in whom he believed, who gives life to the dead and calls into existence the things that do not exist" (Rom. 4:17). With regard to the New Testament teaching on the doctrine of *creatio ex nihilo*, Gerhard May writes: "What the New Testament statements about the creation intend is quite legitimately interchangeable with the idea of *creatio ex nihilo*."[19]

Creatio Ex Nihilo in the Church Fathers

The two early church fathers who are credited with developing the doctrine of *creatio ex nihilo* are Irenaeus and Theophilus. Due to their contribution along with the churches' anti-gnostic stance, the doctrine became a self-evident premise by the end of the second century AD. We see in the works of Tertullian and Hippolytus that the doctrine of creation out of absolutely nothing is already the fixed Christian position. It is clear that by the time of Origen, who was credited with making the first great attempt to systematically develop the Christian doctrine of creation, matter was not viewed as original, as it was created out of nothing by God. For Origen, *creatio ex nihilo* was the foundation of the notion of divine providence; without it the idea of providence was impossible. Thus, as early as the third century AD, the doctrine of *creatio ex nihilo* was regarded as a fundamental tenet of Christian theology.[20] Furthermore, as William Brown has stated, "From Ambrose to the Latin authors of the Middle Ages, Gen. 1:1 alone was considered the sufficient and irrefutable means for refuting the Platonic doctrine of the eternity of matter."[21]

Conclusion

The opening phrase of the Bible, "in the beginning," very clearly implies the concept of *creatio ex nihilo* or "creation from nothing." Harvard University Professor Jon Levenson has stated that the traditional Jewish and Christian view of *creatio ex nihilo* can only be maintained if one translates the opening biblical

---

18. See John H. Sailhamer, *Genesis Unbound* (Sisters Oregon: Multnomah, 1996), 174.
19. Gerhard May, *Creatio Ex Nihilo: The Doctrine of "Creation out of Nothing" in Early Christian Thought,* trans. A. S. Worrall (Edinburg: T & T Clark, 1994), 26.
20. See May, *Creatio Ex Nihilo*, 177–79.
21. Brown, *Structure*, 35.

phrase as "in the beginning."[22] This opening phrase indicates of course that God existed "before the beginning," whereas the material world did not. The heavens and earth are not an emanation of God. "According to Genesis 1:1, creation had a beginning, but God does not. If Genesis 1:1 says that God created all that exists "in the beginning," then before the "beginning" nothing must have existed."[23]

Thus only God is eternal; everything else was created by him. God created the universe "out of nothing." Perhaps no verse in Scripture is as profound as Genesis 1:1. It is the fundamental doctrine of Christianity. This fundamental doctrine may be expressed by two truths from Genesis 1: God created all things and God sustains what he has created. Though creation is not part of God, it is utterly dependent upon God for existence and provision (Neh. 9:6; Acts 17:25, 28). This act of creation and providence emphasize God's omnipotent and omniscient presence in creation. The oft-repeated phrase "and God made" displays God's complete transcendence. All the universe and every human being has been created by him.[24]

REFLECTION QUESTIONS

1. What are the characteristics of the Precreation Chaos Theory?

2. What is the unique verb of creation in the Old Testament?

3. What is distinctive about this verb?

4. How prevalent is the notion of *creatio ex nihilo* in the history of interpretation?

5. What New Testament passages refer to the concept of creation out of nothing?

---

22. See Jon D. Levenson, *Creation and the Persistence of Evil* (San Francisco: Harper & Row, 1988), 5.
23. Sailhamer, *Genesis Unbound*, 105. See Dietrich Bonhoeffer, *Creation and Fall: A Theological Interpretation of Genesis 1–3* (London: SCM Press, 1959), 16; Derek Kidner, *Genesis: An Introduction and Commentary* (Downers Grove: InterVarsity Press, 1972), 43.
24. Ecclesiastes 12:1; Isaiah 44:2, 24; 49:5; Jeremiah 1:5; cf. Job 4:17; 10:8–12; 31:15; 32:22; 33:4; 35:10; 36:3; 37:7; 40:15; Psalm 119:73; 139:13–16; Proverbs 22:2; Isaiah 17:7.

What Is the Connection of Genesis 1:1 to Genesis 1?

The relationship of Genesis 1:1 to Genesis 1 may not be as clear as one might initially expect. Broadly speaking there are four primary evangelical positions regarding the relationship between Genesis 1:1 to the entire chapter of Genesis 1. One view is that Genesis 1:1 should be understood as a title or perhaps a summary of the contents of Genesis 1. This view has been advocated by many and is a central component to Bruce Waltke's Precreation Chaos Theory.[1] The second major position is that Genesis 1:1 is more than a title or summary—it actually describes the initial act of creation. This position has been regarded as the traditional understanding of Genesis 1:1. A third view, a novel position advocated by John Sailhamer, posits that Genesis 1:1 refers to a different creative act than what begins in Genesis 1:2, thus resulting in two distinct creations in Genesis 1. Thus, Genesis 1:1 is to be separated from the creative events of Genesis 1:3–31. Sailhamer refers to his position as Historical Creationism.[2] A fourth position understands Genesis 1:1 along with Genesis 1:2 as the background of the creation account, with the main action beginning in Genesis 1:3. One advocate of this position, John Collins, provides a helpful translation of Genesis 1:1–2 to draw out the distinctiveness of this position:

> (1) God had in the beginning created the heavens and the earth. (2) Now as for the earth, it was formlessness and

---

1. See Bruce K. Waltke, *Creation and Chaos* (Portland, Oregon: Western Baptist Theological Seminary, 1974).
2. See John H. Sailhamer, *Genesis Unbound* (Sisters, Oregon: Multnomah, 1996).

emptiness, and darkness was over the surface of the deep, and the Spirit of God was hovering over the surface of the water.[3]

Virtually all agree that the following narrative, Genesis 1:[2]3–31 describes the manner in which God sets in order the situation that exists in Genesis 1:2. This is accomplished through the pervasive use of the narrative-tense verb in the account. "After Genesis 1:1–2 the main line of the narrative of creation is carried along by the *waw* consecutive, just as the *waw* consecutive is consistently used in the Book of Genesis."[4] To a great extent the solution to the question of the relationship of Genesis 1:1 to the rest of Genesis 1 comes down to the interpretation of two key phrases in Genesis 1:1—the phrases "in the beginning" and "heavens and earth."

In the Beginning

The first question in the understanding of Genesis 1:1 has to do with the interpretation of the first word in Genesis 1:1, the word (technically phrase) *bereshith*. This phrase has most often been translated "in the beginning," but in some modern English versions, we find that translators have chosen to translate the word with a phrase such as "when God began to create."[5] This interpretation is not new. It was the view of prominent medieval Jewish commentators Ibn Ezra (1167) and Rashi (1105). It has been argued that *reshith*, "beginning" lacks the article, but this does not mean that the word is not used in the absolute sense, "in *the* beginning." Temporal phrases often lack the article in Hebrew (e.g., Gen. 3:22; 6:3–4; Isa. 40:21; 41:4, 26; Mic. 5:1; Hab. 1:12). *Reshith* never has the article when it is used in a temporal sense, and it is clear that the noun *reshith* has the absolute sense in Isa. 46:10.[6] Walter Eichrodt has stated that the use of this noun in Isaiah 46:10 is to be

---

3. See C. John Collins, "Reading Genesis 1:1–2:3 as An Act of Communication: Discourse Analysis and Literal Interpretation," in *Did God Create in Six Days?*, ed. Joseph A. Pipa, Jr. and David W. Hall (Taylors, SC: Southern Presbyterian Press, 1999), 134.

4. Robert V. McCabe, "A Critique of the Framework Interpretation of the Creation Week," in *Coming to Grips with Genesis*, ed. Terry Mortenson and Thane H. Ury (Green Forest, AR: Master, 2008), 217–18.

5. The word "beginning" has been understood to refer to a noun in construct with the following verb *bara*, "to create." Normally a construct noun is followed by another noun and expresses the "of" relationship in English, as in the phrase "Son of God."

6. See Gordon Wenham, *Genesis 1–15*, WBC 1 (Waco, Texas: Word, 1987), 3. Moreover, there is Greek inscriptional evidence that suggests that the first word of Genesis is definite and thus introduces a main clause (Claus Westermann, *Genesis 1–11*, trans. John J. Scullion S. J. [Minneapolis: Fortress, 1994], 94). See William R. Lane, "The Initiation of Creation," *VT* 13 (1963): 68; Victor P. Hamilton, *The Book of Genesis Chapters 1–17*, NICOT (Grand Rapids: Eerdmans, 1990), 107; Ken Mathews, *Genesis 1–11*, NAC (Nashville: B&H), 138n.103.

determined by its correlation with *akharith* ("end"), i.e., the final situation.[7] Eichrodt commented on the important contribution of Isaiah 46 to this discussion when he stated,

> The use of *mere'shith* in Isa. 46:10 appears to be determined by its correlation with *akharith*. . . . On the basis of v. 9 it is clear that the prophet thinks of something existent from primeval times, the *ri'shonoth me'olam* . . . the prophet combines God's disposition over beginning and end. But one cannot refer to this pair of words just to Cyrus's rise and ultimate success, of which vs. 11 speaks. The power to summon Cyrus is deduced here, as in 42:24ff; 48:12–15, from the primordial majesty of Yahweh the Creator, who can make known from the beginning (*miqqedem*) that which has not yet been created (v. 10a) and who therefore causes the end to be proclaimed from the very beginning. . . . the transcendent God has determined the end together with the beginning, and therefore commands the entire development of the world.[8]

Isaiah's use of *reshith* (Isa. 46:10) thus refers to the beginning both of time and of history itself. The Lord the Creator is the one who causes the end to be proclaimed from the very beginning. Put differently, according to Derek Kidner the expression in the beginning in Genesis 1:1 shows "that the beginning is pregnant with the end, and the whole process present to God who is First and Last."[9]

The analogous expression *merosh* (from the same root as *reshith*) in Proverbs 8:23 certainly refers to the beginning of all creation.[10] The context

---

7. In this regard *reshith* stands in opposition to *tekhillah* which stands in contrast only to subsequent situations (S. Rattray and J. Milgrom, "ראשית *reshith*," *TDOT* 13:269). Sailhamer's preference of *rishonah* (an adjective) and *tekhillah* to refer to an absolute beginning actually appear as less favorable because neither of these terms expresses opposition to *akharith* as the consummation of time as it does in Isaiah 46:10. *Akharith* is also used with "days" (*yamim*) at the end of Genesis (49:1) to correspond to *reshith* which is associated with creation "days" (*yom/yamim*) in Genesis 1:1. *Akharith* is also paired with its antonym *reshith* in Deuteronomy 11:12; Job 42:12; Ecclesiastes 7:8. In Daniel 8:17–19 *akharith* is used in the context of the "end of time."

8. Walter Eichrodt, "In the Beginning," *Israel's Prophetic Heritage: Essays in Honor of James Muilenburg*, ed. Bernard W. Anderson and Walter Harrelson (New York: Harpers & Brothers, 1962), 5.

9. Derek Kidner, *Genesis: An Introduction and Commentary* (Downers Grove: InterVarsity, 1972), 43. Sailhamer observes that the choice of the word *reshith* in Genesis 1:1 is related to the fact of its close association with the word *akharith* ("end"). See John Sailhamer, *Genesis*, EBC, 2nd ed. (Grand Rapids: Zondervan, 2008), 53.

10. See Eichrodt, "In the Beginning," 3–4; Wenham, *Genesis 1–15*, 12.

of *bereshith* standing at the start of the account of world history makes an absolute sense highly appropriate here. The Massoretes understood the word to be absolute, for they accented the word with the disjunctive accent called a *tiphkha*, which is normal for words in the absolute state, rather than a conjunctive accent. The conjunctive accent would be normal for words in the construct state.[11] The use of the disjunctive accent creates a pause. It separates subsequent words rather than combining them together. This supports the traditional translation "in the beginning."[12]

But the view that the first sentence in the Bible constitutes a fundamental statement of God's activity already existed in the early Greek translation of the Old Testament in the Septuagint. In addition, both of the standard Hebrew lexicons list the meaning "beginning, what comes first," as the most frequent nuance of *reshith*.[13]

Moreover, John 1:1 reflects an interpretation that understands Genesis 1:1 as a main clause. It is widely accepted that the opening words, *en archē* (John 1:1), correspond to the beginning words of the Genesis 1:1 account, *bereshith* (Gen. 1:1; en *archē* [LXX]). This would be John's way of saying that the *Logos*, Christ, existed with the Father at the time of the creation of the universe.[14] The term 'beginning' (*archē* in Greek) often appears in Septuagint and New Testament contexts where reference is made to God's work of creation.[15] With no exceptions all the ancient versions, Jewish midrashim (commentaries), apocryphal, and pseudepigraphic works understood the first word *bereshith* as an absolute.[16]

In traditional Jewish references to creation, reference is made to "the beginning" of Genesis 1 in contexts where the sovereignty of God is the focus (4

---

11. See Westermann, *Genesis 1–11*, 97–98. While Hosea 1:2 is often cited as parallel to Genesis 1:1 with a noun in construct followed by a finite verb, the issue of the disjunctive accent in Genesis 1:1 is distinctive and unravels what appears otherwise to be the perfect parallel in Hosea 1:2.

12. See Edward J. Young, *Studies in Genesis One* (Philadelphia: P&R, 1964), 5; Lane, "The Initiation of Creation," 66; Hamilton, *Genesis Chapters 1–17*, 106–7; Henri Blocher, *In the Beginning*, trans. by David G. Preston (Downers Grove: InterVarsity, 1984), 62n.12. There is an alliterative connection with the words as the first two words of Genesis 1:1 begin with the identical first three letters.

13. See Eichrodt, "In the Beginning," 1–2; *HALOT* 2:1169; BDB, 912.

14. See Edward J. Young, *In the Beginning* (Edinburgh: The Banner of Truth Trust, 1976), 24; Bruce Waltke, with Charles Yu, *An Old Testament Theology* (Grand Rapids: Zondervan, 2007), 180n.14.

15. Genesis 1:1; Proverbs 8:22; Sirach 24:9; 39:25; Jubilees 2:2, 4; Ezra 3:4; 6:38; cf. 6:1–6; 2 Enoch 24:2; Matthew 19:4; 24:21; Mark 10:6; 13:19; 2 Peter 3:4; Hebrews 1:10; Revelation 3:14. See Masanobu Endo, *Creation and Christology* (Tübingen: J. C. B. Mohr [Paul Siebeck], 2002), 206; Westermann, *Genesis 1–11*, 94.

16. See Gary Anderson, "The Interpretation of Genesis 1:1 in the Targums," *CBQ* 52 (1990): 22; C. Westermann, *Genesis 1–11*, 94. See P. Schäfer, "BERESIT BARA' 'ELOHIM: Zur Interpretation von Genesis 1,1 in der Rabbinischen Literatur," *JSJ* 2 (1971): 161–62.

Ezra 6:6; Sir. 15:14). Second Baruch 21:4 states that God is the Creator "who *from the beginning* of the world called that which did not yet exist and they obey him." The term "the beginning" is thus related to the idea of "creation *ex nihilo*." Second Enoch 24:2 also focuses on the unique identity of God, who produces the creatures *ex nihilo*: "Before anything existed, from the beginning, whatever exists I created from the non-existent, and from the invisible into the visible" (see 4 Ezra 3:4; 6:38). Eichrodt suggests that the relative interpretation of the expression "when God began to create" would place an emphasis on the autonomy of the chaotic matter at the beginning of creation contrary to the whole concern of this creation story.[17]

Heavens and Earth as the Title of Genesis 1:1

Bruce Waltke and Brevard Childs argue that the phrase "heavens and earth" is a phrase that signifies the entire organized universe and thus cannot be thought of as part of a chaotic state as described in Genesis 1:2 (Gen. 2:1, 4; Deut. 3:24; Isa. 65:17; Jer. 23:24).[18] This is surely the basic understanding of the phrase as it is used throughout the Old Testament. However, as the first occurrence of the phrase in the Old Testament, as well as the unique historical circumstance of creation, this should not be pressed for Genesis 1:1. As Gordon Wenham states, "Here it suffices to observe that if the creation of the world was a unique event, the terms used here may have a slightly different value from elsewhere. . . . Commentators often insist that the phrase 'heaven and earth' denotes the completely ordered cosmos. Though this is usually the case, totality rather than organization is its chief thrust here. It is therefore quite feasible for a mention of an initial act of creation of the whole universe (v. 1) to be followed by an account of the ordering of different parts of the universe (vv. 2–31)."[19] To insist that the phrase "heavens and earth" must refer only to a perfect and finished universe would be to enslave the expression to its uses elsewhere and thus ignore the contextual requirements of Genesis 1. As Ken Matthews has stated, "Heavens and earth here indicates the totality of the universe, not foremostly an organized, completed universe."[20]

---

17. See Eichrodt, "In the Beginning," 10.
18. See Bruce K. Waltke, "The Literary Genre of Genesis, Chapter One," *Crux* 27, no.4 (December 1991): 4, idem and Cathi J. Fredricks, *Genesis* (Grand Rapids: Zondervan, 2001), 59. Waltke has referred to this view as the "precreation chaos" view.
19. Wenham, *Genesis 1–15*, 13, 15. See Meredith G. Kline, "Space and Time in the Genesis Cosmogony," *Perspectives on Science and Christian Faith* 48, no. 1 (March 1996): 5.
20. Mathews, *Genesis 1–11*, 142. The phrase constitutes a merism as it refers to the totality of the cosmos in its created form (see Michael Deroche, "Isaiah XLV 7 and the Creation of Chaos?" *VT* 42, no. 1 [1992]: 17). A merism is a statement of opposites to incorporate the whole or totality. The combination of the polar opposites indicates more than just the separate meaning of the two component parts.

Understanding this unique circumstance, we should conclude that "the heavens and the earth" in Genesis 1:1 is thus a designation of the essential essence of the world before the detailed forming and ordering, which is described in the rest of the chapter, took place. The term "the heavens and the earth" in verse 1 refers to the substance of the universe from which the entire universe was formed. This is the first occurrence of the phrase "heavens and earth" and one could naturally ask how else the initial stage of the universe might be described? Thus, the argument that the "heavens and earth" must refer to a completed heavens and earth and hence must be a title to the chapter must yield to a better explanation.

Genesis 1:1—Initial Creation Act or Background?

To some extent, the issue of whether Genesis 1:1 refers to a title or summary statement or describes the initial event of creation is one of literary separation. As a title or summary, Genesis 1:1 would stand separate from the rest of the chapter, summarizing the contents. The view that Genesis 1:1–2 provides background information to the creation narrative would also suggest that Genesis 1:1–2 is somewhat separated from the creative process in Genesis 1:1–5. Similarly, Sailhamer's view that Genesis 1:1 describes a different creation is also naturally separated from the verses that follow. The distinctive alternative is that Genesis 1:1 is the first step of the act of creation, describing the creation process itself. As such, it would be more inherently a part of the immediate context and thus have an important role in relation to the meaning.

Hermann Gunkel popularized the understanding of Genesis 1:1 as a summary statement. In more recent times, Bruce Waltke has advocated it. Waltke has claimed that Genesis 1:1 is a summation of the entire creation account of Genesis 1:2–2:3, not something that occurred before the six days nor in part of the first day.[21] Both Gunkel and Waltke argue for a literary separation of Genesis 1:1 from the rest of the chapter because Genesis 1:1 describes what could be considered as a perfect creation, but in Genesis 1:2 what is described is something that is out of sorts or as Waltke has stated: "The cosmos of verse 1 and the chaos of verse 2 cannot have co-existed."[22] Thus, Genesis 1:1 is not to be equated or continued with what is described in Genesis 1 but stands apart from the rest as the title, merely summarizing the events that took place during creation week. Waltke and others make this distinction largely because of their interpretation of the phrase "heavens and earth" in Genesis 1:1. Because this phrase describes the organized universe or the cosmos, it could never refer to the organized world described in Genesis 1:2. Therefore, Genesis 1:1 should be separated from Genesis 1:2 and is not part of the same

---

21. See Waltke, Fredricks, *Genesis*, 58.
22. Waltke, "The Literary Genre of Genesis, Chapter One," 4.

context. Genesis 1:2, introducing a disjunctive, circumstantial clause, thus should be subordinated to Genesis 1:3 rather than Genesis 1:1.

But as Aalders has noted, the phrase "and the earth" which begins verse 2 refers back to verse 1 which indicates that Genesis 1:2 is not the beginning of the creation narrative and therefore verse 1 cannot be considered to be a formal heading for what is to follow.[23] Anton Pearson has argued that Genesis 1:1 should not be understood as a title or summary:

> The first verse of Genesis 1 cannot be regarded . . . as a mere heading of a whole selection nor . . . as a summary statement, but forms an integral part of the narrative, for: (1) It has the form of narrative, not of superscription. (2) The conjunctive particle connects the second verse with it; which could not be if it were a heading. No historical narrative begins with "and" (vs. 2). The "and" in Ex. 1:1 indicates that the second book of Moses is a continuation of the first. (3) The very next verse speaks of the earth as already in existence, and therefore its creation must be recorded in the first verse. (4) In the first verse the heavens take the precedence of the earth, but in the following verses all things, even sun, moon, and stars seem to be appendages to the earth. Thus if it were a heading it would not correspond with the narrative. . . . the above evidence supports the view that the first verse forms a part of the narrative. The first verse of Genesis records the creation of the universe in its essential form. In v. 2, the writer describes the earth as it was when God's creative activity had brought its material into being, but this formative activity had not yet begun.[24]

Moreover, Meredith Kline argued that Genesis 1:1 cannot be a summation of the entire contents of the creation account in Genesis 1 because the connection of Genesis 1:1 with Proverbs 8:22–23 identifies the "beginning" as prior to the events described in Genesis 1:2–31. The alternative, that Genesis 1:1 describes the initial act of creation, is supported by the great Reformers Calvin and Luther.[25] According to these scholars, the verse describes God's first act in

---

23. In fact, Genesis 1:2 begins with the same word (*erets*) that ends Genesis 1:1; see G. Charles Aalders, *Genesis*, 2 vols. (Grand Rapids: Zondervan, 1981), 1:52.

24. Anton Pearson, "An Exegetical Study of Genesis 1:1–3," *Bethel Seminary Quarterly* 2 (1953): 20–21.

25. See Kline, "Space and Time in the Genesis Cosmogony," 5; Martin Luther, *The Creation: A Commentary on the First Five Chapters of the Book of Genesis*, trans. Henry Cole (Edinburgh: T&T Clark, 1858), 27; John Calvin, *The First Book of Moses Called Genesis*, trans. Rev. John King (Grand Rapids: Baker, repr. 1979), 69–70.

creating the world.[26] Proponents of this position often state that the creative act of Genesis 1:1 constituted the first act of day one of creation. "The beginning of the first day is not indicated, although from Exodus 20:11, we may warrantably assume that it began at the absolute beginning, Genesis 1:1."[27] This view is seen in the Talmud: "Rav Judah transmitted in the name of Rav: 'Ten things were created on the first day, namely: heaven and earth, *tohu* and *bohu*, light and darkness, wind, water, the nature of day and the nature of night'" (*b. Hag.* 12a). All these created entities are mentioned in the first five verses of the book of Genesis and thus "heaven and earth" would have been created on day one (Jub. 2:2; 4 Esdras 6:38).[28] Sailhamer maintains that Genesis 1:1 represents a different act of God than what is found in the creation week and thus understands day one of the creation week to begin with Genesis 1:2.[29]

The fourth view which applies discourse analysis to the text is similar to the title view in that it does not refer to Genesis 1:1 as what took place on day one of the creation week. It is unlike the title view, however, in that the first two verses (Gen. 1:1–2) are read together as background without a sharp distinction between Genesis 1:1 and Genesis 1:2. The perfect tense of the first verb in the Bible (*bara*, "created") is often employed in a narrative to provide background information to a narrative that is then "carried along" by the use of the *wayyiqtol* verb form. The latter has been called the "narrative tense" or the "narrator's tense." The first creative act in verse 1 thus provides informing background information for the narrative which covers Genesis 1:3–2:3. Thus, the action of the narrative begins with Genesis 1:3—identical to Waltke's Precreation Chaos model. Also, similar to the title view, the length of time of these background conditions cannot be specified.[30] According to the traditional interpretation, the perfect tense of *bara* in Genesis 1:1 indicates the first event in the sequence in a narrative and is the first event on the first day of creation.[31] This view along with Collin's approach from discourse

---

26. This is confirmed by the Septuagint translation of Genesis 1:1. See William P. Brown, *Structure, Role and Ideology in the Hebrew and Greek Texts of Genesis 1:1–2:3*, SBLDS 132 (Atlanta: Scholars Press, 1993), 31.

27. Young, *Studies in Genesis One,* 104.

28. See Ephraim E. Urbach, *The Sages: Their Concepts and Beliefs*, trans. Israel Abrahams, 2 vols. (Jerusalem: Magnes, 1979), 1:195; James H. Charlesworth, *The Old Testament Pseudepigrapha*, 2 vols. (Garden City, NY: Doubleday, 1983, 1985), 1:536; 2:55. The list in Jubilees 2:2 of the seven things that were created on the first day accounts for all of the nouns of the LXX Genesis 1:1–5, leaving none to have existed prior to day one. See S. D. Diere, *A New Glimpse of Day One: Intertextuality, History of Interpretation, and Genesis 1.1–5* (Berlin: Walter de Gruyter, 2009), 278–79.

29. See *Genesis Unbound,* 109. See also Question 15 ("What Is the Historical Creationism Theory?").

30. See Collins's, "Reading Genesis 1:1–2:3 as an Act of Communication," 134, 144.

31. See Paul Joüon, *A Grammar of Biblical Hebrew*, trans. T. Muraoka, 2 vols. (Rome: Editrice Pontificio Istituto Biblico, 1991), 2:390.

analysis seem to provide the best options for understanding the relationship of Genesis 1:1 to Genesis 1.

According to Harvard University Professor Jon Levenson, the traditional Jewish and Christian doctrine of *creatio ex nihilo* can be found in this chapter only if one translates its first verse as "In the beginning God created the heaven and the earth" and understands it to refer to some comprehensive creative act on the first day.[32]

What we know from Genesis 1:1 is that the universe did not always exist but had a beginning. Creation had a beginning, but God did not. God created the universe at a point in time in the ancient past. Thus, the universe is not eternal (Ps. 33:6; John 1:3; Heb. 11:3); only God is eternal (Isa. 44:24; Jer. 10:16; Ps. 90:2).

REFLECTION QUESTIONS

1. What do the four views regarding the relationship of Genesis 1:1 to Genesis 1 have in common?

2. What is the contribution of Isaiah 46:10 to the meaning of the first word of the Bible?

3. How should the phrase "heavens and earth" in Genesis 1:1 be understood?

4. Should Genesis 1:1 be considered as a title or summary of Genesis 1? Explain.

5. Is there any connection between the understanding of the phrase "in the beginning" to the concept of creation out of nothing? Explain.

---

32. See Jon D. Levenson, *Creation and the Persistence of Evil* (San Francisco: Harper & Row, 1988), 5.

What Is the Relationship of Genesis 1 to Genesis 2?

The rise of the critical study of the Bible arose in no small part from the observation that the Pentateuch contained duplicate accounts of the same event. The first duplicate account, it was argued, came from the first two chapters of Genesis where there are allegedly two distinct creation accounts.

From the outset, other scholars maintained that the first two chapters of Genesis did not reflect two different sources but rather are interrelated. The creation account in Genesis 2:4–25 was viewed as an expansion of Genesis 1:1–2:3 with special focus on the institution of marriage and the family. The method of the approach taken here will be to explore the meaning of Genesis 2:4–25 and then compare and contrast this passage with Genesis 1:1–2:3.

Unproductive Land (Gen. 2:4–7)

Genesis 2:4 begins with the phrase "earth and heavens." The reader quickly realizes that this is a reversal of the phrase "heavens and earth" in Genesis 1:1. This reversal puts "earth" at the forefront and may indicate that the author is moving from the broad treatment of the cosmic creation to the specific focus on the creation of man and woman.[1]

As the narrative begins, Genesis 2:5 tells us that wild uncultivated plants, i.e., "shrub" and "plant,"[2] were not yet on the earth, because the LORD God had not caused rain and there was no man to work the ground. Although

---

1. The major versions including the Septuagint, the Syriac, the Samaritan Pentateuch, and the Aramaic Targum Neofiti have "heaven and earth" rather than "earth and heaven" to harmonize with Genesis 1:1.

2. The distinction between "shrub" (*siakh*) and "plant" (*esev*) seems to lie in whether they may be eaten or not. A shrub appears to denote the low bushy plants characteristic of the arid areas bordering on the Fertile Crescent (21:15; Job 30:4, 7), whereas "plant" covers wild and cultivated plants that may be eaten (cf. 1:29–30; 3:18). See Gordon J. Wenham, *Genesis*

commentators are not in agreement as to what these plants were, most agree that they at least look forward to the garden which God will plant (Gen. 2:8–9).[3]

Regardless, the lack of vegetation was due to the absence of rain and of a man to irrigate the ground (Gen. 2:5b). There was a "spring" or "mist" (*edh*) that watered the land at this time. This spring is understood now by many scholars to refer to subterranean waters that rise to the surface (Gen. 2:6). Thus, the term refers to the subterranean water that comes up *to* the surface of the earth, rather than referring to mist or vapor that comes up *from* the surface of the earth.[4]

The problem raised seems not to be the lack of water but the lack of adequate control of water by man for tilling purposes. This well-watered situation is certainly in keeping with Eden, where God planted a garden (Gen. 2:8). This spring is to be distinguished from the river that flows out of Eden (Gen. 2:10–14).

When God planted a garden "in Eden in the east," the *edh*-water which had been covering the whole surface of the land had receded at Eden and the land was dry enough for God to make a garden. The garden in Eden, "the well-watered place," according to David Tsumura then was naturally drained of the water by a river, thereby producing arable land.[5]

To provide a remedy for this situation God formed man from the dust of the ground (Gen. 2:7).[6] The word *yatsar*, "formed," is frequently used for

---

1–15, WBC 1 (Waco, Tex.: Word, 1987), 58; *HALOT* 2:1321; Bruce Waltke and Cathi J. Fredricks, *Genesis* (Grand Rapids: Zondervan, 2001), 84n.11.

3. The *waw* + subject + predicate construction at the beginning of Genesis 2:5 marks this material introducing a description as background information. These plants were to be the very part of nature that would later be affected by the Fall (Gen. 3:8–24). According to John Sailhamer, the shrub and the plant correspond to the "thorns and thistles." See John H. Sailhamer, *The Pentateuch as Narrative* (Grand Rapids: Zondervan, 1992), 97; Joseph A. Pipa, Jr., "From Chaos to Cosmos: A Critique of the Non-Literal Interpretations of Genesis 1:1–2:3," in *Did God Create in Six Days?* ed. Joseph A. Pipa, Jr. and David W. Hall (Taylors, SC: Southern Presbyterian Press, 1999), 158–59.

4. See David Toshio Tsumura, *The Earth and the Waters in Genesis 1 and 2*, JSOTSup 83 (Sheffield, UK: JSOT Press, 1989), 113, 117; Francis I. Andersen, "On Reading Genesis 1–3," in *Backgrounds for the Bible*, ed. Michael Patrick O'Connor and David Noel Freedman (Winona Lake, Ind.: Eisenbrauns, 1987), 139. This interpretation is basically supported by the ancient versions (LXX, Aquila, Vulgate, Peshitta). The word *edh* appears elsewhere in the Old Testament only in Job 36:27.

5. The root *shaqah*, "watered," in Genesis 2:6 is never used in the sense of "destructive" flooding like a great deluge but usually in a positive sense (see Tsumura, *The Earth and the Waters*, 120–22).

6. That man was created from the dust is alluded to in many parts of the Old Testament (Job 10:9; Isa. 29:16; Pss. 90:3; 104:29, etc.) (see Wenham, *Genesis 1–15*, 59). *Afar* ("dust") is frequently found parallel to clay in Job: 4:19; 10:9; 27:16; 30:19. See Umberto Cassuto, *A Commentary on the Book of Genesis*, 2 vols. (vol. 1, *From Adam to Noah, Genesis I–VI:8*), trans. Israel Abrahams (Jerusalem: Magnes 1961–64), 1:105.

the action of the potter. Thus man's creation is portrayed in terms of God molding the clay soil into shape. The word *yatsar* connects artistic, inventive activity that requires skill and planning (cf. Isa. 44:9–10). It usually describes God's work in creation. After man's physical body was shaped by God, God animated man by breathing "into his nostrils the breath of life" making him a living being (Gen. 2:7). The word for "breath/breathe" (*nafakh*) is used in the Bible for the life imparted to man. It is never used this way for animals.

The closest parallel to this "divine inbreathing" is found in Ezekiel 37:9. It is the divine inbreathing both in Genesis 2:7 and in Ezekiel 37 that gives life. The same root (*nafakh*) is used in the phrase "breathe on these slain, that they may live." Thus, man was created from the dust and was quickened by divine inbreathing, but after the fall he would return to the dust.[7]

Man in the Garden (Gen. 2:8–17)

The new subject in this section is the garden of Eden. The man that God had formed[8] was placed inside this garden.[9] Genesis 2:8 is further developed in Genesis 2:9–17. Genesis 2:9–14 describes the nature of the garden and Genesis 2:15–17 expands on man's role in it.

In this garden God caused to grow every tree pleasant to sight and good for food, as well as the tree of life and the tree of the knowledge of good and evil (Gen. 2:9).[10] The enjoyment of the trees through the senses of sight and taste must be understood as part of God's plan.

Beginning with Genesis 2:10, a somewhat detailed description of the four rivers that flowed out of Eden is provided. These lands were rich in gold and precious jewelry, and their location was closely aligned with the land later promised to Abraham and his descendants. Later biblical prophets made the connection between the garden of Eden and the Promised Land (Ezek. 36:35;

---

7. There is a wordplay in the text on the name Adam/man (*adham*) and ground (*adhamah*) to emphasize man's relationship to the ground. He was created from it; his job is to cultivate it (Gen. 2:5, 15); when he dies, he returns to it (Gen. 3:19).

8. The verb can be translated as a pluperfect indicating that man "had been formed" before the garden was planted. See William J. Dumbrell, "Genesis 2:1–17: A Foreshadowing of the New Creation," in *Biblical Theology: Retrospect and Prospect*, ed. Scott J. Hafemann (Downers Grove: InterVarsity, 2002), 55.

9. The LXX translates *gan* ("garden") by *pardes*, itself a loan word from Persian. *Pardes* is the word from which we get the English word "paradise." The uniqueness of Eden from the rest of the world is clear from Genesis 3:24. The Ugaritic verb *'dn* (cognate to "Eden") can be explained as meaning "to make abundant in water-supply" (Gen. 13:10) and secondarily "to enrich, prosper, make luxuriant (see Ps. 36:9)" (see Tsumura, *The Earth and the Waters*, 135–36). The Vulgate translated the phrase "garden of Eden" by *paradises voluptatis*, "a delightful paradise."

10. Note how Genesis 2:9 takes up again the themes in Genesis 2:5a.

Joel 2:3; Isa. 51:3; Zech. 14:8; Rev. 22:1–2).[11] The garden was east of Canaan as supported by its association with the Tigris and Euphrates (Gen. 2:14).

Genesis 2:15 resumes the contents of Genesis 2:8, reinforcing the view that Genesis 2:9–14 is parenthetical to the main argument of the passage. But it also harkens back to Genesis 2:5 when as yet there were no plants and no man to till (*avadh*) the ground. Soon after man is commissioned to work the ground in the garden, he is given a commandment not to eat of the tree of the knowledge of good and evil. Disobedience to this command would result in certain death (Gen. 2:17).[12]

Woman Provided for the Man (Gen. 2:18–25)

While the creation of man is told briefly, in a single verse, the creation of woman is described in six verses. With the beginning of this section, we are somewhat startled to see that not everything is good in God's eyes in spite of God's sevenfold declaration that all he had made was good in Genesis 1:1–31. To correct this situation God promised to provide a helper for the man. The word for "helper" (Hb. *ezer*) most often is used in the Bible to refer to the help that God himself supplies. In the context of Genesis 2, the meaning of the term particularly applies to the essential "help" of a woman in her role in the bearing of children. Thus, she is a helper "fit for him." That is, she not only complements the man but is of the same essential nature as the man in bold contrast to the animals that he will name.

After God's declaration about man's condition, God presented the various animals of creation before the man so that he might give them names. It is as though God was attempting to create a companion for man who is much like man, as the animals were formed in the same way (*yatsar*) and from the same source (*adhamah*), "ground." This review of the subhuman creation only makes the man conscious of his own uniqueness and loneliness as he observes the universal paring in nature of male and female.[13] As "framework hypothesis" advocate Mark Ross observes,

> The fact that the mention of the creation of the animals follows an account dealing with man does not necessarily mean that the creation of the animals actually followed in time the creation of man. . . . The reason for *mentioning* them subsequent to Adam's creation, but prior to the creation of the woman, is found in the *inclusio* which frames that part of the narrative dealing

---

11. See Sailhamer, *Pentateuch*, 99. There is no consensus about the identity of Pishon and Gihon (Gen. 2:11–13). See Wenham, *Genesis 1–15*, 65.
12. See Question 25 on the nature of the original sin.
13. Note the repetition of the *ezer kenegdo*, "a helper fit for him," in Genesis 2:18 in Genesis 2:20. See Nahum M. Sarna, *Genesis*, JPSTC (Philadelphia: Jewish Publication Society, 1989), 22.

with Eve's creation. The concern is to provide a helper suitable to Adam, the absence of which v. 18 calls "not good". . . . The survey of the whole animal kingdom was principally motivated to draw out the fact that Adam was not a mere animal, made after his kind as they were made after their kind.[14]

God then induced the man into a heavy sleep (*tardemah*) and removed a rib from which he created the woman (Gen. 2:21). The woman can now stand at his side as his helper-counterpart. Only she is qualified to be a suitable companion as only she is made from his rib. In her essential nature she is man's equal as she is created to be his helper and complement.[15] God brings the woman to the man (as he had brought the animals to the man) to place emphasis on the fact that it is only the woman who is a *ezer kenegdo* (a helper for him). "Rather than squandering his most precious gift on one who is unappreciative, God waits until Adam is prepared to appreciate the gift of woman."[16] This first marriage, with its setting in the holy garden and its design by God, is the model for the sacred institution of marriage. This creation of the woman and God's bringing her to the man instituted marriage as proven by the citation of Genesis 2:23–24 in Ephesians 5:28–31.

Man speaks for the first time in Genesis 2:23. He describes the woman in terms that indicate the essential equality of husband and wife.[17] This likeness that the man and the woman share in Genesis 1 may find an analogy with the "likeness" between the man and his wife in Genesis 2. The pronunciation of the woman's name *ishshah* is understood to be derived from his own name *ish*, another indication that she is his equal. While he gave each of the animals a name, it is only the woman who has a name that is virtually identical to his.

Genesis 2:24 is a very significant comment and observation by the narrator explaining the significance of Genesis 2:18–23. Because the woman was taken from the man's body, the bond between husband and wife takes precedence over all other relationships, particularly the relationship one has with his parents. This change of loyalty is extremely significant in that the honoring of parents was considered the highest human obligation.[18] From the facts that

---

14. Mark Ross, "The Framework Hypothesis: An Interpretation of Genesis 1:1–2:3," in *Did God Create in Six Days?* ed. Joseph A. Pipa, Jr. and David W. Hall (Taylors, SC: Southern Presbyterian Press, 1999), 124 (emphasis original).

15. See Wenham, *Genesis 1–15*, 69, 87. The closing of the man's wound (*basar*; Gen. 2:21) anticipates its use in Genesis 2:24 where it refers to the one flesh (*basar*) relationship.

16. Waltke and Fredricks, *Genesis*, 89.

17. The use of the demonstrative pronoun *zoth* ("this") three times emphatically points out that the woman alone is the one who corresponds to the man and can be his companion (see *HALOT* 1:264).

18. See Sarna, *Exodus*, 23; Wenham, *Genesis 1–15*, 70–71. In fact, the explanation of Genesis 2:24 may have had the purpose of correcting those cultures where the parental bonds

God created the woman for the man and that God brings the woman to the man, we can conclude that God established the institution of marriage and that every marriage is ordained by God.

At the end of this narrative account, the narrator adds that the man and the wife were naked and yet not ashamed. Before the fall there was no fear of exploitation or anxiety as the man and wife could live peacefully in their integrity and without sin. They could view each other and their sexuality with wholeness and without shame.[19] As Wilhem VanGemeren has noted: "From the beginning, the family unit was God's means of extending his blessed presence and fellowship to the ends of the earth. He dealt with husband and wife as a family. Creation was not complete until this unit had been established."[20]

Similarities Between Genesis 1 and Genesis 2

There are numerous parallels between the account of creation in Genesis 1:1–2:3 and Genesis 2:4–25. Both of these texts begin with a general statement introducing the respective passages with a reference to the creation of the "heavens and earth" (Gen. 1:1 and 2:4a).

Immediately after this initial introduction to creation, both passages direct our attention to the condition of the land before the creation of mankind. Genesis 1:2 begins by stating that the earth was "without form and void" while Genesis 2:5 mentions that there was no bush or shrub in the land. Immediately after the earth or land is referenced, both accounts then refer to the existence of water (*tehom* ["the deep"] and *edh*) that is present in this very early initial state of the earth.[21] Thus, both narratives begin with a description of the conditions that existed prior to the creation of man.

The unique importance of human beings is clearly seen in Genesis 1 and Genesis 2. In Genesis 1 man is made in the "image" of God (Gen. 1:26–27). In Genesis 2 God forms man and makes him distinct from other parts of creation by breathing "into his nostrils the breath of life" (Gen. 2:7). In Genesis 1, man's creation in the "image of God" involved his creation as male and female (Gen. 1:27). In Genesis 2, this theme is continued by showing that man's creation "in God's image" entailed a "partnership" with his wife.[22]

---

were given higher priority over marital bonds even after the marriage had taken place (see Waltke and Fredricks, *Genesis*, 90).

19. See Waltke and Fredricks, *Genesis*, 90. It would seem much more probable that Genesis 3 is explaining why man must wear clothes, rather than that 2:25 is idealizing nudity. Genesis 2:25 reiterates the contentment of the couple with God's provision (see Wenham, *Genesis 1–15*, 72).

20. Willem VanGemeren, *The Progress of Redemption: From Creation to the New Jerusalem* (Carlisle, UK: Paternoster, 1995), 50. This account of the creation of the woman in Genesis 2:18–23 is unique to the nation of Israel as other ancient Near Eastern texts have no account of the creation of woman (see Waltke and Fredricks, *Genesis*, 88n.29).

21. See Tsumura, *The Earth and the Waters*, 85–86.

22. See John H. Sailhamer, *Genesis Unbound* (Sisters, Ore.: Multnomah, 1996), 154–55.

In both creation accounts, God grants man mastery over the animal kingdom. In chapter 1, this idea is formulated explicitly (Gen. 1:26, 28); in Genesis 2, man's dominion is inferred from the power of naming animals that God has invested to man.

Differences Between Genesis 1 and Genesis 2

In spite of the numerous similarities between the accounts of creation in Genesis 1 and Genesis 2, there are some discontinuities between these chapters as well. First, it is easy to recognize that there is nothing in Genesis 2:4–25 that corresponds to the absolute statement of Genesis 1:1: "In the beginning God created the heavens and the earth."[23] Chapter 2 assumes the creation of the earth, the heaven and the sea, the account of which is given in chapter one.

In addition the focus of the two accounts is completely different. Genesis 2:4–25 is not a second account of the creation of the heavens and the earth, but is rather an account that focuses on the planting of a garden and human life in that garden (Gen. 2:9–25). In this understanding it is more strongly connected with what follows in Genesis 3 than what is described in Genesis 1:1–2:3.[24]

There are also differences of details between the accounts of creation in Genesis 1:1–2:3 and Genesis 2:4–24. While the negative description at the early stage of creation in Genesis 2:5–6 was similar to the initial creative state in Genesis 1:2, the descriptions are not completely parallel. In Genesis 1:2 the entire earth was underwater, while in Genesis 2:5–6, the water was covering only a part of the earth that is described as "land" (*adhamah*). The "land" (*adhamah*), was watered by the *edh*-water that came from the "earth" (*erets*).

The term *erets* ("earth") has a much wider semantic field than the term *adhamah* ("ground"), comprising both the surface of the earth, on which the Lord God sends rain from above (Gen. 2:5), and the underground, where the subterranean waters "come up" (Gen. 2:6).[25] "Land" (*adhamah*) on the other hand is limited. In Genesis 2:9, it is not the whole earth that is referred to but only that region in which the Lord God chose to make the garden.

Without reference to the sun, the moon and stars, or the sea, Genesis 2 is certainly not a true cosmological text. This is not the same literary genre as Genesis 1, which describes the creation of humankind at the grand climax of the creation. Moreover, God stands apart from his creation by speeches and

---

23. See, e.g., Brown, *Structure,* 69. In addition, the beginning of Genesis 2:4 differs from Genesis 1:1 as Genesis 2:4b gives an indication of time unlike Genesis 1:1. Hence, the relationship between Genesis 2:4b and Genesis 2:7 differs from the relationship between Genesis 1:1 and 1:3. See Claus Westermann, *Genesis 1–11,* trans. John J. Scullion S. J. (Minneapolis: Fortress, 1994), 97.
24. See Kenneth A. Mathews, *Genesis 1–11:26,* NAC 1A (Nashville: B&H, 1996), 183.
25. Moreover, the separation between the upper water and the lower water, which is described in Genesis 1:6–7 in the biblical context, is assumed in Genesis 2:5–6 (see Tsumura, *The Earth and the Waters,* 89, 122).

commands in Genesis 1, whereas he seems more directly and intimately involved with his creation through actions in the Genesis 2 account.

Also, in contrast to Genesis 1, Genesis 2 appears to preclude chronological order. In Genesis 2 the animals were created (Gen. 2:19) after man (Gen. 2:7) and yet they were created before the woman (Gen. 2:22). This may suggest that we are to understand the focus on Genesis 2 is only on the garden of Eden.[26] Genesis 1 describes the earlier stage in the one creation process where the waters cover the earth. Genesis 2 reflects the later stage as seen in Gen. 1:9–10 when the waters have separated and the dry land has appeared.

Conclusion

In conclusion, we posit that Genesis 1 gives a general description of the creation of humankind in the framework of the creation of the entire world while Genesis 2, on the other hand, gives a detailed description of humankind and their immediate context on the earth in the garden of Eden. The relationship between Genesis 1 and Genesis 2 may be explained as a generic-specific relationship.[27] In addition, the first chapter stressed the importance of the word of the Lord as the powerful means of creation (everything obeyed God's decree); the second chapter employs the word as the test of obedience. The word of the Lord in this unit comes in the form of a command to be obeyed, one that the man and the woman are able to obey in view of their created nature.

REFLECTION QUESTIONS

1. What is the closest biblical parallel to God's inbreathing into man the breath of life?

2. What rivers flowed out of Eden?

3. What institution is introduced in the garden of Eden?

4. What are the similarities between Genesis 1 and Genesis 2?

5. What are the differences between Genesis 1 and Genesis 2?

---

26. See Sailhamer, *Genesis Unbound*, 89.
27. See Cassuto, *Genesis*, 1:89–92.

What Is the Meaning of the Seventh Day?

Genesis 2:1–3, the last paragraph in the creation account, records the seventh day of the creation week. The seventh day, the Sabbath, could be viewed as the culmination of the creation account. The first three days present the creation in its generalities, and the second three days present those features that specifically impinge upon the human habitat. The symmetry of the text (3 days plus 3 days plus 1 day) indicates that the concluding Sabbath day is the culmination of the creation days of this creation account. The acts of creation are the works of God; but on the seventh day he ceased from work and rested. The entire creation account is thus theocentric: God is the subject; he is the singular agent of will. The Sabbath becomes his witness to his work of creation (cf. Ex. 20:8–11).[1]

Genesis 2:1–3 brings the creation account to conclusion in a beautifully arranged way by repeating the phrases of Genesis 1:1 in a chiastic manner, "God created" (Gen. 2:3) the "heaven and earth" (Gen. 2:1). This arrangement is an emphatic statement of the fact that the creation week has been completed.[2]

Creation Comes to an End (Gen. 2:1)

Genesis 2:1 is a summary conclusion of the preceding six days of the creation week in Genesis 1 and states that the creation of the heavens and the earth was completed along with all their hosts. The Hebrew word for "hosts" (*tsava*) usually indicates the sun, moon, and stars (Deut. 4:19; 17:3; 2 Kings 17:16; Neh. 9:6) but also can refer to angels (1 Kings 22:19; Neh. 9:6; Ps. 148:2) as well as an army (Gen. 21:22).

---

1. See Michael Fishbane, *Text and Texture* (New York: Schocken, 1979), 10–11.
2. See Gordon Wenham, *Genesis 1–15*, WBC 1 (Waco, TX: Word, 1987), 34–35.

God Does Not Work on the Seventh Day (Gen. 2:2)

Genesis 2:2 begins by repeating the content of Genesis 2:1 but adds that this completion had taken place by the seventh day. The text does not indicate that God worked on the seventh day, a statement that would be contradicted in the immediate context, but that by the seventh day, God had already completed his work.[3] As Umberto Cassuto stated: "God was on the seventh day in the position of one who has already finished His work, consequently He abstained from work on the seventh day."[4]

The noun *melakhah*, "work," occurs 166 times in the Old Testament. The meaning of the noun can be classified in four distinct categories: (1) skilled work, craftsmanship; (2) general work (including physical labor); (3) the result of work; and (4) mission, commission, errand, or business. The term is frequently used to refer to skilled labor, including work on the tabernacle and the performance of cultic tasks. But the word is often used to describe ordinary human work, with Genesis 39:11 perhaps being the best example from the life of Joseph: "But one day, when he went into the house to do his *work*." Most of the uses hence refer to human work with less than 4 percent referring to God's activity. The use of this particular term is somewhat surprising as the unequivocal focus of the creation is on God's work and the unique nature of his creation. It is likely that the word choice emphasizes the correspondence between God's work and man's and thus foreshadows the Sabbath law where the same term *melakhah* is used in reference to the activity man is forbidden to perform on the Sabbath.[5]

After God had finished his work by the seventh day, the text states, God "rested" on the seventh day. The verb often translated as "rested" in Genesis 2:2 more literally means "to cease," indicating that it was on the seventh day of the creation week that God ceased his creative activity. This use of the verb with this meaning may be illustrated in such passages as Joshua 5:12; Nehemiah 6:3; Isaiah 14:4; 24:8; and Jeremiah 31:36. The most well-known occurrence of the verb with this meaning is Genesis 8:22: "While the earth remains, seedtime and harvest, cold and heat, summer and winter, day and

---

3. Thus the first verb of Genesis 2:1 *waykal* should be understood as having a pluperfect force, "God had finished" by the seventh day. See Wenham, *Genesis 1–15*, 35; Victor Hamilton, *Genesis 1–17*, NICOT (Grand Rapids: Eerdmans, 1990), 142. The phrase "God had finished his work" is echoed by the phrase "Moses finished his work" with regard to the tabernacle in Exodus 40:33. See Question 14 for a fuller discussion of the connection of the temple with creation.

4. Umberto Cassuto, *A Commentary on the Book of Genesis*, 2 vols. (vol. 1, *From Adam to Noah, Genesis I–VI:8)*, trans. Israel Abrahams (Jerusalem: Magnes 1961–64), 1:62. Because it is possible to understand the phrase as saying that God actually worked on the seventh day, several major versions including the Samaritan Pentateuch, the Septuagint and the Peshitta changed "seventh day" to "sixth day" in Genesis 2:2a.

5. See Jacob Milgrom and David Wright, "מלאכה *melakhah*," *TDOT* 8:326; Ian Hart, "Genesis 1:1–2:3 As a Prologue to the Book of Genesis," *TynBul* 46, no. 2 (1995): 316.

night, shall not *cease.*" The relationship and connection of the verb with the noun Sabbath is patently clear in such passages as Exodus 23:12; 34:21; and Leviticus 23:32 where the notion of Sabbath is related to the concept of "ceasing" or "desisting" activities, i.e., not working. The term Sabbath is related to the verb *shavath* as indicated by the frequent combination of these two terms as well as the clear assonance (similarity of sound) that exists between this noun and verb. That there is a relationship between the two words is also suggested in Exodus 23:12 and 34:21 even though the noun "Sabbath" is not present in these passages. These texts mention the seventh day in context with the verb *shavath* ("to cease"). Thus, the Sabbath day is the day when a person suspends or ceases his normal routine of labor. The meaning of "rest," as an indication of "ceasing from work" is best illustrated in Nehemiah 6:3: "And I sent messengers to them, saying, 'I am doing a great work (*melakhah*) and I cannot come down. Why should the work stop (*shavath*) while I leave it and come down to you?'"[6]

The legislation of the Ten Commandments informs us that the completion of the creation work meant that God "rested" (*nwkh*) from his work on the seventh day. God rested in the sense that his creative activity came to an end. Resting means not creating. God did not withdraw from the world, but ceased creating. As Franz Delitzsch commented, "He now rested, not with the intent of henceforth withdrawing from the world, —He was indeed from that time onwards the governor of the world and the director of its history,—but He rested as Creator; His creative activity was now concluded, His rest belongs to that order of the world which is binding upon the creatures. . . ."[7]

God Made the Seventh Day Unique (Gen. 2:3)

The cessation of creative activity on the seventh day by God made this day distinct compared with the first six days of creation. Thus God blessed (*barakh*) the Sabbath day and declared it holy (Gen. 2:3; see Ex. 20:11b).

This is not the first occurrence of the verb "to bless" in the creation account (see Gen. 1:22, 28).[8] God blessed his creation, but on the seventh day

---

6. See J. Tigay, "שבת *shabbath*," in *Encyclopaedia Biblica*, 9 vols. (Jerusalem: Bialik, 1950–1988), 7:505; John H. Walton, *Genesis*, NIVAC (Grand Rapids: Zondervan, 2001), 146; F. Stolz, "שבת *shbth*," *TLOT* 3:1297; E. Haag, "שבת *shabbath*," *TDOT* 14:388; Mark F. Rooker, *The Ten Commandments: Ethics for the Twenty-First Century*, NACSBT (Nashville: B&H, 2010), 78–79; Claus Westermann, *Genesis 1–11*, trans. John J. Scullion S. J. (Minneapolis: Fortress, 1994), 173.

7. Franz Delitzsch, *A New Commentary on Genesis*, trans. Sophia Taylor, 2 vols. (T&T Clark, 1888; reprint Minneapolis: Klock & Klock, 1978), 1:107.

8. Unlike the blessings of Genesis 1:22, 28 which are blessings mentioned with explicit outcomes, the blessing of the Sabbath is not defined and pertains to time itself. See Nahum M. Sarna, *Genesis*, JPSTC (Philadelphia: Jewish Publication Society, 1989), 15.

he blessed a day, the Sabbath. The Hebrew word "bless" (*barakh*) occurs 327 times in the Old Testament. It refers to a continuous, present power that affects the future. The blessing of God results in vitality, prosperity, abundance, or fertility. A blessing is a direct act of God that causes what is blessed to perform and produce at the optimum level, fulfilling its purpose.[9] God's blessing is a bestowal of his kindness that results in success.

God blessed the Sabbath day although he had not blessed any other of the creation days. But he did more than bless; he also "made it [the Sabbath] holy." God declared that the first six days of creation were good; only the Sabbath day he declared to be holy. The basic meaning of the word "holy" (*qdhsh*) is to "be distinct, withheld from ordinary use, treated with special care, to belong to the sanctuary." It denotes something that belongs to the sphere of the sacred as it refers to things that belong to God. It may be used of people (Jer. 1:5), places (Ex. 29:37), things (Ex. 30:29), and times (Lev. 25:10) that were separated from the mundane affairs of everyday life and dedicated to the service of the Lord. The antonym of "holy" is something that is profane or common, existing in its natural state. Thus, holiness is associated with God and is an expression of his perfection. Holiness is not inherent in creation, but an entity is determined to be "holy" only as God dictates. It requires an act of God to bring something from its normal state into the sphere of holiness. Thus, anything that is described as "holy" in the Old Testament has been determined so by God's election and choice and dedicated to him in the prescribed manner.[10]

It is significant that the word "holy" occurs both at the beginning (Ex. 20:8) and at the end of the Sabbath law (Ex. 20:11). This root is repeated at the beginning and end of the Sabbath law to stress the uniqueness of this day. The Sabbath day was withdrawn from ordinary days as on the Sabbath day there was to be no labor taking place. As Michael Fishbane has noted, "The seventh day is thus clearly set off from the *work* of the previous six. Its repose and calm stand in stark contrast to the acts of the days of creation: the Sabbath is a day of 'rest' (as opposed to the predominance of 'making' on the other days), a day blessed as a whole (as opposed to the blessings of the specific works on the fifth and sixth days)."[11]

Furthermore, unlike the previous six days, the number of this day, the "seventh day," is referenced three times indicating its importance in relation to the other creation days. Each phrase in Genesis 2:1–3 contains seven Hebrew words, with reference to the "seventh day" in the middle of each

---

9. See Westermann, *Genesis 1–11*, 161; J. Scharbert, "ברך *brk*," *TDOT* 2:287, 294, 298–99; C. Keller and G. Wehmeier, "ברך *brk*," *TLOT* 1:270–71, 277; M. Brown, "ברך *brk*," *NIDOTTE* 1:759.
10. See Wenham, *Genesis 1–15*, 36.
11. Fishbane, *Text and Texture*, 9 (emphasis original).

phrase. Finally, there are a total of thirty-five words in this paragraph about the seventh day.[12] Waltke observed the significance of the number seven and gave examples of its occurrences throughout Scripture beginning with the creation account:

> Creation in six days and divine rest on the seventh (Gen. 2:3; Ex. 20:8–11); the sabbatical year; after seven sabbatical years, a Year of Jubilee (Lev. 25); the seven-day Feast of Tabernacles (23:34) and Feast of Unleavened Bread (Ex. 34:18); the seven branches of the lampstand (Ex. 25:31–39); the seven day's march with the seven priests around Jericho climaxing on the seventh day with a march seven times around (Josh. 6:3–4); and the seven river dippings of the proud, leprous Naaman in order to restore his skin (2 Kings 5:14). Seven may also signify simple completeness, such as Cain's sevenfold revenge and Lamech's boast to avenge himself seventy-seven times (Gen. 4:24; cf. Prov. 6:31; 24:16).[13]

The creation of the seven-day week sets the pattern for the significance of the number seven throughout the remainder of Scripture. The concept of a seven-day week was an innovation unique to Israel.[14]

The seventh day is set apart from the first six days, not only by stating specifically that God "blessed" it and "sanctified" it. On this day he blessed and sanctified but does not "speak" nor "work" as he had on the previous days. In fact, it is recorded three times that God did not work.

Sabbath and Worship

As a day that was sacred or holy to the Lord, the Sabbath day was a day of religious observance (Isa. 1:13; 58:13; Jer. 17:19–27). First of all, the bread of the Presence in the tabernacle was set out every seven days each Sabbath (Lev. 24:5–9). In addition, on the Sabbath day an Israelite might visit a sanctuary or a prophet (2 Kings 4:23; Isa. 1:13). Special sacrifices as well as additional spiritual matters and religious ceremonies were also to take place on this holy day (Lev. 24:8; 1 Chron. 23:31; 2 Chron. 8:13; 31:3).[15] Numbers 28:9–10 specifies additional sacrifices on the Sabbath: two extra lambs as a burnt offering after the usual morning sacrifice. Second Kings 16:18 implies that the king of Israel visited the temple on the Sabbath. Lamentations 1:10 and 2:6 appear to indicate

---

12. For a treatment of the number seven in this paragraph on the Sabbath, as well as throughout the creation account, see Cassuto, *Genesis*, 1:14–15.
13. Bruce K. Waltke and Cathi J. Fredricks, *Genesis* (Grand Rapids: Zondervan, 2001), 111n.5.
14. See Sarna, *Genesis*, 14.
15. See J. Tigay, *The JPS Torah Commentary: Deuteronomy*, 68; idem, "שבת *shabbath*," 511. In addition, Psalm 92 was to be read every Sabbath day.

that the congregation was normally in the sanctuary on the Sabbath. Psalm 90:1 also assumes collective worship on the Sabbath. Like other festal occasions in the worship calendar (see Leviticus 23), the Sabbath was called a holy convocation (*miqra qodhesh*). But given its weekly observance the Sabbath is distinct from the other festivals from the fact that it is the most frequently occurring holy convocation in the year (Lev. 23:2).

Initial Sabbath celebrations were in individual homes, but later the religious community could gather collectively to worship on the Sabbath in the temple. It was a day of holiness and joy and was a festive assembly. For the Israelites, the Sabbath was also a day of worship and service to the Lord their God, and it testified to his sovereignty over creation. All types of work were forbidden, including plowing and harvesting, gathering food and firewood, lighting fires, and commercial activities (Ex. 16:23–30; 34:21; 35:3; Num. 15:32–36; Neh. 13:15–21; Amos 8:5; Jer. 17:21–22).[16] Work was also forbidden on religious days and festivals as these special occasions were "Sabbath-like" (Ex. 12:16; Lev. 16:29; 23:8, 28).

Moreover, the importance of the Sabbath may be seen by the fact that it is often juxtaposed with the prohibition of idolatry (Ex. 23:12; Lev. 19:3–4; 26:1–2; Ezek. 20:16–24). The violation of the Sabbath law was tantamount to breaking the covenant. According to the Midrash, the Sabbath was equal to all other legal precepts (*Exod. Rab.* 25:12).[17]

Umberto Cassuto commented on the worshipers' memory of God's unique creation of the world that was memorialized each Sabbath day:

> Rise on this day above the plane of ordinary activities, liberate yourself from the burden of work of the six preceding days, and dedicate it not to your body but to your soul, not to material things but to things of the spirit, not to your relationship to nature, but to your relationship to the Creator of nature. Thereby you will imitate the ways in which the Lord your God works, and you will bear constant witness to the fact that he alone created the whole world in all its parts, and that he is not to be identified with any portion of the world or with any of the forces of nature, but he transcends the sphere of nature.[18]

---

16. The commandment is not prohibiting any sort of exertion, or the preparing of food, or the feeding or watering of animals, or anything else necessary to get through the day in an agrarian culture. It prohibits duplicating on the Sabbath any of the usual labor of the other six days that can possibly be stopped without actually causing someone or something harm (see D. Stuart, *Exodus*, NAC 2 [Nashville: B&H, 2006], 449).

17. See Merrill Unger, "The Significance of the Sabbath," *BSac* (January, 1966): 58; Tigay, *Deuteronomy*, 68.

18. Umberto Cassuto, *A Commentary on the Book of Exodus*, trans. I. Abrahams (Jerusalem: Magnes, 1974), 246.

Putting it somewhat differently, John Calvin stated: "God did not command men simply to keep holiday every seventh day, as if he delighted in their indolence; but rather that they, being released from all other business, might the more readily apply their minds to the Creator of the world."[19]

What Does the Sabbath Mean for Today?

First century AD historian Flavius Josephus stated, "Every week men should desert their occupations and assemble to listen to the Law" (*Ag. Ap.* 2.175; see also *Ant.* 16.43). Thus, the worship component of the Sabbath day was carried over into the days of the first century AD during the time of the events of the New Testament. Jesus attended the synagogue where the Old Testament Scriptures were read each Sabbath (cf. Mark 1:21, 29; 3:1; Luke 4:44; 13:10). Apparently, this characterized his religious life (Luke 4:16). The Apostle Paul demonstrated the same consistency as he routinely entered synagogues on the Sabbath, where he took the opportunity to preach the Christian gospel (e.g., Acts 13:14, 42, 44; 17:2; 18:4).[20]

But in the days of the New Testament, the observance of the Sabbath day had changed. The New Testament recorded the fulfillment of the prophecies of Jesus Christ concerning the Sabbath. The Sabbath was a type of Christ (Col. 2:16–17) who alone brings believers rest in this life and in the life to come. The Sabbath law is not binding upon the church, and its observance or non-observance is a matter of personal conscience (Rom. 14:5–23).[21] This typological understanding of the Sabbath is supported by the fact that the Sabbath law (the fourth commandment) is the only one of the Ten Commandments not repeated in the New Testament. As a shadow it was fulfilled in Christ's ministry— but it also awaits a future fulfillment.

In the book of Hebrews, the Sabbath rest, according to Bruce Waltke, gives concrete expression to the church's realized eschatology (Heb. 4:1–11). The author first quotes Genesis 2:2, that God "rested on the seventh day from all his work that he had done" and then follows up this quote with another Old Testament quote, "They shall not enter my rest" (Ps. 95:11). Rest had been promised to those who enter the land of Canaan as indicated in Deuteronomy 12:9–10. Thus, in Hebrews 4, God's rest in creation is joined to the failure of the Israelites to enter the promised land because of their unbelief. The author goes on to say, however, that there remains a rest for the people of God that is available today (Heb. 4:9), but this rest must be connected to the rest in the creation narrative. The Sabbath rest assures believers that, just as God entered

---

19. John Calvin, *Commentaries on the First Book of Moses Called Genesis* (Grand Rapids: Baker, 1979), 106.
20. See Gerhard Hasel, "Sabbath," *ABD*, 5:854; S. Westerholm and C. Evans, "Sabbath," *DNTB*, 1035.
21. Waltke and Fredricks, *Genesis*, 67, 72–73.

his rest after working for six days, so also they live in the hope that they shall enter an eternal rest. New Testament saints already by faith enter that rest by their union with Christ. As Jon Laansa maintains, the entrance of believers into the heavenly temple is a present privilege, while the entrance into rest (*katapausis*) remains in the future. To say that a Sabbath remains means no more than that a great salvation is in store for the people of faith.[22]

Conclusion

Even though the New Testament believer is not commanded to perform the ceremonial aspects of the Sabbath law, the teaching of the Sabbath has a relevance to the New Testament believer's life. First, and perhaps foremost, the Sabbath teaches us about the sovereignty of God. By abstaining from work one day a week, we express our belief that ultimately we are not dependent upon our own work and human efforts but that God is sovereign in our lives. Our work and our lives are under his control. Just as the firstfruits and the tithe were offered to God as a recognition that the whole produce of the earth really belongs to the Lord, the dedication of one day in seven is an expression that every minute of our lives belongs to God who gives us our lives (see Ex. 20:10; 35:2). "In ceasing from labor, one is reminded of one's true status as a dependent being, of the God who cares for and sustains all his creatures, and of the world as a reality belonging ultimately to God."[23] Sabbath-like observance places a clear limit on human autonomy. The fact that we should work, our ability to do work, and the work we have been assigned are all part of his sovereign plan for us (Gen. 2–3; 1 Thess. 5:11; 2 Thess. 3:10). The principles of work, rest, and worship that emerge from the Sabbath law are relevant today.

The first principle of the Sabbath law is that of the responsibility to work. While there is a focus on rest in the fourth commandment and in Genesis 2:1–3, the law also endorses the principle that human beings should be about work six days in a week. As Abraham Heschel observed, "The duty to work for six days is just as much a part of God's covenant with man as the duty to abstain from work on the seventh day."[24] When we engage in work for six days a week, we follow God's example in the creation. As we follow the lead of the consummate Craftsman, our work should be characterized by integrity and produce a quality product (see Ex. 31:6; 35:35). Even though work has been affected by the fall, we should work with a zeal and industriousness that is honoring to God and not be characterized by idleness, laziness, and slothfulness (Prov. 6:6–11; 21:25). All work and all occupations (providing they do not promote illicit activity) are significant and honorable before the Lord. The fourth commandment

22. See Jon Laansma, *I Will Give You Rest* (Tübingen: Moher Siebeck, 1997), 315–17.
23. C. Slane, "Sabbath," *EDBT*, 697. See A. McNeile, *The Book of Exodus*, 3rd ed. (London: Methuen, 1931), 118.
24. A. Heschel, *The Earth Is the Lord's and the Sabbath* (New York: Harper & Row, 1966), 28.

affirms human labor and exalts the dignity of work. The "three matters which are strongly emphasized in Genesis 1:1–2:3, the six-day creation, the image of God, and the Sabbath, are intrinsically linked—by the 'work mandate.'"[25]

The fact that the work and rest pattern was established on the work of God himself as explained in the Sabbath law (Ex. 20:8–11) indicates that this principle for mankind has universal significance and application. Man's divinely appointed task to have dominion over God's created order (Gen. 1:26) carried with it the privilege of sharing in God's rest.

Thus, days of work have their goal in a day of rest. The sanctification of the Sabbath institutes an order for humankind according to which time is divided into work time and holy time, a time for work and a time for rest. By sanctifying the seventh day, God instituted a polarity between the everyday and the solemn day, between days of work and days of rest, which was to be determinative for human existence. This is a gift of the Creator to his people and is not merely an anticipation of the Israelite Sabbath. People "sanctify" the Sabbath by observing it one day a week. God bestows a blessing upon the person who observes a Sabbath day by abstaining from working on it.[26]

The stress on the completion of the work in Genesis 2:1–3 is directed toward humans; the echoes of the language of the Sabbath law confirm this. And while all days may be treated the same under the new covenant (Rom. 14:5), the principle of a day of rest is applicable for believers today.

The fourth commandment calls for a day to offer worship and praise to God. It calls for a day set aside for God that we might remember his creation and his redemption. It is a day where we acknowledge God's ownership not only of ourselves but of all creation. As we enter a time of deep reflection on this day of worship, we turn "from the world of creation to the creation of the world."[27] We turn in worship to God to celebrate those acts of God whereby our lives have come to be valued. It is a day wherein we reflect upon the fact that our Lord is the Creator, Redeemer, and Lord of all. Setting aside a day of rest symbolizes the fact that human worth and purpose are not to be derived from toil. Human worth is derived from the relationship with the Creator. Or as Dietrich Bonhoeffer concluded, rest means transfiguration, "it means turning our eyes absolutely upon God's being God and towards worshipping him."[28]

---

25. Hart, "Genesis 1:1–2:3 As a Prologue to the Book of Genesis," 330.

26. See W. Eichrodt, *Theology of the Old Testament,* 2 vols., trans. J. A. Baker, OTL (Philadelphia: Westminster, 1961), 1:133; Peter Craigie, *The Book of Deuteronomy,* NICOT (Grand Rapids: Eerdmans, 1976), 157n.18; Westermann, *Genesis 1–11,* 170–72.

27. Heschel, *The Earth Is the Lord's and the Sabbath,* 10.

28. Dietrich Bonhoeffer, *Creation and Fall: A Theological Interpretation of Genesis 1–3* (London: SCM Press, 1959), 40. See R. Collins, *Christian Morality: Biblical Foundations* (Notre Dame, IN: Notre Dame University Press, 1986), 55; P. Barker, "Sabbath, Sabbatical Year, Jubilee," *DOTP,* 698.

REFLECTION QUESTIONS

1. What does the verb "rest" mean?

2. What is unique about the Sabbath day?

3. What is the significance of the number seven?

4. What were the views about the Sabbath in the New Testament?

5. What should be the Christian attitude toward work?

What Does Genesis Teach About the Purpose of Man's Creation?

As the book of Genesis is the book of beginnings, one would naturally expect that the early accounts of the creation of man and the universe would address the important issue of the purpose of man's creation. Certainly some indication of man's purpose is given in Genesis 1 as man is uniquely placed in dominion over the animal kingdom. As man was created in God's image, he is given a will that allows him to manage God's creation as illustrated in Genesis 2 where he names the animals.[1] Thus, the text indicates that exercising dominion over the earth as a representative of God is at least part of the purpose for creating man. The purpose of man derived from his responsibility to exercise dominion in Genesis 1 is virtually without controversy (see Question 23, "What Does It Mean That Man Is Made in God's Image"). Yet, it has also been argued that Genesis 2:15 may offer a profound contribution by addressing the issue of man's purpose in life.

Context and Translation of Genesis 2:15

After the description of the unproductive land (Gen. 2:4–7), man is formed by God and placed in the garden of Eden (Gen. 2:8–17). Included in the narrative is a parenthetical section that gives a description of the rivers of the garden of Eden in Genesis 2:10–14.[2] Genesis 2:15 then picks up and essentially repeats Genesis 2:8a. In Genesis 2:15, as the narrative resumes, we are informed that man is placed in the garden "to work it and keep it." This purposeful placement of man in the garden is reflected in all English translations of the Bible. Yet, there is some evidence, particularly in Jewish tradition,

---

1. See Michael Fishbane, *Text and Texture* (New York: Schocken, 1979), 18.
2. The section is introduced by a *waw* disjunctive in Hebrew, which supports the view that the section should be taken as parenthetical.

which would indicate that the placement of man in the garden was not for the expressed purpose of cultivating and maintaining this piece of land.

Objections to the Traditional Translation of Genesis 2:15

The first objection to the traditional translation of Genesis 2:15 has to do with the antecedent of the suffix "it," a feminine pronominal suffix occurring twice in the phrase, "to work *it* and to keep *it*." As normally understood, a suffix modifies the nearest antecedent. In this verse the nearest antecedent is the reference to the "garden of Eden." Hence, we find in the traditional translation the phrase "to work it and keep it" with "it" referring to the garden. A difficulty arises, however, as it has been pointed out that the noun garden (Hb. *gan*) is considered to be not a feminine noun but rather a masculine noun by its attested usage in other parts of the Hebrew Bible.[3]

The second objection has more to do with the cohesion of the larger narrative of Genesis 2:4–3:24. At the end of this section, after the fall has occurred and the punishment for sin has been announced, man is relegated to "working the ground" outside the garden of Eden (Gen. 3:23). Thus, "to work the ground" is contrary to man's purpose in the garden. Instead it is a result of the fall and is a judgment particularly directed toward the man.[4]

The third objection to the traditional translation has to do with the meaning of the pair of verbs, rendered "work" (Hb. *avadh*), and "keep" (Hb. *shamar*), particularly in their usage in the Pentateuch. These verbs may have a technical connotation, but when they occur together, particularly in the Pentateuch, they convey a meaning that indicates a religious service. As G. K. Beale observed:

> It is true that the Hebrew word usually translated 'cultivate'
> can refer to an agricultural task used by itself (e.g., 2:5; 3:23).
> When, however, these two words (verbal [*avadh* and *shamar*]
> and nominal forms) occur together in the Old Testament
> (within an approximately 15-word range), they refer either to
> Israelites 'serving' God and 'guarding [keeping]' God's word
> (approximately 10 times) or to priests who 'keep' the 'service'

---

3. A few scholars have argued that there is no suffix at all and the longer infinitive forms represent an ancient way of writing infinitive forms. See Umberto Cassuto, *A Commentary on the Book of Genesis*, 2 vols. (vol. 1, *From Adam to Noah, Genesis I–VI:8*), trans. Israel Abrahams (Jerusalem: Magnes, 1978), 1:122; John H. Sailhamer, "Genesis," in *The Expositors Bible Commentary*, rev. ed. (Grand Rapids: Zondervan, 2008), 79. However, Sailhamer in his work *Genesis Unbound* maintains that the suffix should be viewed as feminine with the understood antecedent being the Law (Hb. *torah*) (*Genesis Unbound* [Sisters Oreg.: Multnomah, 1996], 75). The word *torah* is nowhere to be found in the immediate context, and indeed does occur only one time in the book of Genesis in Genesis 26:5.
4. See Cassuto, *Genesis*, 1:122.

(or 'charge') of the tabernacle (see Num 3:7–8; 8:25–26; 18:5–6; 1 Chr 23:32; Ezek 44:14). The Aramaic translation of Genesis 2:15 (*Tg. Neofiti*) underscores this priestly notion of Adam, saying that he was placed in the Garden 'to toil in the Law and to observe its commandments' (language strikingly similar to the above Numbers' reference; likewise *Tg. Pseudo-Jonathan Genesis* 2:15).[5]

Numbers 3:7–8 and 8:26 are especially interesting where the two verbs *avadh* and *shamar* are juxtaposed as they are in Genesis 2:15. Thus, rather than being translated "work it and keep it," the phrase should be rendered something like "worship and obey" in Genesis 2:15. As William Dumbrell has stated, "The only other time the OT uses both verbs together is in connection with the Levitical service and guarding of the sanctuary (Num. 3:7–8; 8:25–26). In the context of Genesis 2:15, the meaning of *avadh* is 'till' or 'cultivate,' but the regular use of the verb as 'worship' later in the OT imports into the Genesis 2 context the aspect of human response in what seems to be this sanctuary, where the presence of God is directly experienced."[6] This understanding could be supported from the next verse that does not reference any aspect of cultivation but rather speaks of obedience to God's command (Gen. 2:16).

Critique of the Alternate Understanding of Genesis 2:15
Feminine Suffix and the Garden
There are several ways to address the issue of the apparent lack of gender agreement of the word "garden" with the feminine suffix. First of all, while nouns in Hebrew are either masculine or feminine, when it comes to places or locations, the gender appears to vary between masculine and feminine.[7] Moreover, in an unpublished paper, Gordon P. Hugenberger has examined the use of garden (*gan*) in the Old Testament and has concluded that the only clear example of "garden" being masculine occurs in Song of Solomon 4:16.[8] Another possibility is the view that the feminine suffix refers not to "garden" but rather to "Eden," which would be considered feminine. While this is not

5. G. K. Beale, *The Temple and the Church's Mission: A Biblical Theology of the Dwelling Place of God,* NSBT 17 (Downers Grove: InterVarsity, 2004), 67; idem, *A New Testament Biblical Theology* (Grand Rapids: Baker Academic, 2011), 617–18. Similarly in Sifré to Deuteronomy, Pisqa 41.6 we find the view that "to work it" refers to the study of the Law, and "to guard it" refers to keeping religious duties. See Jacob Neusner, *Sifre to Deuteronomy: An Analytical Translation* (Atlanta: Scholars Press, 1987), 130.
6. William J. Dumbrell, "Genesis 2:1–17: A Foreshadowing of the New Creation," in *Biblical Theology: Retrospect and Prospect,* ed. Scott J. Hafemann (Downers Grove: InterVarsity, 2002), 59.
7. GKC, 392 (§122l).
8. See Gordon P. Hugenberger, "Is Work the Result of the Fall? A Note on Genesis 2:15," n.d.

the most common way to understand the referent of the suffix, according to the *Intermediate Grammar* by Waltke and O'Connor this is the correct view here in Genesis 2:15 where "the place name determines the gender of the phrase."[9] Ronald Hendel, on the other hand, has argued that in early preexilic texts the suffix could be understood as masculine.[10] There is also the possibility that the feminine suffix is to be retained and infer that it refers back to the feminine noun, *adhamah*, "ground" (Gen. 2:5). In this context the root *avadh* occurs with *adhamah* as the object in Genesis 2:5; 3:23. These texts surround Genesis 2:15 so it could be argued that the idea of "ground" is assumed here though it is not repeated. Moreover and very importantly, the Septuagint, the earliest translation of the Hebrew Old Testament included the "it" suffix.[11]

Cohesion of the Narrative

The view that Genesis 2:15 has nothing to do with cultivating and maintaining the garden views human work to be the consequence of the fall. This, of course, would be in tension with the long-standing position, expressed already in the Septuagint centuries before Christ, that work is not a result of the curse, but on the contrary an integral part of being human and in being in relationship with God. Claus Westermann in his study of Genesis has commented that work is an essential part of human existence and that a life without work would not be worthy of human beings. He further comments that the view of humankind in Genesis 2 is distinct from the view of human beings in mythological literature, particularly in the significance of human work:

> The Sumerian and Akkadian Myths refer human work to the world of the gods from the very beginning; this is typical of myth: the gods need people for the heavy work. Gen. 2:15 strips work of any mythical connection with the world of the gods. Work is part of human existence because the living space which the creator has assigned to his people demands this work. Human work then, as a mandate from God to his creatures, is a necessary part of the exchange between God and his people. Work is a determining factor in a God-created

---

9. *IBHS* 104 (§6.4.1d).

10. Thus, reading the vowel -*ô* instead of the vowel -*â* (the addition of vowels to the Hebrew text was not finalized until the tenth century AD). See Ronald S. Hendel, *The Text of Genesis 1–11: Textual Studies and Critical Edition* (New York/Oxford: Oxford University Press, 1998), 44.

11. The same can be said for the Aramaic Targum, Targum Onkelos, the most literal of the Aramaic Targum translations.

person. The dignity which belongs to civilization rests on the mandate of God to his creatures.[12]

The nature of the man's punishment in the fall, as Mathews states, is not "working the ground" in Genesis 3:23 but rather laboring outside the garden with a ground that is cursed and therefore less cooperative.[13] Hamilton adds that work is mentioned in the creation account before sin is, and if man had never sinned, he would still have worked.[14]

Work and Keep

While the rare possibility exists for reading these verbs as infinitives without suffixes, Hugenberger has noted that these particular verbs in Genesis 2:15 (*avadh* and *shamar*) occur in this exact form as infinitives in no other place in the Old Testament. The verb *avadh* does occur as an infinitive in over thirty additional places and *shamar* occurs as an infinitive in over fifty other places, yet never with the lengthened form as is maintained in Genesis 2:15.[15]

The root for "work" (Hb. *avadh*) occurs often in the Old Testament and is frequently used for cultivation elsewhere in Genesis as in Genesis 2:5; 3:23; 4:2, 12. It is also true that, in the range of usage of the verb, the term is used in the religious sense of serving God (Deut. 4:19) as well as administering tabernacle duties (Num. 3:7–8; 4:23–24, 26). Likewise, "keep" (Hb. *shamar*) is used to refer to observing God's commands (Num. 17:9; Lev. 18:5) as well as for the important task of "guarding" the tabernacle (Num. 1:53; 3:7–8).[16] But elsewhere in the Old Testament when *shamar* refers to obeying, it is accompanied by a direct object—the very issue that Cassuto and Sailhamer deny for Genesis 2:15. These meanings of "worship and obey" are well and fine in liturgical texts, but the context of Genesis 2–3 is not liturgical. As noted *avadh* has been used of "working the ground" just a few verses earlier (Gen. 2:5). Human work is not to be diminished. When creation is restored, manual labor will characterize the eschatological paradise (Isa. 2:4; 65:21–25; Ezek. 36:9, 34; Amos 9:13–14; Mic. 4:3).[17]

Conclusion

As demonstrated above, taking into account the immediate context of Genesis 2:15, it seems reasonable to surmise that the original audience would

---

12. Claus Westermann, *Genesis 1–11*, trans. John J. Scullion S. J. (Minneapolis: Fortress, 1994), 222.
13. See Kenneth A. Mathews, *Genesis 1–11:26*, NAC 1A (Nashville: B&H, 1996), 209n.94; Nahum M. Sarna, *Genesis*, JPSTC (Philadelphia: Jewish Publication Society, 1989), 28.
14. See Victor P. Hamilton, *The Book of Genesis Chapters 1–17*, NICOT (Grand Rapids: Eerdmans, 1990), 171.
15. Hugenberger, "Is Work the Result of the Fall?"
16. See Gordon J. Wenham, *Genesis 1–15*, WBC 1 (Waco, Tex.: Word, 1987), 67.
17. Ibid., 86.

certainly have understood the work specified in Genesis 2:15 to be that of a local farmer. The work of agriculture or farming has been a major, if not the major, labor occupation in world history until just a few centuries ago. Yet, it would be wrong to restrict the author's intention to only this type of work. As Westermann has said, "It can be said that every human occupation shares in some way in this 'tilling and keeping.'"[18] Paradise was not a life of leisure. Nahum Sarna observed, "The man is not indigenous to the garden. He is fashioned elsewhere and finds himself in it solely by the grace of God. True, his needs are easily taken care of, but his life in the garden is not to be one of indolence. He has duties to perform. It is his responsibility to nurture and conserve the pristine perfection of the garden. This he must do by the labor of his hands. Yet, strenuous exertion is not required, for nature responds easily to his efforts."[19] Manual work should be viewed as concomitant with man exercising dominion. In fact, J. Moltmann argued that Genesis 2:15 indicates that man's dominion was in fact like the cultivating and protective work of a gardener.[20]

In this regard, man's labor in the garden is indeed a kind of divine service, for it is done for God and in his presence. In addition, there are many indications in the garden narrative that the garden of Eden is comparable to the later tabernacle. It has been noted how the main verbs *avadh* and *shamar* in Genesis 2:15 are also used with regard to service in the tabernacle. This indicates, on the one hand, that man's ordinary work is a service to God. In addition, it also indicates that the occurrence of these verbs in juxtaposition in Genesis 2:15 is at least an allusion to the service in the tabernacle.[21] Like the garden of Eden (Gen. 3:8), the tabernacle was a place where God walked with his people (Lev. 26:12).[22]

The allusions to the tabernacle as the special place of God's presence heightens the tragedy of what was lost in the garden, particularly the loss of fellowship between God and human beings. This fellowship was critical for God's original purpose in creating man and would not be restored until the coming of one who tabernacled among us (John 1:14).

---

18. Westermann, *Genesis 1–11*, 221.
19. Sarna, *Genesis*, 20. The meaning of man's work must also be balanced by the observance of the Sabbath rest during the work-week. See Question 9 and Mark F. Rooker, *The Ten Commandments: Ethics for the Twenty-First Century* (Nashville: B&H, 2009), 100.
20. See Hart, "Genesis 1:1–2:3 As a Prologue to the Book of Genesis," 323n.26 (J. Moltmann, *God in Creation* [London: SCM, 1985], 30).
21. Ibid., 333. See Wenham, *Genesis 1–15*, 86.
22. See Wenham, *Genesis 1–15*, 90. This interplay between the garden of Eden and the tabernacle was noted in rabbinic literature (*Gen. Rab.* 16:5). See Jacob Neusner, *Genesis Rabbah*, vol. 1(Atlanta: Scholars Press, 1985), 176, and see particularly Gordon J. Wenham, "Sanctuary Symbolism in the Garden of Eden Story," in *Proceedings of the Ninth World Congress of Jewish Studies* 9 (1986): 19–25.

REFLECTION QUESTIONS

1. What has man's purpose been associated with?

2. What are the issues with the translation "to work it and keep it"?

3. What is another possible way to translate the phrase "work it and keep it"?

4. What should be our attitude toward work?

5. What is the connection between the garden of Eden and the tabernacle?

PART 3

QUESTIONS ABOUT
THE DAYS OF CREATION

What Is the Gap Theory?

The gap theory, sometimes called ruin-restoration creationism, is a form of old earth creationism that posits that after God's creation in Genesis 1:1 there was an unknown gap of time between the first two verses of Genesis. Sometime after Genesis 1:1, Satan rebelled and God pronounced a cataclysmic judgment upon the once perfect earth.[1] This judgment brought about the conditions described in Genesis 1:2. Beginning in Genesis 1:3 God began to transform the earth now in a chaotic state and continued this transformation throughout the remainder of the creation narrative. Weston Fields summarizes the essence of the theory along with other details when he states,

> God created a perfect heaven and perfect earth. Satan was ruler of the earth which was peopled by a race of 'men' without any souls. . . . Because of Satan's fall, sin entered the universe and brought on the earth God's judgment in the form of a flood (indicated by the water of 1:2), and then a global ice age when the light and heat from the sun were somehow removed. All the plant, animal, and human fossils upon the earth today date from this 'Lucifer's flood' and do not bear any genetic relationship with the plants, animals, and fossils living upon the earth today.[2]

The gap theory places millions of years of geologic time (including billions of fossilized animals) and the origins of most geologic strata between Genesis 1:1 and Genesis 1:2.

---

1. Satan's fall appears to be described in Isaiah 14:12–15 and Ezekiel 28:11–19 (see also John 8:44).
2. Weston W. Fields, *Unformed and Unfilled: A Critique of the Gap Theory of Genesis 1:1,2* (Winona Lake, Ind.: Light and Life, 1973), 7.

History of the Gap Theory

Thomas Chalmers (1780–1847), a professor at the University of Edinburgh and patriarch of the Free Church of Scotland, is credited with popularizing gap creationism. Chalmers traced the origin of the theory to the seventeenth century Dutch Arminian theologian Simon Episcopius. Gap creationism became increasingly popular near the end of the eighteenth century and first half of the nineteenth century because the newly established science of geology had determined that the earth was far older than a literal interpretation of Genesis would allow. The gap theory was a significant attempt by Christian scholars to reconcile the time scale of world history found in Genesis with the popular belief that geologists provided "undeniable" evidence that the world is exceedingly old (billions of years). Gap theorists oppose evolution, but believe in an ancient origin of the universe.

The most influential nineteenth century writer to popularize the gap theory was G. H. Pember in his book *Earth's Earliest Ages*, first published in 1884. Pember stated, "Since, then, the fossil remains are those of creatures anterior to Adam, and yet show evident tokens of disease, death, and mutual destruction, they must have belonged to another world, and have a sin-stained history of their own, a history which ended in the ruin of themselves and their habitation."[3]

The twentieth century writer who published the most academic defense of the gap theory was Arthur C. Custance in his work, *Without Form and Void*.[4] But the gap theory gained particular popularity as it was the view taken by the editors of the *Scofield Bible* in 1907.[5] By the mid-twentieth century Bernhard Ramm could state, "The gap theory has become the standard interpretation throughout Fundamentalism, appearing in an endless stream of books, pamphlets, Bible studies, and periodical articles. In fact, it has become so sacrosanct with some that to question it is equivalent to tampering with Sacred Scripture or to manifest modernistic leanings."[6] In the following discussion we will interact with the interpretive positions of the gap theory and follow with a critique of these positions.

---

3. G. H. Pember, *Earth's Earliest Ages* (Old Tappan, N.J., 1884), 35. The ruin is described in Genesis 1:2. Satan was the ruler of the earth that was populated by a race of "men" without any souls (Fields, *Unformed and Unfilled*, 7). Many advocates of this position place the dinosaurs in this gap.
4. Arthur C. Custance, *Without Form and Void* (Brockville, Canada: Doorway Publications, 1970).
5. *The New Scofield Reference Bible* (New York: Oxford University Press, 1907), 1n.5, 752–53n.2.
6. Bernard Ramm, *The Christian View of Science and Scripture* (Grand Rapids: Eerdmans, 1955), 197.

Create Versus Make

Because gap theorists maintain that there are two creation ac
Genesis 1, they propose that two prominent Hebrew verbs, *bara*
and *asah* ("do" or "make") are used in distinct ways in the chapter. The distinction between the two verbs is that *asah* does not refer to creation but
rather the giving of a new role to something already in existence. Thus "creation" is restricted to Genesis 1:1 where *bara* is used. *Bara* refers to the
original creation; *asah* does not mean to create, but rather to make. So in
Exodus 20:11 when it is stated that God made (*asah*) heaven and earth in six
days, we are not to assume that this has reference to the original creation—
"For we are told that in the beginning God *created* the heaven and the earth;
but the Scriptures never affirm that He did this in the six days. The work
of those days was . . . quite a different thing from original creation: they
were times of restoration, and the word *asah* is generally used in connection with them."[7] Thus Exodus 20:11 refers to the work of six creation days
not as a time of creation *ex nihilo* ("out of nothing") but as a time in which
a ruined cosmos was re-ordered as a fit habitation for man. Not only does
this understanding of Exodus 20:11 seem forced, but the understanding of
asah to have no reference to creation is at odds with the use of this verb in
the creation account.

The root *asah* is used numerous times in the creation account (Gen.
1:7, 16, 25, 26, 31; 2:2–3). It is usually understood to mean "to do" or "to
make." But throughout the creation account the verb is used virtually
synonymously with the verb *bara* (Gen. 1:1). The verb *asah* appears to be
equivalent in meaning with *bara* in Genesis 1:7 where God makes the expanse to divide the waters. It also appears to be synonymous with *bara*
as it is used with reference to the creating of the heavenly bodies (Gen.
1:16) or the animals that live on the land (Gen. 1:25). Both verbs *bara* and
asah are used in conjunction with the creation of mankind (Gen. 1:26–27).
Moreover, outside Genesis 1 *asah* is used in reference to the creation of
heaven and earth (Ex. 20:11; Neh. 9:6). Nehemiah 9:6 alludes to the original creation from nothing in Genesis 1:1 but employs the word *asah*. The
verb is also used at the conclusion of the six days of creation to refer to all
that God had made (Gen. 1:31). Moreover, the close association between
asah and *bara* can be recognized by their occurrence together at the close
of the seven day creation week in Genesis 2:3. *Asah* and *bara* thus often
appear to be interchangeable and are parallel in Genesis 2:4, Exodus 34:10,
Isaiah 41:20, 43:7, and Ps. 148:1–5.[8]

---

7. Pember, *Earth's Earliest Ages*, 22–23 (emphasis original).
8. See James Barr, "The Image of God in the Book of Genesis—A Study of Terminology,"
   BJRL 51 (1968–69): 25. See Genesis 1:11–12; 1:21, 25; 1:26–27; 2:2–4; Job 41:25; Isaiah
   57:16; Jeremiah 31:16 (Fields, *Unformed and Unfilled*, 56, 61–62, 65–70; *HALOT* 1:890).

The Grammar of Genesis 1:2

Gap theorists affirm that the grammar allows, or even requires, a chronological hiatus between the events described in Genesis 1:1 and Genesis 1:2. Hence, they insist that the first phrase of Genesis 1:2 be rendered as "the earth *became* formless and void."[9] Thus, gap theorists insist that Genesis 1:2 be read as subsequent, or sequential, to Genesis 1:1. However, this understanding would require that Genesis 1:2 begin with the Hebrew verb form that indicates sequence in a narrative, the verb form known as the *waw* consecutive. Genesis 1:2, however, begins with the conjunction (*waw*) and then the noun (the earth). This construction is known as the *waw* disjunctive in a narrative passage. The *waw* disjunctive does not depict sequence, but rather adds explanatory details to the account.[10] It introduces a circumstantial clause, a clause that expresses the circumstances accompanying the principal statement (Gen. 1:1). Thus, Genesis 1:2 explains more clearly the condition or the circumstances attending God's creative act. Genesis 1:2 is thus a description of the earth as originally created. Fields aptly summarizes the grammatical issue of the gap theory: "The use of the *waw disjunctive* in Genesis 1:2, as well as the fact that the passage consists of three circumstantial clauses, indicates that the clauses of which it is composed are a description of the action of the main verb (namely, the action of creating the heaven and the earth in Gen. 1:1), *not a chronologically sequential development after 1:1.* Verse 2 sets the scene, making *the earth* our vantage point; whatever the total pattern, this is our concern."[11] Keil and Delitzsch reiterate that all three clauses describe the condition of the earth immediately after the creation of the universe.[12]

Genesis 1:2 should be taken as a positive description, not a negative one. And though the earth was not yet suitable for man to inhabit, "there is no reason, so far as one can tell from reading the first chapter of Genesis, why

---

9. This rendering finds no support by the earliest translation of the Old Testament, the LXX.
10. Grammarians understand this as an explanatory *waw* (GKC, 484 [§154a, n. 1]).
11. Fields, *Unformed and Unfilled*, 86 (emphasis original). The only *waw* disjunctive in Genesis 1 is the one in Genesis 1:2. This is also the only occurrence of the Greek conjunction *de*. There are three waw disjunctives in Genesis 2 (2:6, 10, 12) and they are also translated by *de* (Fields, *Unformed and Unfilled*, 83; see GKC, 456 [§142d]; C. John Collins, "Reading Genesis 1:1–2:2 as An Act of Communication: Discourse Analysis and Literal Interpretation," in *Did God Create in Six Days?* ed. Joseph A. Pipa, Jr. and David W. Hall [Taylors, SC: Southern Presbyterian Press, 1999], 149).
12. See C. F. Keil and F. Delitzsch, "Genesis," in *Commentary on the Old Testament* (Grand Rapids: Eerdmans, 1973), 1: 49. See also Claus Westermann, *Genesis 1–11*, trans. John J. Scullion S. J. (Minneapolis: Fortress, 1994), 102, 106; Fields, *Unformed and Unfilled*, 83–84. Since the three clauses are coordinate, Westermann and Schmidt would argue that they should be viewed in the same light, either positively or negatively. See also Gordon J. Wenham, *Genesis 1–15*, WBC 1 (Waco, Tex.: Word, 1987), 17; D. F. Payne, "Approaches to Genesis i 2," *Transactions* 23 (1969–70): 66.

God might not have pronounced the judgment, 'very good,' over the condition described in the second verse."[13]

According to the traditional interpretation, however, Genesis 1:2 states the condition of the earth as it was when it was first created until God began to form it into the present world.[14]

Formless and Void

Gap theorists affirm that the phrase *tohu wavohu* ("formless and void") implies a judgmental destruction and therefore not an original state of the earth. Isaiah 34:11 and Jeremiah 4:23 contain the only other biblical attestations of the phrase *tohu wavohu* "formless and void" (Gen. 1:2).[15] These passages are said to substantiate the understanding of "formless and void" in Genesis 1:2 in a negative sense as the phrase occurs in both of these passages in the context of judgment oracles. Gap theorists use Genesis 1:2 to suggest that God did not make a *tohu* in the original creation; but because it became a *tohu* in Genesis 1:2 it needed a new creation. Thus, Genesis 1:2 describes a judgment brought about by God.

Furthermore, gap theorists argue that Isaiah 45:18 supports their understanding of *tohu* as being the result of judgment:

> For thus says the LORD who created the heavens
> (He is the God who formed the earth and made it,
> He established it *and* did not create it a waste place [*tohu*]),
> *but* formed it to be inhabited) (NASB).

Does not this passage seem to imply, gap theorists argue, that God was not responsible for creating such a chaotic state as described in Genesis 1:2?

The answer to this objection appears to be found in the purpose of God's creation from the context of Isaiah 45:18. It could be argued from the context of the passage that it was not God's intention or purpose to create or leave the earth in a desolate *tohu* condition. On the contrary, he created the earth "to be inhabited" (Isa. 45:18).[16] Far from contradicting the initial chaos theory

---

13. Edward J. Young, "The Interpretation of Genesis 1:2," *WTJ* 23 (1960–61): 174; see Westermann, *Genesis 1–11*, 94, 102.

14. See Edward J. Young, "The Relation of the First Verse of Genesis One to Verses Two and Three," *WTJ* 21 (1959): 144n.20.

15. The term *bohu* only occurs in combination with *tohu* while *tohu* may occur by itself.

16. See John Peter Lange, "Genesis," in *Lange's Commentary on the Holy Scriptures* (Grand Rapids: Zondervan, 1978), 499; Edward J. Young, "The Interpretation of Genesis 1:2," 154; R. N. Whybray, *Isaiah 40–66*, New Century Bible (Greenwood, S.C.: Attic Press, 1975), 110–11; Fields, *Unformed and Unfilled*, 123–24. This text would thus correspond to the creation account in Genesis 1 where we also see that God did not leave the earth in this state. Thus, John Calvin, *Commentary on the Book of the Prophet Isaiah*, 4 vols., trans. Rev.

(the traditional view), Isaiah 45:18 actually helps to clarify the meaning of *tohu* in Genesis 1:2 as we see *tohu* contextually contrasted with *lasheveth*, "to inhabit."[17] One should infer from this contextual usage that *tohu* is the antonym of "inhabiting."[18] This would provide a clue as to the meaning of the problematic phrase in Genesis 1:2. The earth, immediately after God's initial creative act, was in a condition that would not be habitable for mankind. God did not create the world for it to be empty. He created it to be formed and filled, a suitable abode for his creatures. Gap theorists miss the point altogether when they argue that because Isaiah says God did not create the world a *tohu*, it must have become *tohu* at some later time. Isaiah 45:18 is about God's purpose in creating, not about the original state of the creation. Tsumura nicely summarizes the contribution of Isaiah 45:18 to the understanding of Genesis 1:2:

> . . . *tohu* here is contrasted with *lasheveth* in the parallelism and seems to refer rather to a place which has no habitation, like the terms *hemamakh* "desolation" (cf. Jer. 4:27; Isa. 24:12), *kharev* "waste, desolate" and *azuvah* "deserted." There is nothing in this passage that would suggest a chaotic state of the earth "which is opposed to and precedes creation." Thus, the term *tohu* here too signifies "a desert-like place" and refers to "an uninhabited place." . . . It should be noted that *lo tohu* here is a resultative object, referring to the purpose of God's creative action. In other words, this verse explains that God did not create the earth so that it may stay desert-like, but to be inhabited. So, this verse does not contradict Genesis 1:2, where God created the earth to be productive and inhabited though it "was" still *tohu wavohu* in the initial state.[19]

The context of Isaiah speaks of God's grace in restoring Israel: he did not choose his people in order to destroy them. He is the Lord who created the

---

William Pringle (Grand Rapids: Eerdmans, 1947), 3: 418; Delitzsch, "Genesis," 227; John L. McKenzie, *Second Isaiah*, AB (Garden City, N.Y.: Doubleday, 1968), 83.

17. See John Skinner, *The Book of the Prophet Isaiah, Chapters XL–LXVI* (Cambridge: Cambridge University Press, 1898), 65.

18. For discussion of the use of antonyms or binary opposites in delimiting and clarifying the meaning of terms in context, see John Lyons, *Introduction to Theoretical Linguistics* (Cambridge: Cambridge University Press, 1968), 460–70; John Barton, *Reading the Old Testament* (Philadelphia: Westminster, 1984), 109–12.

19. David Toshio Tsumura, *The Earth and the Waters in Genesis 1 and 2*, JSOTSup 83 (Sheffield, UK: JSOT Press, 1989), 33–34. This would also pertain to the phrase in Isaiah 34:11. The threat would be that the land would become a desolation and waste and thus unfit for inhabitants. See E. J. Young, *The Book of Isaiah II*, NICOT (Grand Rapids: Eerdmans, 1969), 438.

earth not to be a chaos, but to be formed and filled during the remaining days of creation.

David Tsumura concludes his extensive treatment of the meaning of *tohu wavohu* in Genesis 1:2 and provides a helpful summary of the meaning of the phrase when he states, "In conclusion, both the biblical context and extra-biblical parallels suggest that the phrase *tohu wavohu* in Genesis 1:2 has nothing to do with 'chaos' and simply means 'emptiness' and refers to the earth which is an empty place, i.e., 'an unproductive and uninhabited place.'"[20] He continues, "There is nothing in this passage that would suggest a chaotic state of the earth which is opposed to and precedes creation."[21] This understanding of Genesis 1:2 fits well with the overall thrust and structure of Genesis 1:1–2:3, and it undermines a major tenet of the gap theory that Genesis 1:2 describes a state of judgment.

Conclusion

Western Bible commentaries written before the eighteenth century, before the belief in an old age for the earth became popular, knew nothing of any gap between Genesis 1:1 and Genesis 1:2. Because the gap theorists cannot accept the conclusions of evolution, nor that the days in the Genesis record correspond to geologic periods, they assume the proposition that God reshaped the earth and re-created all life in six literal days after "Lucifer's flood," hence the name "ruin-reconstruction." However, any rebellion of Satan during this gap of time appears to conflict with God's description of his completed creation on day six as being "very good" (Gen. 1:31). Scripture nowhere states that God judged the world when Satan fell.[22]

Exodus 20:11 affirms that everything in heaven and earth and in the sea was made in six days. There could have been nothing left over that was not made during the six days. "Exodus 20:11 establishes a chronological limit upon the interpretation of the first chapter of Genesis which completely vaporizes not only the gap theory in any form whatsoever, but also any theory which does not postulate the formation of the entire universe within the framework of the six days of creation."[23] The use of *tohu* and/or *bohu* in Isaiah 34:11 and Jeremiah 4:23 is a "verbal allusion." These passages on judgment allude to the formless and empty earth at the beginning of creation to suggest the extent of God's judgment to come. God's judgment will be so complete that the result will be that the land will become like the earth before it was formed

---

20. Tsumura, *The Earth and the Waters*, 156. For similar understanding in post-biblical Jewish literature, see Jacob Newman, *The Commentary of Nahmanides on Genesis Chapters 1–6* (Leiden, Netherlands: E. J. Brill, 1960), 33.
21. Tsumura, *The Earth and the Waters*, 33–34.
22. See Bruce K. Waltke, *Creation and Chaos* (Portland, Ore.: Western Conservative Baptist Seminary, 1974), 24.
23. Fields, *Unformed and Unfilled*, 58.

and filled—formless and empty. This does not imply that the state of the creation in Genesis 1:2 was arrived at by some sort of judgment or destruction as imagined by gap theorists. As Robert Chisholm, Jr. wrote, "By the way, allusion only works one way. It is unwarranted to assume that Jeremiah's use of the phrase in a context of judgment implies some sort of judgment in the context of Genesis 1:2. Jeremiah is applying the language of Gen. 1:2 to the judgment he foresees; he is not interpreting the meaning of Genesis 1:2."[24]

Isaiah 34:11 and Jeremiah 4:23 do speak of a wasteness and emptiness resulting from judgment for sin; this meaning is not implicit in the expression itself but is gained from the contexts. No such reference is required by the context of Genesis 1:2.

The simple, straightforward meaning of Genesis 1:1–2 is that, when God created the earth at the beginning, it was initially formless, empty, and dark, and God's Spirit was there above the waters. It was through his creative energy that the world was then progressively formed and filled during the six days of creation.

REFLECTION QUESTIONS

1. What English Study Bible helped the gap theory gain popularity?

2. What is the grammatical problem with the gap theory?

3. What is the meaning of the phrase "formless and void"?

4. Where else does the phrase "formless and void" occur, besides Genesis 1:2?

5. When did the gap theory become a viable interpretation?

---

24. Robert Chisholm, Jr., *From Exegesis to Exposition* (Grand Rapids: Baker, 1998), 52.

What Is the Day-Age Theory?

The day-age theory of creation is an interpretation of the creation account in Genesis that maintains that the six creation days in Genesis 1 are not literal twenty-four hour days, but rather represent much longer periods, perhaps millions or even billions of years. Proponents of this view include theistic evolutionists who accept the theory of evolution and progressive evolutionists who generally reject naturalistic and materialistic evolution. But according to both positions, the days of Genesis represent "an age." Thus the day-age theory is the attempt to insert geological time into the biblical text during the creation week. The sequence and duration of the creation's "days" represent or symbolize the sequence and duration of events that scientists theorize happened in the creation of the world. The Genesis account thus provides somewhat of a summary of how modern science views the creation of the world and/or universe. Creation days are literal, in the sense that they are six sequential, long periods of time. Integrating biblical and scientific data, day-age proponents assert that the physical creation events reported in Genesis appear in appropriate sequence and in scientifically defensible terms. The hyphenated name of this theory "day-age" precisely describes the essence of this position as it is a combination of the biblical view of Genesis 1 (creation "day"), as well as an "age" or epoch of time often demanded by modern science. Of all the modern models for understanding the creation of the earth and universe, the advocates of this view maintain, only the day-age theory of creation provides a coherent testable creation model.[1]

Scientific Basis for Day-Age Theory

In the mid-nineteenth century, American geologist Arnold Guyot discovered that modern science and Scripture were in harmony with regard

---

1. See Hugh Ross and Gleason A. Archer, "Day-Age View," in *The Genesis Debate: Three Views on the Days of Creation*, ed. David G. Hagopian (Mission Viejo, Calif.: Crux, 2001), 125.

to the world's creation as long as one interpreted the days of Genesis 1 as epochs in cosmic history.[2] Similarly, but much more extensively in modern times, astronomer Hugh Ross has defended the day-age hypothesis on many occasions, particularly in his book *Creation and Time*. Recent scientific discoveries in astronomy and biology have caused us to reconsider the age of the earth as the evidence points to an earth and universe that could be billions of years old.

Astronomers have argued for years that it takes a certain amount of time for light to travel a given distance. Based on the vast distance of a star and the constant velocity of the speed of light, the light from stars we now see must have been emitted billions of years ago. Given the vast measured distance, scientists can confirm that it takes light sometimes as long as seventeen billion years to be seen upon the earth. Thus the age of the universe should be calculated in billions of years.[3]

The earth's crust contains an abundance of compositional elements and biological resources that are crucial for human life to exist. These life resources include limestone, marble, ozone, oxygen, water, top soil, coal, oil, gas, salt, phosphate, gypsum, and kerogen (including tar sands and oil-rich shales). According to the day-age model these resources were laid down in the systematic course of creation events occurring over the few billion years of earth's history. Millions of generations of life would be needed to prepare for the advent of the first human being.[4]

Thus, the advent of lower forms of life predates the arrival of the *homo sapiens*. Speciation (the formation of new species) was abundant before the advent of humanity when God supernaturally created large numbers of new phyla, families, orders, genera, and species. This order is in harmony with Genesis 1. When man arrived on the scene, the creation of new species and genera became limited to what appears to be a natural process. This corresponds with the Genesis record of rest on the seventh day ("epoch"). The limited speciation we do see during God's "rest" after the creation of man is consistent with the words used to describe God's creative activity during the six creation days.[5]

To demonstrate that the earth and the universe have existed for billions of years, day-age theorists use these discoveries in astronomical and biological realms. By way of conclusion, Norman Geisler has summarized

2. See Ronald Numbers, *The Creationists: From Scientific Creationism to Intelligent Design*, exp. ed. (Cambridge: Harvard University Press, 2006), 21–23.
3. See Hugh Ross, *Creation and Time: A Biblical and Scientific Perspective on the Creation-Date Controversy* (Colorado Springs: NavPress, 1994), 95–100.
4. These resources, it is surmised, are orders of magnitude beyond anything possible in a young-earth creation paradigm (see Hugh Ross, *The Genesis Question* [Colorado Springs: NavPress, 1988], 151–54; "Day-Age View," 137, 142).
5. See Ross and Archer, "Day-Age View," 141.

these and other scientific arguments for the position that the world has existed for billions of years. He states, "There are scientific arguments that the world has existed for billions of years. The age of the universe is based on: (1) the speed of light and the distance of the stars; (2) the rate of expansion of the universe; (3) the fact that early rocks have been radioactively dated in term of billions of years; (4) the rate that salt runs into the sea and the amount of salt there, which indicates multimillions of years."[6]

Biblical Basis for Day-Age Theory

In his work *The Fingerprint of God,* Hugh Ross provided thirteen scriptural arguments for long creation days:

1. Genesis 1 fits the form and, hence, the function of biblical chronology.

2. A long period of time is clearly acceptable with the definitions of *yom, erev,* and *boqer.*

3. The unusual syntax of the sentences enumerating specific creation days suggests indefinite time periods.

4. The seventh day in Genesis 1 and 2 is not closed out.

5. The events of the sixth day cover more than twenty-four hours.

6. The wording of Genesis 2:4 suggests a long time span for the creation week.

7. In describing the eternity of God's existence, Bible writers compare it to the longevity of the mountains or of the "foundations of the earth."

8. Truthfulness and a purpose to reveal truth, both in the creation and written Word, are fundamental attributes of God. He does not lie.

9. The Bible affirms that the creation reveals God's existence, his handiwork, his power, and his divine nature.

10. The Bible writers' statements about the vastness of the universe also serve as indicators of its age.

11. The Sabbath day for man and Sabbath year for the land are based on analogy with God's workweek.

---

6. Norman Geisler, *Systematic Theology,* vol. 2: *God and Creation* (Minneapolis: Bethany House, 2003), 644.

12. The onset of "death through sin" does not restrict the length of creation days.

13. The subjection of the creation to "its bondage of decay" does not restrict the length of creation days.[7]

Critical to the day-age theory, as seen above, is the understanding that the word "day" (Hb. *yom*) is not to be understood as a twenty-four hour period but as an extended length of time, perhaps an epoch. Ross and Archer point out that this extended use of the word "day" occurs already in the creation account in Genesis 2:4: "These are the generations of the heavens and the earth when they were created, in the day that the LORD God made the earth and the heavens." As the word "day" here refers to all six creation days it cannot be restricted to a period of only twenty-four hours.[8] This understanding finds additional biblical support in Psalm 90:4: "For a thousand years in your sight are but as yesterday when it is past," and 2 Peter 3:8: "with the Lord one day is as a thousand years, and a thousand years as one day."

Moreover, when one observes all the activities that took place on day six (Gen. 2:15–23), it is clear that all that is described would not fit in a normal twenty-four hour day period. Geisler summarizes the issues:

> It would appear that the sixth "day" of creation was considerably longer than a solar day. Consider everything that happened during this one "day." *First*, God created all the many hundreds (or thousands) of land animals (Gen. 1:24–25). *Second*, God "formed" man of the dust of the earth (Gen. 2:7). This Hebrew word (*yatsar*) means "to mold" or "form," which implies time. *Yatsar* is used specifically of the work of a potter (cf. Jer. 18:2f.). *Third*, God said, "I *will* make a helper suitable for him" (Gen. 2:18, emphasis added). *Fourth*, Adam observed and named this whole multitude of animals (Gen. 2:19). . . . This is hardly enough time for Adam to study each animal and determine an appropriate name for it. Assuming a minimum of only two minutes each, the process would have taken six hundred hours (or twenty-five days). *Fifth*, Adam searched for a helpmate for himself, apparently among all the creatures God had made. "But for Adam no suitable helper *was found*" (implying a time of searching). (Gen. 2:20, emphasis added). *Sixth*, God put Adam to sleep and operated on him, taking out one of his ribs and healing the flesh (Gen. 2:21). This too

---

7. See Hugh Ross, *The Fingerprint of God,* 2nd ed. (Orange, Calif.: Promise Publishing, 1991), 146–55.

8. See Ross and Archer, "Day-Age View," 147.

involved additional time. *Seventh*, Eve was brought to Adam, who observed her, accepted her, and was joined to her (Gen. 2:22–25). In conclusion, it seems highly unlikely that all of these events—especially the fourth one— were compressed within a twenty-four hour period or, more precisely, within the approximately twelve hours of light each day afforded.[9]

In addition to naming the perhaps thousands of animals, Adam needed the time to perceive his loneliness before the creation of Eve. Thus, the days of Genesis actually refer to long periods of time and can be harmonized with the major periods of evolutionary geological history. Many weeks, months, or perhaps even years of activities must have taken place in this latter portion of the sixth day. Similarly, Psalm 95 and Hebrews 4 confirm that the seventh day having no evening or morning, represents a period of minimally several thousand years. This reinforces the position again that the creation days are not to be understood as referring to a twenty-four hour period. But the days of creation are sequential; the six epochs revealed in Genesis 1 occurred in the order revealed. Since the work-rest pattern of the creation account is clearly sequential, it should be concluded that the day-by-day events of creation also appear in sequence.[10]

Evaluation for Day-Age Theory
The Scientific Argument
     The fundamental tenet of the day-age theory is that the creation of the universe took place over long periods of time. While this point may be conceded due to the abundance of scientific evidence, Carl F. H. Henry made the important observation that neither Christians nor secularists believed in the vast antiquity of the universe before the nineteenth century.[11] This indicates that the position is not well documented in the history of biblical interpretation. As an example, rabbinic literature, along with the early church fathers, appears to be unanimous in accepting a normal, twenty-four hour day for Genesis 1.[12]

---

 9. Geisler, *Systematic Theology*, 643–44. As Robert Newman noted, "If every one of the approximately 15,000 living species of such animals (not to mention those now extinct) were brought to Adam to be named, it would have taken ten hours if he spent only two seconds on each" (see Robert C. Newman and Hermann J. Eckelmann, Jr., *Genesis One and the Origin of the Earth* [Downers Grove: InterVarsity, 1977], 129).
10. See Ross and Archer, "Day-Age View," 144–45, 153–54. Other poetic accounts of creation in the Bible such as Job 36–41 and Psalms 8, 19, 33, and 148 reflect on Genesis 1 events in artistically beautiful and nonsequential terms. The authors of these passages treat Genesis 1 as a nonfictious, a literally true record of events (so Ross and Archer, "Day-Age View," 155).
11. See Carl F. H. Henry, *God, Revelation and Authority*, vol. 6 (Wheaton, Ill.: Crossway, 1999), 142. Ross, however, would maintain that ignoring the great antiquity of the universe would require a wholesale revision of the laws of physics ("The Day-Age Reply," 209).
12. See J. Ligon Duncan III and David W. Hall, "The 24-Hour Response," in *The Genesis Debate: Three Views on the Days of Creation*, ed. David G. Hagopian (Mission Viejo, C:

To counter the idea that the universe is millions or billions of years old, many young earth advocates have often argued that God's creating work was accompanied by an appearance of age. Thus, when God created a tree, it already had annual rings indicating that it was actually older than it was in fact.[13] But, without question, the essential component of the day-age theory is the understanding of the days of Genesis 1 as referring to long periods of time.

Meaning of the Word "Day"

Critical to the day-age theory is the meaning of the word "day" referring to an age or epoch of millions or billions of years. This position appears to be the most difficult to defend. With regard to the meaning of the word "day," John Collins, who does not hold to a twenty-four hour day in Genesis 1, argues that the view that the creation day is an age or epoch is not tenable:

> In my judgment the "day-age" position (view 4) suffers from a serious semantic problem. Generally speaking, the Hebrew word *yom* "day" has several attested senses. In the singular it can designate (1) the period of daylight, (2) a period of 24 hours, and (3) a period of time of unspecified length. To be lexically responsible, we should try to indicate criteria by which a reader would discern one sense or another in a given context. Senses 1 and 2 are fairly easy to discern, in Hebrew as well as in English; that is to say, these are the senses that require the least supporting information from the context. Sense 3 exists in English too; and we detect it in both languages based on qualifiers such as "day of the Lord," "day of Jerusalem," "day of wrath," "in that day," etc. Such qualifiers are not present here in Genesis 1:1–2:3, so it would be better to find an interpretation that does not rely on sense 3. I have elsewhere argued that the expression "on the day that" (Heb. *beyom* + infinitive construct) in Genesis 2:4 does not provide the needed evidence for sense 3 being present here.[14]

Crux, 2001), 168, 171. In arguing that the church fathers *explicitly* affirmed a twenty-four hour day, Duncan and Hall may have overstated the evidence. See Peter Bouteneff, *Beginnings: Ancient Christian Readings of the Biblical Creation Narratives* (Grand Rapids: Baker, 2008).

13. See John C. Whitcomb and Henry M. Morris, *The Genesis Flood* (Grand Rapids: Baker, 1961), 233. This was first proposed by British biologist Philip Gosse in his book *Omphalos, An Attempt to Untie the Geological Knot* published in 1857 (see Ross, *The Fingerprint of God*, 143).

14. John Collins, "Reading Genesis 1:1–2:2 as An Act of Communication: Discourse Analysis and Literal Interpretation," in *Did God Create in Six Days?* ed. Joseph A. Pipa, Jr. and David W. Hall (Taylors, S.C.: Southern Presbyterian Press, 1999), 147–48; see idem, "How Old Is the Earth? Anthropomorphic Days in Genesis 1:1–2:3," *Presb* 20, no. 2 (Fall 1994): 110.

The classic texts cited by day-age advocates to prove that the Hebrew word "day" is more than twenty-four hours are Psalm 90:4 and 2 Peter 3:8. In both texts, however, the word "day" is understood literally as a twenty-four hour day. Otherwise there would be no comparison. The texts simply show that with respect to the eternality of God there is no difference whatsoever between a day and a thousand years.[15] God is timeless. In addition, the Sabbath law where man was to imitate God by working six days and resting on the seventh is problematic when one maintains that the days represent billions of years (Ex. 20:11).[16]

If each day represented billions of years, then the question would be raised as to what took place in the evening (dark). How could animals have survived billions of years in darkness before the light of the next day? Wayne Grudem observed another problem with "days" representing epochs of time: "The greatest difficulty for this view is that it puts the sun, moon, and stars (Day 4) millions of years *after* the creation of plants and trees (Day 3). . . . [P]lants do not grow without sunlight, and there are many plants (Day 3) that do not pollinate without birds or flying insects (Day 5), and there are many birds (Day 5) that live off creeping insects (Day 6)."[17] Similarly, John Sailhamer opined, "Finding geological ages in the 'days' of creation stretches the imagination of even many sympathetic readers."[18]

The issue of the abundance of activities on the sixth day is a valid issue. However, we do not know how many kinds of animals Adam named. It may have been only a limited number. It seems that the animals that Adam named were restricted to domesticated animals and birds. Apparently, he did not name fish and insects, etc. God's purpose for Adam in this exercise was not to give an exhaustive taxonomy but to learn that for him "there was not found a helper fit for him" (Gen. 2:20) physically or psychologically.[19]

Conclusion

Hugh Ross's thirteen scriptural supports for the day-age theory are not at all distinctive and could easily be used as support for other biblical creation theories. With regard to position eight regarding God's commitment to truthfulness and his purpose to reveal the truth in creation, this applies particularly to Ross's objection to the "appearance of age" issue. The implication is that if God created with the appearance of age he could be accused of being deceptive. This in effect makes God subject to the ethics of scientific

---

15. See Joseph A. Pipa, Jr., "From Chaos to Cosmos: A Critique of the Non-Literal Interpretations of Genesis 1:1–2:3," in *Did God Create in Six Days?* ed. Joseph A. Pipa, Jr. and David W. Hall (Taylors, S.C.: Southern Presbyterian Press, 1999), 180.

16. For further discussion, see Question 16 ("What Is the Twenty-Four Hour Theory?").

17. Wayne Grudem, *Systematic Theology* (Grand Rapids: Zondervan, 1994), 299–300.

18. John H. Sailhamer, *Genesis Unbound* (Sisters, Ore.: Multnomah, 1996), 111.

19. See Pipa, "From Chaos to Cosmos," 180–81.

procedure—it is as though God would need to be worried about how his creation might upset humans' attempt to date the universe.

However, as Duncan and Hall have pointed out, perhaps the most serious flaw with this view is that it elevates reason (through science) to the degree that it gives "equal ultimacy to revelation and reason."[20] Advocates of the day-age theory interpret Genesis 1 as though its purpose is to provide a detailed, scientifically verifiable model of cosmic origins. This hardly seems in harmony with the narrative's purpose in its ancient context. The "view asks too much harmonization with *modern* scientific theories for us to see its connection with what the *ancient* account was actually for."[21]

REFLECTION QUESTIONS

1. What is the evidence for an old earth?

2. What is the evidence that the Hebrew word "day" refers to an epoch period of time?

3. What verses suggest that the Hebrew word "day" refers to more than a twenty-four hour period?

4. Is it possible that all the events that took place on day six could have occurred in a twenty-four hour period? Explain.

5. What relevance does the Sabbath commandment (Ex. 20:8–11) have for the understanding of the length of the creation days?

20. "The 24-Hour Response," *The Genesis Debate*, 174.
21. Collins, "Reading Genesis 1:1–2:3 as An Act of Communication," 148 (emphasis original). See Lee Irons with Meredith G. Kline, "The Framework Response," in *The Genesis Debate: Three Views on the Days of Creation*, ed. David G. Hagopian (Mission Viejo, Calif.: Crux, 2001), 180.

What Is the Framework Theory?

According to framework advocate Mark Ross, the framework hypothesis is "a view of Genesis 1:1–2:3 which claims that the Bible's use of the seven-day week in its narration of the creation is a literary (theological) framework and is not intended to indicate the chronology or duration of the acts of creation."[1] The framework interpretation of creation asserts that God used the image of an ordinary seven-day week to provide a metaphorical or figurative framework of God's creative acts in Genesis 1. While the six days of creation are normally understood as six solar days, the advocates of this view argue that there are clues in Genesis that indicate that the days are figurative, not literal twenty-four hour days. The literary framework of Genesis 1 presents a topical, nonsequential order for the days of creation, rather than a literal and sequential order. The employment of this method enables the reader to appreciate the real theological message of the passage.

The Poetic Nature of the Days of Genesis 1

The name "framework" is primarily derived from the fact that the advocates of this position argue that the framework and symmetry of the creation days suggest that Genesis 1 has a literary focus and this is demonstrated through the framework and structure of the six creation days. The proponents of this view present the structure of the literary nature of this position in two columns representing an intentional symmetry between the creation days.[2]

---

1. Mark Ross, "The Framework Hypothesis: An Interpretation of Genesis 1:1–2:3," in *Did God Create in Six Days*? ed. Joseph A. Pipa, Jr. and David W. Hall (Taylors, S.C.: Southern Presbyterian Press, 1999), 113.
2. Many commentators have observed this general structure. See Umberto Cassuto, *A Commentary on the Book of Genesis* (vol. 1, *From Adam to Noah, Genesis I–VI:8*), trans. Israel Abrahams (Jerusalem: Magnes, 1961), 17; Gordon J. Wenham, *Genesis 1–15*, WBC 1 (Waco, Tex.: Word, 1987), 7; Allen Ross, *Creation and Blessing* (Grand Rapids: Baker,

Day 1	Light	Day 4	Luminaries
Day 2	Firmament: sky & seas	Day 5	Inhabitants: sea & winged creatures
Day 3	Dry land, vegetation	Day 6	Land animals, Man
		Day 7	Sabbath

The association of this triadic scheme with this interpretive approach has led for this method to be called the "framework" hypothesis. The symmetrical design and connection between days one and four, two and five, and three and six are evident and have a topical and theological connection and purpose rather than a chronological one.

The literary designs are also evident in the repeated formulae that occur throughout the creation week. Throughout the creation days we find a divine speech ("God said"), a creative act ("let there be"), fulfillment ("there was," "it was so," "God created"), evaluation ("God saw that it was good"), and conclusion ("there was evening and there was morning," day x). It is argued that the literary nature of the account suggests that the creation days are not literal, and thus not twenty-four hour days. This is warranted, it is alleged, as the text is poetic or at least exalted prose. But at the heart of the framework hypothesis, just as in the twenty-four hour and day-age approaches, is the understanding of the creation days and their sequence. So there are two essential criteria defining the framework interpretation—a metaphorical interpretation of the days that in turn allows for a nonsequential ordering of the creative events.[3] The advocates of the framework hypothesis attest that reference to creation days four, six, and seven prove that these days are not be taken as literal.

Solar Days Begin on Day Four

As was seen from the chart above, there is a schematic connection between creation days one and four. These days deal with the same topics of light/darkness as well as day/night. In addition, on each of these days the verb *bdl* ("to separate") is used to separate the light and the darkness on day one (Gen. 1:4) and the day and the night on day four (Gen. 1:14) and the light and the darkness through the agency of the luminaries (Gen. 1:18) on day four. Thus, the divine purposes for creating the light on day one and the luminaries on day four are identical. According to the framework hypothesis, day four should not be considered in any way subsequent or sequential to day one but rather day four provides a more detailed description of what actually took place on day one. While day one has recorded the results of the creating of

---

1988), 104. The present chart most closely resembles Nahum M. Sarna, *Genesis,* JPSTC (Philadelphia: Jewish Publication Society, 1989), 4.

3. See Lee Irons with Meredith G. Kline, "The Framework View," in *The Genesis Debate: Three Views on the Days of Creation,* ed. David G. Hagopian (Mission Viejo, CA: Crux, 2001), 224.

light, it is actually in day four that we are made aware of the physical mechanism God used to produce these results. "In terms of chronology, day four thus brings us back to where we were in day one, and in fact takes us behind the effects described there to the astral apparatus that account for them."[4] Thus, days one and four suggest the same creative activity. According to Lee Irons and Meredith Kline, this recapitulation that occurs on days one and four justifies taking the whole creative week as figurative and nonsequential.[5] Days one and four appear to be contemporaneous.

Moreover, the fact that days one through three are described as normal days, even though the sun has not yet been created, indicates that these days cannot be understood in their normal sense as a literal twenty-four hour day. Consequently, this nonliteral use of the days in creation days one to three suggests that all these days are figurative or metaphorical.

Day Six with Genesis 2

The narrative order of Genesis 2 seems to stand in contradiction in some instances to the narrative order of Genesis 1. One of the most striking cases is the notion that the creation of man preceded the creation of animals (Gen. 2:19). After Adam was created, God declared that it was not good for the man to be alone and that a helper suited to him needed to be provided (Gen. 2:18). Before that would happen, however, the whole of the animal kingdom was paraded before the man so that he could give them names. This survey reinforced Adam's solitariness and uniqueness and that a helper suitable to him was not found. On one hand, Adam appears to be created before the animals (which conflicts with Genesis 1), while on the other hand, there seems to be far too much activity for Adam before the creation of Eve on day six. Can we expect this to take place within the confines of one day, the sixth day of creation and presumably all within the daylight hours? As Bruce Waltke has stated, "It is difficult to imagine that Adam named all the animals (both domestic and wild), underwent an operation, woke up, and composed a poem all within the daylight hours of the sixth day. It seems clear that the two chapters were not written to be read sequentially and according to strict chronology."[6] There is no indication in the text that some miracle took place or that some special dispensation occurred that would allow for all this activity to take place on day six. Thus, it is argued, this description does not seem to harmonize with the chronological account found in Genesis 1, as well as indicating that the sixth day of creation must have been extraordinarily longer than twenty-four hours.

---

4. Meredith G. Kline, "Space and Time in the Genesis Cosmogony," *Perspectives on Science and Christian Faith* 48, no. 1 (March 1996): 8.

5. See Irons with Kline, "The Framework View," 229–30.

6. Bruce K. Waltke and Cathi J. Fredricks, *Genesis* (Grand Rapids: Zondervan, 2001), 76n.82.

The Seventh Day is a Non-solar Day

The Sabbath day is distinct from all the other creation days (see Question 9, "What Is the Meaning of the Seventh Day?"). One distinctive of this day is seen in the fact that only this day does *not* have the refrain morning or evening, day x (seven). Framework advocates are prone to state that the seventh day has an eternal dimension. As an eternal day it provides the pattern for mankind's weekly observance of the Sabbath day (Ex. 20:11). The book of Hebrews, it is argued, interprets God's rest as a nonliteral day, as an eschatological heavenly rest to which believers can enter by faith in Christ (Heb. 4:4, 9–10). This Sabbath rest is still offered today (Heb. 3:7, 13) and is thus an ongoing eternal reality. Because the Sabbath is not an ordinary day the advocates of the framework hypothesis believe they have additional support for understanding all the days of Genesis 1 as nonliteral.[7]

Evaluation of the Framework Hypothesis

Even though there is a certain symmetry and rigidity exhibited in Genesis 1 that appears to give the account a somewhat poetic form, framework hypothesis interpreters acknowledge that the most natural reading of the text would result in a literal as well as chronological understanding. Furthermore, not all who recognize the symmetry of the triads espouse the framework interpretation as we have defined it—that is nonliteral days accompanied by a nonsequential narrative. It is possible that a narrative might have striking thematic parallelisms and still convey a literal, sequential chronology. Yet, in truth there is little to support the notion that Genesis 1 is actually poetry in the first place. As Edward Young stated, "Genesis one is written in exalted, semi-poetical language; nevertheless, it is not poetry. For one thing, the characteristics of Hebrew poetry are lacking, and in particular there is an absence of parallelism. It is true that there is a division into paragraphs, but to label these strophes does not render the account poetic."[8] Thus, artistic form in no way prevents the communication of facts.

Moreover, the overall framework itself does not correspond as cogently as many who maintain the framework hypothesis believe. Wayne Grudem has pointed out that the correspondence of days one and four, two and five, and three and six often breaks down. For example, the sun, moon, and stars created on the fourth day are placed in the firmament, which did not exist on day one; it was not created until day two. The correspondence between days two

---

7. John Collins seeks to interpret Exodus 20:11 in light of Exodus 31:17 where Moses says that when God ceased his work of creation he "was refreshed." Since the phrase "was refreshed" is obviously anthropomorphic, Exodus 20:11 may be anthropomorphic as well. See Joseph A. Pipa Jr., "From Chaos to Cosmos: A Critique of the Non-Literal Interpretations of Genesis 1:1–23 in *Did God Create in Six Days?* ed. Joseph A. Pipa, Jr. and David W. Hall, 171.
8. Edward J. Young, *Studies in Genesis One* (Philadelphia: P&R, 1964), 82–83.

and five is also not exact. The fish and the birds created on day five do not fill the space created on day two but rather on day three. Thus, as a consequence, there is also an issue when one compares days three and six. There is nothing created on day six that fills the form created on day three, the seas. These considerations contradict the notion that the materials created in the second trio of three days were to fill the forms and spaces of what was created on the first three days.[9]

On the other hand, the creation account of Genesis 1:1–2:3 gives every indication of being a typical Hebrew narrative. Like other Hebrew narratives, the account is dominated by the use of the *wayyiqtol* tense, also known as the *waw* consecutive. This type of verb normally conveys sequence of the mainline of a narrative and has been called the "narrator's tense." In Genesis 1:1–2:3 the *wayyiqtol* form occurs some fifty-five times in only thirty-four verses. With few exceptions, the occurrence of the *waw* consecutive in Genesis 1:1–2:3 is used to indicate a chronological sequence of events. This high frequency of the occurrence of other *waw* consecutive verbs is completely consistent with the other narrative passages in the book of Genesis.[10]

Evaluation of Day One and Day Four

The correspondences between days one and four need not suggest that they be viewed as identical. As Edward Young stated,

> Day four and day one do not present two aspects of the same subject. Indeed, the differences between the two days are quite radical. On one day light is created (*wayhi*); on day four God makes light-bearers. No function is assigned to the light of one, but several functions to the light-bearers. God himself divides the light which he has created from the darkness; the light-bearers are to divide between the light and the darkness. It is important to note this function. The light and the darkness between which the light-bearers are to make a division *are already present*. They have manifested themselves in the evening and morning which closed each day. . . . This one consideration in itself is sufficient to refute the idea that days one and four present two aspects of the same subject. The light-bearers are made for the purpose of dividing between already existing light and darkness.[11]

---

9. See Wayne Grudem, *Systematic Theology* (Grand Rapids: Zondervan, 1994), 302.
10. See Robert V. McCabe, "A Critique of the Framework Interpretation of the Creation Week," in *Coming to Grips with Genesis,* ed. Terry Mortenson and Thane H. Ury (Green Forest, Ark.: Master, 2008), 216–25.
11. Young, *Studies in Genesis One*, 96–97 (emphasis original).

In addition, to suggest that days one and four refer to the same creative activity is to ignore the grammar of the passage, particularly the use of the *waw* consecutive form which suggests these days are chronological and should be read in sequence. The fact that the days are numbered along with the repeated occurrence of the refrain, "evening and morning" reinforces the notion that the days are to be understood as following a sequence.

The purpose of the fourth day is to assign the luminaries as the governors of the heavenly bodies of the light and darkness. These regulate the separation of the day and the night, as well as differentiate monthly and annual time. According to the narrative, light existed before the sun.[12]

Evaluation of Day Six

One way to reconcile the seeming tension between day six and Genesis 2 is to insist that Genesis 2 is topical rather than chronological. Thus, the mention of the creation of the animals after the creation of man does not necessarily mean that the creation of the animals actually followed in time the creation of man. The reason could be a literary one in which the animals are mentioned subsequent to Adam's creation, but prior to the creation of Eve, to bring resolution to the tension in the narrative that it was not good for man to be alone, that he needed someone suitable for him.

An alternative approach to the problem of animals being created after man may have its source in the verbal form in Genesis 2:19. It is possible that this *waw* consecutive verbal form may be viewed as a pluperfect or past perfect. Hence the ESV translation: "the LORD God *had formed* every beast of the field and every bird of the heavens."[13] The *waw* consecutive thus presents the idea of logically anterior circumstances (a pluperfect) and is not in conflict with Genesis 1. The verb lends itself to this interpretation when read in the larger context of Genesis 1:1–2:3.

The difficulty of having too many activities for Adam to perform on day six may partially be resolved by suggesting that he did not actually name all the animals God created but rather a representation of them. It would seem to be unlikely that he named fish and insects for example. The word *every* or *all* would then be used figuratively much as it is used in the New Testament as in Mark 1:5 in reference to John the Baptist: "And all the country of Judea and all Jerusalem were going out to him and were being baptized by him in the river Jordan, confessing their sins."

---

12. See Pipa, "From Chaos to Cosmos," 177; see also Job 38:19–20. Rashi held the view that the fourth day involved forming the lights that were made in Genesis 1:3.
13. See NIV; Paul Joüon, *A Grammar of Biblical Hebrew*, trans. and rev. T. Muraoka, 2 vols. (Rome: Pontifical Institute, 1991), 2:393; *IBHS* 552–53; C. John Collins, "The Wayyiqtol as 'Pluperfect': When and Why," *TynBul* 46, no. 1 (1995): 117–40.

Evaluation of the Seventh Day

The Sabbath day is the day when God ceased from his creative activity.[14] Thus, in Genesis 2:2, the author declared that God brought the creative process to an end. That is, he ceased his creative work on that particular day. God does not "rest" from *all* labor, as he "made" (*asah*) coats of skins for Adam and Eve (Gen. 3:21). He *does* permanently cease from creating the world, but not from all temporal creative activity.[15] As Young states, "The text here clearly presents the seventh day as another in the well-defined series of days within the original creation week. In fact, this 'seventh day' is the conclusion to the week, not only in that it is the seventh day of only seven days, all properly enumerated. But also, on that day we have the historical cessation of the divine creative activity."[16] The seventh day structure differs from the other six on more than just the absence of the evening/morning refrain. It omits all the elements of the fivefold structure mentioned above. The point of these omissions was to emphasize that day seven was the end of God's creative activity, as the two uses of *shavath*, "to cease," clearly demonstrate.

Moreover, Exodus 20:11 and 31:17 indicate that the creation days are normal twenty-four hour days. The "dayness" of the six days, as well as the seventh, is essential to the meaning of the Sabbath commandment. Consequently, the fourth commandment, the Sabbath law, is a particular problem for the framework hypothesis. "Exodus 20:11 is a crucial problem for the framework theory. As figurative it would imply that God's creative activity is described in terms of a human workweek. But the fourth commandment states the reverse. God's activity is not described in terms of man's. Man's workweek is shaped by God's activity."[17] How could man imitate God's activity in the weekly cycle if God's activity was not accurately described in Genesis 1? Thus, the eternal rest in Hebrews 4 cannot be equated with day seven of the creation. Kenneth Gentry and Michael Butler explain: "Some 1500 years after Moses wrote Genesis the writer of Hebrews refers to the original, creational Sabbath in Heb. 4:4b to *develop* the concept of an ongoing or eschatological Sabbath. But this *theological point* may not be imposed upon the *historical* meaning of Genesis 2:2. Certainly Hebrews applies Genesis 2:2 to the argument for an ongoing and/or eschatological Sabbath; but he does so only *typologically*. His argument in Hebrews 4:4 no more proves the original day in Genesis 2:2 is ongoing, than his typological proof for Christ's eternity in Hebrews 7 proves Melchizedek actually lacked human genealogy."[18]

---

14. The verb *shavath* means the cessation of creativity. The verb has this same sense in its only other Genesis occurrence (Gen. 8:22).
15. In John 5:17, Jesus referred to the weekly recurring earthly Sabbath and noted that God himself works on it.
16. Young, *Studies in Genesis One*, 177–78n.73.
17. Noel Weeks, *The Sufficiency of Scripture* (Edinburgh: Banner of Truth Trust, 1988), 112.
18. Kenneth L. Gentry, and Michael R. Butler, *Yea, Hath God Said?: The Framework Hypothesis/Six Day Creation Debate* (Eugene, Ore.: Wipf and Stock, 2002), 63 (emphasis original).

Neither the omission of the evening-morning conclusion for day seven nor the use of Genesis 2:2 in Hebrews 4 provides support for the seventh day of the creation week as eternal or unending. It is a literal day that concluded a week of six literal, consecutive days.[19]

Conclusion

We conclude by mentioning that there is not a single theological truth from the creation account that depends upon a framework reading of the text. Moreover, no particular insight has been discovered in the framework analysis that is also not apparent in other approaches to the study of creation in Genesis 1. In this regard the framework hypothesis has failed to deliver. It is virtually impossible to escape the drumbeat of the ongoing march of the creation days and the sequence of time in Genesis 1. This is particularly supported by the language of the text that is dominated by the *wayyiqtol* tense, the main tense of narration that forms the backbone of the narrative as it is the verb that is used to perform the sequence of events. Each creative act of each created day is introduced by the *waw* consecutive.[20] Wayne Grudem effectively summarizes the shortcomings of the framework hypothesis:

> Finally, the strongest argument against the framework view, and the reason why comparatively few evangelicals have adopted it, is that the whole of Genesis 1 strongly suggests not just a literary framework but a chronological sequence of events. When the narrative proceeds from the less complex aspects of creation (light and darkness, waters, sky, and dry land) to the more complex aspects (fish and birds, animals and man) we see a progressive build up and an ordered sequence of events that are entirely understandable chronologically. When a sequence of numbers (1–2–3–4–5–6) is attached to a set of days that correspond exactly to the ordinary week human beings experience (Day 1, Day 2, Day 3, Day 4, Day, 5, Day 6, Day 7, with rest on Day 7), the implication of chronological sequence in the narrative is almost inescapable.[21]

If Moses was trying to emphasize and focus on chronology and sequence in the creation account, it is difficult to imagine a clearer presentation than what we find in Genesis 1:1–2:3.

---

19. See McCabe, "A Critique of the Framework Interpretation of the Creation Week," 246.
20. See Pipa, "From Chaos to Cosmos," 182.
21. Grudem, *Systematic Theology*, 303.

The rather recent appearance of the framework hypothesis upon the interpretive scene has raised suspicion among not a few interpreters that behind this approach is an attempt to be more in harmony with those who have embraced modern cosmological theories about the creation of the universe.[22]

REFLECTION QUESTIONS

1. Should Genesis 1 be viewed as a poetic text? Explain.

2. How is the fourth day of creation used to support the framework hypothesis?

3. How is the sixth day of creation used to support the framework hypothesis?

4. How is the seventh day used to support the framework hypothesis?

5. How would you evaluate the main ideas of the framework hypothesis?

---

22. See J. Ligon Duncan III and David W. Hall, "The 24-Hour Response, "in *The Genesis Debate: Three Views on the Days of Creation*, ed. David G. Hagopian (Mission Viejo, Calif.: Crux, 2001), 265.

What Is the Temple Inauguration Theory?

The temple inauguration theory asserts that Genesis 1:1–2:3 portrays creation in terms that would be recognized to the people of the ancient world as a temple building account. It is a description of creation as a cosmic temple. The seventh day of the creation account, according to this theory, would mark the beginning of God inhabiting his cosmic temple. This theory is based on parallels found in ancient Near Eastern cosmogonies along with implicit biblical evidence.

Creation and Temple Inauguration in the Ancient Near East

The concept of temple inauguration appears to have been widespread among the peoples of the ancient Near East.[1] Scholars have often cited the Babylonian creation account of the *Enuma Elish*, dated in the early part of the second millennium BC, as evidence of the practice of the temple inauguration phenomenon. Early in the account numerous gods are annoyed by the noise of lesser gods who are engaged in some kind of hard labor. The gods are not able to find relief from the noise and thus have rest. The primeval waters Apsu and Tiamat are particularly disturbed by the turmoil produced by the lower gods. Apsu then exclaims,

> By day I find no relief, nor repose by night.
> I will destroy, I will wreck their ways,
> That quiet may be restored. Let us have rest (*ANET*, 61)

---

1. Mircea Eliade has observed that there is nearly a universal connection of temples with creation (see Mircea Eliade, *The Myth of the Eternal Return or, Cosmos and History*, trans. Willard R. Trask [Princeton: Princeton University Press, 1954], 12–21).

As rest continued to be denied, Tiamat and those associated with her became engaged in a conflict with Marduk. After Marduk defeated Tiamat he created the world and then organized it. In this new cosmos, which has now been delivered from the chaos, the gods are no longer disturbed, for they will all be at rest. Now, the noisy work will no longer be performed by the lower gods, but by Marduk's special creation, man (*ANET*, 61). The creation account culminates with the construction of Marduk's temple Esagila, a place of rest and repose, at which time there is a celebration because the world is now in order.[2]

What is immediately apparent in this myth is that the temple inauguration is depicted as a victory over chaos. According to Bruce Waltke, other creator gods in the ancient world built temples as a sign of their victory over the wild forces of chaos. This pattern of a combat at the sea, the miraculous appearance of dry land, the construction of the temple, and the enthronement of the deity, is also reflected in Canaanite and Egyptian literature.[3]

A second component of the temple inauguration theory is the connection of the creation with the erection of the temple. There is a long tradition in the ancient Near East that binds temple building and world building. The temple and the world stand in an intimate and intrinsic connection. According to Jon Levenson, "[T]he two projects cannot ultimately be distinguished or disengaged."[4] A world without a temple was a world that was in a precosmic condition. Or as John Walton expressed it, "The cosmos and temple were conceived together and thus are virtually simultaneous in their origins."[5]

Egyptian temples served as models of the cosmos where the floor represented the earth and the ceiling the sky. Similarly, Genesis 1 can be seen as a creation account focusing on the cosmos as a temple.[6] Perhaps the interchange of the cosmos and the temple is best seen in Isaiah 66:1–2a:

---

2. See N.-E., Andreasen, *The Old Testament Sabbath: A Tradition-Historical Investigation*, SBLDS (Missoula, Mo.: Society of Biblical Literature, 1972), 174–75, 180; Jon D. Levenson, *Creation and the Persistence of Evil* (San Francisco: Harper & Row, 1988), 99.

3. See Bruce K. Waltke and Cathi J. Fredricks, *Genesis* (Grand Rapids: Zondervan, 2001), 68; Levenson, *Creation and the Persistence of Evil*, 76; see also Question 5 ("What Is the Relationship of Genesis 1–2 to Other Creation Accounts?").

4. Jon D. Levenson, "The Temple and the World," *JR* 64 (1984): 287–88; see William J. Dumbrell, "Genesis 2:1–17: A Foreshadowing of the New Creation" in *Biblical Theology: Retrospect and Prospect*, ed. Scott J. Hafemann (Downers Grove: InterVarsity, 2002), 57.

5. John H. Walton, *The Lost World of Genesis One* (Downers Grove: IVP Academic, 2009), 79.

6. See Walton, *Lost World*, 81, 84. Perhaps it is not a coincidence that the Hebrew Bible begins with an account of the creation of heaven and earth by the command of God (Gen. 1:1) and ends with the command of the God of heaven "to build him a Temple in Jerusalem" (2 Chron. 35:23; see Levenson, "The Temple and the World," 295). Second Chronicles is the last book in the Hebrew Bible.

Thus says the LORD:
"Heaven is my throne,
and the earth is my footstool;
what is the house that you would build for me,
and what is the place of my rest?
All these things my hand has made,
And so all these things came to be,
declares the LORD.

Whereas Genesis 1 sees the sanctuary as a world, Isaiah 66:1–2 sees the world as a sanctuary.[7] There is a rabbinic tradition that the world "was created from Zion" (*Yoma* 54b). Similarly, Josephus viewed the temple as a microcosm of the world (*J.W.* 3, 7:7).

A third component of the temple inauguration theory involves the connection of creation with the accomplishment of rest. The creation of the world and the completion of a temple each bring about an environment where God can find "rest" (Ex. 20:11; Ps. 132:8). Just as Marduk established rest after creation and the erection of a temple, we find rest to be the consequence of creation in Egypt as well as in Canaan. For the god to rest in a temple indicated stability for the world. Once this stability was achieved the operations of the cosmos could be undertaken.[8] Whereas the Hebrew term for rest does not occur in Genesis 2:1–3, it is used to describe the creation week in Exodus 20:11 in the law regarding Sabbath observance. Moreover, in Psalm 132:7–8, 13–14 the same root for "rest" (Hb. *nukh*) is used to describe God's rest in the temple. Thus, Jon Laanasma states, "When the traditions of both YHWH's *menukhah* in the temple and his Sabbath rest following creation seem to exhibit definite links with the very same Near Eastern mythological traditions, the temptation is strong to merge the two OT traditions into one and to claim that YHWH'S rest following creation (as in Ex. 20:11) is none other than his *menukhah* in the temple" (Ps. 132).[9] Thus, in the world of the ancient Near East, a temple could be viewed as a place for divine rest.

Another important component of the temple inauguration theory has to do with the connection of creation to a period of seven days. The number seven appears pervasively in temple accounts in the ancient Near East. Gudea, king of the Sumerian city Lagash toward the end of the twenty-second century BC, held a seven-day festival of dedication for one of the temples that he built. Baal's temple in Canaan was also said to have been built in seven days.

---

7. See Levenson, "The Temple and the World," 296.
8. See Andreasen, *The Old Testament Sabbath*, 182; Walton, *Lost World*, 73; Levenson, *Creation and the Persistence of Evil*, 107; Andreasen, *The Old Testament Sabbath*, 178, 181; *ANET*, 4–6.
9. Jon Laansma, *I Will Give You Rest* (Tübingen: Moher Siebeck, 1997), 72.

According to Levenson, there was in Israel as well a clear association between temple building and the seven-day celebration that explains why temple inauguration may be the correct way to understand Genesis 2:1–3: "If in early Israel there was a seven-day festival in the fall and again (although with differences) in the spring and if this festival in either form or both was at least in part a celebration of the New Year, with the reactualization of cosmogony and enthronement, as was the case in some places and times in Mesopotamia, then it would be natural to think of the creation of the world as occurring within a seven-day period."[10]

Furthermore, 1 Kings 8, which depicts Solomon's dedication of his temple, informs us that this took place in the seventh month, during the Feast of Tabernacles, the seven-day feast in the seventh month. Levenson again concludes that it is likely that the construction of the temple is presented here as a parallel to the construction of the world in seven days (Gen. 1:1–2:4). Hence, the building of the temple appears to have been modeled on the seven-day creation of the world, which again is also in line with the building of temples in seven days elsewhere in the ancient Near East. Whereas in the Babylonian creation epic, the *Enuma Elish*, the construction of the temple of Marduk, Esagila, crowns and consummates creation, the Sabbath does the same in Israel.[11]

Creation and Tabernacle Parallels

Michael Fishbane has noted three significant close connections between the divine work of Genesis 2:1–3 and the human work of Exodus 39–40 in the construction of the tabernacle. First, the rare expression *ruakh elohim* ("spirit of God") appears in Genesis 1:2, before the transformation of the desolate waste into the created world; but it occurs as well in Exodus 31:3 in reference to Bezalel's inspired role in the construction of the tabernacle. Secondly, in both the creation account and the construction of the tabernacle narrative there is a singular and decisive emphasis on Sabbath rest—the stress in Genesis 2:1–3 is on divine rest, whereas the emphasis in Exodus 31:12–17 and 35:2–3 is in human cessation from labor. And finally, there is the impressive fact that the tabernacle was erected in the first day of the first month of the year (Ex. 40:2, 27), which naturally invites comparison to the creation of the world. All of these comparisons suggest that the tabernacle symbolized an extension of the process begun at creation.[12]

---

10. Levenson, *Creation and the Persistence of Evil*, 72; see ibid., 78–80; Walton, *Lost World*, 87. A reference to seven days is not mentioned in the *Enuma Elish* account although the inscription appears on "seven" tablets.

11. See Levenson, "The Temple and the World," 287–89; idem, *Creation and Persistence of Evil*, 78–70.

12. See Michael Fishbane, *Text and Texture* (New York: Schocken, 1979), 12.

But there are many other features that are shared between the creation account and the tabernacle/temple narratives. These include the gold and the onyx stones that are in the garden. There was gold in the garden (Gen. 2:11), and gold was widely used in covering the furniture of the tabernacle, including the ark, alter of incense, and lampstand in the Holy of Holies. Everything in the Holy of Holies was covered with gold, and as one moved away from the Holy of Holies the materials used decreased in value. The most sacred items of the tabernacle were thus covered with gold. There were also onyx stones in the garden that were also a part of the tabernacle furnishings (Gen. 2:12 with Ex. 25:7). These onyx stones were also part of the shoulder piece of the ephod worn by the Israelite priest (Ex. 28:9; 39:6–7).

The Tree of Life in the garden may correspond to the lampstand in the tabernacle. This identification is further supported by the fact that Genesis 1 uses the unusual word "lights" (*meoroth*, 5 times) instead of "sun" and "moon." Elsewhere in the Pentateuch, "lights" (*meoroth*) is used only for the "lights" on the tabernacle lampstand.[13]

The placing of the cherub to guard the entrance to the garden of Eden at the end of the creation story (Gen. 3:22–24) has several echoes in the description of the structure of the tabernacle. The cherub stationed east of the garden to guard the way to the garden corresponds to the tabernacle and temple which were also entered on the east side. In the tabernacle/temple two cherubs are one piece with the mercy seat and look down on the ark. The cherubs are also embroidered on the veil which separates the Most Holy Place and the Holy of Holies (Ex. 26:31). In the temple two cherubs guarded the inner sanctuary (1 Kings 6:23–28). Pictures of the cherubs decorated the walls of the Jerusalem temple (1 Kings 6:29).

Moreover, the total instructions for the tabernacle are divided into seven sections, which is reminiscent of the creation account, particularly the seven times repeated statement, "God saw that it was good." Each section begins with the phrase, "The Lord said to Moses" (Ex. 25:1; 30:11; 30:17; 30:22; 30:34; 31:1; 31:12). The last and seventh section of the tabernacle instructions in fact addresses keeping the Sabbath. Richard Hess beautifully summarizes the correspondence between the garden and the tabernacle when he states,

> Both the garden of Genesis 2 and the Tabernacle/Temple are entered from the East, have jewels and gold, portray God as walking back and forth, and charge people with guarding or keeping it. . . . It has also been observed that the construction of the Tabernacle has allusions to the initial act of creation in

---

13. See Greg K. Beale, *The Temple and the Church's Mission: A Biblical Theology of the Dwelling Place of God*, NSBT 17 (Downers Grove: InterVarsity, 2004), 34; idem, *A New Testament Biblical Theology* (Grand Rapids: Baker Academic, 2011), 628–29.

it. Moses "saw all the work . . . as the Lord commanded" and "blessed" the people (Ex. 39:43) just as the Lord blessed the seventh day when he finished his work. "As the Lord commanded Moses" is repeated seven times, recalling the repetition of phrasing in the creation of the world over the seven-day period. In Exodus 40:34–38 the Sabbath is celebrated just as God celebrated the Sabbath at the end of creation.[14]

It is no surprise then that *Targum Onqelos* would draw the imagery of temple building into his account of the creation of the Sabbath.[15]

The fact that the creation and the tabernacle are associated can be further supported from the fact that Adam has been perceived to function as a priest in the garden. This can be supported by the first command given to Adam in Genesis 2:15. He was commanded to work the garden and to keep it. Elsewhere in the Pentateuch this expression describes the activity of priests. As a priest and guardian of the garden, Adam should have guarded the garden from the serpent. Moreover, the occurrence of the verbs *avadh* and *shamar* in Genesis 2:15 is at least an allusion to sacrifices. On the basis of Exodus 3:12 and Numbers 28:2, the Jewish Midrash Genesis Rabbah 16.5 equates man's work in the garden with sacrifices. In the only other part of the Pentateuch where these two words occur together (Num. 3:7–8; 8:26; 18:5–6), it is used of the Levites' duty in guarding and serving in the sanctuary. When the two words (verbal [*avadh* and *shamar*] and nominal forms) occur together in the Old Testament, they refer either to Israelites "serving" God and "guarding [keeping]" God's word (approximately 10 times) or to priests who "keep" the "service" (or "charge") of the tabernacle (see Num. 3:7–8; 8:25–26; 18:5–6; 1 Chron. 23:32; Ezek. 44:14). This is supported by the Aramaic translation of Genesis 2:15 (*Tg. Neof.*) that describes Adam's role to be one of "working in the Law and to observing its commandments."[16] In addition, after the fall God clothes Adam with garments (*kothnoth*; Gen. 3:21). The same Hebrew term is used for the priests' attire in Exodus 28:4, 29 and of the high priest's clothing in Leviticus 16:4.

Perhaps the strongest connection between the creation and the tabernacle can be seen on the similarity of the conclusion of both accounts.[17]

---

14. Richard S. Hess, "The Roles of the Woman and the Man in Genesis 3," *Themelios* 18 (1993): 18n.8.
15. Gary Anderson, "The Interpretation of Genesis 1:1 in the Targums," *CBQ* 52 (1990): 26; see also the rabbinic midrash Tanhuma Pequde 2.
16. See Gordon J. Wenham, "Sanctuary Symbolism in the Garden of Eden Story," in *Proceedings of the Ninth World Congress of Jewish Studies*, 1986), 21; Beale, *The Temple and the Church's Mission*, 67, 81; Waltke and Fredricks, *Genesis*, 80–81, 87.
17. See Levenson, *Creation and the Persistence of Evil*, 85–86.

CREATION	TEMPLE
And God saw everything that he had made, and behold, it was very good. (Gen. 1:31)	And Moses saw all the work, and behold, they had done it; as the LORD had commanded, so had they done it. Moses blessed them. (Ex. 39:43)
Thus the heavens and the earth were finished, and all the host of them (Gen. 2:1)	Thus all the work of the tabernacle of the tent of meeting was finished. (Ex. 39:32)
And on the seventh day God finished his work that he had done, and he rested on the seventh day from all the work that he had done. (Gen. 2:2)	So Moses finished the work. Then the cloud covered the tent of meeting, and the glory of the LORD filled the tabernacle. (Ex. 40:33b–34)
So God blessed the seventh day and made it holy, because on it God rested from all his work that he had done in creation. (Gen. 2:3)	And Moses saw all the work, and behold, they had done it; as the LORD had commanded, so had they done it. Moses blessed them. (Ex. 39:43)
So God blessed the seventh day and made it holy, because on it God rested from all his work that he had done in creation. (Gen. 2:3)	Then you shall take the anointing oil and anoint the tabernacle and all that is in it, and consecrate it and all its furniture, so that it may become holy. You shall also anoint the alter of burnt offering and all its utensils, and consecrate the altar, so that the altar may become most holy. You shall also anoint the basin and its stand, and consecrate it. (Ex. 40:9–11)

Eden Foreshadows the Tabernacle

As the tabernacle represents the dwelling place of God, it can be viewed as a restoration of Edenic privilege where man walked with God. The garden of Eden thus foreshadows the tabernacle where Israel was to meet with God. The garden thus should be viewed as an archetypal or ideal sanctuary. The occurrence of the verbal form *mithhallekh*, "to walk to and fro" (Gen. 3:8) is used to describe the divine presence in the later tent sanctuaries in Leviticus 26:12; Deuteronomy 23:15; 2 Samuel 7:6–7. The Lord walked in Eden as he subsequently walked in the tabernacle. It thus typified the fellowship God had with man, which was the purpose of his creation.[18] As William Dumbrell has

---

18. See Wenham, "Sanctuary Symbolism," 20; John H. Sailhamer, *Genesis Unbound* (Sisters, Ore.: Multnomah, 1996), 77.

stated, "Temple theology, which attests to the sovereign presence of God with his people, takes its rise in Eden."[19]

Conclusion

An underlying assumption behind the temple inauguration theory is that there are uniform beliefs among the Israelites and individuals of the ancient Near East. In the middle of the last century, however, G. Ernest Wright argued that the differences between the Israelite way of thinking about reality and the way in which Israel's neighbors approached reality were so significant that no genetic explanations could account for them.[20]

While there are surely parallels to the ancient Near Eastern myths, what makes the Bible unique is that it maintains its theological positions and worldview exclusively and throughout. From a pagan worldview, due to the capricious nature of the gods, it is entirely possible to maintain several contradictory views at once. Walton's defense of the temple inauguration theory depends upon downplaying the much greater differences between Genesis 1 and other ancient Near Eastern cosmologies and focusing only on the rather superficial similarities between them. Nahum Sarna time and again has shown that dissimilarities between Old Testament and ancient Near Eastern accounts are greater than the similarities.[21]

As argued above, another major assumption behind the temple inauguration theory has to do with the assumption of chaos before creation. However, a casual reading of Genesis 1 and 2 indicates that the story of the creation of the cosmos is described in an atmosphere of complete tranquility. Even though matter was originally described as "without form and void" (*tohu wavohu*, Gen. 1:2), this need not lead us to conclude that God faced adversity or had to encounter any resistance on the part of animated chaotic matter or had to overcome the forces of evil in order to make the world. The cosmos is not the body of defeated chaos, as in the Babylonian story, nor is it the result of the sexual activity of the god or gods, as in several of the Egyptian accounts.[22]

A critical weakness of the temple inauguration theory is the admitted lack of explicit evidence that the Bible alludes to this alleged ancient practice celebrating God's victory over evil forces and the erection of a temple at the end of the creation week. As Levenson concedes, "The absence of an explicit biblical

---

19. Dumbrell, "Genesis 2:1–17," 64–65. Passages such as Isaiah 66:1; Psalm 95:11; 132:14 appear to indicate that the resting place is the Holy Land itself, which is sometimes conceived as a vast sanctuary (see Levenson, *Creation and the Persistence of Evil*, 107).

20. See G. Ernest Wright, *The Old Testament against Its Environment* (London: SCM, 1950); John N. Oswalt, *The Bible Among the Myths* (Grand Rapids: Zondervan, 2009), 11.

21. See Nahum Sarna, *Understanding Genesis* (New York: Jewish Theological Seminary of America, 1996); idem, *Exploring Exodus: The Heritage of Biblical Israel* (New York: Schocken, 1986); Oswalt, *The Bible Among the Myths*, 69n.8.

22. See Oswalt, *The Bible Among the Myths*, 67–68.

association of New Year's Day with creation must not be taken to exclude implicit associations."[23] The possible connection of the idea of rest based upon Psalm 132 was acknowledged by Laansma, but in the end he also refused to take the connection as proof of this phenomenon, as he admits,

> . . . at no point does the idea of a Sabbath rest, or the Sabbath institution generally, bear a direct connection with the *menukhah* . . . . and the temple or tabernacle is never characterized as YHWH's "resting place" (*menukhah*) in direct connection with the Sabbath. A text where these two traditions come together in a promising way is Isa. 66 where, in v. 1, creation as YHWH's temple—one of the only two usages of "my resting place" outside of Ps. 95:11 (cf. Ps. 132:14)—is found in the same context as one of the clearest expressions of eschatological Sabbaths (plural; v. 23); yet even here there is no direct connection drawn between the two.[24]

Thus, there is no direct biblical evidence for a connection between God's rest in the temple with God's rest after creation.

Walton admits that the definitive biblical evidence that Genesis 1 was used in a festival for temple inauguration is lacking even though Moshe Weinfeld had suggested that Genesis 1 could have served very effectively as the liturgy of such a festival.[25] But Exodus 20 clearly indicates that it is not the obscure temple inauguration that is being celebrated in the Sabbath law but more simply and generally God's sovereignty over creation.

It makes more biblical sense that the Israelites had believed that God lived in heaven both before and after the creation week. Thus the week of creation does not address God's need for a physical habitat where he can rest.

Eden is the representation not only of the tabernacle and the temple but of what the world is to become. The New Jerusalem is presented in terms of the Holy of Holies of the Jerusalem temple (Revelation 21–22; see again Ezek. 36:33–36). So also John's description of the New Jerusalem places a stress on the gold and precious stones that picture the glorious presence of God among his people (Rev. 21:18). The prevalent biblical theme of God's presence with us began in the garden (Gen. 3:8), continued in the tabernacle/temple, and pointed to the time when the incarnate God would "tabernacle" among us (John 1:14). The tearing of the veil at his death (Mark 15:38; Heb. 10:19–20) has now provided the most intimate fellowship and access.

23. Levenson, *Creation and the Persistence of Evil*, 73.
24. Laansma, *I Will Give You Rest*, 74–75.
25. See Walton, *Lost World*, 91.

REFLECTION QUESTIONS

1. Explain the relationship of creation and temple building in the culture of the ancient world.

2. What are some detailed parallels between the creation account and the narrative about the construction of the tabernacle?

3. What are the parallels between the conclusion of the creation account and the conclusion of the construction of the tabernacle account?

4. What is the connection between the garden of Eden and the tabernacle?

5. What is the connection between the tabernacle and the New Testament?

What Is the Historical Creationism Theory?

Many Christians believe a conflict exists between the authority of Scripture and the findings of modern science. John Sailhamer, who holds to the doctrine of the inerrancy of Scripture, has brought to light an approach to Genesis 1 and 2 that he claims has deep historical interpretive roots and yet is not in conflict with modern scientific views. This view he calls "historical creationism."[1]

Support for Historical Creationism

According to Sailhamer, Genesis 1 refers to two great acts of God. The first occurs in Genesis 1:1 when God created the "heavens and the earth." The phrase "heavens and earth" is a merism. A merism is created by the combination of two words that are polar extremes to express totality. In a merism, the combination of two words to express a totality becomes more significant than just the combination of two individual words. Genesis 1:1 indicates a time when the earth, the animals, the sun, moon and stars all came into being. Thus, the phrase "heavens and earth" refers to "everything" and is the Hebrew way of referring to the universe. This creation took place as the opening phrase of Genesis 1:1 states "in the beginning."

Sailhamer claims that the Hebrew word for "beginning" (*reshith*) does not refer to a moment of time, but rather to a "duration of time." This is seen particularly in passages such as Job 8:7; Genesis 10:10; and Jeremiah 28:1. Jeremiah 28:1 is particularly significant: "In that same year, at the beginning [*reshith*] of the reign of Zedekiah king of Judah, in the fifth month of the fourth year, Hananiah the son of Azzur, the prophet from Gibeon, spoke to me in the house of the LORD." As Sailhamer notes, the "beginning" of Zedekiah's reign "included

---

1. See John H. Sailhamer, *Genesis Unbound* (Sisters, Ore.: Multnomah Books), 1996.

events which happened four years after he had assumed the throne."[2] Therefore, because *reshith* does not mean an instant or point of time, but rather a duration or indefinite period of time, we cannot be sure when God created the universe nor how long it took. Had the author wanted to refer to a starting point, or point of time, he had other Hebrew terms that would better fit this purpose, particularly the terms *rishonah* and *techillah* both of which can also be translated "beginning." Had the author used either of these words, he could have expressed the notion of creation in the first moment of time. Because the intention of the opening phrase of Genesis 1 is to refer to an indefinite period of time, it is possible that the time covered in Genesis 1:1 took millions or billions of years. Thus, Genesis 1:1 refers to a "time before time" when the universe was created but before man came to be.[3] Man came to be in the second great act of Genesis 1 (Gen. 1:2–31). Nevertheless, because we cannot pinpoint the time of creation, there is no conflict between Genesis 1 and modern science.

Beginning with Genesis 1:2, the second great act of God in Genesis 1 is described. This creation (Sailhamer prefers "preparation") is depicted from Genesis 1:2–31 and is now addressing something other than the creation of the universe. The verse begins with the phrase "The earth was without form and void." The word normally translated "earth" in Genesis 1:2 is the Hebrew word *erets*. The first word of Genesis 1:2 *erets* was the last word of Genesis 1:1, but now it is *not* occurring in a merism. Thus, the term has its own individual meaning separate from its meaning when it occurred as part of a merism, "the heavens and the earth." This word, *erets* ("earth, land, ground"), has a range of meaning that can even be seen in Genesis 1. In Genesis 1, for example, the Hebrew word *erets* is also used to signify the "dry land" as opposed to a body of water or the seas (Gen. 1:10).

Sailhamer acknowledges that the range of meaning of the term *erets* indicates that the word could be understood as the "earth" in a global sense. The word *erets* refers to the earth in the sense of the planet in passages such as Genesis 18:25, "the Judge of all the earth" as well as in Psalm 2, "The kings of the earth set themselves" (Ps. 2:2). This meaning of *erets*, however, is not the normal or most common meaning, particularly in Genesis. In Genesis 1:2 the term *erets* has the specific meaning of "land" rather than "earth." Thus, the term "land," the land of Israel, is the main focus in the rest of Genesis 1 and the term *erets* in Genesis 1:2 is to be distinguished from the phrase heaven and "earth" (*erets*) in Genesis 1:1. The narrative begins to address the preparation of the land for the man and woman. Genesis 1:2–31 thus refers to God's acts during the six creation days in preparing the land for human habitation in the garden of Eden.[4]

---

2. Ibid., 39, 56.
3. Ibid., 14, 32, 41.
4. Sailhamer acknowledges that when God began this work in Genesis 1:2 to prepare "the

The separate acts of God in Genesis 1 are distinguished by the different verbs in the two descriptions. In Genesis 1:1, the verb translated "to create" (*bara*) is a verb that may refer to the concept of "creation out of nothing." This is of course what Genesis 1:1 describes. Beginning in Genesis 1:2, however, the dominant verb used is the verb *asah*, which could be understood as "to prepare."[5] A new creation is not being described as much as a preparation of the land, the garden of Eden for Adam and Eve. Thus, when we read in the Ten Commandments the phrase, "For in six days the LORD made (*asah*) heaven and the earth" (Ex. 20:11), the reference must be to the second great act of God in Genesis 1 because the verb *asah* is used. Thus, this verse in the Ten Commandments echoes God's preparation of the earth in Genesis 1:2–31, even though it contains the phrase "heaven and earth."[6] Sailhamer claims that Exodus 20:11 does not say that God created the heavens and earth in six days but that God *prepared* the sky, land and seas and then filled them in six days.

As the accounts of Genesis 1:2–31 and Genesis 2 are related and are to be understood to describe the same event, Genesis 2 more specifically clarifies that this land (which begins to be discussed in Gen. 1:2) is the garden of Eden. This land not only contained the garden of Eden but also is the promised land that was to be given to Israel. "The implication is that the account of the creation of the 'land' in Genesis 1 is actually about the garden of Eden."[7] Sailhamer argues that this more limited scope of the Hebrew term *erets* would be what was understood by the original audience of Israelites. In the pre-scientific age, the ancients did not think of the term *erets* as an orbiting planet around the sun. On the contrary, they would have only thought of a limited piece of land surrounded by a body of water. This is reflected in ancient maps where the promised land was considered to be the center of the inhabited world. The ancients clearly had limited geographic perspectives.[8] This limited understanding of *erets* is further reinforced by the use of *erets* in phrases like the "land [*erets*] of Egypt" (Gen. 45:8). Similarly, in Jeremiah 27:5–6 the land (*erets*) that God was about to give Nebuchadnezzar, Sailhamer argues, was the land which he had made in Genesis 1, the land of Israel. Thus, the

---

land" it was likely that there were numerous other places in existence that were already suitable for human habitation, but does not elaborate (ibid., 150, 48).

5. The verb *bara* is used in Genesis 1:21, 27 however (see Question 7, "What Is the Relationship of Genesis 1:1 to Genesis 1?").

6. Even though we have the use of the exact phrase "heaven and earth" in Exodus 20:11, it is not a merism because the expression is followed by descriptive phrases (so Sailhamer, *Genesis Unbound*, 106).

7. Ibid., 90. Sailhamer does not comment on the fact that different names for God are used in Genesis 1 and 2 (Elohim in Gen. 1:1–2:3 and Yahweh Elohim in Gen. 2:4–25). This distinction between the two accounts could support the view that two different subjects are being addressed—the name Elohim for the cosmic creation of the world and universe in Genesis 1 and the covenant name Yahweh Elohim in Genesis 2 for the God who has a relationship with human beings.

8. Ibid., 45.

understanding of *erets* would more likely refer to a limited land rather than referring to the entire earth. The initial readers would have understood the reference to be the land of Israel in Genesis 1:2.

This reference to "land," and the occupation of the land of Israel, is one of the major themes in the Pentateuch. Throughout most of Genesis and the Pentateuch the word *erets* was a reference to the promised land. Most of the narratives in the Pentateuch are concerned with the occupation of this "land."[9]

The association of the promised land and the garden of Eden is supported by the fact that the boundaries and descriptions of these areas are virtually identical. For example, the description of the garden in Genesis 2:10–14 is the same as the land described to Abram in Genesis 15. The areas marked off by the two rivers in Genesis 15, the river of Egypt and the Euphrates, echoes the description of the region of the garden of Eden in Genesis 2, which refers to the Gihon, Tigris, and Euphrates (Gen. 2:13–14). These locations are specific boundaries of the land promised to Abraham (Gen. 15:18). Sailhamer asserts that Moses intentionally indicated that these two regions should be identified.[10] "The Covenant is grounded in the events of creation. The author of Genesis 1 wants to show that the stretch of land which God promised to Israel in the Sinai Covenant—the land where Abraham and his family sojourned, the land of Canaan—was the same land God had prepared for them at the time of creation."[11] The prophets understood this identification of the promised land with the garden of Eden. This is clearly seen in their description of the blessing of the end time as a return to Eden (Isa. 51:3; Ezek. 36:35; Joel 2:3; Zech. 14:8). The same prediction is also made in the New Testament (Rev. 22:1–2).

Understanding Genesis 1:2–31 as a reference to the creation of the garden of Eden has early support by Jewish medieval commentator Rashi as well as by the Christian exegete Lightfoote.[12] This connection led to the early Jewish view that Adam was created in the same area where later the temple was built (Jerusalem) as well as the association of Jerusalem/Zion with the center of the world (*b. Yoma* 54b).

Evaluation of Historical Creationism

Sailhamer's approach to the creation account in Genesis 1 should be commended as it offers a close and serious reading of the Hebrew text. As he interacts and struggles with the text, he seeks to determine the meaning of the

---

9. Ibid., 50–54, 109.
10. John H. Sailhamer, *The Pentateuch as Narrative* (Grand Rapids: Zondervan, 1992), 99; see *Genesis Unbound*, 15. In addition, the exile from the garden matches the exile from the promised land, toward the east. An angel guarded the eastern entrance to the garden just as an angel guarded the eastern entrance to the promised land. See Genesis 3:24; 31:1–2, 22–32; Joshua 5:13–15.
11. Sailhamer, *Genesis Unbound*, 83.
12. Ibid., 216.

text from the original author's point of view. He believes that the focus of interpretation should remain on the text itself. Too often interpreters have read outside information into the text, such as understanding "formless and void" (*tohu wavohu*) in Genesis 1:2 as a reference to chaos. This notion can be tied to Greek influence (or possibly Babylonian) and would probably be foreign to an ancient Israelite. The notion of "formless and void" from biblical use is, as Sailhamer argues, more along the line of describing an "uninhabitable land" (Deut. 32:10; Jer. 4:23–26). Another example where Sailhamer's close scrutiny of the biblical text has shed light on our understanding is his lengthy examination of the term *erets* ("land, earth, ground"). Sailhamer convincingly points out that the term land (*erets*) most often refers to a localized area, not the entire world, in Genesis and also in the Pentateuch. And, in doing so he has convincingly made a case for the virtual identity of the garden of Eden and the promised land.

Moreover, Sailhamer clearly understands that Genesis 1 is to be read as historical, that is, it describes something that has taken place. This, of course, puts him at odds with those who understand Genesis 1 to be mythological or a piece of literature that is just trying to convey a theological truth. Also one must appreciate his insights regarding how the original readers would have understood the text. Sailhamer logically and convincingly argues the original readers lived in a different age than our own, a pre-scientific age. This, of course, would have an effect on their own understanding, and we should not try to assume that they saw the world entirely as we do in the modern age.

While there are numerous positive aspects about "historical creationism," questions remain. First of all, Sailhamer's understanding of *reshith*, "beginning," as a reference to a duration of time is open to challenge. The meaning of this term is critical to "historical creationism" as it reinforces the notion of two separate creation acts, one as described in Genesis 1:1, while the second act is the six day "creation/preparation" throughout the remainder of Genesis 1. It should be pointed out that while it is clear that *reshith* in Jeremiah 28:1 seems to clearly refer to a duration of time rather than a point in time, Sailhamer seems to have overstated the case when he implies that *reshith* had a very special technical use to refer to the "indeterminate period of time before the official reckoning of a king's reign."[13] *Reshith* occurs in fifty-one places in the Old Testament and in two-thirds of the occurrences the word is used in reference to "the best, choicest part," or "firstfruits." The use of *reshith* as the "beginning" of a king's reign occurs only four times in the Old Testament (all in Jeremiah, Jer. 26:1; 27:1; 28:1; 49:34), less than 10 percent of the term's total occurrences. Only in Jeremiah 28:1 is it clear that *reshith* refers to a "duration of time" in reference to a king's reign. But in its temporal occurrences the term is recognized as having a range of meaning which includes, according to

---

13. Ibid., 39.

theological lexicons and dictionaries, the notion of the beginning or starting point. The use of *reshith* in Deuteronomy 11:12, "from the *beginning* of the year until the end of the year," could be an example of *reshith* as referring to time as a starting point. At least it is not clear cut that had Moses wanted to refer to a point in time that *rishonah* and *techillah* would have unequivocally been better choices. As the term *reshith* also indicates "the best," or "first-fruits," when it refers to time, it should be understood as the temporal extreme. The use of *reshith* in Isaiah 46:10 appears to be comparable to Genesis 1:1, and the term has been understood in that passage to refer to "the beginning of time per se."[14] Also, given the fact that Sailhamer maintains that *bara* refers to *creatio ex nihilo*, "creation out of nothing" (Gen. 1:1), there is a question why *reshith* would be used (it is the word immediately before *bara*) if the focus of *reshith* was on duration of time. Does not an event that takes place uniquely in a singular instant in time by necessity take place in a single moment? Furthermore, in understanding *reshith* to refer to a duration of time, Sailhamer refers to Genesis 1:1 curiously as a "time before time."[15]

Perhaps more consequential to historical creationism (or the promised land theory) is the understanding of the term *erets*, translated as "earth, land, ground." The word *erets*, which occurs numerous times in Genesis 1, occurs 2,504 times in the Old Testament and is the fourth most common noun in the Old Testament.[16] The term, like many Hebrew substantives, including *reshith*, has a wide range of meaning. It is not always easy to determine whether *erets* refers to earth or land. But German scholars H. H. Schmid and Magnus Ottosson list scores of occurrences of the use of *erets* in the Old Testament particularly in relation to the Lord's sovereignty, to support the notion of the Lord's sovereignty over the entire earth (*erets*).[17] Luis Stadlemann agrees that the use of *erets* primarily means the entire area as opposed to heaven or the underworld. In this sense, the word *erets* denotes the whole area as opposed to parts or sectors of it.[18] As Stadlemann concluded, "What we observe in the use of *erets* and *aratswth* (pl. of *erets*) is a gradual distinction introduced in later biblical texts, whereby the singular form, formerly used to designate both the whole world and particular territories, came to be employed to indicate the

---

14. See *HALOT* 2:1169; S. Rattray and J. Milgrom, "ראשית *reshith*," *TDOT* 13:269; H. P. Müller, "ראש *rosh*," *TLOT* 3:1190; Bill T. Arnold, "ראשית " *NIDOTTE* 3:1025. Amazingly, Sailhamer suggests that *reshith* appears to refer to a "starting point" on the last page of his book, *Genesis Unbound*, 250.

15. Sailhamer, *Genesis Unbound*, 38. The notion of a "time before time" is problematic. This involves referring to a temporal period before time exists. You cannot speak of "time" if time does not exist.

16. H. H. Schmid, "ארץ *erets*," *TLOT* 1:173.

17. See Ottosson, "ארץ *erets*," *TDOT* 1:394–96; Schmid, "ארץ *erets*,"177.

18. Genesis 18:18, 25; 22:18; 2 Kings 19:15, 19; Isaiah 37:16, 20; Jeremiah 25:26, 29–30; 26:6; Zechariah 4:10, 14.

'earth,' whereas the plural was taken in the sense of 'countries, territories of nations.'"[19] It is also somewhat curious that Sailhamer does not address the occurrences of *erets* (earth or land) in the flood account (e.g., Gen. 7:3; 8:9; 9:11) as he is focused on the meaning of *erets*, particularly in Genesis.[20]

Also of great significance is the different meaning of *erets* in Genesis 1:1 and in the rest of Genesis 1. In Genesis 1:1, *erets* is part of a merism, "the heavens and earth," whereas in the rest of Genesis 1, *erets* does not occur in this phrase but rather occurs by itself, which Sailhamer argues allows it to have a different meaning than the meaning of "heaven and earth" of Genesis 1:1, i.e., the universe. In Exodus 20:11, the phrase "heavens and earth" does not constitute a merism as in Genesis 1:1 because, Sailhamer argues, it is followed by additional phrases, "the sea, and all that is in them." Because "heaven and earth" is followed by additional phrases in Exodus 20:11, it is no longer a merism.[21] Even though the text reads "heavens and earth," "this passage in Exodus does not use the merism, 'heavens and earth' to describe God's work of six days."[22]

What is more problematic with this view, is the occurrence of the identical phrase, "For in six days the Lord made the heaven and earth" in Exodus 31:17 without a following descriptive phrase.[23] According to Sailhamer's explanation of Exodus 20, this has to be a merism because there is no following list. But if it is a merism, it is stating that God made (*asah*) the universe in six days. This statement is in direct conflict and contradicts "historical creationism." The position of "historical creationism" is that the universe was not created in six days but was created back in Genesis 1:1. Sailhamer goes to great lengths to redefine "heavens and earth" because the verb used in Exodus 20:11 and 31:17 is the verb *asah*, not *bara*. According to Sailhamer, *asah* creation does not refer to creation of the universe but is used of preparation of the land in Genesis 1. To maintain the distinction Sailhamer argues that these two "creations" are described by two separate verbs—*bara* in Genesis 1:1 and *asah* in Genesis 1:2–31. However, passages such as 2 Kings 19:15; 2 Chronicles 2:12[11]; and Isaiah 37:16 all describe creation of the universe ("heavens and earth") by use of the verb *asah*.

---

19. Luis I. J. Stadelmann, *The Hebrew Conception of the World* (Rome: Biblical Institute Press, 1970), 128. Waltke agrees and understands *erets* in Genesis 1:2 to refer to the planet (see Bruce K. Waltke and Cathi J. Fredricks, *Genesis* [Grand Rapids: Zondervan, 2001], 59).

20. Ibid., 48.

21. Perhaps other examples of a merism being negated by subsequent descriptive clauses would be needed to support this thesis.

22. Sailhamer, *Genesis Unbound*, 106.

23. Sailhamer mentions that Exodus 31:17 is an abbreviated form of Exodus 20, but as it, like Exodus 20 alludes to creation this is not clear. Exodus 20 and Exodus 31 both link back to the creation account of Genesis 1:1–2:3: "for in six days God created the heavens and the earth" (Ex. 20:11; 31:17). In fact, Sailhamer states that Exodus 20 frequently alludes back to Genesis 1 (*Genesis Unbound*, 50).

But even more detrimental to the historical creationism (or the promised land view) is the occurrence of the next merism in Genesis—the phrase "heavens and earth" in Genesis 2:1. This phrase forms an inclusion with Genesis 1:1 indicating that the creation account is a unit that is coming to a close. Thus, the phrase "heavens and earth" in Genesis 2:1 indicates that the entire creation account is a unity describing one creation (not two) about the "heavens and earth" and is not only referring to the promised land. Genesis 1:1–2:3 is a unified pericope about one unified creation account of the universe.

Broader Questions

Other questions for historical creationism are more general in nature. Since Genesis 1:2–2:3 is addressing the issue of preparing the garden of Eden (promised land) for man, the question arises as to when the rest of the earth became habitable for man. Was it in Genesis 1:1?[24] If so, one might seek the reason for this as the rest of the planet was habitable for man and yet man did not come to inhabit the earth until the promised land was prepared perhaps billions of years later. Also, in reference to the creation of man on day six, we are told that he was created to have dominion over the whole *erets* (Gen. 1:26, 28). If the text is saying that man's dominion is only over the promised land, the more cosmic understanding of the purpose of man becomes problematic and needs to be explained (see Questions 10, "What Does Genesis Teach about the Purpose of Man's Creation?" and 23, "What Does It Mean That Man Is Made in God's Image?").

Included in preparing the land for man was the creation of the sky over the Promised Land as well as stocking the seas with life.[25] Did the sky only *not* exist over the Promised Land before Genesis 1:2, and did the Mediterranean Sea have a vast supply of fish except where the waters met the coast line of Israel?[26]

Another issue is Sailhamer's appeal to the history of interpretation in support of the position of "historical creationism." Sailhamer's citation of early support for this view does not come close in any respect to suggest that the affirmation of this position was overwhelming. He argues as though this position was well known if not dominant in the history of interpretation.[27] The fact that Rashi and Lightfoote are the only solid supports for this view speaks of the

---

24. Sailhamer states that many other places may have already been suitable for man before God prepared the garden and the promised land but appears to acknowledge that this is speculation on his part (ibid., 150).
25. Again, Sailhamer acknowledges that there had been a sky and land in the beginning, apart from the land of Israel apparently (ibid., 108).
26. Sailhamer includes the preparation of the Mediterranean Sea with the preparation of the land of Israel (see *Genesis Unbound*, 126).
27. Ibid., 159–64.

rarity of the position rather than a justification for it.[28] Jack Lewis's investigation, on the other hand, clearly indicates that the view that Genesis 1 refers to the creation of the universe in six days has been the clear majority view in the history of interpretation.[29]

Conclusion

While there are issues that need to be addressed, many may find plausible explanations to the questions I have raised. Sailhamer is to be commended for his focus on the biblical text and trying to reach a rapprochement with modern science. His work is insightful and innovative. Also his understanding of the significance of the land as a critical component of God's covenant with Israel is a positive focus of this view. As for historical creationism's relationship to other creation views, many may find conceptual affinities with the gap theory: primarily the idea of creation in Genesis 1:1 and a separate creation act starting with Genesis 1:2 (see Question 11).

REFLECTION QUESTIONS

1. What are the main points of the historical creationism view?

2. What does the "land" refer to in Genesis 1:2, according to historical creationism?

3. What is the historical support for historical creationism?

4. The dimensions of the garden of Eden are equivalent to what region?

5. When were human beings created according to historical creationism?

---

28. I could not find any Jewish or rabbinic support for the view that *erets* in Genesis 1 is referring to Eden/the promised land in the 2,232 pages of Meir Zlotowitz's comprehensive two volume work, *Bereishis—Genesis: A New Translation With a Commentary Anthologized from Talmudic, Midrashic, and Mishnaic Sources,* 2nd ed. (Brooklyn, N.Y.: Mesorah Publications, 2009).

29. Jack P. Lewis, "The Days of Creation: An Historical Survey of Interpretation," *JETS* 32, no. 4 (1989): 433–55.

What Is the Twenty-Four Hour Theory?

Down through the history of biblical interpretation, the meaning of the word "day" (Hb. *yom*) in Genesis 1 has been widely debated among interpreters from all kinds of theological perspectives. The twenty-four hour theory of creation is an interpretation of Genesis 1 that understands the creation days to refer to a twenty-four-hour period of time, or a solar day. While the Hebrew word for day (*yom*) has a range of meaning, it is the argument of the twenty-four-hour creation day advocates that in Genesis 1, it is the literal—not the extended—meaning of *yom* that is clearly in view.

Support for a Literal Twenty-Four-Hour Day in Genesis 1

In Genesis 1 the creation days are referenced with a number to refer to each successive day of the creation week (1:5, 8, 13, 19, 23, 31). Elsewhere in Scripture when the word "day" (*yom*) is used with a number, it always refers to a twenty-four-hour day.[1] The same is true when the word occurs in the singular (day vs. days) and is not found within a compound grammatical construction, such as the object of a preposition or the object of an infinitive construct.[2] Moreover, there are additional reasons from the context of Genesis 1 to suggest that the day is a normal twenty-four-hour period—specifically, the employment of the formula "evening and morning" occurring with the six creation days (1:5, 8, 13, 19, 23, 31). The occurrence of the phrase "evening and morning," with or without the occurrence of the word "day," refers consistently to literal twenty-four-hour days in the Old Testament.[3] The word "evening" would refer to the dark part of the day while "morning" would indicate

---

1. The word *yom* occurs about 150 times with a number in the Old Testament. See E. Jenni, "יוֹם *yom*," *TLOT* 2:528.
2. See M. Saebø, "יוֹם *yom*," *TDOT* 6:21; Robert V. McCabe, "A Critique of the Framework Interpretation of the Creation Week," in *Coming to Grips With Genesis*, ed. Terry Mortenson and Thane H. Ury (Green Forest, Ark.: Master, 2008), 226n.62.
3. See McCabe, "A Critique of the Framework Interpretation of the Creation Week," 226–27.

the light part of the day. It is reasonable that this descriptive phrase that defines or describes the creation days is meant to convey the idea that a normal day of twenty-four hours is in view.

A second line of support for understanding that literal twenty-four-hour days are in view in Genesis 1 has to do with the Sabbath law in the Ten Commandments. The law of the Sabbath requires man to work for six days during the week, but then rest on the seventh day (the Sabbath) from all his labors. The reason for this pattern according to the record of the Ten Commandments in Exodus 20 is that God worked six days and then rested, ceased from his labors, on the seventh day (Ex. 20:8–11). As humans are called to imitate God by this work pattern, it is understood that the model for the Sabbath is based on literal twenty-four-hour periods of time and the basis for this understanding comes from the use of days in Genesis 1. E. J. Young comments on the logic of this reasoning when he states, "In Ex. 20:11 the activity of God is presented to man as a pattern, and this fact presupposes that there was a reality in the activity of God which man is to follow. How could man be held accountable for working six days if God himself had not actually worked for six days?"[4] Hence, the Ten Commandments take the word "day" as referring to twenty-four-hour periods within the weekly cycle, as God provided an example for mankind's labor.

Another possible support for literal twenty-four-hour days in Genesis 1 comes from the significance of a literal seven-day period in the records of the ancient Near East. John Stek has summarized some of the more significant occurrences of a seven-day period in ancient Near Eastern literature:

> As regards the seven-day structure, any other temporal order would appear to have been unfitting in that ancient world. Throughout the ancient Near East, the number seven had long served as the primary numerical symbol of fullness/ completeness/perfection, and the seven-day cycle was an old and well-established convention. Out of the many examples available, we may note from Ugaritic literature (1) the seven-day journey of King Keret to the city of Udum the Great and his seven-day siege of that city, (2) the seven days required for completing Baal's royal palace, and (3) King Danel's seven-day appeal to the gods and his subsequent seven days of feasting. According to the Epic of Gilgamesh, it took seven days to build Utnapishtim's "ark," and the flood that followed raged for seven days and took a similar period to subside. Functionally, the Sabbath structure of creation "time" added

---

4. Edward J. Young, *Studies in Genesis One* (Philadelphia: P&R, 1964), 47. See Allen P. Ross, *Creation and Blessing* (Grand Rapids: Baker, 1988), 109.

symbolic reinforcement of the explicit themes of the completeness of God's creative work and the "goodness" of the created realm.[5]

Evaluation of a Literal Twenty-Four-Hour Day in Genesis 1

The Word "Day"

The proponents of a nonliteral twenty-four-hour day normally bring forth two primary issues with regard to the length of the days in Genesis 1. The first has to do with the understanding of the length of the creation days, while the second deals with what these proponents argue is the implausibility of the twenty-four hour view.

The opponents of the twenty-four-hour day in Genesis 1 are quick to point out that the Hebrew word day (*yom*) has an extended meaning and does not always refer to a literal twenty-four-hour period. This can already be indicated in the early chapters of Genesis. First of all, it is clear that in Genesis 1 the word "day" does not always mean a twenty-four-hour period. In fact the word may refer to a time period less than twenty-four hours. In Genesis 1:5, 14–16, the word "day" refers to not a solar day but rather the time of daylight as opposed to night. On the other hand, the word "day" appears to refer to more than a twenty-four-hour period by its use in Genesis 2:4, when it is preceded by the preposition "in": "in (or when) the Lord God made the earth and the heavens" (similarly in Gen. 2:17). In Genesis 2:4, "day" appears to apply to the entire six-day creation period. Moreover, the word *yom* clearly has an extended sense beyond a twenty-four-hour period when it is used in the expression of "day of," as in the phrase "Day of the Lord." The phrase refers clearly to a distinct period of time. The word *yom* also has the extended meaning of referring to a period of time (Judg. 14:4; Gen. 29:14) and may describe the eventful historical character of an important event and its effects, as in the "days of Gibeah" (Hos. 9:9; 10:9).[6]

In addition, two important biblical texts address the subject of the length or duration of time intended by the word "day." Psalm 90:4 and 2 Peter 3:8 appear to indicate that a day is equivalent to a thousand years with respect to God. Some argue that this understanding of the word "day" proves that understanding *yom* as a twenty-four-hour period is incorrect.

Another major reason that scholars and interpreters deny that the word *yom* refers to a twenty-four-hour period is because it does not seem to

---

5. John H. Stek, "What Says the Scriptures?" in *Portraits of Creation: Biblical and Scientific Perspectives on the World's Formation* (Grand Rapids: Eerdmans, 1990), 239. See also Gordon J. Wenham, *Genesis 1–15*, WBC 1 (Waco, Tex.: Word, 1987), 19; Todd Beall, "Contemporary Hermeneutical Approaches to Genesis 1–11," in *Coming to Grips With Genesis*, ed. Terry Mortenson and Thane H. Ury (Green Forest, Ark.: Master, 2008), 158.
6. Saebø, "יום yom," 30; Jenni, "יום yom," 529.

harmonize with the creative events of Genesis 1:1–2:3. Interpreters have argued that understanding the word *yom* as a twenty-four-hour period of time does not appear to harmonize with what we find in the description of what takes place on days four, six, and seven.

It is without doubt that the word *yom* has extended meanings that are distinct from its use in referring to a twenty-four-hour period. For example, in Genesis 2:4 the word *yom* appears in a prepositional phrase *beyom* ("in the day"). This prepositional phrase is in construct with an infinitive forming a temporal clause. It is an idiomatic expression for "when."[7] And yet, when the term occurs outside a temporal clause and in connection with "evening and morning," it has the meaning of a full, normal day.[8]

Of course, the classic texts for the term "day" (*yom*) as applied to an "age" or "epoch" are Psalm 90:4 and 2 Peter 3:8. In both texts, however, "day" is to be taken literally. Otherwise there would be no comparison. In Psalm 90:4 the phrase "as yesterday" is parallel with the following phrase, "as a watch in the night." This phrase is actually referring to a period less than twenty-four hours. The texts simply show that with respect to the eternity of God, there is no difference between a day or even a shorter period of time and a thousand years.[9] Similarly, in 2 Peter 3:8 the phrase "one day is as a thousand years, and a thousand years as one day" demonstrates that God is not limited to time when it comes to fulfilling his promises.

Day Four

The teaching about day four has led many to understand the meaning of the word "day" as figurative. Since the sun was not created until day four, how could the references to the first three days be understood as literal twenty-four-hour periods? Thus, it is argued, "day" has a different meaning in Genesis 1 (especially days one, two, and three) than how it is normally understood. As we typically define the term, the word "day" cannot be defined or said to be in existence except by its relation to the sun. Thus, Ken Mathews states,

> Although understanding "day" as solar has the advantage of its simplicity, there are many indications that "day" in its customary sense may not be intended. The most obvious indication is the sun's absence for the first three days. That "day" might not have its normal meaning here is not surprising

---

7. See Saebø, "יוֹם *yom*," 15; Jenni, "יוֹם *yom*," 529; BDB, 400; Umberto Cassuto, *A Commentary on the Book of Genesis*, 2 vols. (vol. 1, *From Adam to Noah, Genesis I–VI:8*), trans. Israel Abrahams (Jerusalem: Magnes 1961–64), 1:99, 100.

8. BDB, 398; Saebø, "יוֹם *yom*," 23.

9. See Joseph A. Pipa, Jr. "From Chaos to Cosmos: A Critique of the Non-Literal Interpretations of Genesis 1:1–2:3," in *Did God Create in Six Days?* ed. Joseph A. Pipa, Jr. and David W. Hall (Taylors, S.C.: Southern Presbyterian Press, 1999), 180.

since other Hebrew terms, such as "heaven" and "earth," also have varying meanings in the narrative (e.g., vv. 1, 8). *Yom* is a designation for the "daylight" of the first creative day, not a reference to a full solar day (v. 5), and it is used as a temporal expression for the entire creative period of six days in the *toledoth* section (2:4a). If we keep in mind the colloquial use of the language, "day" cannot have its common meaning before the sun is created. The very expression "evening and morning" demands the planetary arrangement of our solar system that does not come into existence until the fourth day.[10]

Genesis 1:14–19 declares that the heavenly bodies were not created until the "fourth day" and placed in their familiar positions. It does not appear that Moses is saying that hitherto hidden heavenly bodies now became visible on earth.[11]

The argument that the word "day" cannot be understood to refer to a twenty-four-hour period because the sun was not created until day four has been countered in two ways. First of all, as John Sailhamer has noted, the syntax of the description of the formation of the sun, moon, and stars on day four is distinct from the previous three creation days. The text is not actually saying that the creation of the "lights" took place on day four but rather it explains the purpose of the created lights—they had been made to divide the day and night and "for signs and seasons, and for days and years" (Gen. 1:14). The lights had actually been created "in the beginning" (Gen. 1:1).[12]

A second possible way to understand the existence of "solar" days before the creation of the sun is to maintain that the creation of light is not necessarily connected with the luminaries, particularly the sun. Victor Hamilton recognizes this in substance, saying, "The Bible begins and ends by describing an untarnished world that is filled with light, but no sun (cf. Rev. 22:5). Should not the one who is himself called "light" (1 John 1:5) have at his disposal many sources by which he dispatches light into his creation?"[13] Furthermore, Terence Fretheim argues that it is likely that the Hebrews believed that the ultimate source of light was other than the heavenly bodies (cf. Isa. 60:19–20;

---

10. See Ken Mathews, *Genesis 1:1–11:26*, NAC (Nashville: B&H, 1996), 149. See Howard J. Van Till, *The Fourth Day* (Grand Rapids: Zondervan, 1986).
11. So Meredith G. Kline, "Because It Had Not Rained," *WTJ* 20 (1958): 153.
12. See John H. Sailhamer, *Genesis Unbound* (Sisters Ore.: Multnomah, 1996), 252n.13. See also, Wenham, *Genesis 1–15*, WBC, vol. 1, 23. For the difference in syntax, see Sailhamer, *Genesis,* EBC, 2nd ed. (Grand Rapids: Zondervan, 2008), 65.
13. Victor P. Hamilton, *The Book of Genesis Chapters 1–17*, NICOT (Grand Rapids: Eerdmans, 1990), 121n.7. See also Benjamin Shaw, "The Literal Day Interpretation," in *Did God Create in Six Days?* ed. Joseph A. Pipa, Jr. and David W. Hall (Taylors, S.C.: Southern Presbyterian Press, 1999), 205.

Ps. 104:2; Job 38:19; Rev. 22:5).[14] Jon Levenson argues that Isaiah 60:19–20 teaches in effect that the light that existed on the first three days of creation (i.e., without the sun) will return in the eschaton and once again the sun will not be needed.[15] Thus, the "lights" and stars are presented only as instruments for measuring time in Genesis 1:14–18 and have no power to affect human destiny. They are servants rather than masters of time.

The days four, five, and six are described no differently than days one, two, and three, indicating that they are alike. If the sun was created on day four there does not appear to be any measurable change as to the nature of the days in days one, two, and three.[16]

Day Six

When one examines the activities and experiences that took place on the sixth creation day, it is difficult to believe that they all could be accomplished in a twenty-four-hour period. Many scholars argue that it is hard to believe that Adam, in spite of his supposed vast mental ability, could have received instructions from God (Gen. 2:15–17), named all the animals in accordance with their natures (Gen. 2:18–20), fallen into a deep sleep (Gen. 2:20), and experienced enough passing of time to exclaim "now at last" (Gen. 2:23) when Eve was created. It has been suggested that naming many hundreds of species of animals alone must have required several months. Does not rational thinking lead one to conclude that all these activities need more than twenty-four hours?[17]

The argument that a comparison of Genesis 1 and 2 would appear to include too many activities to occur on day six creates a genuine dilemma for the twenty-four hour position. Joseph Pipa has addressed this issue by pointing out that we do not actually know how many kinds of animals Adam named. The general description is that of domesticated animals, birds, and beasts. Apparently, he did not name fish and insects, for example. Pipa states that God's purpose in this exercise was not to give an exhaustive taxonomy but to learn experimentally that for him "there was not found a helper suitable for him" (Gen. 2:20).[18]

---

14. Terence E. Fretheim, "Were the Days of Creation Twenty-Four Hours Long?" in *The Genesis Debate*, ed. Ronald Youngblood (Grand Rapids: Baker, 1990), 23.

15. Jon D. Levenson, *Creation and the Persistence of Evil* (San Francisco: Harper & Row, 1988), 125.

16. See Charles G. Aalders, *Genesis*, 2 vols. (Grand Rapids: Zondervan, 1981), 1:66; H. C. Leupold, *Exposition of Genesis*, 2 vols. (Grand Rapids: Baker, 1942), 1:52–53.

17. See Gleason Archer, Jr., "A Response to the Trustworthiness of Scripture in Areas Relating to Natural Science," in *Hermeneutics, Inerrancy and the Bible*, ed. E. D. Radmacher and R. D. Preus (Grand Rapids: Zondervan, 1984), 325–26; C. John Collins, "How Old Is the Earth? Anthropomorphic Days in Genesis 1:1–2:3," *Presb* 20, no. 2 (1994): 119; idem, "Reading Genesis 1:1–2:3 as An Act of Communication," in *Did God Create in Six Days?* ed. Joseph A. Pipa, Jr. and David W. Hall (Taylors, S.C.: Southern Presbyterian Press, 1999), 148–49.

18. Pipa, "From Chaos to Cosmos," 180–81.

Day Seven

Because the seventh day does not repeat the formula, "evening and morning," it has been thought to be distinct from the previous six days of creation. It is argued that the day does not come to an end as in the previous six creation days and thus should be viewed as an eternal divine Sabbath. As such the sabbatical week is an earthly metaphor for the heavenly archetype. The writer of Hebrews picks up on this spiritual nature of the Sabbath (Heb. 4:3–11). Hebrews 4:9–11 tells us that there still remains a Sabbath rest for the people of God. Thus, Hebrews 4:9–11 endorses the idea of a continuing Sabbath but indicates that there are dimensions of the Sabbath day that have never been completely realized in human experience. Consequently, the biblical writers portray the seventh day of Genesis 2:2–3 as continuing into the present.[19] As Bruce Waltke has stated, "The Sabbath rest assures saints that, just as God entered his rest after the working for six days, so also they live in the hope that when they cease from their labors after their fleeting days they too shall enter an eternal rest."[20] As the climactic seventh day of the six-day series, it does not refer to a literal twenty-four-hour period and thus this implies that all six days are nonliteral.

The argument that the seventh day is not a literal twenty-four-hour period is based on the omission of the phrase "evening and morning" on the seventh day. Thus, the seventh day must be ongoing, or eternal. Yet, it also should be observed that the seventh day differs from the previous six creation days by more than just the omission of the phrase "evening and morning." In fact none of the other phrases that occur consistently throughout the other six creation days are mentioned: God said, "let there be," fulfillment, evaluation, and two-fold conclusion (evening and morning, day x). The overall structuring device was not utilized because God was no longer creating after day six. These formulae are excluded from day seven as day seven marks the end of the creation activity.[21]

The eternal rest as presented in Hebrews is based on an analogy to God's creative rest on the first Sabbath in Genesis 2:1–3. The rest of God in Genesis 2:2–3 is completely different than the rest in Hebrews 4:3–11. The Sabbath-rest of Hebrews 4:3–11 is a rest that the people can actually experience, a spiritual rest. Hebrews 4:3–11 establishes that God's eternal rest is an analogy drawn from God's rest on the literal seventh day in Genesis 2:1–3. The author of Hebrews is thus not *expositing* the text's original meaning, but *extending*

---

19. See Meredith. G. Kline, "Space and Time in the Genesis Cosmogony," *Perspectives on Science and Christian Faith* 48, no. 1 (March 1996): 11; John H. Sailhamer, "Genesis," EBC, rev. ed. (Grand Rapids: Zondervan, 2008), 72; William J. Dumbrell, "Genesis 2:1–17: A Foreshadowing of the New Creation," in *Biblical Theology: Retrospect and Prospect*, ed. Scott J. Hafemann (Downers Grove: InterVarsity, 2002), 55; Collins, "How Old is the Earth?" 11.

20. Bruce K. Waltke and Cathi J. Fredricks, *Genesis* (Grand Rapids: Zondervan, 2001), 72–73.

21. See McCabe, "A Critique of the Framework Interpretation of the Creation Week," 225, 242.

it. Thus, Hebrews 4 does not preclude day seven of the creation week as a historic literal day.[22]

As mentioned above, the view of a nonliteral, eternal Sabbath based on the Sabbath day of Genesis 2:2 is in tension with Exodus 20:9–11 and Exodus 31:17. The application of Exodus 20:11 and 31:17 dealing with the Sabbath ordinance seems to rule out an open-ended interpretation of day seven. Both passages have been clearly understood as references to man imitating the divine pattern established in the first week of temporal history by working on six consecutive, normal days and resting on a literal seventh day. As McCabe states, "With a legitimate use of the analogy of Scripture, Exodus 20:11 and 31:17 unequivocally indicate that God did not create on heavenly time, but on earthly time."[23] Moreover, how does the fall and the curse fit in to this pattern of the ongoing Sabbath day of Genesis 2:2–3?

A Mediating Position

Among those interpreters who maintain that the evidence for a literal twenty-four-hour day is lacking in Genesis 1, many have suggested that the day should be taken in a figurative or metaphorical sense as the days cannot be viewed as solar days. Bruce Waltke stated, "To be sure the six days in the Genesis creation account are our twenty-four-hour days, but they are metaphorical representations of a reality beyond human comprehension and imitation."[24] In speaking of days, God is accommodating Himself to humanity in terms human beings would understand. Similarly Gordon Wenham notes that day must have its basic sense of a twenty-four-hour day, but the literary nature of the text suggests that the word "day" not be understood in its normal way. This also applies to the understanding of the Sabbath. There is a correspondence between God's work and man's and God's rest as a model for the Sabbath, but we should not take this to mean that the six days of creation are the same as human days. John Sailhamer similarly views the creation days of Genesis 1, in a non-literal fashion: "As mega-history we must understand the biblical narrative to use analogies that ultimately transcend our everyday experience. The 'days' of Genesis 1 are thus real and literal twenty-four-hour days, but they depict events that lie outside of our everyday experience. . . . By identifying God's act of creation with an element or a feature of our own experience of the world, we lose sight of the actual work of God in creation."[25]

22. See Kenneth L. Gentry and Michael R. Butler, *Yea, Hath God Said? The Framework Hypothesis/Six Day Creation Debate* (Eugene, Ore.: Wipf and Stock, 2002), 63; McCabe, "A Critique of the Framework Interpretation of the Creation Week," 245.
23. See McCabe, "A Critique of the Framework Interpretation of the Creation Week," 243–44.
24. Bruce K. Waltke, "The Literary Genre of Genesis, Chapter One," *Crux* 27, no. 4 (December 1991): 8; Waltke and Fredericks, *Genesis*, 61. Similarly, Kline, "Space and Time in the Genesis Cosmogony," 7, 10; Collins, "How Old is the Earth?" 117, 120.
25. Sailhamer, *Genesis Unbound*, 243–44; see Wenham, *Genesis 1–15*, 19, 40.

Conclusion

It needs to be affirmed that in the Hebrew Bible the normal understanding of *yom* is a day of the week. There are, to be sure, places where it may refer to an unmeasured period of time or to an era such as in the prophets' phrase "in that day," or to an unusually long period of time, even up to a millennium (Ps. 90:4). The burden of proof, however, is on those who do not attribute to *yom* in Genesis 1 its normal and most common interpretation, especially when *yom* is always described as being composed of an evening and morning. Many nonevangelical critical scholars of the Old Testament including James Barr, Gerhard van Rad, and Claus Westermann agree that the days of Genesis 1 are meant as literal twenty-four-hour days. As Westermann stated, "The words 'evening and morning' describe an actual day of twenty-four hours; otherwise the succession of six days ending with Sabbath loses its meaning."[26] Also John Stek, who in the end takes a mediating position states, "Surely there is no sign or hint within the narrative itself that the author thought his 'days' to be irregular designations —first a series of undefined periods, then a series of solar days—or that the 'days' he bounded with 'evening and morning' could possibly be understood as long eons of time."[27]

The biggest challenge to the twenty-four-hour day theory seems to be the massive amount of activities that must have taken place on day six. This is a real issue, and not all will be convinced with Pipa's explanation that not all animals were brought before Adam, but only representative types from various kinds. And yet we can agree with Derek Kidner that "it also seems over-subtle to adopt a view of the passage which discounts one of the primary impressions it makes on the ordinary reader."[28] Similarly Claus Westermann comments, "The average reader who opens his Bible to Genesis 1 and 2 receives the impression that he is reading a sober account of creation, which relates facts in much the same manner as does the story of the rise of the Israelite monarchy, that is, as straightforward history."[29]

The text itself indicates that these are regular days. "It is extremely difficult to conclude that anything other than a twenty-four-hour day was intended."[30]

---

26. Claus Westermann, *Genesis 1–11*, trans. John J. Scullion S. J. (Minneapolis: Fortress, 1994), 90; see Gerhard Von Rad, *Genesis*, rev. ed. (Philadelphia: Westminster, 1972), 65; Hamilton, *Genesis 1–17*, 53. Moreover, does the claim that the Sabbath is not a literal twenty-four-hour day due to the omission of the phrase "evening and morning" not imply that the previous six days are literal twenty-four hour days?
27. Stek, "What Says the Scriptures?" 237–38.
28. Derek Kidner, *Genesis: An Introduction and Commentary* (Downers Grove: InterVarsity, 1967), 54–55.
29. Claus Westermann, *The Genesis Accounts of Creation* (Philadelphia: Fortress, 1964), 5.
30. John Walton, *Genesis*, NIVAC (Grand Rapids: Zondervan, 2001), 81; see Andrew E. Steinmann, "אחד as an Ordinal Number and the Meaning of Genesis 1:5," *JETS* 45, no.4 (December 2002): 584.

REFLECTION QUESTIONS

1. What are the main arguments for understanding the creation days as twenty-four-hour periods?

2. What is the relevance of appealing to the number seven in ancient Near Eastern texts for the discussion of the length of days?

3. What is the difficulty of arguing for a twenty-four-hour day in view of creation day four?

4. What is the difficulty of arguing for a twenty-four-hour day in view of creation day six?

5. What is the difficulty of arguing for a twenty-four-hour day in view of the Sabbath day?

PART 4

QUESTIONS ABOUT THE AGE OF THE EARTH

Are There Gaps in the Biblical Genealogies?

In his book *Genealogy and History in the Biblical World*, Robert Wilson defines the term genealogy as "a written or oral expression of the descent of a person or persons from an ancestor or ancestors."[1] Genealogies are generally classified into two major groups or categories—linear genealogies or segmented genealogies. Linear (or vertical) genealogies trace an unbroken line of descendants from A to Z. Segmented (or horizontal) genealogies, on the other hand, trace more than one line of descent from a common ancestor, so that more than one individual appears in each generation.[2]

Up until the time of the Enlightenment, biblical scholars and laymen read the genealogies literally and at face value, often reading the genealogies to calculate the beginning of the history of the world and of mankind. The most influential of these chronological schemes was that which was worked out by Archbishop Ussher in his work, "Annales Veteri et Novi Testament" (1650–1654).

According to Ussher's calculations the creation of the world occurred in the year 4004 BC. Post-Enlightenment scholarship, on the other hand, has largely abandoned any notion that the genealogies bore any authentic witness and has called their historical reliability into question. Ignaz Goldziher and Bernard Stade, for example, argued that the early biblical writers used

---

1. Robert R. Wilson, *Genealogy and History in the Biblical World* (New Haven and London: Yale University Press, 1977), 9.
2. See Robert B. Robinson, "Literary Functions of the Genealogies of Genesis," *CBQ* 48 (1986): 597n. 4. Genesis 5 and 11 fit the pattern of the linear lists, linking individuals from one era to another. Genesis 5 starts with Adam and ends with Noah, while Genesis 11 begins with Shem and ends with Terah. Genesis 10, on the other hand, more closely illustrates the segmented pattern. Genesis 25:12–18 and 36:1–43 also are segmented genealogies. See Allen P. Ross, *Creation and Blessing* (Grand Rapids: Baker, 1988), 229.

mythical names to fabricate a biography of their ancestors and that the genealogies were in fact a fiction that had little connection with actual historical
individuals.[3] Julius Wellhausen, considered the pioneer of the modern critical
approach to the Old Testament, wrote, "Genealogical form lends itself to the
reception of every sort of materials. In the patriarchal legend, however, the
ethnographic element is always predominant. Abraham alone is certainly not
the name of a people like Isaac and Lot . . . he might with more likelihood be
regarded as a free creation of unconscious art."[4]

Biblical and Ancient Near Eastern Genealogies

In spite of the well-known tendency of Mesopotamian scribes to com-
pile and preserve lists, relatively few genealogies appear in Sumerian and
Akkadian sources. As somewhat of a consequence, Richard Hess has noted
that "none of the comparative ancient Near Eastern examples proposed by
scholars actually have a precise parallel with any of the genealogical forms
found in Genesis 1–11."[5] The Old Testament is unique with regard to this
genre as it contains about twenty-five genealogies of varying complexity, a
fact suggesting that genealogy played an important role in Israelite life and
thought.[6]

The Purpose and Function of Biblical Genealogies

In his work, *The Purpose of the Biblical Genealogies*, Marshall Johnson
lists nine separate functions of biblical genealogies. Three of these purposes
are particularly germane to the purpose of the Genesis genealogies. The purpose of genealogies are: (1) to establish and preserve the homogeneity of the
race; (2) to provide the principle of the purpose of the continuity of God's
people during a time of national disruption; and (3) to serve apologetic purposes.[7] Biblical genealogies are closely connected to their contexts and to the
narratives in which they occur.[8] As such they have a literary function that
serves both a rhetorical and theological purpose.

---

3. See Wilson, *Genealogy and History in the Biblical World*, 2.
4. Julius Wellhausen, *Prolegomena to the History of Ancient Israel* (Cleveland and New York:
   Meridian, 1957), 320. Similarly, Martin Noth claimed that biblical genealogies were primarily literary creations. See Wilson, *Genealogy and History in the Biblical World*, 7.
5. Richard Hess, "The Genealogies of Genesis 1–11 and Comparative Literature," in *I Studied
   Inscriptions from before the Flood*, ed. Richard S. Hess and David Toshio Tsumura (Winona
   Lake, Ind: Eisenbrauns, 1994), 59.
6. See Wilson, *Genealogy and History in the Biblical World*, 57; idem, "Genealogy, Genealogies,"
   ABD 2:929–30.
7. See Marshall D. Johnson, *The Purpose of the Biblical Genealogies* (Cambridge: Cambridge
   University Press, 1969), 77–82, 253.
8. *Toledoth* headings (e.g., "generations of") can introduce either narrative sections dealing
   with the principal characters in Genesis (2:4; 6:9; 11:27; 25:19; 37:2) or genealogical lists
   (5:1; 10:1; 11:10; 25:12; 36:1, 9). See T. Desmond Alexander, "Messianic Ideology in the

Literary Features of the Biblical Genealogies
Structural Design
The genealogies in Genesis exhibit several features that exhibit structural designs. This is clearly seen in Genesis 5 where in listing each patriarch we find the repeated formula that is composed of: (1) the patriarch's name, (2) his age at the birth of his first son, (3) the length of his remaining life (with a statement that he begat other children), and (4) his age at death.

After the chapter's introduction giving the setting of this genealogy as the creation of man in God's image (Gen. 5:1b–2), there is a tenfold linear genealogy from Adam to Noah (Gen. 5:3–31) followed by a segmented eleventh generation (Gen. 5:32) that functions as a summary statement. The genealogy in Genesis 5 thus serves to link the first founder of humanity, Adam, with its refounder, Noah.[9]

The genealogy of Genesis 10 differs from previous biblical genealogies that focused on individuals. Now we are given a genealogy of nations. The introductory (Gen. 10:2, 6, 21) and concluding refrains (Gen. 10:5, 20, 31) in connection with each of the three sons of Noah clearly mark off a tripartite arrangement, linking the tribes and nations with Noah's prophecy (Gen. 9:24–27). Allen Ross has noted other tripartite arrangements among these major genealogies in Genesis 1–11, "The genealogy of Cain ends with three sons (Jabal, Jubal, and Tubalcain). The genealogy from Adam to Noah (Gen. 5) includes ten names, and the last person on the list (Noah) has three sons (Shem, Ham, and Japheth). The genealogy from Noah to Terah (Gen. 11) also includes ten names (counting Noah), and the last person on the list (Terah) has three sons as well (Abram, Nahor, and Haran)."[10] Thus, it is beyond doubt that there is a clear structural design in the layout and literary nature of these early genealogies.

Discontinuity
When a context or section demonstrates clearly demarcated patterns, variations in the structure capture our attention. While there are many similarities between the genealogies of Genesis 4 and 5 for example, speeches are attributed to only two of the people listed—the two Lamechs. Lamech the descendant of Cain sang a taunt song of his prowess in killing a youthful warrior, but Lamech the descendant of Seth named Noah in the hope that he would bring people comfort from the pain of the curse (Gen. 5:29).[11] Furthermore, the author digresses from the rigid pattern of

Book of Genesis," in *The Lord's Anointed*, ed. Philip E. Satterthwaite, Richard S. Hess, and Gordon J. Wenham (Grand Rapids: Baker, 1995), 22.

9. See Gordon J. Wenham, *Genesis 1–15*, WBC 1 (Waco, Tex.: Word, 1987), 125.

10. Allen P. Ross, "The Table of Nations in Genesis 10—Its Structure," *BSac* 137 (October–December 1980): 342.

11. See Ross, *Creation and Blessing*, 168. In Genesis 5:29 we find another literary feature, a pun

the structural design of Genesis 5 in three other places—at the beginning with Adam, in the seventh panel with Enoch, and at the end with Noah. Adam is created in God's image (Gen. 5:1–2; see Gen. 1:26–28) while the records of the godly Enoch and Noah do not end with the refrain of death. These individuals thus stand out in the genealogy and receive the focus of attention. Even though we find a tight structural pattern in Genesis 5, the deviations from the pattern get our notice as they alert us to the biblical writer's purpose.

We see further discontinuities in Genesis 10. Within this listing of nations the author shows a special interest in the exact boundaries of the area of Canaan (Gen. 10:19; cf. Num. 34:1–12). This indicates that the land lay at the heart of his purpose in writing the book. This was the land promised to Abraham. Allen Ross has well noted the extra details in describing the land of Canaan in Genesis 10, "[T]he preoccupation with the Canaanites in the land of promise shows the concern of the writer to fit the Table to the message of the book: the fulfillment of God's promise to bless Israel as a nation in that land, and to bless those nations that bless her, and curse those who are antagonistic to her."[12]

The ancestor Eber receives special and unique treatment in Genesis 10. He is not only mentioned out of chronological order (see Gen. 10:21, 24), but he is mentioned even before Shem's sons (Gen. 10:22). The mention of Eber's two sons (Peleg and Joktan) in Genesis 10:25 provides the narrative clue to the structure of Genesis 10 and 11 and, by doing so, is distinctive in the genealogical context. The genealogy of Shem in 10:21–31 is traced from Shem to the sons of Joktan, the brother of Peleg. After the account of the building of the city of Babylon, the genealogy of Shem is taken up again and traced through Peleg to Abraham (Gen. 11:10–26). One line of Shem ends in Babylon and the other in the land with Abraham.[13] These discontinuities within the genealogy appear to indicate that chronology was not the critical consideration in the genealogical lists.

Number Seven

Another literary feature found in biblical genealogies is the preference for the number seven. Enoch, the seventh in Seth's line walks with God (Gen. 5:24), in contrast to the seventh in Cain's line, Lamech, the bigamist and vengeful murderer who boldly sings of his violent deeds (Gen. 4:23–24). In Genesis 11:14–26 we find that the great patriarch Abraham is reckoned as the

---

or play on words as Lamech prophecies that his son Noah (*nuch*) will bring relief (*nchm*) to the world. The similarly sounding words highlight the connection.

12. Ross, "The Table of Nations in Genesis 10—Its Content," 30–31; see Wenham, *Genesis 1–15*, 226; John H. Sailhamer, *The Pentateuch as Narrative* (Grand Rapids: Zondervan, 1992), 133.

13. See John H. Sailhamer, "Genesis," EBC, rev. ed. (Grand Rapids: Zondervan, 2008), 142.

seventh from Eber.[14] In the list of Jacob's sons in Genesis 35:23–26, the order of birth is not chronological so that Joseph can occupy the seventh position. It is also worthy of note that Boaz occupies the seventh position in Ruth 4:18–22. To place Boaz in this esteemed position, the genealogist of Ruth was forced to begin the genealogy not with Judah, the ancient ancestor of the tribe, but with Judah's descendant Perez. Related to the prestige of the number seven in biblical genealogies is the use of "seventy" (7x10), which is the number of the male descendants of Jacob at the end of Genesis (Gen. 46:27; see Deut. 10:22). Thus, the number of the descendants of Israel is equivalent to the number of nations of the world: fourteen from Japheth, thirty from Ham, and twenty-six from Shem (Genesis 10). God assigns the nations their territories (Deut. 32:8; also Amos 9:7) and has determined the times set for them and the exact places where they should live (Acts 17:26).

Outside the Genesis genealogies it is to be noted that Moses was the seventh descendant from Abraham (see Ex. 6:16–20). Moreover, Jesus was the seventy-seventh (7x11) descendant of Adam, while Abraham was the twenty-first (7x3) and David was the thirty-fifth (7x5) (Luke 3:23–38).[15]

Telescoping in Biblical Genealogies

In Exodus 6:12 we read that the Israelites refused to listen to Moses. The author then rather abruptly begins a genealogy of the sons of Jacob (Ex. 6:14–25). Instead of listing all twelve of Jacob's sons, the author stops with Jacob's third son, Levi and his descendants. The truncated genealogy ends with the notation that the Moses and Aaron who are not being followed at this critical time are indeed from the tribe of Levi (see Ex. 6:26). It is clear that the brief genealogical survey was to underline Moses' priestly heritage and thus reinforce his authority over the people. The original genealogy has been intentionally truncated in order to serve a very specific narrative function. In addition, there is further evidence of telescoping in this genealogy as only five generations from Jacob to Moses are mentioned, whereas we know from 1 Chronicles 7:23–27 that there were at least ten generations from Jacob to Moses. This difference illustrates that genealogies were not meant to be exhaustive but were adjusted to serve the author's purpose.

Another example of telescoping occurs in 1 Chronicles 7:13 where Bilhah's grandsons are spoken of as her own sons. Likewise, in Genesis 46:18, the children that Zilpah bore to Jacob include great-grandsons.

We also see a clear example of telescoping in the first chapter of the New Testament, Matthew 1, in the genealogy of Jesus. Matthew 1:8 declares that "Joram was the father of Uzziah." From the Old Testament record of the Judean

---

14. The designation "Hebrew" (Hb. *ivri*; see Gen.14:13) is derived from "Eber" (Hb. *ever*).
15. See Jack M. Sasson, "Generation, Seventh," *IDBS*, 354–356; idem, "A Genealogical 'Convention' in Biblical Chronography?" *ZAW* 90 (1978): 171–85.

kings, however, we find that three generations were omitted by this statement. The actual order is Joram, Ahaziah, Joash, Amaziah, and Uzziah. Joram thus fathered the line that culminated in Uzziah. Similarly, in Matthew 1:11 Josiah is said to be the father of Jechoniah when in fact he was the Jechoniah's grandfather.[16] This use of telescoping in Matthew 1 made it possible to obtain fourteen (2x7) ancestors in each of the three historic "ages." It is once again clear that genealogies were not exclusively created for the purpose of conveying historical information.[17]

Consequently, it is doubtful if the genealogies in chapters 5 and 11 can be used with confidence to construct a comprehensive chronology for the early chapters of Genesis. It is questionable that the sum of these years could be used to arrive at the age of mankind. Genesis 5 is selective in creating its ten-generation depth. The ten-name scheme telescopes the number of descendants but creates what appears to be a comprehensive historical chronology. Further analysis reveals, however, that the genealogies in Genesis 5 and 11 give clear indication that they have been condensed.[18] The same techniques employed in the Genesis genealogies appear to have been used in the genealogy of Jesus in Matthew 1.

Conclusion on Telescoping

As Mitchell and Millard have noted: "There is thus no reason to suppose that all the genealogies in the Bible purport to be complete, since their purpose was more the establishment of descent from some particular ancestor or ancestors, a purpose unaffected by the omission of names, than the reckoning of exact chronologies."[19] Benjamin Warfield noted years ago that it was ex-

---

16. See Wilson, "Genealogy, Genealogies," 932; David M. Howard, *An Introduction to the Old Testament Historical Books* (Chicago: Moody, 1993), 251; Victor P. Hamilton, *The Book of Genesis Chapters 1–17*, NICOT (Grand Rapids: Eerdmans, 1990), 254n.16. The word Hebrew word *ben* ("son") could mean not only son but also "grandson" and "descendant," and in like manner the verb *yalad* could mean not only "bear" in the immediate physical sense but also "become the ancestor of."

17. See Wilson, *Genealogy and History*, 199.

18. See Hamilton, *The Book of Genesis Chapters 1–17*, 254; Kenneth A. Mathews, *Genesis 1–11:26*, NAC 1A (Nashville: B&H, 1996), 302; Kenneth Kitchen, *Ancient Orient and Old Testament* (Chicago: InterVarsity, 1966), 37–38; idem, *The Bible in Its World* (Downers Grove: InterVarsity, 1977), 33.

19. T. C. Mitchell, and Alan R. Millard. "Genealogy," in *NBD*, 3rd ed. (Downers Grove: InterVarsity, 1996), 400. Thus, it may be argued that the inclusion of additional information such as the age of a patriarch at the birth of his descendant as well as how long a patriarch may have lived after the birth (Genesis 5 and 11) does not militate against the view that these genealogies contain abridgements. See W. H. Green, "Primitive Chronology," *BSac* 47 (April 1890): 285–303; reprinted in Walter C. Kaiser, ed., *Classical Essays in Evangelical Old Testament Interpretation* (Grand Rapids: Baker, 1972), 13–28; Mitchell and Millard, "Genealogy," 400. For a well-argued alternative view, see Travis R. Freeman, "Do the Genesis 5 and 11 Genealogies Contain Gaps?" in *Coming to Grips with Genesis*, ed. Terry

tremely precarious to draw chronological inferences from genealogical tables; these genealogies must be valued trustworthy only for the purposes for which they are recorded. They were not recorded to provide a complete record of all the generations through which the descent of the persons to whom they are assigned runs.[20]

Telescoping seems to be the most common way of adjusting Near Eastern genealogies. Recent studies by anthropologists and archaeologists have shown that there were gaps in the genealogical tradition of such regions as the Sudan, Rhodesia, Polynesia, and Arabia.[21]

If No Gaps

If one refuses out of hand to acknowledge that genealogies contain gaps, he would have to affirm that all the events of Genesis 9–11 would occur within three centuries and all of Abraham's ancestors would have been living when he was born. Shem was 450 years old at the time of Abraham's birth and was 525 years old when Abraham began his migration to Canaan. According to the genealogy, if there were no gaps, Shem outlived Abraham by thirty-five years while both Shem and Eber would have been contemporaries with Jacob! In reading the Genesis text, the clear impression is given that the life of Abraham took place many generations after Shem, the son of Noah, had passed off the scene.[22]

Longevity[23]

One perennial issue with regard to the Genesis genealogies has to do with the long life spans of the early antediluvian patriarchs. Because the early biblical individuals live for an incredible and almost unbelievable length of time, the reliability and historicity of the early records themselves have been questioned. First, it should be observed that these long life spans were not unique to the Bible. Other ancient Near Eastern texts attribute even longer lives to earlier generations; e.g., the Sumerian King List mentions eight

Mortenson and Thane H. Ury (Green Forest, Ark.: Master, 2008), 291–92, 305, 308; Samuel R. Külling, *Are the Genealogies in Genesis 5 and 11 Historical and Complete, that is, Without Gaps?* (Riehen, Switzerland: Immanuel-Verlag, 1996); Brevard Childs, *Introduction to the Old Testament As Scripture* (Philadelphia: Fortress, 1979), 146.

20. See Benjamin Breckenridge Warfield, *Biblical and Theological Studies* (Philadelphia: P&R, 1968), 240.

21. See Wilson, *Genealogy and History in the Biblical World*, 133–34; William F. Albright, *The Biblical Period from Abraham to Ezra* (New York: Harper, 1963), 9.

22. See Bruce K. Waltke and Cathi J. Fredricks, *Genesis* (Grand Rapids: Zondervan, 2001), 188; Eugene H. Merrill, "Chronology," in *Dictionary of the Old Testament: Pentateuch*, ed. T. Alexander and David W. Baker (Downers Grove, IL: InterVarsity, 2003), 119–20.

23. The Hebrew Bible, the Septuagint, and the Samaritan Pentateuch differ on the ages of the antediluvians (see Merrill, "Chronology," 116; Ronald S. Hendel, *The Text of Genesis 1–11* [New York, Oxford: Oxford University Press, 1998], 64; Waltke and Fredricks, *Genesis*, 114).

kings who reign for 241,000 years. By contrast the total number of years in Genesis 5 (by comparison) is a modest 1,656 years. Some have suggested that the long life spans of the early patriarchs should be understood as symbolic; or that the numbers are encoded with some unknown significance; or that the figures were calculated by a different numeric method. No writer, however, has offered a convincing explanation, and none of the proposed alternatives can be substantiated with any certainty. The traditional understanding is that the numbers should be taken at face value and assumes that something changed in the cosmology of the earth or in the physiology of humans (or in both) after the flood, that resulted in a rapid decline in longevity. Outside the book of Genesis, only Job (140), Moses (120), Joshua (110), and Jehoida (130) lived longer than a century of years. However, these biblical figures are not to be considered as unhistorical merely because these long life-spans have been attributed to them.[24]

Conclusion

We must conclude that we cannot date with certainty the time of the creation of the world nor of the beginning of mankind based on the examination of the biblical genealogies. The genealogies do not provide complete lists of generations. Furthermore, we do not find in the larger contexts of these genealogies any concern about computing the length of time since creation or the flood like we find in references to the Exodus (Ex. 12:40) or the building of the temple (1 Kings 6:1). The motive for the creating and inserting of the genealogies into the biblical narrative was certainly not a chronological one.[25]

Even though there is evidence of telescoping, gaps, and selection in the biblical chronology of the genealogies, we still have the impression from the biblical genealogies that not an enormous amount of time has passed since the beginning of creation. After an analysis of the gaps and omissions in the Genesis genealogies, Benjamin Warfield still refused to concede that the genealogical record indicated that man came into existence millions of years ago.[26]

---

24. See Kitchen, *Ancient Orient and Old Testament*, 40–41; idem, *The Bible in Its World*, 33; Waltke and Fredericks, *Genesis*, 112; John H. Walton, *Genesis*, NIVAC (Grand Rapids: Zondervan, 2001), 281; Mathews, *Genesis 1–11:26*, 311.
25. See Kenneth Kitchen, *On the Reliability of the Old Testament* (Grand Rapids: Eerdmans, 2003), 441; Warfield, *Biblical and Theological Studies*, 241, 243. At the same time the genealogies do yield a minimum length of time for the period they cover (see Green, "Primitive Chronology," 23–24).
26. Warfield, *Biblical and Theological Studies*, 248.

REFLECTION QUESTIONS

1. What is the difference between a linear genealogy and a segmented genealogy?

2. How do the biblical genealogies compare with those from the ancient Near East?

3. What are the literary features found in biblical genealogies?

4. What is telescoping? How is it relevant to the discussion of the age of the earth?

5. Do biblical genealogies contain gaps? Explain.

What Have Been the Attempts to Determine the Age of the Earth?

Historically, the debate has not been between creation and evolution, but creation and eternalism. During the apostolic and patristic eras, the pagans did not argue simply for an ancient earth, they contended that the universe was eternal. Even though Aristotle believed that the world was caused by God, he did not believe that God created the world in *time*, in the usual understanding of the word "create." God, as the perfect, unchangeable being, did not act in time. Since he is the eternal source of the world, Aristotle reasoned, the cosmos and its elements must also be eternal. Such a view is called *eternalism*. During the first centuries of the church, neo-Platonic philosophers would use Aristotle's arguments to attack the Christian doctrine of creation. For example, in his book, *On the Eternity of the World*, Proclus gives eighteen arguments against creation in favor of an everlasting universe.[1] From biblical times up through the medieval era, the greatest challenge to the doctrine of creation was eternalism.[2]

Eternalism, by its very nature, is fatalistic. The ancient pagans believed that the world operated within an eternal framework of oscillating and recurring cycles. The early cultures—Sumerian, Indian, and Chinese—universally held to the notion of never-ending, repeating, cyclic time. The Babylonians, Persians, and Greeks all held to 36,000-year cycles while the Hindus believed that the cycles were as long as 4.3 million years.[3] The Mayans taught that the world had been created, destroyed, and re-created at least four times, with the

1. Proclus, *On the Eternity of the World,* trans. Helen S. Lang and A. D. Marco (Berkeley: University of California Press, 2001).
2. Pitirim A. Sorokin, *Social and Cultural Dynamics: Fluctuation of Systems of Truth, Ethics, and Law,* vol. 2 (New York: Bedminster, 1962), 211–43; 385–439.
3. John Baillie, *The Belief in Progress* (New York: Charles Scribner's Sons, 1951), 45–47; Sorokin, *Social and Cultural Dynamics,* 415.

last re-creation occurring on February 5, 3112 BC[4] The pagans understood time as a circle rather than an arrow.

Early Christian writers such as Tertullian and Augustine responded to the threat of eternalism by demonstrating that the Bible taught that God created in time and that he created the world *ex nihilo* (i.e., out of nothing).[5] John Philoponus, a sixth century Christian philosopher, exposed the internal inconsistencies of Aristotle's arguments and demonstrated that the notion of a world created in time is more logically tenable than belief in an eternal universe.[6] By the end of the patristic period the doctrine of creation had won the day. However, the resurgence of eternalism accompanied the scientific revolution and the Enlightenment of the seventeenth and eighteenth centuries. This needs to be kept in mind as we survey the attempts to ascertain the universe's age.

The Efforts of Biblical Scholars to Determine the Age of the Earth

Many of the patristic fathers believed 2 Peter 3:8 ("With the Lord a day is like a thousand years, and a thousand years are like a day") taught that the universe would last seven thousand years. They saw the seven days of creation in Genesis 1 as presenting the seven ages of the earth, with each age approximately 1,000 years long. Many believed that they were living in the sixth stage just prior to Jesus's return. They concluded that the earth had been created at approximately 5000 to 5500 BC, and therefore Christ would return sometime between AD 500 and 1000.[7] Theophilus of Antioch (d. 191) placed creation at 5529 BC[8]

However, a number of the early fathers—such as Justin Martyr, Irenaeus, and Augustine—interpreted the seven days of creation in nonliteral terms.[9] Philo, a Jewish philosopher in Alexandria who was a contemporary of Paul, took an allegorical approach to interpreting the Genesis

---

4. Patrick Wyse Jackson, *The Chronologer's Quest: Episodes in the Search for the Age of the Earth* (Cambridge: Cambridge University Press, 2006), 10.
5. Tertullian, *The Treaty against Hermogenes* (New York: Paulist, 1956), 31–48; Augustine, *The City of God against the Pagans* (Cambridge: Cambridge University Press, 1998), 12.14.
6. John Philoponus, *Against Aristotle on the Eternity of the World*, trans. Christian Wildberg (Ithaca, N.Y: Cornell University Press, 1987); Richard Sorabji, *Philoponus and the Rejection of Aristotelian Science* (Ithaca, N.Y: Cornell University Press, 1987).
7. Richard Kyle, *The Last Days Are Here Again: A History of the End Times* (Grand Rapids: Baker, 1998), 37.
8. Theophilus of Antioch, *To Autolycus* 3.28, http://www.ccel.org/ccel/schaff/anf02.iv.ii.iii. xxviii.html (accessed 10/04/12).
9. Justin Martyr, *Dialogue with Trypho* 81, http://www.newadvent.org/fathers/01286.htm (accessed 10/03/12); Irenaeus, *Against the Heresies*, 5.9.23, http://www.newadvent.org/fathers/0103523.htm (accessed 10/03/12); Augustine, *The Literal Meaning of Genesis*, vols. 1 and 2 (New York: Paulist, 1982).

account.[10] Clement of Alexandria and Origen did likewise.[11] Nevertheless, most patristic authors, such as the Cappadocian fathers, took a more literal approach.[12]

For the medieval scholars the age of the earth appears to have been of little concern. The theologians often discussed the nature of the water above the firmament or how light shone during the first three days even though the sun was not created until the fourth, but they gave very little attention to the world's age.[13] The Reformers also gave the question scant attention. For example, both Luther and Calvin held that the world was less than 6,000 years old but neither attempted to work out a chronology.[14] Astronomical issues, such as the validity of the Copernican model of the solar system, garnered more attention.

It is during the post-Reformation era that biblical scholars began the attempt to precisely determine the world's age. They seem to have been driven by eschatological concerns similar to those of the patristic fathers. Many of the early editions of the King James Bible had "4004 BC" listed in the margin of the opening chapter of Genesis. The date was taken from James Ussher's (1580–1656) *Annals of the World* published in 1650. At that time many disagreed with Ussher. At least 140 different contemporaries provided alternative dates, ranging from 3004 BC to 6484 BC[15] Ussher went beyond assigning the year though; he also picked the very day. The cover of *Annals of the World* declares:

> In the beginning God created Heaven and Earth, *Gen. 1. v.* 1.
> Which beginning of time, according to our chronologie, fell
> upon the entrance of the night preceding the twenty third
> day of *Octob*, in the year of the Julian Calendar, 710.[16]

10. Philo, *A Treatise on the Account of the Creation of the World as Given by Moses,* 12–14.
11. Colin Gunton, "Between Allegory and Myth: the Legacy of the Spiritualizing of Genesis" in *The Doctrine of Creation: Essays in Dogmatics, History and Philosophy,* ed. Colin Gunton (Edinburgh: T&T Clark, 1997), 47–62.
12. Peter C. Bouteneff, *Beginnings: Ancient Christian Readings of the Biblical Creation Narratives* (Grand Rapids: Baker, 2008), 121–68. By Cappadocian fathers we mean Basil of Caesarea, Gregory of Nazianzus, and Gregory of Nyssa.
13. One exception appears to have been Robert Grosseteste, the 12th century bishop of Lincoln. He calculated the creation to have occurred around 3997 BC See Jackson, *The Chronologer's Quest,* 15. See also Robert Letham, "'In the Space of Six Days': The Days of Creation from Origen to the Westminster Assembly," *WTJ* 61 (1999): 149–74.
14. Martin Luther, "Lectures on Genesis, Chapters 1–5," in *Luther's Works,* vol. 1 (St. Louis: Concordia, 1958); John Calvin, *Commentaries on the First Book of Moses Called Genesis* (Grand Rapids: Eerdmans, 1948).
15. Jackson, *The Chronologer's Quest,* 14–19; Nicolaas A. Rupke, "Geology and Paleontology," in *Science and Religion: A Historical Introduction,* ed. Gary Ferngren (Baltimore: John Hopkins University Press, 2002), 179–85.
16. Quoted in Jackson, *The Chronologer's Quest,* 24.

In other words, Ussher was saying that creation took place on Saturday, October 22, 4004 BC John Lightfoot (1602–1675) would make the additional claim that Adam was created the following Friday at 9 a.m.[17]

The Enlightenment and the Rise of Naturalistic Theories

The Impact of Newtonian Physics

With the rise of Newtonian physics came the reappearance of eternalism. In the seventeenth century, Isaac Newton (1642–1727) formulated the laws of gravity, physics, and mathematics that successfully described the planetary orbits of the solar system. It would be difficult to overstate the impact his achievements had on the scientific revolution and how western culture viewed the world. Newton's law of gravity stated that each object in the universe exerts an attraction on all other objects. The gravitational force between any two objects is directly proportional to their size and inversely proportional to the distance between them. The law of gravity, thus stated, brings up a problem that was immediately recognized in Newton's day. If there is a universal attraction, why is not everything crunched together? Newton answered that the cosmos must be infinite in extent and content, thus there is no central location to which everything can gather. An infinite universe implies that it has an infinite age. Newton was a devout theist, but the deists of his day argued that his model of the universe seemed to require eternalism.[18] This model would become known as "the steady state cosmology."[19] Later, during the Victorian era, eternalism will play a crucial role in the acceptance of evolution.

The Impact of Modern Geology

Most historians of science consider James Hutton's (1726–1797) publication of *The Theory of the Earth* (1795) to be the birth of modern geology. Hutton argued that nature exhibits the "principle of uniformity," that is, all geological history can be explained by the very same natural, gradual processes we witness today. Hutton proposed *uniformitarianism* as an alternative to *catastrophism* (the view that most of the geological record is the result of catastrophic events, the main event being Noah's flood). Mountains, canyons, and the geological column were formed over great expanses of time. Hutton argued for a theory of the "eternal present" when he declared, "In nature we find no vestige of a beginning,—no prospect of an end."[20] The deists of the Enlightenment would later use Hutton's position as further evidence for eternalism.

---

17. Ibid., 28.
18. Colin Gunton, *The Triune Creator: A Historical and Systematic Study* (Grand Rapids: Eerdmans, 1998), 126–30.
19. Robert Jastrow, *God and the Astronomers* (New York: Warner, 1978), 2–12.
20. Quoted in Davis A. Young and Ralph F. Stearley, *The Bible, Rocks, and Time: Geological Evidence for the Age of the Earth* (Downers Grove: InterVarsity Press, 2008), 88.

Geologists who followed Hutton also argued for a "deep history of time." None were more significant than Charles Lyell (1797–1875), whose writings would have a great impact on Charles Darwin. In his three volume work, *Principles of Geology* (1830–33), Lyell persuasively argued that the geologic column demonstrated that the earth was very old and had changed its form slowly, mainly from conditions such as erosion. His method of dating the ages of rocks by using fossils embedded in the stone as time indicators became the standard practice for geologists. From 1860 to 1914, geologists published over twenty different estimates for the age of the earth, based on various sediment accumulation methods. The estimates ranged from 3 million years to 1.5 billion years.[21]

Acceptance of an Ancient Earth among Christians of the Victorian Era
The Acceptance of an Ancient Earth

Even before Darwin published *On the Origin of Species*, most Christian scholars and scientists had come to accept that the cosmos was ancient. Lord Kelvin (1824–1907), for example, the influential nineteenth century British physicist and devout Christian, calculated the cooling rate of the earth's core to arrive at the conclusion that the planet was 20 to 60 million years old.[22] In America, Princeton theologian B. B. Warfield (1851–1921), who coined the term "biblical inerrancy," accepted the antiquity of both the world and humanity. He argued against using the biblical genealogies to attempt to determine the age of the universe, declaring, "[N]othing can be clearer than that it is precarious in the highest degree to draw chronological inferences from genealogical tables." Warfield concluded, "The question of the antiquity of man is accordingly a purely scientific one, in which the theologian as such has no concern."[23] Both Kelvin and Warfield embraced some form of theistic evolution. According to some sources, by 1850 only 50 percent of American Christians believed in a young earth.[24]

Christian geologists offered a number of alternative explanations to the traditional reading of Genesis in order to allow for the longer ages the geological evidence seemed to require. The two most prominent approaches were the gap theory (also known as the ruin-restoration theory) and the day-age approach.[25] Thomas Chalmers (1780–1847), a Scottish minister and amateur scientist, proposed a gap of indeterminate time between the first two verses

21. Jackson, *The Chronologer's Quest*, 188.
22. Ibid., 197–210.
23. B. B. Warfield, "On the Antiquity and the Unity of the Human Race," in *The Works of Benjamin B. Warfield*, vol. 9 (1932; repr., Grand Rapids: Baker, 2003), 237–45.
24. Ronald L. Numbers, "Cosmogonies," in *Science and Religion: A Historical Introduction*, ed. Gary Ferngren (Baltimore: John Hopkins University Press, 2002), 241–42. See also Terry Mortenson, *The Great Turning Point: The Church's Catastrophic Mistake on Geology—before Darwin* (Green Forest, Ark.: Master, 2004), 33–36.
25. See Questions 11 and 12.

of Genesis. Several prominent nineteenth-century geologists such as William Buckland, Adam Sedgwick, and Edward Hitchcock became advocates of the theory.[26] The great Baptist pastor, Charles Spurgeon, appealed to the gap theory in his preaching:

> Can any man tell me when the beginning was? Years ago we thought the beginning of this world was when Adam came upon it; but we have discovered that thousands of years before that God was preparing chaotic matter to make it a fit abode for man, putting races of creatures upon it, who might die and leave behind the marks of his handiwork and marvelous skill, before he tried his hand on man.[27]

Over the course of the nineteenth century, Christian geologists became less enthusiastic about the gap theory and turned increasingly to the day-age theory, with Scottish geologist Hugh Miller (1802–1856) as its leading proponent.[28] Other geologists who held to the day-age position included Princeton's Arnold Guyot (1804–1887) and Yale's James Dwight Dana (1813–1895).

One other significant concordist theory was developed in the nineteenth century.[29] Though it received little support at the time, it has become perhaps the dominant approach among current young-earth creationists. In 1857, Philip Henry Gosse published *Omphalos*. The title is the Latin word for navel, and it referred to the question of whether or not Adam possessed one. Gosse argued that Adam indeed had a belly button, because he was created as a fully functioning adult male. This functionality gave Adam the appearance of age that he did not in reality have. Similarly, reasoned Gosse, the universe was created fully mature, and this quality gives the world an appearance of age. Practically all current young-earth creationist theories employ the mature creation argument in one way or another. Because of its current significance, we will examine the argument more thoroughly in Question 22. It is worth noting that *Omphalos* was published two years before Darwin published *The Origin of Species*, which demonstrates that the age of the earth had already become an issue before the challenges of evolution came to bear.

---

26. Davis A. Young, "Scripture in the Hands of Geologists (Part Two)," *WTJ* 49 (1987): 262–72.
27. Charles Spurgeon, "Election," http://www.spurgeon.org/sermons/0041.htm (accessed 10/08/12).
28. Young, "Scripture in the Hands of Geologists (Part Two)," 262–72.
29. A "concordist" theory is an attempt to reconcile the creation account in Genesis 1–2 with the findings of the natural sciences. For further discussion see Question 1.

The Implications of Eternalism

While Christians were dealing with the notion of an ancient earth, non-Christians explored the ramifications of an eternal universe. Eternalism played a crucial role in the arguments made for Darwinism by its early advocates. Darwinists conceded that the odds of something as complex as living beings coming about by random chance were extremely low, even minuscule. However, if the cosmos is eternal, then it does not matter how unlikely an event may be. Given an infinite amount of time, if an event has any possibility of happening *at all*—no matter how remote—then inevitably it will happen. In an everlasting universe, it does not matter how many multiplied trillions of years it might take. Eventually every possible scenario will get its day. We are here; so obviously our existence is possible. Therefore, concluded the Darwinists, as absurdly improbable as it is, an eternal and infinite universe renders our evolution inevitable.

Nineteenth century Germany would see some of the most vociferous advocates of Darwinism take eternalism to its logical conclusion. In his *The Riddle of the Universe*, Ernst Haeckel (1834–1919) would argue that an infinite and eternal world means that humanity must abandon the outmoded "ideals of God, freedom, and immortality."[30] Perhaps Fredrich Nietzsche (1844–1900) saw most clearly where eternalism led. He argued for what he called "the eternal recurrence theorem." An infinite universe does not just render our improbable existence inevitable. It means that we have occurred again and again in the past, and we will recur in the future *ad infinitum*. We are caught in an endless loop. Life has no purpose, nor can it have any. Nietzsche embraced *nihilism*, the view that "life leads to nothing" and that existence is "useless, empty, and absurd."[31] However, discoveries and advances in physics and astronomy at the beginning of the next century would overturn both steady-state cosmology and eternalism.

The Modern Era: The Big Bang And Young-Earth Creationism

The twentieth century will see the rise of two completely different paradigms for understanding the age of the earth: the big bang hypothesis and young-earth creationism. Actually, the time can be pinpointed even more closely. Both paradigms will ascend during the 1960s.

---

30. Hans Schwarz, *Creation* (Grand Rapids: Eerdmans, 2002), 19. Schwarz quotes Friedrich Engels as asserting, "We have the certainty that matter remains eternally the same in all its transformations, that none of its attributes can ever be lost" (67).

31. "In infinity, at some moment or other, every possible combination must once have been realized; not only this, but it must once have been realized an infinite number of times. . . . If all possible combinations and relations of forces had not already been exhausted, then an infinity would not yet lie behind us. Now since infinite time must be assumed, no fresh possibility can exist and everything must have appeared already, and moreover an infinite number of times" (Fredrich Nietzsche, quoted in Frank J. Tipler, *The Physics of Immortality: Modern Cosmology, God and the Resurrection of the Dead* [New York: Doubleday, 1994], 74–103).

The Rise of the Big Bang Hypothesis

In 1916, Albert Einstein presented a paper in which he applied his general theory of relativity to the universe as a whole. The results implied that the universe had a beginning—a conclusion that Einstein himself resisted. In the 1930s, astronomer Edwin Hubble demonstrated that the universe appeared to be expanding. He noticed that the light from all neighboring galaxies is red-shifted, which indicates that those galaxies are rapidly moving away from us. The galaxies appear to be like dots on an expanding balloon. As the balloon fills with air, the surface becomes larger and the dots move farther and farther away from one another. Hubble concluded that something similar appears to be happening to all the galaxies. Evidence was building that the cosmos is not eternal.

In 1965 Arno Penzias and Robert Wilson discovered that the universe is bathed in faint, background radiation. This radiation indicated that there was a universal fiery explosion that was calculated to have occurred 13.7 billion years ago. For most astronomers and astrophysicists, Penzias and Wilson's discovery provided the crucial evidence that confirmed the big bang hypothesis. From the 1960s on, the big bang theory has been the reigning paradigm within the scientific community.[32]

Robert Jastrow recounts how most physicists and astronomers initially were hostile to the big bang theory. In fact, the expression "big bang" was a term of derision coined by astronomer Fred Hoyle, who remained a lifelong proponent of eternalism. Astronomer Arthur Eddington declared in 1931, "[T]he notion of a beginning is repugnant to me."[33] Chemist Walter Nernst argued that adherence to eternalism was necessary when he wrote, "To deny the infinite duration of time would be to betray the very foundation of science."[34] Jastrow points out that such opposition was motivated by philosophical presuppositions rather than scientific evidence. He ends his book on the subject with the now well-known observation:

> For the scientist who has lived by his faith in the power of reason, the story ends like a bad dream. He has scaled the mountains of ignorance; he is about to conquer the highest peak; as he pulls himself over the final rock, he is greeted by a band of theologians who have been sitting there for centuries.[35]

---

32. This does not mean that there is universal acceptance. In 2004, thirty-three scientists published a letter in *New Scientist* which expressed skepticism about the big bang hypothesis and complained that adherents of the steady state view are not receiving comparable research funding (see http://www.cosmologystatement.org [accessed 10/06/12]).
33. Jastrow, *God and the Astronomers*, 102.
34. Ibid., 103.
35. Ibid., 105–6.

Many who accept the big bang theory have not given up on eternalism. A number of cosmologists now suggest that our universe is part of a multiverse (i.e., reality is made up of an infinite number of universes, of which our universe is just one).[36]

The Rise of Young-Earth Creationism

As we noted earlier, most Christians, including evangelicals, accepted the view that the universe was millions and perhaps billions of years old. This is true up through the first half of the twentieth century. R. A. Torrey (1856–1928), who helped to found both Moody Bible Institute and Biola University and who edited a series of books called *The Fundamentals* (from which we get the term "fundamentalist"), held to the gap theory. Even William Jennings Bryan, of the Scopes Monkey Trials fame, held to a day-age interpretation of Genesis 1.

Two of the most ardent anti-evolutionists of the twentieth century were W. B. Riley (1861–1947) and Harry Rimmer (1890–1952). Riley, editor of *The Christian Fundamentalist* and president of the Anti-Evolution League of America, held to the day-age position. Riley insisted that there was not "an intelligent fundamentalist who claims that the earth was made six thousand years ago; and the Bible never taught any such thing."[37] Rimmer, a self-educated layman and apologist known for his debating skills, held to the gap theory. In a celebrated series of debates, the two men argued for their respective positions with Rimmer generally considered to have been the victor.[38]

Until 1960, the view that the proper interpretation of Genesis requires that the earth be less than 10,000 years old was advocated almost exclusively by George McCready Price, an apologist for Seventh-Day Adventists. Seventh-Day Adventists believe that the writings of their denomination's founder, Ellen G. White, are divinely inspired and are to be treated as Scripture. White claimed she received a vision in which God carried her back to the original week of creation. There, she said, God showed her that the original week was seven days like any other week.[39] Price worked tirelessly to defend White's position as the only view that did not compromise biblical authority.

In 1961, John Whitcomb (1924–) and Henry Morris (1918–2006) published *The Genesis Flood,* which has sold over 300,000 copies and launched

---

36. See Martin Rees, "Other Universes: A Scientific Perspective," in *God and Design: The Teleological Argument and Modern Science,* ed. Neil A. Manson (New York: Routledge, 2003), 211–20; Steven Weinberg, "Living in the Multiverse," in *The Nature of Nature: Examining the Role of Naturalism in Science,* ed. Bruce L. Gordon and William A. Dembski (Wilmington: ISI Books, 2011), 547–57.
37. Quoted in Ronald Numbers, *The Creationists* (New York: Alfred Knopf, 1992), 45.
38. Ibid., 66–72.
39. Ibid., 73–79.

the modern creationist movement.[40] Whitcomb and Morris argued that Ussher's approach to determining the age of the universe was generally sound and that the universe must be less than 10,000 years old. Combining flood geology with the mature creation hypothesis, *The Genesis Flood* presented a compelling case for young-earth creationism. It would be difficult to exaggerate this book's impact in shaping evangelical attitudes toward the question of the age of the earth. In many circles, adherence to a young earth is a point of orthodoxy.[41]

Conclusion

The debate between creation and eternalism continues. The big bang hypothesis gives strong support to the notion of the universe having a beginning. Some Christians welcome this development while others point out that the hypothesis also posits this beginning to have occurred over 13 billion years ago. Evangelicals are divided as to whether the big bang scenario can be reconciled with the Genesis creation account and subsequent genealogies. The particular issues in that discussion are the topics of the next four questions.

REFLECTION QUESTIONS

1. What are the implications of the pagan idea of eternalism?

2. What scientific developments during the Enlightenment led to an acceptance of an eternal universe?

3. What is the eternal recurrence theorem and what are its implications?

4. Why did Einstein and many other scientists of his day resist the evidence that the universe had a beginning?

5. What two events in the 1960s produced two conflicting views of the age of the world?

---

40. John Whitcomb and Henry Morris, *The Genesis Flood: The Biblical Record and Its Scientific Implications* (Phillipsburg: P&R, 1961).
41. For example, Liberty University affirms that the "universe was created in six historical days" as part of its doctrinal statement (http://www.liberty.edu/index.cfm?PID=6907 [accessed 10/09/12]).

What Are the Evidences that the Universe Is Young?

When making the case for a young earth, advocates of young-earth creationism (YEC) give three lines of arguments: (1) the biblical witness, (2) the theological implications, and (3) the empirical evidence. When considering the biblical witness, YEC proponents point out that a straightforward reading of the creation and fall in Genesis 1–3, the genealogies provided in Genesis 4–5, and the scope and effects of the flood in Genesis 6–9 all appear to indicate a world of recent origin. Theologically, YEC advocates argue that old-earth creationism (OEC) undermines the authority of Scripture, that OEC would mean that death and disease existed prior to the fall, that OEC threatens the Adam/Christ correlation made by the New Testament (Rom. 5; 1 Cor. 15), and that OEC impugns the character of God. The biblical and theological arguments are covered in other chapters,[1] while this chapter focuses on the scientific and physical evidences presented by YEC proponents.

The Inherent Limitations in Doing Origins Science

YEC adherents distinguish between origins science and operational science.[2] Origins science is understood to be the attempt to answer "a history question using science," namely the history of the world's origin. Operational science, by contrast, studies the ongoing functions, properties, and relations of the physical world. Kurt Wise argues that, while we have the cognitive and empirical tools available for operations science, humans do not

---

1. See Question 26 ("Was There Animal Death before the Fall?") and Question 27 ("What Effect Did the Fall Have on Creation?").
2. Tim Chaffey and Jason Lisle, *Old Earth Creationism on Trial: The Verdict Is In* (Green Forest: Master, 2008), 111–14, 121.

have the ability to do origin science.[3] Why is this? Wise gives three reasons. First, simply put, we were not there. Second, our physical limitations severely impede our investigations. Third (and perhaps most importantly), we are hindered by the effects of the fall. The fall further limited our already finite physical and mental capacities, and now humanity's moral inclinations are predisposed against God. For these reasons, Christians, submitting to the authority of Scripture, must start with the presupposition of a young earth and then interpret the empirical evidence in the light of the biblical witness.

The Scientific Evidences for a Young Earth

Paul Garner lists three lines of evidence for a young earth: (1) evidences in the solar system, (2) evidences in the earth, and (3) evidences in the human race. We will use his categories as we look at representative arguments which seem to be the most employed by Garner and other YEC proponents.[4]

Astronomical Evidences

YEC proponents point to a number of phenomena indicating the cosmos may be young. Four evidences stand out:

- *The shallowness of the moon dust.* If the moon were billions of years old, its layers of dust should be much deeper.[5] Prior to the Apollo space program, the depth of meteoric dust was predicted to be anywhere from 50 to 180 feet thick. Astronauts found instead the levels to range from 2 to 13 feet.

- *The changing temperature of the sun.* Some YEC proponents point to evidence that the sun appears to be shrinking at a rate of .01 percent per century.[6] Extrapolated backwards, this means that billions of years ago the sun would have been too hot for life on earth. Other YEC advocates point to evidence of the opposite problem, called the "faint sun paradox." Thermonuclear theory predicts that 3.5 billion years ago the sun was too cool to keep the earth from freezing.[7]

---

3. Kurt Wise, *Faith, Form, and Time: What the Bible Teaches and Science Confirms about Creation and the Age of the Universe* (Nashville: B&H, 2002), 3–4.
4. Paul Garner, *The New Creationism: Building Scientific Theories on a Biblical Foundation* (Webster: Evangelical, 2009), 105–17.
5. Paul D. Ackerman, *It's a Young World after All: Exciting Evidences for Recent Creation* (Grand Rapids: Baker, 1986), 15–25.
6. Ibid., 55–65.
7. Danny Faulkner, "No. 4: Faint Sun Paradox (The 10 Best Evidences from Science that Confirm a Young Earth)," *Answers* 7, no. 4 (October-December 2012): 51.

- *The short life span of comets.* Comets burn off material every time they pass the sun. They cannot survive billions of years. Their burn rates prove their recent age.[8]

- *The delicate nature of planetary rings.* Saturn's rings are composed of dust and ice. The maximum life span for these rings appears to be only in the thousands of years.[9]

Geological Evidences

The Genesis flood figures prominently in the arguments made by YEC advocates. This may explain why they appear to place more emphasis on geological evidences than astronomical evidences. Eight arguments can be noted:

- *The salt levels in the ocean.* Over 450 million tons of sodium enters the oceans every year, but only about 120 million tons are removed annually by natural processes.[10] If the oceans were three billion years old (as taught in standard geological texts) then the level of saline in the ocean should be much higher.

- *The sediment levels in the ocean.* "If sediments have been accumulating on the seafloor for three billion years, the seafloor should be choked with sediment many miles deep."[11] Yet the sedimentary depth is less than one-quarter mile.

- *The erosion rates of the continents.* The standard model holds that the continents are 3.5 billion years old. Twenty billion tons of sediment is carried into the ocean annually. This rate is fast enough to have leveled the continents 340 times in the time allotted by the standard model.[12]

- *The decaying magnetic field.* Earth's magnetic field is quickly wearing down. Given the current rate of decay, it cannot be more than 20,000 years old.[13]

---

8. Danny Faulkner, "No. 8: Short-lived Comets (The 10 Best Evidences from Science that Confirm a Young Earth)," *Answers* 7, no. 4 (October-December 2012): 55.

9. Garner, *The New Creationism*, 110.

10. Ibid., 112–13; also see Andrew Snelling, "No. 9: Very Little Salt in the Sea (The 10 Best Evidences from Science that Confirm a Young Earth)," *Answers* 7, no. 4 (October-December 2012): 56.

11. Andrew Snelling, "No. 1: Very Little Sediment on the Seafloor (The 10 Best Evidences from Science that Confirm a Young Earth)," *Answers* 7, no. 4 (October-December 2012): 47.

12. Garner, *The New Creationism*, 114–15.

13. Andrew Snelling, "No. 5: Rapidly Decaying Magnetic Field (The 10 Best Evidences from Science that Confirm a Young Earth)," *Answers* 7, no. 4 (October-December 2012): 52.

- *The presence of carbon 14 in fossils and coal.* Carbon 14 has a relatively short half-life of 5,730 years, so it should not be present in fossils that are more than a few hundred thousand years old. Yet carbon 14 has been detected in fossils and coal that are supposedly millions of years old.[14]

- *The inconsistencies in radiometric dating.* Geologists use a number of methods when attempting to determine the date of geological formations. The most common techniques are the potassium-argon method and the uranium-lead method. YEC adherents claim that radiometric testing is based on questionable assumptions and has resulted in readings that are demonstrably wrong. Tests done on rocks that were formed in recent volcanic eruptions have produced results declaring the rocks to be millions of years old.[15]

- *The soft tissue in fossils.* YEC adherents contend that almost all fossils contained in the geological record were created during Noah's flood. They point to the recent discovery of the remnants of blood vessels and protein collagens in a *Tyrannosaurus Rex* fossil.[16] Fossils deposited 65 million years ago could not still have soft remains.

A central feature to YEC is the argument that the preponderance of geological features on the surface of the earth is the result of the flood recorded in Genesis 6–9. Whether Noah's flood was worldwide or regional is such a crucial question that we devote Questions 30 and 31 to addressing this issue.

Population Evidence

Seven billion people presently live today. The human population grows at a rate of approximately 1.14 percent. Even if one assumes a growth rate of only 0.5 percent, the time it would take for the population to grow from two to seven billion is around 4,000 years. If humans had been around for over a million years then the population would be exponentially greater than what it is today. The present population and growth rate points to a recent origin of the human race.[17]

---

14. Andrew Snelling, "No. 7: Carbon-14 in Fossils, Coal, and Diamonds (The 10 Best Evidences from Science that Confirm a Young Earth)," *Answers* 7, no. 4 (October-December 2012): 54–55.
15. Chaffey and Lisle, *Old Earth Creationism on Trial*, 131–36.
16. David Menton, "No. 3: Soft Tissue in Fossils (The 10 Best Evidences from Science that Confirm a Young Earth)," *Answers* 7, no. 4 (October-December, 2012): 50.
17. Garner, *The New Creationism*, 116.

The Responses by Old-Earth Adherents
Criticisms in General

Opponents of the YEC position criticize both the evidence set forth by YEC advocates and the way they approach the evidence. They accuse YEC advocates of "cherry picking," that is, selecting the few examples that might possibly bolster their position while ignoring the preponderance of data that goes against their view. Opponents have pointed out the failure of many of YEC arguments. A number of the examples set forth in the 1960s and 70s, during the early days of the YEC movement, have not fared well. As Fowler and Kuebler observe, in this area YEC proponents have "a tough row to hoe."[18]

John Collins chides the YEC proponents for taking a "haphazard" approach to the empirical evidence. If certain evidence seems to bolster the YEC position, then it is taken at face value. If it points to an ancient universe, then the evidence is either dismissed as invalid or it is claimed to have been created with the appearance of age.[19] Such an approach is in danger of being anti-science and even anti-realism. Old-earth adherents have provided replies to each of the arguments given in the previous section. To the credit of some YEC organizations, such as Answers in Genesis (AIG), they recognize that there are reasonable old-earth answers to the evidences they present. AIG has acknowledged these answers and, in some cases, has withdrawn some arguments altogether.

Replies to Astronomical Arguments

- *The shallowness of the moon dust.* In an article entitled "Far Out Claims about Astronomy," AIG acknowledged that the level of moon dust does not support the young earth position. Past rates of accumulation are unknown, so therefore "moon dust cannot be used as an age indicator one way or the other."[20]

- *The changing temperature of the sun.* Hugh Ross replies that these objections overlook significant data. When the oscillating nature of the sun is taken into account, along with the variations in the earth's atmosphere, then these objections disappear.[21]

---

18. Thomas Fowler and Daniel Kuebler, *The Evolution Controversy: A Survey of Competing Theories* (Grand Rapids, 2007), 194–96.

19. We examine the appearance of age theory or mature creation argument exclusively in Question 22.

20. http://www.answersingenesis.org/articles/am/v3/n1/far-out-claims (accessed 10/13/12).

21. Hugh Ross, *A Matter of Days: Resolving a Creation Controversy* (Colorado Springs, NavPress, 2004), 190–92; Faulkner, "No. 4: Faint Sun Paradox," 51. See also http://www.sciencedaily.com/releases/2010/03/100331141415.htm (accessed 10/13/12).

- *The short life span of comets.* Ross replies, "Comets not only last much longer but they are also vastly more abundant than young-earth proponents presume."[22] The Kohoutek comet orbits the sun every 80,000 years, while orbits of other comets are calculated in the millions of years with life spans in the billions of years.

- *The delicate nature of planetary rings.* NASA scientists admit they do not know the age of Saturn's rings.[23] However, even if the rings were shown to be young, that would not indicate that the planet was too. Like the moon dust, Saturn's rings do not tell us how old the universe is.

Reply to Geological Arguments

- *The salt levels in the ocean.* The argument assumes that at present the ocean is getting saltier. Yet there is no evidence this is the case. It appears that salt levels in the ocean have fluctuated over time. Geologists do not use the ocean's saline content as a means to determine the earth's age.[24]

- *The sediment levels in the ocean.* Sediment levels are uneven. At the mid-Atlantic range (where new ocean floor is being formed), the level is relatively shallow. At some places in the continental margins, the sediment measures thousands of feet thick, which is in keeping with the old-earth model.[25]

- *The erosion rates of the continents.* This objection fails to take into account the rate of tectonic uplift that equals and often exceeds the rate of erosion. The Himalayas mountain range, for example, is presently rising faster than it is eroding.[26]

- *The decaying magnetic field.* The magnetic field is not decaying, rather it is oscillating. The earth periodically reverses polarity. This is actually evidence for an ancient earth, since these reversals can be demonstrated to have happened.[27]

---

22. Ross, *A Matter of Days,* 201; see also Faulkner, "No. 8: Short-lived Comets," 55–56.
23. http://saturn.jpl.nasa.gov/science/index.cfm?SciencePageID=57 (accessed 10/13/12).
24. Snelling, "No. 9: Very Little Salt in the Sea," 56. See also http://thenaturalhistorian. com/2012/09/08/salty-sea-part-3-young-earth-creationism/ (accessed 10/13/12).
25. Snelling, "No. 1: Very Little Sediment on the Seafloor," 47–48. See also http://www.usd. edu/esci/age/content/creationist_clocks/ocean_floor_sediment.html (accessed 10/13/12).
26. Ross, *A Matter of Days,* 186–87.
27. Ibid., 189–90; Snelling, "No. 5: Rapidly Decaying Magnetic Field," 52.

- *The presence of carbon 14 in fossils and coal.* Ancient coal deposits contain minute levels of uranium. When uranium decays one of the things it produces is carbon 14.[28] Finding carbon 14 in fossils and coal deposits is not unexpected.

- *The inconsistencies in radiometric dating.* Presently there are more than forty different radiometric methods. Their findings show a remarkable level of convergence. Inaccuracies occur only when tests are applied outside their respective limitations. Discordant dates are explained by contamination and sample size.[29]

- *The soft tissue in fossils.* The debate surrounding the discovery of soft tissue in a *Tyrannosaurus Rex* fossil is ongoing. Some scientists dispute the finding altogether, while others suggest that certain proteins can survive the normal decay process. However, at this point the evidence does seem to indicate that the organic remains are genuine.[30]

Reply to the Population Argument

The argument depends on the assumption that the population has always increased on a reasonably consistent manner. Certain historical events show that this is an unwarranted assumption. For example, Europe's population decreased by a third during the black plague of the fourteenth century. However, even though OEC proponents believe the earth is ancient, they agree with YEC adherents that humans have been on the earth for only thousands of years.

The Lack of Scientific Evidence for a Young Earth

A Candid Admission

Many thoughtful YEC proponents admit that the physical, empirical evidence for a young earth is weak. While making the case for recent creationism, Nelson and Reynolds candidly admitted:

> Presently, we can admit that as recent creationists we are defending a very natural biblical account, at the cost of abandoning a very plausible scientific picture of an "old" cosmos. . . . In our opinion, old earth creationism combines a less natural textual reading with a much more plausible scientific vision. They have

28. Snelling, "No. 7: Carbon-14 in Fossils, Coal, and Diamonds," 54–55. See also http://www.c14dating.com/corr.html (accessed 10/13/12).
29. Ross, *A Matter of Days,* 175–79, 194–95.
30. Kate Wong, "Molecular Analysis Supports Controversial Claim for Dinosaur Cells," http://blogs.scientificamerican.com/observations/2012/10/18/molecular-analysis-supports-controversial-claim-for-dinosaur-cells/ (accessed 11/06/12).

many fewer "problems of science." At the moment, this would seem the more rational position to adopt.[31]

Similarly, paleontologist and YEC proponent Kurt Wise concedes that there are "many different indicators that the universe is old" while there are only "a few indicators that suggest the creation is only thousands of years old."[32]

Arguments that Have Been Abandoned

It must be recognized that many of the initial arguments made for YEC have been abandoned by proponents. John Whitcomb and Henry Morris' book, *The Genesis Flood*, launched the modern creationist movement.[33] However, many of its key arguments have not stood the test of time. Without naming *The Genesis Flood*, an Answers in Genesis blog post entitled "Arguments We Don't Use" concedes that many of the book's central claims have been disproved.[34] Examples are numerous. Whitcomb and Morris argued that the world was originally created with a vapor canopy which supplied the water for Noah's flood. But such a canopy would have a greenhouse effect that would cause the temperature on earth to be intolerably hot.[35] They suggested that we can see the light from other galaxies because the universe is actually very small, or because light is able to take a shortcut through space.[36] Whitcomb and Morris based their claim on an article that some say was a spoof.[37] They suggested that the second law of thermodynamics (entropy) was the curse of the fall. However, Adam and Eve's digestive tracts would not have worked without the second law being in force (nor would practically anything else have worked, for that matter).[38]

The real "bombshell" of the book was the claim that human and dinosaur footprints had been found side-by-side in the Paluxy River bed near

---

31. Paul Nelson and John Mark Reynolds, "Young Earth Creationism," in *Three Views on Creation and Evolution*, ed. J. P. Moreland and John Mark Reynolds (Grand Rapids: Zondervan, 1999), 73.

32. Wise, *Faith, Form, and Time*, 70–71.

33. http://www.answersingenesis.org/articles/2005/09/14/the-genesis-flood-pt1 (accessed 10/12/12).

34. http://www.answersingenesis.org/get-answers/topic/arguments-we-dont-use (accessed 10/12/12). John Collins observes that perhaps the article should have been entitled "Arguments We *No Longer* Use" (see John Collins, *Science and Faith: Friends or Foes?* [Wheaton: Crossway, 2003], 239).

35. http://www.answersingenesis.org/home/area/tools/flood-waters.asp (accessed 10/12/12).

36. John Whitcomb and Henry Morris, *The Genesis Flood: The Biblical Record and Its Scientific Implications*, 1st ed. (Philadelphia: P&R, 1961), 370. Later editions have removed the claim.

37. Robert Schadewald, "Moon and Spencer and the Small Universe," *Creation Evolution Journal* 2, no. 2 (Spring 1981): 20–22.

38. http://www.answersingenesis.org/get-answers/topic/arguments-we-dont-use (accessed 10/12/12).

Glen Rose, Texas. The assertion created a sensation and helped to make *The Genesis Flood* a bestseller. YEC advocates now recognize that the footprints were a hoax.[39]

The RATE Project

From 1997 to 2005, a team of YEC scientists conducted a series of rigorous geological tests for the purpose of challenging the validity of radiometric methods for dating rock samples. The endeavor was called the RATE Project (Radioisotopes and the Age of The Earth).[40] They argued that the conflicting results from the different radiometric methods demonstrated their unreliability. However, they conceded that their tests showed that over 500 million years worth of radioactive decay has occurred. This posed a real dilemma. The project's own tests pointed to an ancient earth. At this point the group's operating presupposition kicked in: "One principle agreed on by all the RATE members is that the earth is young, on the order of 6,000 years old. This is not simply a working hypothesis to be tested as to whether it is true or false."[41] The project group therefore concluded that the radioactive decay rate must have been a billion times faster during the creation week and Noah's flood. However, the group conceded that such a phenomenon would violate all known scientific laws and would have had the side-effect of vaporizing the earth. If the RATE group's starting assumptions were impervious to empirical results, then what was the purpose of doing the tests?

The response from critics of the RATE Project has ranged from harsh to dismissive. Randy Isaac, executive director of the American Scientific Affiliation, denounced the conclusions as deceptive and lacking in integrity.[42] In his assessment of the project, Charles Foster concludes, "Being as kind as possible, it is impossible not to note that the creationist ideas about the age of the earth are contradicted by every single piece of evidence available."[43]

A Tacit Admission

As the results of the RATE Project indicate, YEC proponents are finding it necessary to argue that the early universe operated under a radically different set of natural laws. Andrew Snelling, a YEC geologist and member of the RATE Project, argued that special supernatural laws were in effect during the creation week. He concludes, "What is clear from the biblical record is that

---

39. http://www.icr.org/article/paluxy-river-mystery/ (accessed 10/12/12).

40. Don DeYoung, *Thousands . . . Not Billions* (Green Forest: Master, 2005).

41. Ibid., 174.

42. Randy Isaac, "Assessing the RATE Project," *Perspectives in Science and Christian Faith,* 59, no. 2 (June 2007): 143–46.

43. Charles Foster, *The Selfless Gene: Living with God and Darwin* (Nashville: Thomas Nelson, 2009), 48.

the perception of a human observer on the earth during the Creation Week would have been that countless millions of years of earth history at uniformitarian rates had been compressed into six days of normal human existence."[44] He argues that similar phenomena occurred during the year of Noah's flood.[45] The other tack taken by Snelling and other YEC adherents is to appeal to "mature creation" hypothesis (i.e., the universe was created with the appearance of age). We will devote Question 22 to addressing this question.

Critics of YEC contend that appeals to changes in the laws of nature and to the appearance of age are tacit admissions that the empirical evidence is against the young-earth model. Davis Young and Ralph Stearley, old-earth proponents, call on YEC advocates to give up attempts to scientifically prove the universe is young. They admonish, "The only recourse that [YEC advocates] have to save the theory is to appeal to pure miracle and thus eliminate entirely the possibility of historical geology. We think that would be a more honest course of action for young-earth advocates to take."[46]

In the 1960s and 70s, during the early days of the modern creationist movement, YEC proponents referred to their position as *scientific creationism*. Henry Morris, the movement's founder, contended that an unbiased examination of the scientific evidence would lead one to the young-earth view. The YEC model has the virtue of (1) being simpler, (2) being more consistent, (3) being "more effective in correlating the available data," (4) "fitting the observed facts," and (5) "provid[ing] the only basis for real meaning in life."[47] Today, most YEC advocates no longer use the label *scientific creationism* to describe their position. John Morris, Henry Morris' son and successor, has admitted that he knows of no scientist who has embraced a young earth on the basis of the empirical evidence alone.[48]

Conclusion

Young-earth creationists admit that they find themselves in a very difficult position. They concede that the empirical case for a young earth is weak. YEC proponents Nelson and Reynolds admit, "Recent creationists should humbly agree that their view is, at the moment, implausible on purely

---

44. Snelling, 2:468. See also 614, 629, 639.
45. Ibid., 847. "Thus, it is concluded that hundreds of millions of years worth of radioisotope decay (at today's measured rates) must have occurred during the Flood year, only about 4,500 years ago."
46. Davis A. Young and Ralph F. Stearley, *The Bible, Rocks, and Time* (Downers Grove: InterVarsity, 2008), 474.
47. William Lane Craig, "Evangelicals and Evolution: An Analysis of the Debate between the Creation Research Society and the American Scientific Affiliation," *JETS* 17, no. 3 (Summer 1974): 135–36.
48. Ross, *A Matter of Days*, 206.

scientific grounds."[49] They believe the biblical case for a young earth is strong, but an empirical case is not. YEC proponents see this situation to be a fulfillment of 2 Peter 3:3–7. They understand Peter to be predicting that a scientific apostasy would occur that embraces a uniformitarian understanding of nature and a rejection of Noah's worldwide flood. We will examine the extent of Noah's flood in Questions 30 and 31. Some evangelical leaders see the age of the earth as a hill on which to die. Others disagree.[50] We have not yet examined what is perhaps the primary or strongest argument for a young universe; the mature creation or appearance of age theory. We have devoted Question 22 to examining this theory.

REFLECTION QUESTIONS

1. What are implications of the YEC distinction between origins science and operations science?

2. What do OEC proponents mean when they accuse YEC advocates of "cherry-picking"?

3. Which of the empirical evidences seem to support most strongly the YEC position? The OEC position?

4. How significant is the admission by many YEC proponents that the scientific evidence for a young earth is weak? Explain.

5. What role did presuppositions play in the YEC interpretation of the RATE project's results?

---

49. Nelson and Reynolds, "Young Earth Creationism," 51.
50. John MacArthur is an example of the former and Wayne Grudem is an example of the latter. See John MacArthur, *The Battle for the Beginning: Creation, Evolution, and the Bible* (Nashville: Nelson, 2001), 18–19; Wayne Grudem, *Systematic Theology* (Grand Rapids: Zondervan, 1994), 307–8.

What Are the Evidences that the Universe Is Old?

Most scientists accept that the universe is approximately 13.7 billion years old and that the earth is about 4.5 billion years old. A very strong cumulative case can be made for an ancient universe. Even many (if not most) young-earth creationism (YEC) proponents admit this. But they are convinced that a correct interpretation of Genesis 1–11 requires adherence to a young earth. This conviction leads them to reject the scientific consensus, no matter how compelling that consensus may appear to be.[1] Ken Ham probably speaks for most YEC advocates when he describes acceptance of an old earth as a "virus" that is "responsible for the 'death' of many church members."[2]

Nevertheless, the list of prominent Christians who embrace old-earth creationism (OEC) is impressive. Statesmen such as Billy Graham, C. S. Lewis, and Francis Schaeffer accept or accepted an ancient earth. Theologians such as J. I. Packer, Wayne Grudem, and Millard Erickson affirm OEC. Norman Geisler, William Lane Craig, Alvin Plantinga, and numerous other Christian philosophers all believe the earth is ancient. Pastors such as John Piper and Tim Keller hold to an ancient earth. In addition, many Old Testament scholars—including Walter Kaiser, John Sailhamer, and C. John Collins—adhere to an old universe.

As we noted in Question 18, virtually all early fundamentalist and evangelical leaders held to an ancient earth.[3] For example, B. B. Warfield, who coined the term "biblical inerrancy," held to theistic evolution. R. A. Torrey,

---

1. See the discussion in Question 1 on the distinction between presuppositionalism and fideism.
2. Ken Ham, "Eisegesis: A Genesis Virus," http://www.answersingenesis.org/articles/cm/v24/n3/eisegesis. (accessed 11/01/12).
3. Ronald Numbers, *The Creationists: The Evolution of Scientific Creationism* (New York: Knopf, 1992).

who helped to found both Moody Bible Institute and BIOLA, and who edited The Fundamentals (from which we get the term "fundamentalist"), held to the gap theory. In a celebrated debate over the creation account in Genesis between two early noted fundamentalists, W. B. Riley and Harry Rimmer, neither advocated young-earth creationism. Even William Jennings Bryan, of the Scopes Monkey Trials fame, held to a day-age interpretation of Genesis 1. The accusation that adherence to an ancient earth produces "spiritual death" appears to be unfounded.

Scripture and the Age of the Earth

Advocates of old-earth creationism (OEC) generally approach the relationship of Scripture and the age of the earth in one of four ways. Some, including David Snoke, concede that the scientific evidence has affected the way in which they interpret the Genesis creation account. But they claim they have good warrant for doing so, and they are still submitting to Scripture as the final authority.[4] Others, such as Mark Wharton, contend that the Genesis account can be reasonably interpreted from an OEC perspective, even if the YEC approach may be the more natural interpretation.[5] Still others, such as John Walton, argue that the Genesis account does not speak to the age of the earth, so the believer is free to follow the empirical evidence of the subject wherever it may lead.[6] Finally, some OEC proponents, such John Lennox, contend that the Genesis account gives evidence that long periods of time were involved. Therefore the biblical record itself leads the believer to expect evidences of an ancient cosmos.[7]

What should be the definition of "old?" Since YEC teaches that earth cannot be much more than 6,000 years old, then for the purposes of this chapter any evidence that points to an age beyond 4000 BC will be viewed as pointing to an "old earth." Other chapters look at the attempts to provide interpretations of the

---

4. David Snoke, *A Biblical Case for an Old Earth* (Grand Rapids: Baker, 2006). "At the very outset, let me say that my experience in science has affected my interpretation of the Bible. . . . I believe that an old-earth view is compatible with the Bible. Nevertheless, I admit that my interpretation is a 'possible' one, not an 'obvious' one" (11–12). See also Davis Young, "Where Are We? Perceived Tensions between Biblical and Scientific Cosmogonies," in *Portraits of Creation: Biblical and Scientific Perspectives on the World's Formation*, ed. Howard J. Van Till, et al. (Grand Rapids: Eerdmans, 1990), 1–4.
5. Mark Whorton, *Peril in Paradise: Theology, Science, and the Age of the Earth* (Waynesboro: Authentic Media, 2005), 11–12.
6. John Walton, *The Lost World of Genesis One: Ancient Cosmology and the Origins Debate* (Downers Grove: InterVarsity), 94.
7. John Lennox, *Seven Days that Divide the World: The Beginning According to Genesis and Science* (Grand Rapids: Zondervan, 2011), 39–63. Lewis and Demarest agree, declaring, "Ultimately, responsible geology must determine the length of the Genesis days, even as science centuries earlier settled the issue of the rotation of the earth about the sun" (Gordon Lewis and Bruce Demarest, *Integrative Theology*, vol. 2 [Grand Rapids: Zondervan, 1996], 29).

biblical texts which allow an ancient universe.[8] So in this chapter we will survey only the scientific arguments given by OEC proponents.

Evidences that the Universe and the Earth Are Ancient

The empirical evidences typically presented by OEC advocates can be gathered under four headings: (1) large scale, (2) layered, (3) complex, and (4) independent.

Large-Scale Evidences that the Universe Is Ancient
The large scale evidences can be lumped together into three groups:

- *The large amount of evidences.* OEC advocates point to the enormous volume of independent lines of data which indicate an ancient earth and cosmos. When eight Bible-believing geologists recently published an article in *Modern Reformation* arguing for the OEC position, they stated that they faced two challenges. One was to present technical evidences in a clear and concise manner, and the other was to choose from the "literally thousands of good candidates from every corner of the globe."[9] OEC proponents often take the approach of making a cumulative case argument (i.e., piling one example upon another) for their position. For the nonspecialist, the parade of geological evidences provided by OEC advocates can become tedious.

- *The astronomical evidences.* The second line of large-scale evidences is the astronomical evidences. The size of the universe is, well, astronomical. Our Milky Way galaxy measures 100,000 light-years across. Our galaxy is only one of many billions of galaxies, each containing billions of stars. Since it takes millions of years (and more) for the light from these galaxies to reach earth, then the universe cannot be only 6,000 years old.

  Astronomers use triangulation methods that show, by direct means, that the universe is exponentially many times older than 10,000 years. Direct triangulation measures reveal that the Large Magellanic Cloud is 160,000 light years away, which is relatively close. Similar methods have measured the distance of galaxies from which the light took as long as 54 million years to reach the earth.[10]

---

8. See Questions 11 through 16 in Part 3.
9. David Campbell, et al., "PCA Geologists on the Antiquity of the Earth," http://www.modernreformation.org/default.php?page=articledisplay&var1=ArtRead&var2=1137&var3= (accessed 11/06/12).
10. Hugh Ross, *A Matter of Days: Resolving a Creation Controversy* (Colorado Springs: NavPress, 2004), 162.

OEC advocates note the lack of attention given to the greater part of the universe in Genesis 1–2. Significantly, the Genesis account devotes only five words (in English translations) to the creation of the stars and the galaxies. Moses, seemingly in passing, states, "He made the stars also" (Gen. 1:16, NKJV). Five words given to describing the formation of over 99 percent of the universe. For OEC advocates, this indicates God did not intend to convey any technically exact information about the scope or nature of the universe or a precise, scientific account of its formation.

- *The geological evidences.* A third line of large-scale evidences is the geological column. The successive layers of rock formations make up a column of immense length. The geologic column in the Grand Canyon is over 12,000 feet in depth. Parts of the world exhibit columns 45,000 feet deep.[11] Embedded in the geological column are fossils. The fossil record presents enormous numbers of extinct creatures and plants that lived in the past. The fossil record indicates that successions of "flora and fauna" lived on earth at intervals—single-celled and multi-celled creatures, fish, dinosaurs, mammals, insects, and more. And the record presents a volume and quantity of extinct creatures too great to have lived together on earth for a brief period of only 1,500 years.[12]

Layered Evidences that Require Long Time Periods to Accumulate
A number of geological artifacts appear to be the products of gradual, incremental processes that occurred over an immense period of time. Some of these processes happened with such regularity that they can be used as clocks and calendars to determine the age of the geological relic.

- *Geological phenomena are created by annual processes.* Geologists can determine the age of certain artifacts simply by counting their annual layers or rings. Many lake beds have yearly silt layers, called "varves," that are created by microorganisms interacting with the runoff produced by spring thaw. The varves in some lakes are more than 100,000 layers deep, which seems to indicate that the lakes are at least 100,000 years old.[13] Certain ancient lakes contain varves more than

11. Davis A. Young and Ralph F. Stearley, *The Bible, Rocks, and Time: Geological Evidence for the Age of the Earth* (Downers Grove: InterVarsity, 2008), 217.
12. Thomas Fowler and Daniel Kuebler, *The Evolution Controversy: A Survey of Competing Theories* (Grand Rapids: Baker, 2007), 194–96.
13. Campbell, "PCA Geologists on the Antiquity of the Earth."

one million layers deep which descend to a depth of more than four miles.[14] Similarly, ice core samples of glaciers from the Arctic and Antarctic circles reveal annual strata more than 110,000 layers deep.[15] Likewise, salt beds in deserts show evidence of being produced by long, gradual episodes of evaporation in ancient seas. Many of these beds are over a mile deep.[16]

- *Layered evidences created by living things.* Coral reefs grow gradually, at an incremental rate between five and eight millimeters per year. Yet many reefs are thousands of meters deep, indicating immense age. Reefs exist in the Pacific Ocean that are more than 4,500 feet thick and estimated to be more than 200,000 years old.[17] Remarkably, "the record of coral reef layers extend back 400,000,000 years."[18]

Another, more modest example is the bristlecone pine tree, which is believed to be the oldest living thing on earth. Some of these scrubby trees have rings which go back 8000 years, which would not be possible if the earth was created 6000 years ago (and was flooded 4500 years ago).[19]

Complex Evidences that Were Formed in Stages

OEC adherents point to both small-scale and large-scale examples of geological artifacts that exhibit a complexity that would seem to require long periods of time.

- *Small-scale examples.* Some of the small-scale examples often cited are the holes and ridges found in some sedimentary rocks on the ocean floor. After the sediment hardened into rock, burrowing sea creatures hollowed out tubes in which they colonized the stone. This had to have occurred in stages, and as YEC proponent Paul Garner concedes, "These surfaces seem to require time to develop."[20]

- *Large-scale examples.* Large-scale examples include the Sierra Nevada Mountains and the Michigan Basin. The Sierra Nevada mountain

---

14. Young and Stearley, *The Bible, Rocks, and Time,* 310. See also Denis O. Lamoureux, *I Love Jesus and I Accept Evolution* (Eugene, Ore.: Wipf and Stock, 2009), 96.
15. Ross, *A Matter of Days,* 183.
16. Young and Stearley, *The Bible, Rocks, and Time,* 302–4.
17. Lamoureux, *I Love Jesus and I Accept Evolution,* 96.
18. Ross, *A Matter of Days,* 183.
19. Mark Wharton and Hill Roberts, *Holman QuickSource Guide to Understanding Creation* (Nashville: Holman, 2008), 235–36.
20. Paul Garner, *The New Creationism: Building Scientific Theories on a Biblical Foundation* (Darlington: Evangelical, 2009), 86–87.

range is a complex structure that reveals a complicated history. It exhibits a composite structure that demonstrates layers of molten rock that alternates with layers of sedimentary rock. Some sediments are conglomerates, composed of aggregate which have been smoothed down by prior events. In other words, many latter layers were formed out of the debris of earlier layers. This obviously could not have happened in one catastrophe like a single flood (i.e., Noah's flood). OEC proponents Davis Young and Ralph Stearley contend that even without appealing to radiometric dating, the Sierra Nevadas can be demonstrated to require hundreds of thousands and millions of years to construct.[21]

Similarly, the geologic layers of the Michigan Basin manifest characteristics that seem to require great age, three of which are noted by OEC advocates. First, each layer is a unified package with internal consistency (i.e., coal layers are not mixed with coral reef layers, and so on). Second, each layer serves as a subtle time piece that can be dated with precision. And third, each layer shows evidence of gradual accumulation and deposition, rather than evidence of a violent flood.[22]

Independent Evidences that Point to an Ancient Earth

OEC proponents point out that the multiple thousands of evidences in space and on earth—from galaxies to geological phenomena—which consistently point to an ancient universe and earth are independent of one another. These independent lines make a reinforcing, cumulative case. The expansion of the Atlantic Ocean floor is often presented as a localized example of how many different, discrete, and independent data all indicate that the earth is ancient.[23] Lava is welling up at the middle of the Atlantic Ocean, slowly pushing the American continents and the European/African continents apart. The ocean floor near the mid-Atlantic ridge is relatively young. That which is farther out toward the continents shows signs of being gradually older. A large number of independent evidences confirm that the process of plate tectonics is taking eons of time. The gradually increasing level of sediments, the corresponding radiometric dates, the evidences of magnetic fields periodically alternating, and the matching fossils—all these artifacts dovetail to reinforce the ancient earth view. OEC proponents point out that each line of evidence is obtained independently of the other. This fact, they contend, gives strong support to the OEC position.[24]

21. Young and Stearley, *The Bible, Rocks, and Time*, 366–73.
22. Ibid.
23. Campbell, "PCA Geologists on the Antiquity of the Earth."
24. Wharton and Roberts, *Holman QuickSource Guide to Understanding Creation*, 111–13.

The Responses by Young-Earth Adherents

YEC proponents have been quick to reply to the arguments for an ancient universe. Some of the replies are substantial, so we will devote separate chapters to them.

The Large Scale Evidences

- *The large amount of evidences.* Many YEC advocates concede that they are swimming against a tide of empirical evidences.[25] Young-earth geologist Andrew Snelling admits, "There are, of course, many lines of geological evidences that appear to strongly imply that the earth and its various rock strata are millions and even billions of years old, immensely older than the straightforward biblical interpretation."[26] Snelling and other YEC advocates, however, argue that astronomers and geologists who accept an ancient age for the universe are doing so because they are operating with biases that operate as blinders. These biases cause them to dismiss young-earth interpretations without giving them due consideration. As we saw in the previous chapter, YEC proponents argue that proper interpretation comes down to a matter of proper presuppositions.

- *The astronomical evidences.* YEC astronomers and astrophysicists such as Jason Lisle and Russell Humphreys recognize that the immense size of the universe presents a serious challenge to the YEC position.[27] We will devote the next two chapters to looking at solutions proposed by YEC supporters to the starlight and time problem.

- *The geological evidences.* To answer the arguments presented by OEC geologists, YEC geologists point to the flood narrative as given in Genesis 6–9. They argue that a straight forward reading indicates a worldwide flood—a flood that modern geology has failed to take into account. YEC proponents such as John Whitcomb, Henry Morris, and Andrew Snelling argue that, instead of gradually forming over eons, the preponderance of geological

---

25. Kurt Wise, *Faith Form, and Time: What the Bible Teaches and Science Confirms about Creation and the Age of the Universe* (Nashville: B&H, 2002), 89.
26. Andrew Snelling, *Earth's Catastrophic Past*, 2 vols. (Dallas: ICR, 2009), 2:798. In his discussion of radioactive methods for dating rocks, Snelling states, "There is no question that the vast majority of the geochronometers mentioned above have given estimates for the age of the earth and its strata immensely greater than any possible estimate based on biblical chronology" (799).
27. See Jason Lisle, *Taking Back Astronomy: The Heavens Declare Creation and Science Confirms It* (Green Forest: Master, 2006); D. Russell Humphreys, *Starlight and Time: Solving the Puzzle of Distant Starlight in a Young Universe* (Green Forest: Master, 1994).

phenomena was created rapidly by Noah's flood.[28] Because of the promi-
nence the Genesis flood plays in YEC models, two chapters (Questions 30
and 31) are devoted to the debate about the extent of the flood.

The Layered Evidences

YEC geologists argue that the layered evidences found in lake beds and
glaciers could have been deposited much faster than most geologists have
been willing to permit. In 1980, Mount St. Helens (located in the Pacific
Northwest region of the United States) experienced a major volcanic eruption. YEC advocates point to the layered formations created by the aftermath
of the eruption as an example of how stratified sediment can be created rapidly in a matter of days rather than requiring eons.[29]

The Complex Evidences

YEC geologist Andrew Snelling argues that all evidence marshaled
against YEC geology is based on assumption of uniformity (i.e., that present
day processes were operative in the past). This assumption is simply a matter
of choice, "since there is no external objective scientific yardstick for determining which assumptions are the best to adopt."[30] Therefore the complex
evidence will inevitably be viewed as support for the ancient-earth thesis.
Snelling argues that special, supernatural laws were in force during creation
week and during Noah's flood, with the result that things that would have
taken billions of years to occur actually occurred in one week.[31]

The Independent Evidences

In reply to the OEC case built on examples such as the evidence derived
from the Atlantic Ocean floor, YEC proponents again argue that presuppositions are at work, and that possible interpretations that allow for a young earth
are available. Snelling concedes that the empirical data points to tectonic and
geological processes and events that normally would take millions of years
to occur.[32] However, he again argues that this interpretation fails to take into
account the miraculous. Because supernatural conditions were in effect, all
evidences, no matter how independent they may be, are all equally affected.

---

28. See John Whitcomb and Henry Morris, *The Genesis Flood* (Philadelphia: P&R, 1961);
    Andrew Snelling, *Earth's Catastrophic Past*, 2 vols.
29. Paul Garner, *The New Creationism: Building Scientific Theories on a Biblical Foundation*
    (Darlington: Evangelical, 2009), 86–87.
30. Snelling, *Earth's Catastrophic Past*, 1:296.
31. Snelling, *Earth's Catastrophic Past*, 2:468, 614.
32. Ibid., 629, 639.

"But You Weren't There"

In the previous chapter we noted the YEC argument against science's ability to do origins science. Humans are inherently limited from doing origins science, the argument goes, since we were not there to observe what happened. Astrophysicist and OEC proponent Hugh Ross replies that the past is exactly what astronomers are looking at. He states, "Astronomers don't have the present; they have only the past. They cannot observe or record present events. But they can observe and record all manner of past events. . . . Because of the time it takes for light to travel from stars, galaxies, and other sources to astronomers' telescopes, these telescopes operate like time machines carrying us into the past."[33] The observable astronomical testimony, Ross concludes, is that the universe is unfathomably immense and ancient.

Conclusion

So how old is the earth? The OEC advocates make a strong cumulative case for an old universe and earth. Even YEC advocates admit this, though they reject the OEC position. Wayne Grudem probably is correct when he observes, "Although our conclusions are tentative, at this point in our understanding, Scripture seems to be more easily understood to *suggest* (but not to require) a young earth view, while the observable facts of creation seem increasingly to favor an old earth view. Both views are possible, but neither one is certain."[34] Grudem calls on members of both camps to work together with humility and Christian charity. He then makes the following admonition:

> Progress will certainly be made if old earth and young earth scientists who are Christians will be more willing to talk to each other without hostility, *ad hominem* attacks, or highly emotional accusations, on the one hand, and without a spirit of condescension or academic pride on the other, for these attitudes are not becoming to the body of Christ, nor are they characteristic of the way of wisdom, which is "first pure, then peaceable, gentle, open to reason, full of mercy and good fruits, without uncertainty or insincerity," and full of the recognition that "the harvest of righteousness is sown in peace by those who make peace" (James 3:17–18).[35]

33. Hugh Ross, *A Matter of Days: Resolving a Creation Controversy* (Colorado Springs: NavPress, 2004), 172–73.
34. Wayne Grudem, *Systematic Theology* (Grand Rapids: Zondervan, 1994), 307–8 (emphasis original).
35. Ibid.

We believe Grudem has given good advice that we would be wise to follow.

REFLECTION QUESTIONS

1. What approaches do OEC proponents take when considering Scripture and the age of the earth?

2. The Genesis 1 account gives almost no attention to the formation of the stars. What significance do OEC advocates give to this fact?

3. What is the significance of the geological evidence being "layered" and "complex"?

4. Both OEC proponents and YEC proponents focus a great deal of attention on whether or not the lines of evidence are truly independent. Why would this matter?

5. How do OEC proponents respond to the "but you weren't there" objection?

If the Universe Is Young, How Can We See Stars So Far Away?

Like our Milky Way, Andromeda is a spiral galaxy. It is the closest spiral galaxy to us, and at a distance of 2.5 million light-years, this beautiful neighbor is relatively nearby. "Light-years" is a convenient way for astronomers to describe the immense distances between intergalactic objects. To say that the Andromeda Galaxy is 2.5 million light-years away means that it takes that long for light from Andromeda to travel to Earth. The Milky Way and Andromeda are just two of the many billions of galaxies populating the universe. And most galaxies are billions of light-years away—much farther than even Andromeda. Astronomers observe some objects that appear to be 13 billion light-years away; yet we can see them. These vast distances pose an obvious problem to the young-earth model, which posits that the universe is only 6,000 years old.

Young-earth creationism (YEC) proponents recognize the challenge that the immense size of the universe presents to their position. YEC astrophysicist Russell Humphreys says that he is constantly asked at every conference in which he speaks, "If the universe is so young, how can we see light from stars that are more than 10,000 light-years away?"[1]

This chapter examines four main ways YEC advocates have attempted to solve this dilemma. John Whitcomb and Henry Morris suggest that light might take a shortcut through space. Barry Satterwhite posits a second model theorizing that the speed of light may have been much greater in the past. A third approach is presented by Russell Humphreys. He argues that, due to time dilation caused by Einstein's theory of relativity, billions of years occurred in space during the seven days of creation on earth. In

---

1. D. Russell Humphreys, *Starlight and Time: Solving the Puzzle of Distant Starlight in a Young Universe* (Green Forest: Master, 1994), 9.

other words, Humphreys's position implies that a young earth exists within an old universe. Finally, Jason Lisle offers a fourth hypothesis. This theory argues that starlight traveling toward earth arrives almost instantly, regardless of how far away the light source is. Rather than accepting that light moves at a constant speed regardless of its direction, this view posits that, because the earth is in a privileged position, light headed toward our planet travels at an infinite speed.

There is a fifth approach known as the mature creation hypothesis (otherwise known as the "appearance of age" argument). It is probably the most popular approach among YEC advocates, and proponents of the four options listed above all interact with the mature creation hypothesis in one way or another. Because of its importance, we devote the next chapter to exploring the mature creation (or "appearance of age") hypothesis.

The Bending of Space Approach

Remarkably, in their landmark work *The Genesis Flood*, John Whitcomb and Henry Morris devote only two pages to the starlight and time problem.[2] They dismiss the issue with an appeal to the "appearance of age" argument. However, they also appeal to an article published in 1953 by Parry Moon and Domina Spencer. In the article, Moon and Spencer argued that light, when traveling great distances through space, was able to take a shortcut, so to speak. Rather than traveling in a straight line, light traveled through "Riemannian space." They concluded, "In this way the time required for light to reach us from the most distant stars is only 15 years."[3]

Moon and Spencer never provided any mathematical support for their hypothesis. And critics pointed out numerous problems with the theory. For example, if the theory were correct, certain nearby stars would take up more of our night sky than the moon.[4] There is some evidence that Moon and Spencer presented their theory with tongue in cheek, and that they never meant the proposal to be taken seriously.[5] Humphreys observes, "The theory was never very popular, perhaps because of its obscurity, and it seems to have died of natural causes."[6]

2. John Whitcomb and Henry Morris, *The Genesis Flood: The Biblical Record and Its Scientific Implications* (Philadelphia: P&R, 1961), 368–70.
3. Parry Moon and Domina Eberle Spencer, quoted in Whitcomb and Morris, *The Genesis Flood*, 370.
4. Perry G. Phillips, "A History and Analysis of the 15.7 Light-Year Universe," *Perspectives on Science and Christian Faith* 40, no. 1 (March 1988): 19–23.
5. Robert Schadewald, "Moon and Spencer and the Small Universe," *Creation Evolution Journal* 2, no. 2 (Spring 1981): 20–22.
6. Humphreys, *Starlight and Time*, 46.

The Deceleration of Light Approach

In 1987, Barry Setterfield and Trevor Norman argued that seventeenth century astronomical data indicated that the speed of light was substantially faster two hundred years ago than it is today.[7] They contended that a line of deceleration can be charted for the speed of light. When Setterfield and Norman charted the line back in time, the upward curve implied that six thousand years ago light traveled much faster than it does today—more than a million times faster. If true, this phenomenon would explain why we can see the light from such distant stars.

Setterfield and Norman's deceleration of light theory suffers from two difficulties. The first dilemma is with the seventeenth century-data. Closer examination by others reveals no real indication of a slowdown in the speed of light.[8] All the variations in measurements can be attributed to the limited technology of that day. A second dilemma is that such a change in the speed of light would have a catastrophic effect on the physical constants of the universe. These constants are finely tuned and are "very delicately balanced."[9] No record of accompanying disruptions has been found, which would indicate that the speed of light has remained constant. These difficulties have caused most YEC advocates to look elsewhere for a solution to the distant starlight problem.

The Dilation of Time Approach

In 1994, physicist Dale Humphreys, in his book *Starlight and Time: Solving the Puzzle of Distant Starlight in a Young Universe*, built an argument for the dilation of time based on Einstein's theory of relativity.[10] He theorized that the universe was much smaller at the initial moment of creation, with the earth located at or near the center. This would have meant that the mass of the entire universe would have been concentrated on the earth. God then stretched out the cosmos, almost instantly, to the size it is today. Such an action would have caused curious gravitational effects of time. Namely, even though only days would have occurred on earth, the rest of the universe would have had billions of years go by. In this manner Humphreys's proposal posits that God created an ancient universe "at the same time" (so to speak) that he created a young earth.[11]

7. Barry Setterfield and Trevor Norman, "The Atomic Constants, Light, and Time," (August 1987), http://www.setterfield.org/report/report.html (accessed 11/24/12).
8. Hugh Ross, *A Matter of Days: Resolving a Creation Controversy* (Colorado Springs: NavPress, 2004), 163–66.
9. Thomas B. Fowler and Daniel Kuebler, *The Evolution Controversy: A Survey of Competing Theories* (Grand Rapids: Eerdmans, 2007), 202–5.
10. Humphreys, *Starlight and Time*, 9–29.
11. Ibid., 25–29.

Humphreys notes that several times the Bible speaks of God "stretching out" or "spreading out" the heavens like a curtain or a tent (Job 9:8; Ps. 104:2; Isa. 40:22; Jer. 10:12; and Zech. 12:1). He argues that these references should be understood literally rather than metaphorically and that they are definite statements about the manner in which God created the cosmos. In addition, Humphreys has a novel interpretation of the firmament (or expanse) and waters above the firmament spoken of in the creation account (Gen. 1:6–8). He understands the firmament to be interstellar space and the waters above the firmament to be located outside the visible universe.[12]

Astrophysicist Hugh Ross, an old-earth proponent, contends that Humphreys's model fails upon close scrutiny.[13] Experts in general relativity point out that the model does "not yield the required gravitational time dilation." Observational evidence of certain astronomical objects—variable stars, supernovae, gamma-ray sources—do not support Humphreys's theory. Jason Lisle, a fellow YEC supporter, points out that Humphreys's theory seems to require that light from distant galaxies is blue-shifted.[14] But we observe the opposite: light from distant galaxies is red-shifted. In addition, the dilation of time model predicts that it's not only the earth that will look young, but the solar system as well. But the sun, the moon, and all the planets "show evidence of billions of years of natural history."[15] YEC advocate Paul Garner observes, "As with any new theory, Humphreys's cosmology has come in for criticism and modification, and it is unclear at present whether his version of the theory will survive the challenge of scientific and biblical analysis."[16]

The Synchronized Arrival of Light Approach

Jason Lisle, an astronomer on staff with Answers in Genesis and the Institute for Creation Research, presents a proposal that he calls the anisotropic synchrony convention (ASC).[17] Like Humphreys's hypothesis, ASC appeals to Einstein's theory of relativity. Einstein's theory teaches that time and space have a dynamic relationship, with the result, counterintuitively, that clocks in relative motion run at different rates. Since there is no absolute time, scientists must choose a standard or convention when synchronizing distant clocks. Einstein's theory assumes that light traveling from two different sources would arrive at the midpoint "at the same time." But this is only an assumption. Lisle argues that one can assume that light traveling from

---

12. Ibid., 53–68.

13. Ross, *A Matter of Days*, 166–68.

14. Jason Lisle, "Anisotropic Synchrony Convention—A Solution to the Distant Starlight Problem," *Answers Research Journal* 3 (2010): 204.

15. Ross, *A Matter of Days*, 166–68.

16. Paul Garner, *The New Creationism: Building Scientific Theories on a Biblical Foundation* (Darlington: Evangelical, 2009), 30.

17. Lisle, "Anisotropic Synchrony Convention," 191–207.

distant stars to earth travel at nearly infinite speeds while traveling only half the standard speed of light when going in the opposite direction. Earth, Lisle concludes, occupies a unique place in the universe so that light from the farthest reaches of the universe arrives almost instantly. In this way the problem of distant starlight is solved.

A number of objections have been raised to Lisle's theory, two of which we will note here. First, fellow YEC proponent Jonathan Sarfati objects to the theory as being *ad hoc*—a makeshift solution that makes unjustified assumptions.[18] Second, several critics point out that, if the earth really were in a privileged place in the universe which caused all light headed toward it to travel at nearly infinite speeds, then certain phenomena should be observed. Namely, earth should possess a gravitational field apart from the one created by its mass. However, none has been detected.[19]

Conclusion

Astronomy is unique among the natural sciences. Unlike geologists or paleontologists, astronomers do not merely use empirical data to construct theories about the past. When they look into their telescopes, astronomers really do empirically observe the past. Because of the time it takes for light to reach the earth from across the vast distances of space, astronomers study events that happened long ago. The size and scope of the universe indicates immense age. None of the solutions to the distant starlight problem offered by YEC scientists is very compelling.

Compared to the attention given by YEC advocates to making geological and biological arguments, the number of astronomical arguments is relatively small. Many lay supporters of the young-earth position do not seem to grasp the seriousness of the problem. Hugh Ross, an outspoken critic of YEC, states, "I'm troubled to think what may happen when the connection between cosmic size and age becomes widely understood."[20] In the survey of YEC approaches to the starlight and time problem, Fowler and Kuebler observe, "[I]f these theories fail, it bodes ill for the entire Creationist paradigm, presumably compelling it to fall back on some type of miraculous creation event, with many of the attendant problems of the 'created in transit' hypothesis."[21]

Indeed, the mature creation argument does seem to be the approach taken by most YEC proponents, and it appears to have the fewest logical and empirical problems. Except for Humphreys, the proponents of the positions outlined

---

18. Jonathan Sarfati, "Anisotropic Synchrony Convention," http://creation.com/asc-cosmology (accessed 11/25/12).
19. Jeff Zweerink, "An Infinite Speed of Light?" http://www.reasons.org/articles/an-infinite-speed-of-light (accessed 11/25/12).
20. Ross, *A Matter of Days*, 173.
21. Fowler and Kuebler, *The Evolution Controversy*, 207.

in this chapter appeal to the appearance of age argument at one time or another. Therefore, the mature creation argument is the focus of the next chapter.

REFLECTION QUESTIONS

1. Why is the "starlight and time" problem considered such a big challenge to the YEC position?

2. What assumption do both Humphreys and Lisle make in their respective theories concerning the location of the earth?

3. Concerning the study of the past, how is astronomy unique among the natural sciences?

4. What are the two challenges to the "dilation of time" approach?

5. What would be an example of the problems associated with the "bending of space" approach?

What Is the Mature Creation Argument?

In the previous three chapters, we have looked at the arguments for the competing views that either the creation is young or that it is old, along with the evidences marshaled by proponents of the respective positions. Young-earth creationism (YEC) advocate Kurt Wise sums up the situation well when he states, "A face-value reading of the Bible indicates that the creation is thousands of years old. A face-value examination of the creation suggests it is millions or billions of years old. The reconciliation of these two observations is one of the most significant challenges to creation research."[1] The mature creation argument has become central in most attempts by YEC researchers to achieve the reconciliation Wise deems necessary.

The *Omphalos* Argument

The mature creation argument originates with Philip Henry Gosse. In 1857 (two years before Darwin published *On the Origin of Species*), Gosse published *Omphalos: An Attempt to Untie the Geological Knot*.[2] Gosse was a respected naturalist and marine biologist. He is considered by many to be the inventor of the aquarium. *Omphalos* was well illustrated and well written, and it revealed a thorough knowledge of geology, paleontology, and biology as understood in that day. Gosse surveyed the various attempts to reconcile the findings of geology with the first eleven chapters of Genesis—the gap theory, the day-age theory, and appeals to Noah's flood, among others. He found all to

---

1. Kurt P. Wise, *Faith, Form, and Time: What the Bible Teaches and Science Confirms about Creation and the Age of the Universe* (Nashville: B&H, 2002), 58.
2. Philip Henry Gosse, *Omphalos: An Attempt to Untie the Geological Knot* (London: John Van Voorst, 1857).

be lacking. He contended that the only viable alternative was the theory that God created a fully functioning mature creation.

The mature creation argument (or "appearance of age" hypothesis) makes the following observation: Anything created by God directly and immediately would have the appearance of an age that it did not actually have. For instance, Adam was created as a fully mature adult male. He would appear, presumably, to be at least eighteen years old. However, in Genesis 1–2, his actual age would have been only a few hours. Like Gosse, YEC proponents Paul Nelson and John Mark Reynolds argue that Adam would have possessed the appearance of age and the appearance of a history—complete with all the evidences of having been born. They state, "He looked as if he had once had an umbilical cord and had been in the womb of a woman. However, being created from the hand of God, he had no such history. Thus Adam has an apparent history different from his actual one."[3] This is why Gosse referred to the mature creation view as the *omphalos* argument (*omphalos* is the Greek word for "belly button").

Gosse made similar arguments concerning plants and animals in the original creation. He points to examples such as the leaf scars on the tree fern.[4] A tree fern's trunk is composed of the scarring remnants of leaves that have fallen away, typically over a thirty-year period. If one stood in the garden of Eden, by necessity it would have appeared to be much older than it actually was. Gosse also contends that hardwood trees created in the garden of Eden would have possessed growth rings. These rings also could have been interpreted as indicators of age (and history) that the trees, in fact, did not have.[5]

YEC advocates apply this line of reasoning to the universe as a whole. Henry Morris argued that when God created a star that is millions of light-years away, he created its light in transit.[6] Vern Poythress can be taken as representative when he extrapolates from Adam to the cosmos.

> I suggest, then, that the mature creation view offers an attractive supplement to the 24-hour-day view. It retains all the main advantages of the 24-hour-day view, by maintaining that God created the universe within six 24-hour days. It supplements this view with a clear and simple explanation for the conclusions of modern astronomy. The universe *appears* to be

---

3. Paul Nelson and John Mark Reynolds, "Young Earth Creationism," in *Three Views on Creation and Evolution,* ed. J. P. Moreland and John Mark Reynolds (Grand Rapids: Zondervan, 1999), 51. See also Philip Gosse, *Omphalos,* 289–90.
4. Gosse, *Omphalos,* 131–33.
5. Ibid., 178–81.
6. Henry M. Morris, *The Remarkable Birth of Planet Earth* (Minneapolis: Dimension, 1972), 62–63. See also Don B. DeYoung, *Astronomy and the Bible: Questions and Answers* (Grand Rapids: Baker, 1989), 80–81; idem, *Astronomy and Creation: An Introduction* (Ashland, Ohio: Creation Research Society, 1995), 48–49.

14 billion years old because God created it mature. Moreover, the universe is *coherently* mature, in the sense that estimates of age deriving from different methods arrive at similar results. This coherence makes some sense. God created Adam mature. Why should we not think that Adam was coherently mature?[7]

When Poythress states that the universe coherently appears ancient, he is arguing that the appearance is comprehensive, that the mature creation argument implies that the entire cosmos will uniformly appear to be old. Most YEC advocates do not apply the mature creation argument as consistently as Gosse and Poythress do.

The Analogy of Jesus Turning Water into Wine

To illustrate the mature creation argument, a number of YEC proponents appeal to Jesus' miracle of turning the water to wine at the marriage feast of Cana (John 2:1–11).[8] They see this miracle operating as an analogy of the creation events of Genesis 1–2. The master of the feast mistakenly thought the wine that Jesus created was older than it actually was (John 2:10). The master assumed at least that the wine had been present since the beginning of the feast. Kurt Wise speculates as to what a person investigating the wine might have concluded. If the investigator had used naturalistic assumptions, he would have mistakenly deduced that the wine must be years old. Wine requires a fermentation process that can take years, and the presence of wine implies a vineyard, with owner and workers. Wise argues that all miracles result in appearances that can be easily misunderstood. However, miracles are not intentionally deceptive. It is not the miracles that are misleading; rather, the naturalistic assumptions are.[9]

The analogy Wise makes has force. The dilemma lies in how comprehensive this analogy must be. Imagine that someone did exactly what Wise suggests and investigated Jesus' miracle of turning water into wine. In order for the analogy to work, it would seem to have to provide an explanation for the possibility that the jars had time-stamped seals that stated a given date for when the wine was poured into the jars. It would also have to provide an explanation if there were labels on the jars stating that the wine was produced at such-and-such vineyards. And if the stated vineyards turned out to exist somewhere in Judea, complete with vines, owners, and workers, then this would have to be considered part of the miracle also. If this turned out to be

---

7. Vern S. Poythress, *Redeeming Science: A God-Centered Approach* (Wheaton, Ill.: Crossway, 2006), 116. Also Philip Gosse, *Omphalos,* 363. Poythress does not himself hold to the mature creation view, but he does coherently present the view in a sympathetic light.

8. In addition to Wise, *Faith, Form, and Time,* 58 and Poythress, *Redeeming Science,* 119–20, see Andrew Snelling, *Earth's Catastrophic Past: Geology, Creation, and the Flood,* 2 vols. (Dallas: ICR, 2009), 2:647–48, 850–53.

9. Wise, *Faith, Form, and Time,* 59.

the case, one could then posit that our Lord, when he turned the water into wine, also miraculously and instantly brought into existence all the components necessary to produce the wine through natural means. But this would seem to compromise the miracle's ability to operate as a sign (John 2:11). In addition, it would re-open the door to the accusation that God provided the miracle with the appearance of age for the purpose of deliberately misleading those investigating it. Yet, in order for the miracle of turning water into wine to operate as an analogy, such an elaborate scenario would seem to be necessary. The mature creation theory entails that God created the universe with a much more elaborate history than that of a mere vineyard.

Objections to the Mature Creation Argument

Opponents to the mature creation argument raise a number of objections. One opponent is Russell Humphreys, which is notable since he also holds to a young earth. He raises five objections.[10]

First, he argues that the theory has no clear biblical support. Advocates of the mature creation view cannot point to a single passage of Scripture that actually states that God created the world with an appearance of age. At best the appearance of age theory can only be described as extra-biblical.

Second, the mature creation argument requires believing that most of the events seen in the heavens never actually happened. This would include phenomena such as exploding supernovae, pulsars, quasars, and light from distant galaxies, just to name a few. The light that supposedly came from those celestial objects actually was created in transit. And the theory does not just affect our understanding of starlight. Because of the sun's dense mass, photons take over ten thousand years to escape from its core. Therefore, according to the mature creation model, the sunlight we see does not *actually come from the sun*.[11] For Humphreys, this turns astronomy into an exercise in "theological literary criticism"—of a fiction God wrote for us in the sky.[12]

A third criticism that Humphreys levels against the mature creation theory is that it seems to have little explanatory power. It is one thing to assume that when God created fully developed trees they had rings. But it is another thing to try to use the mature creation hypothesis to explain why God created billions of galaxies that are millions of light-years away.

Fourth, Humphreys points out that the theory is untestable. Since the appearance of age hypothesis makes no scientific predictions, it can be neither

---

10. D. Russell Humphreys, *Starlight and Time: Solving the Puzzle of Distant Starlight in a Young Universe* (Green Forest, Ark.: Master, 1994), 43–46.

11. Wise admits the mature creation argument implies this. He states, "Even now, some six thousand years after the creation, the light from the sun we are now seeing was not generated by fusion in the sun. It only *looks* as if it were" (see Wise, *Faith, Form and Time*, 65, emphasis original).

12. Humphreys, *Starlight and Time*, 45.

proven nor disproven. And fifth, the mature creation hypothesis impedes further investigation. Humphreys concludes, "It reminds me of the 17th-century theory that the fossils were created by God just to puzzle men and test their faith!"[13]

Old-earth advocate Davis Young adds his criticisms of the mature creation view.[14] First, he points out that the theory is relatively recent, noting, "So far as I am aware, neither the church fathers nor the Reformers ever held to the notion of creation of apparent age."[15] In other words, the novelty of the argument calls it into question. Second, a consistent application of the mature creation view has no more room for a worldwide flood than does old-earth creationism. The appearance of age view seems to "insist on a flood in which the water was miraculously created and annihilated."[16] Finally, Davis warns that "proponents of this literalism must then be willing to accept the consequence that fossil elephant bones, fossil dinosaurs, and fossil trees are illusions created in place, and that such 'fossils' tell us absolutely nothing whatsoever about formerly existing elephants, dinosaurs, or trees."[17]

Vern Poythress has replied to the criticisms made by Humphreys, Young, and others. He first addresses the accusation that the mature creation view makes God appear to be a deceiver. Poythress reiterates the point that the inference of age is an assumption made by us. Age is not a message imbedded within creation.[18] In other words, the problem lies within our assumptions, not in any so-called misleading evidence residing inside the material world. Poythress argues that it is difficult to see how any complex structure could have been created by God that did not have "an appearance of age."

Second, concerning the objection that a mature creation falsely implies that death preceded the fall, Poythress argues that the view implies only that animal death occurred before the fall. He contends that the death of animals prior to Genesis 3 poses no real theological problems.[19] It must be noted that this answer puts Poythress at odds with most other young-earth proponents.

In his reply to the objection that a mature creation delegitimizes scientific investigation, Poythress seems to consider this an acceptable concession. He declares that God is under no obligation to work uniformly in the past "in a

---

13. Ibid.
14. Davis Young, "Scripture in the Hands of Geologists (Part Two)," *WTJ* 9 (1987): 297–300.
15. Ibid.
16. Ibid.
17. Ibid.
18. Poythress, *Redeeming Science,* 116–30. Tim Chaffey and Jason Lisle make a similar argument. They state, "Some creationists have said that Adam was created with the 'appearance of age.' This is a subtle contradiction of terms because as we've said, age cannot be seen. It would be better to say that Adam was created as a mature adult" (Tim Chaffey and Jason Lisle, *Old Earth Creationism on Trial: The Verdict Is In* [Green Forest, Ark.: Master, 2008], 150).
19. Ibid., 122.

way that will perfectly accommodate the desires of scientists!"[20] At any rate, he continues, the believing geologist or astronomer can continue to study events that appear to have occurred in deep time, with the understanding that they happened "*in ideal time.*"[21] In other words, since God created the universe with the appearance of age, then we are free to study it as if it were old.

Poythress also seems to concede the objection that the mature creation view undermines investigation of Noah's flood. He suggests that since the flood was a miraculous event, similar to the resurrection of Christ, then it may simply lie beyond the scope of scientific investigation.[22] If so, he argues, the objection would be moot. However, the founders of the young-earth creationism movement, John Whitcomb and Henry Morris, built their case primarily with appeals to the Genesis flood.[23]

Conclusion

First, *an appearance of age is an appearance of a non-actual history*. Gosse demonstrated this with a litany of examples. Fish scales, tortoise plates, bird feathers, deer antlers, elephant tusks, and many more—all grow in successive stages that tell the story of a particular creature's life.[24] Biologists regularly use these features to determine age of the respective animals. Gosse declares, "I have indeed written the preceding pages in vain, if I have not demonstrated, in a multitude of examples, the absolute necessity of retrospective phenomena in newly-created organisms."[25] If the original creatures were created fully grown, then they were created with an apparent history. By extension, a universe created fully mature will, by necessity, give signs of a history that did not actually happen.

Second, *the mature creation argument is unfalsifiable*. This means it can be neither proven nor disproven. As Bertrand Russell observed, "We may all have come into existence five minutes ago, provided with ready-made memories, with holes in our socks and hair that needed cutting."[26] Since there is no way to prove the theory, we have moved from the realm of science into the

---

20. Ibid., 123.
21. Ibid., 124 (emphasis original).
22. Ibid.
23. John Whitcomb and Henry Morris, *The Genesis Flood: The Biblical Record and Its Scientific Implications* (Phillipsburg, N.J.: P&R, 1961). Yet, as they built their case for a universal flood, they also appealed to the appearance of age argument numerous times (see pages 232–39 and 344–62).
24. Gosse, *Omphalos,* 182–290.
25. Ibid., 349–50.
26. Quoted in Richard Dawkins, *The Greatest Show on Earth: The Evidence for Evolution* (New York: Free Press, 2009), 13.

realm of metaphysics. The mature creation argument truly is a fideistic position, since it places creation beyond investigation.[27]

Third, *the appeal to an appearance of age is an admission that the evidence is against the young earth view.* Gosse conceded this over 150 years ago.[28] If the overwhelming preponderance of empirical data pointed to a recent creation, then YEC advocates would not bother with such a difficult hypothesis as the *omphalos* argument. The very fact that YEC proponents find it necessary to appeal to the mature creation argument is a concession.

Fourth, *the mature creation argument seems almost to embrace a denial of physical reality.* Certain advocates of the argument do not hesitate to describe the universe as an illusion. Gary North declares, "The Bible's account of the chronology of creation points to an illusion. . . . The seeming age of the stars is an illusion. . . . Either the constancy of the speed of light is an illusion, or the size of the universe is an illusion, or else the physical events that we hypothesize to explain the visible changes in light or radiation are false inferences."[29] At this point the arguments for the appearance of age seem uncomfortably gnostic.

Fifth, a consistent application of the mature creation argument will conclude *that there are no evidences of a young earth.* The universe has been coherently, uniformly created with the appearance of age. With the exception of Poythress, almost all young-earth proponents and flood geologists seem to overlook this portion of Gosse's argument. But this was not a minor point to him. It was, in fact, a main part of his thesis.[30] Gosse would have considered the efforts of Answers in Genesis, The Institute for Creation Research, and other YEC organizations unrealistic at best and detrimental at worst. The appearance of age argument seems to imply that the movement launched by Whitcomb and Morris is misguided.

Sixth, Gosse arrived at the conclusion *that we should study the earth as if it were old.* He argued:

> Finally, the acceptance of the principles presented in this volume, even in their fullest extent, would not, in the least degree, affect the study of scientific geology. The character and order of the strata; their disruptions and displacements and injections; the successive floras and faunas; and all the other phenomena, would be *facts* still. They would still be, as now, legitimate subjects of examination and inquiry. I do not know that a single conclusion, now accepted, would need to be given

27. Fideism argues for the validity of holding a position in blind faith. See Question 1 for further discussion of fideism.
28. Gosse, *Omphalos*, 90–100.
29. Quoted in Hugh Ross, *A Matter of Day: Resolving a Creation Controversy* (Colorado Springs: NavPress, 2004), 35.
30. Ibid., 114–27.

up, except that of actual chronology. And even in respect of this, it would be rather a modification than a relinquishment of what is at present held; we might still speak of the inconceivably long duration of the processes in question, provided we understand *ideal* instead of *actual* time;—that the duration was projected in the mind of God, and not really existent.[31]

This is a surprising, even stunning, conclusion. Yet, it is entirely consistent with the logic of the mature creation argument. And at present the mature creation hypothesis appears to be the best argument that young-earth creationism has. The hypothesis may be true, but it will remain unproven and improvable. Part 4 of this book has been devoted to questions concerning the age of the earth. The conclusion must be that, though a cursory reading of Scripture would seem to indicate a recent creation, the preponderance of empirical evidence seems to indicate otherwise.

REFLECTION QUESTIONS

1. Why is the mature creation hypothesis sometimes called the *omphalos* model?

2. What are the strengths and weaknesses of using the analogy of Jesus turning the water into wine?

3. What does it mean to say that the mature creation argument is unfalsifiable?

4. Why does the mature creation argument seem to indicate that we should study the earth as if it is old?

5. When Poythress contends that the inference of age is an assumption made by us, what is the point he is making?

---

31. Ibid., 369–71 (emphasis original).

PART 5

QUESTIONS ABOUT THE FALL
AND THE FLOOD

What Does It Mean that Man Is Made in God's Image?

There are three major views of the meaning of the image of God—the substantive view, the relational view, and the functional view. According to the substantive view, the image is located in some spiritual quality or faculty of man giving man the capacity for self-consciousness, speech, and moral discernment (Gen. 9:6; James 3:9). Many relatively recent Old Testament interpreters have argued that the likeness is to be found in such capacities as personality, understanding, the will and its freedom, self-consciousness, intelligence, spiritual being, spiritual superiority, and the immortality of the soul. The relational view of the image of God asserts that what is meant by the image of God is man's unique ability to relate to other human beings and especially to God (Gen. 1:28–30; 2:15–25). The capacity for a personal relationship with the Creator is understood by the advocates of the relational view to be intrinsic to the concept of the image of God. The third position, the functional view, has more recently come to dominance and argues from the context of Genesis that the image of God in man refers to man having dominion over God's creation (Gen. 1:28–30).[1]

Context of the Image

The uniqueness of man is clearly revealed in the creation account itself, in Genesis 1:26–31. There is a break in the rhythm of the occurrence of the phrase "let there be" (the formula of the seven preceding creative acts) as it is

---

1. See the helpful discussion by Millard Erickson, *Christian Theology*, 2nd ed. (Grand Rapids: Baker, 1998), 517–36; John J. Davis, *Paradise to Prison: Studies in Genesis* (Salem, Wis.: Sheffield, 1975, reissued 1998), 81; D. J. A. Clines, "The Image of God in Man," *TynBul* 19 (1968): 56–57; Claus Westermann, *Genesis 1–11*, trans. John J. Scullion S. J. (Minneapolis: Fortress, 1994), 149.

replaced by the phrase "let us make."[2] Previously in the creation narrative God has been introduced simply as commanding; now, when he approaches the most excellent of all his works, he enters into consultation. "This pause, this announcement, signalizes the creation of humankind as the most momentous of all God's creative acts."[3] In addition, the formulaic phrase "and it was so" is replaced by the threefold blessing of Genesis 1:27:

> So God created man in his own image,
> > in the image of God he created him;
> > male and female he created them.

The threefold repetition of "created" (*bara*), the special term for God's unique creation in Genesis 1:1, the poetical parallelism of the lines, and the fact that the sixth day of creation is the longest of the creation days all indicate that this is the peak of the creation account. "In these ways, the narrator places humankind closer to God than the rest of creation."[4]

Man in God's Image

The most important term for the nature of man is the word "image" (*tselem*). The term is mentioned two times in Genesis 1:27 as well as Genesis 1:26. The word *tselem* occurs seventeen times in the Old Testament, most often with reference to a physical image (e.g., 1 Sam. 6:5) and sometimes with reference to an idol or statue (Num. 33:52; 2 Kings 11:18).

The phrase "image of God" occurs only four times in the Old Testament (Gen. 1:26–27 [2x]; 9:6). Because of the physical nature of the term *tselem*, there have been those who have advocated that the primary focus of man in God's image has to do with man's physical appearance or even upright posture or that man physically resembles God. In other words, they look for a physical explanation of the divine image.[5] As Kenneth Mathews has reasoned however,

---

2. The reference to the plural pronoun "us" was understood to be a reference to the Trinity by the early church fathers. Plurality in the Godhead has already been alluded to by the reference to the "Spirit of God" in Genesis 1:2. See Gerhard F. Hasel, "The Meaning of 'Let Us' in Gn 1:26," *AUSS* 13 (1975): 58; John Calvin, *Commentaries on the First Book of Moses Called Genesis* (Grand Rapids: Baker, 1979), 92.

3. John H. Stek, "What Says the Scriptures?" in *Portraits of Creation: Biblical and Scientific Perspectives on the World's Formation* (Grand Rapids: Eerdmans, 1990), 251.

4. Bruce Waltke and Cathi J. Fredricks, *Genesis* (Grand Rapids: Zondervan, 2001), 64. See C. John Collins, "Reading Genesis 1:1–2:3 as An Act of Communication: Discourse Analysis and Literal Interpretation," in *Did God Create in Six Days?* ed. Joseph A. Pipa, Jr. and David W. Hall (Taylors, S.C.: Southern Presbyterian Press, 1999), 137.

5. Hermann Gunkel was an early advocate of this view. This view has never received much traction when it surfaced in the history of interpretation. See Westermann, *Genesis 1–11*, 149–150; Grunnlaugur A. Jónsson, *The Image of God: Genesis 1:26–28 in a Century of Old*

the fact that the physical representation of God is prohibited in the Mosaic law (Ex. 20:1–2; Deut. 4:16) renders this view completely untenable.[6]

Man in God's Likeness

The meaning of the phrase "in our image" is clarified by the following phrase "after our likeness" (*demuth*; Gen. 1:26). The only other place in Scripture where these two terms "image" and "likeness" (*tselem* and *demuth*) occur together as they do in Genesis 1:27 is in Genesis 5:3, where the words occur in reverse order but with the prepositions "in" and "after" in the same order.[7] This has led to the view that these terms *tselem* (image) and *demuth* (likeness) are synonymous and virtually interchangeable, which was the view of both Martin Luther and John Calvin.[8] Others have made sharp distinctions between these two terms. For example, the medieval commentator Rashi (AD 1040–1105) argued that image referred to a physical mold or stamp while likeness indicated a reference to cognitive and intellectual capacities. Church father Irenaeus (ca. AD 180) understood image and likeness to refer to two different aspects of man's nature. The image referred to what might be called natural qualities (reason, personality, etc.) that make man like God, whereas likeness in contrast referred to supernatural graces like ethical behavior.[9]

The Hebrew term *demuth* (likeness) is used in Hebrew when something is compared to something else. Thus, the term represents an explanation or specification of the meaning of the image. Or as James Barr noted, *demuth* was added both to define and limit the meaning of "image."[10] William Dumbrell explains the meaning of *demuth* ("likeness") in Genesis 1:26: "The addition of the phrase 'after our likeness' in Genesis 1:26 seems designed to exclude the notion of exact copy contained in the word 'image' while seeking

---

Testament Research, Old Testament Series 26 (Uppsala: Almqvist & Wiksell International, 1988), 54, 106, 112, 177.

6. See Kenneth Mathews, *Genesis 1–11:26*, NAC 1A (Nashville: B&H, 1996), 168.

7. Attempts to distinguish the Hebrew prepositions *be* and *ke* have been given up. The synonymity of the prepositions is supported by the Greek and Latin translations of the Old Testament which only used *kata* (Greek) and *ad* (Latin) for both prepositions (Westermann, *Genesis 1–11*, 145; Gerhard von Rad, *Genesis*, rev. ed. [Philadelphia: Westminster, 1972], 58). The interchange of the two prepositions indicates nothing but a stylistic variant. See John F. A. Sawyer, "The Meaning of beselem elohim אלהים בצלם (In the Image of God) in Genesis 1–XI," *JTS* 24 (1973): 421.

8. See Westermann, *Genesis 1–11*, 145–46; Ian Hart, "Genesis 1:1–2:3 As a Prologue to the Book of Genesis," *TynBul* 46, no. 2 (1995): 321; Sawyer, "The Meaning of beselem elohim אלהים בצלם (In the Image of God) in Genesis 1–XI," 420–21; Gordon J. Wenham, *Genesis 1–15*, WBC 1 (Waco, Tex.: Word, 1987), 29–31; James I. Cook, "The Old Testament Concept of the Image of God," in *Grace Upon Grace*, ed. James I. Cook (Grand Rapids: Eerdmans, 1975), 86.

9. See Jon D. Levenson, *Creation and the Persistence of Evil* (San Francisco: Harper & Row, 1988), 111; Wenham, *Genesis 1–15*, 29–31.

10. See James Barr, "The Image of God in the Book of Genesis—A Study of Terminology," *BJRL* 51 (1968–69): 24.

to convey some resemblance either in nature or function. The connotation of the term 'image' is thus weakened by the addition of 'likeness,' probably in the interests of avoiding the potentially idolatrous idea of an unqualified 'in our image.'"[11] Thus any notion of a physical connotation of image would be immediately weakened by the addition of *demuth* ("likeness"). Humanity must be viewed as only a facsimile of God and hence distinct from him. Whereas the image of the deity is equated with the deity in the ancient Near East, here in Genesis 1:26 the word "likeness" distinguishes God from humans in the biblical worldview. After God's resolution to make man in his image, he immediately asserts that man is to have "dominion" over all creatures of the sea, of the heavens, and of the earth (Gen. 1:26).

Further development of what is meant by the "image of God" is provided in Genesis 1:27. In Genesis 1:27 we learn that the image of God consists of both male and female. The unique repetition of the word "create" (*bara*; Gen. 1:1) intensifies and personalizes this significant act. Humanity is uniquely shaped by the hand of God. The term is clearly emphasized as it occurs three times in one verse indicating that here the high point and goal has been reached toward which all God's creativity from Genesis 1:1 onward was directed. Man and woman are made in the image of God, not "according to their kind" (Gen. 1:21, 24–25). The image of God consisting of male and female is a plurality like the divine plurality expressed in Genesis 1:26. Thus, as John Sailhamer has noted, the human relationship between man and woman as male and female "becomes a witness to God's own personal relationship within the Godhead."[12]

After creating the man and the woman in his image, God blessed them and gave human beings the same mandate he had given to the living creatures, birds, and sea creatures on day five, "Be fruitful and multiply and fill the waters (earth)" (see Gen. 1:22). But here in the creation of humankind the mandate is extended by the statement to subdue the earth and have dominion over all other created beings (Gen. 1:28).

The Substantive View of the Image of God

The substantive view of the image of God was held by many of the early church fathers, including Athanasius, Augustine, and the Reformers. Athanasius maintained that the image of God referred to man's rationality, while Augustine believed the image referred to the faculties of human beings including "memory, intellect, and will." This view was first fully developed by Philo. The Reformers, including Luther and Calvin, on the other hand, argued that righteousness and holiness were the essence of the image of God in man.

---

11. William J. Dumbrell, *The Faith of Israel*, 2nd ed. (Grand Rapids: Baker Academic, 2002), 16.
12. John H. Sailhamer, *Genesis Unbound* (Sisters, Ore.: Multnomah, 1996), 146–47. See Waltke, *Genesis*, 65, 67; von Rad, *Genesis*, 57.

Those who have suggested that spiritual qualities constitute the image of God in man include Philo, Otto Procksch, August Dillman, H. H. Rowley, and Benno Jacob. The viewpoint that sees the divine image as consisting in one or more of man's spiritual qualities was the dominant viewpoint of the church throughout the centuries, even early in the twentieth century. The interpretation implied a continuity between God's spiritual nature and man's spiritual nature.[13]

The Relational View of the Image of God

The relational view of man in the image of God presents the belief that man's divine likeness is seen in the fact that he and God can maintain a relationship, that God can talk to man and that man can understand and answer God.[14] Karl Barth has been the person most often associated with the relational view.

Barth argued from the context of Genesis 1 that the relation and distinction in mankind between male and female corresponds to the relation and distinction of the I-Thou relationship in God himself. There is an I-Thou within the Deity, there is also an I-Thou relationship between man and woman. God's image in man is the reciprocal relationship of human being with human being. Also, because man is the being whom God addressed, there is a relationship between human existence and the divine nature. The image of God in man indicates that the human being alone has the special characteristic of human existence by which man is capable of communication with God and can respond to him. Man, the pinnacle of the creation account, is God's unique counterpart. Man's crowning glory is his relation to God. As Sailhamer stated, "God and man share a likeness that is not shared by other creatures. This apparently means that a relationship of close fellowship can exist between God and man that is unlike the relationship of God with the rest of his creation."[15] Moreover, as we read that no suitable partner was found for man in Genesis 2, we understand that man was not like the other creatures. In this narrative where man gives names to the animals (Gen. 2:19–20), we further see this correspondence with God as man alone, like God, has the capacity to communicate through speech. "The human creature not only differentiates itself from its environment through the symbolic

---

13. See Clines, "The Image of God in Man," 54–55; R. Ward Wilson and Craig L. Blomberg, "The Image of God in Humanity: A Biblical-Psychological Perspective," *Themelios* 18 (1993): 9; Jónsson, *The Image of God*, 11, 33; Hart, "Genesis 1:1–2:3 As a Prologue to the Book of Genesis," 317n.5.

14. See Jónsson, *The Image of God*, 59.

15. John H. Sailhamer, "Exegetical Notes: Genesis 1:1–2:4a," *TrinJ* 5 (1984): 80. See Derek Kidner, *Genesis: An Introduction and Commentary* (Downers Grove: InterVarsity, 1972), 50.

medium of language, but establishes therewith diverse orders of differentiation as well. In so doing, man-the-steward, like God-the-creator, creates a world with words."[16]

The image of God thus is not a quality of man like we find in the substantive view. The individual man is not the image of God, since the image comes to expression in the juxtaposition and conjunction of man and man—which is that of male and female. Barth argued that the Old Testament does not teach that the image was lost after the fall.

Barth has had a profound influence on the progress of the *imago Dei* debate in Old Testament studies. Moreover, his conviction that the divine likeness should not be sought in particular qualities of man became a virtual consensus within Old Testament interpretation.[17]

The Functional View of the Image of God

Advocates of the functional view of the image of God maintain that the context of Genesis 1:26–28 supports the idea that the image of God in man is related to the concept that God has given dominion to man over his creation. Immediately after the statement that man is made "after our likeness" (Gen. 1:26), we find the expression "let them have dominion," which may be viewed as a purpose statement and could be rendered "in order that they may have dominion."[18] The notion that "context is the safest guide to meaning" has led to the conclusion that image and likeness are defined by what follows in Genesis 1:26, that is, that man is to have dominion "over the fish of the sea and over the birds of the heavens and over the livestock and over all the earth and over every creeping thing that creeps on the earth." The text is thus saying that exercising royal dominion over the earth as God's representative is the basic purpose for which God created man. The functional interpretation which appeared only very rarely until late in the nineteenth century has now become the predominant position among biblical interpreters.[19]

In the ancient Near East it was customary to think of a king as a representative of a god. The king as an image of the god was viewed as ruling on the god's behalf. The king was thus the representative of the god on earth. Many advocates of the functional view believe this understanding was democratized

---

16. Michael Fishbane, *Text and Texture* (New York: Schocken, 1979), 18. It cannot be denied that speech is a feature which is noticeably absent in all animals. See H. C. Leupold, *Exposition of Genesis*, 2 vols. (Grand Rapids: Baker, 1942), 1, 89–90.

17. See Clines, "The Image of God in Man," 60; Jónsson, *The Image of God*, 72–73, 75.

18. The *waw* before the imperfect in *weyirdu* expresses purpose. See S. R. Driver, *A Treatise on the Use of the Tenses in Hebrew* (Oxford: Clarendon, 1881), 81 (§64); Dumbrell, *The Faith of Israel*, 16.

19. See Jónsson, *The Image of God*, 219. Already a millennium ago the philosopher and commentator Saadya (AD 882–942) associated the image of God in Genesis 1:26–27 with humanity's God-like rule over creation (Levenson, *Creation and the Persistence of Evil*, 112).

by the biblical writer and thereby broadened to include all mankind as made in the image of God. Man, as God's representative on earth, rules and exercises dominion on the earth, on God's behalf, like a king. In other words, the idea of the image of God was universally extended as the image was to include mankind in general as made in the image of God. As the image of God, man is to manage and develop God's creation. He is elevated to a vice-regent of God. An illustration of man exercising dominion over God's creation is found in Genesis 2:19–20. Thus, Marsha Wilfong has noted, "In exercising 'dominion' over the rest of creation, human beings act as God's representatives or stewards. Created in God's image, humankind stands in the place of God in relation to the rest of creation. Like earthly rulers who set up statues of themselves to assert their sovereignty in places where they were not present, so humankind is set upon the earth to assert and to carry out God's sovereign rule over all of creation."[20] The image thus refers to humans as the representative of God. Man is *to be* God's representative of the transcendent God who remains outside the world order. Hence, the meaning of the text is not that man was created in the image of God, he actually is the image of God.[21]

Conclusion

We have seen that all three major views of the meaning of the image of God in man assume man to be distinct from the animals. This is supported by the creation context in Genesis 1–2 and must have a significant contribution to the meaning of the image of God in man. "The truth is that the image marks the distinction between man and the animals."[22] The focus of the creation of woman in Genesis 2 is also founded on the concept that man is distinct from animals, as Adam did not find someone who corresponded to him among the animal kingdom until the woman was created (Gen. 2:20, 23). With regard to the substantive view, man is ontologically different from animals;[23] from the relational view God converses and has a relationship with man and not animals; and with regard to the functional view man is distinct from animals as he rules over them.

20. Marsha M. Wilfong, "Human Creation in Canonical Context: Genesis 1:26–31 and Beyond," in *God Who Creates: Essays in Honor of W. Sibley Towner,* ed. William P. Brown and S. Dean McBride, Jr. (Grand Rapids: Eerdmans, 2000), 45. See I. Hart, "Genesis 1:1–2:3 As a Prologue to the Book of Genesis," 318–19, 322, 324.

21. See Eugene H. Merrill, "A Theology of the Pentateuch," in *A Biblical Theology of the Old Testament,* ed. Roy B. Zuck (Chicago: Moody, 1991), 14–15. Man thus *is* the image of God, understanding the preposition *be* as a *beth essentiae.* See GKC, 378 (§199i).

22. John Skinner, *Genesis,* ICC, 2nd ed. (Edinburgh: T&T Clark, 1930), 32.

23. The substantive view, however, is opposed by much of modern scholarship as man is now viewed as a unity and not a composition of parts. See Clines, "The Image of God in Man," 56–57; Hamilton, *Genesis 1–17,* 137.

As we have observed, the functional position, while in many ways the most recent view, has become the most common way to understand the image of God in man in recent times. The clear attraction of this view is the support of the immediate context that appears to explain the image of God in man as having dominion over the animal kingdom as well as the earth (Gen. 1:26–28). The functional view stressed context; man is stated to have dominion immediately after being created in God's image (Gen. 1:26b). But is the context to be so narrowly construed? The context could also be cited to support the substantive view—the distinctive difference between man and animals pervades the narrative of Genesis 1–2, and the immediate context of man's day of creation on day six has God conversing with man in distinction from the other created creatures. So context is key, but how narrowly or more broadly are we to define the context?

James Barr has observed that the understanding of dominion as constitutive of the meaning of the image of God in man does not seem to fit well with two other close contexts where the image terminology is used. In Genesis 5:3 and 9:6, reference is again made to the image of God, but nothing is made over man's dominion over animals. As Barr stated with regard to Genesis 9:6: "Homicide was to be punished not because man had dominion over the animals, but because man was like God."[24] Thus, context should not be restricted to a just a few juxtaposed verses.

Not a few Old Testament scholars have argued that the functional concept does not define the image of God in man but is rather a consequence of man being created in God's image.[25] To be sure, it is the first thing conferred on man subsequent to his creation in God's image. But as Jónsson stated, "It is noteworthy that some scholars who connect the concept of the divine image with man's status as God's viceroy or representative, nevertheless assert that man's dominion over the rest of creation is only a consequence of the image, not the meaning of the image itself."[26]

Moreover, the exercise of dominion may not be the only consequence of human creation in God's image. Wilfong argues that the ability to correspond with God distinguishes mankind from the rest of creation and should also be regarded as a necessary consequence of being created in God's image.[27] The relational view as argued by Barth and then carried on by Westermann is a worthy rival to the dominant functional interpretation. Already at creation,

---

24. James Barr, "Man and Nature—The Ecological Controversy and the Old Testament," *BJRL* 55 (1972): 20.
25. See Westermann, *Genesis 1–11*, 155; von Rad, *Genesis*, 59; Wenham, *Genesis*, 31–32.
26. Jónsson, *The Image of God*, 222.
27. See Wilfong, "Human Creation in Canonical Context: Genesis 1:26–31 and Beyond," 43. Maybe in a less direct way the substantive view in some sense could also be viewed as a consequence from the fact that dominion must be the result of the exercise of the human will. This may be what Fishbane has in mind (see Fishbane, *Text and Texture*, 18).

man is in dialogue with his Creator which implies that man was created to live face to face with God.[28]

When we turn to the New Testament, we find that the concept of the image of God is associated with moral attributes (Col. 3:10; see Eph. 4:24). This connection would be harmonious with the substantive view. Because of the fall, man can only partially fulfill the regent function or the cultural mandate of the image. This will only be completely fulfilled by the Christ, the Second Adam (Ps. 8; Heb. 2).[29] But the image was not lost in the fall. After the fall, man is still said to be in God's image (Gen. 9:6) and likeness (James 3:9); however, he stands in need of being renewed after the image of him that created him (Col. 3:10; cf. Eph. 4:24).[30]

It is possible that the first reference to the concept of the image of God in Genesis 1 is not making a universal statement about the nature of humankind. It may only be stating that to be human is to bear the image of God. As Wayne Grudem concluded, the expression "the image of God" may simply refer to every way in which man is like God.[31] Similarly, Carl F. H. Henry summarized the nature of man as follows: "Humanity is made for personal and endless fellowship with God, involving rational understanding (Gen. 1:28–29), moral obedience (2:16–17), and religious communion (3:3). Humanity is given dominion over the animals and charged to subdue the earth, that is, to consecrate it to the spiritual service of God and humankind."[32]

While man is made "after the likeness" of God and thus is to be distinguished from him, man is also unique and prominent among all God's creation. As Rabbi Akiba exclaimed: "What sign of God's love that man was created in his image! What still greater love that he was told that he was created in his image!" ('*Abot* 3:15).

REFLECTION QUESTIONS

1. What are the three primary views on the image of God?

---

28. See Jónsson, *The Image of God*, 223–24. Those who hold to the relational view understand the phrase "let them have dominion" not as the purpose of being in God's image (functional view) but the result of being created in God's image (see Westermann, *Genesis 1–11*, 216).

29. See Waltke, *Genesis*, 70.

30. See James I. Cook, "The Old Testament Concept of the Image of God," 87; Kidner, *Genesis*, 50–51.

31. See Wayne Grudem, *Systematic Theology* (Grand Rapids: Zondervan, 1994), 443; Westermann, *Genesis 1–11*, 155; Hamilton, Genesis 1–17, 137. And yet the dominion of man over creation cannot be excluded from the content of the image itself (see Clines, "The Image of God in Man," 97, 101).

32. C. F. H. Henry, "Image of God," in *EDT*, 2nd ed. Walter A. Elwell, ed. (Grand Rapids: Baker Academic, 2001), 593.

2. Which view is the most prominent today?

3. Which view does the context support?

4. How are human beings different from animals?

5. How has the fall affected the image of God in man?

Were Adam and Eve Historical Persons?

In Question 38 ("Can a Christian Hold to Theistic Evolution?"), we survey the various ways that evolutionary creationists view the historicity of the events recounted in Genesis 1–3. There we pay particular attention to the ways different evolutionary creationists understand the historicity of the original couple. In recent days, some evangelicals, such as Peter Enns and Denis Lamoureaux, have either questioned or denied the historicity of the original couple.[1] They contend that evolutionary genetics have rendered the traditional view untenable, but this is no great loss since the affirmation of a literal Adam is not necessary for any essential Christian doctrine.

This chapter focuses on the importance of affirming that Adam and Eve were real persons. Opposing Enns and Lamoureaux, we contend that this matter is of the utmost importance. We believe the historicity of Adam and Eve is so important that the matter should serve as a litmus test when evaluating the attempts to integrate a proper understanding of Genesis 1–3 with the latest findings of science. It must be realized that any position which denies that a real fall was experienced by a real couple will have adverse effects on other significant biblical doctrines. This does not mean that we should stick our heads in the sand concerning the latest developments in genetics. But we should recognize the consequences of trying to alter doctrines that have solid scriptural footing.

C. John Collins, a professor of Old Testament, has recently written a book devoted to the question we are addressing in this chapter. In his *Did Adam and Eve Really Exist?*, Collins argues that we need to retain the *Good summary*

---

1. Peter Enns, *The Evolution of Adam: What the Bible Does and Doesn't Say about Human Origins* (Grand Rapids: Brazos, 2012), 119–35; Denis O. Lamoureux, *I Love Jesus and I Accept Evolution* (Eugene, Ore.: Wipf and Stock, 2009), 80–84, 135–39.

iew of Adam and Eve, or at least something close to it.[2] He
ines of argument for a historical Adam. First, biblically, an ex-
f the relative texts and extrabiblical literature from the Second
seem to require a historical Adam. Second, theologically, the
biblical storyline seems to require a literal original couple. And third, an-
thropologically, the scriptural view of humanity, morality, and religious
experience all also argue for the traditional view of Adam. One helpful
feature of Collins's book is that he makes his case while interacting with the
latest findings in science, particularly the field of genetics. We are adapting
his arguments for this chapter.

Biblical Evidence of the Historicity of Adam and Eve

The Bible presents two lines of evidence for the historicity of the original
couple. First, at a number places, Scripture presents genealogies that begin
with Adam. Genesis 5 provides the linage of Adam through Seth up to Noah
and his sons. Then Genesis 11 continues the genealogy from Shem, who was
Noah's son, to Abraham, who was the father of the Hebrew people. Thus, the
book of Genesis biologically connects Adam with the nation of Israel.

The book of 1 Chronicles takes a similar approach to that of Genesis,
but with much more thoroughness. The first nine chapters of the book are
devoted to providing genealogies of the twelve tribes of Israel, with special
attention given to King David and his descendants. Like Genesis, the first
chapter of 1 Chronicles gives the lineage from Adam to Abraham. In the New
Testament, the Gospel of Luke presents Jesus as the adopted son of Joseph.
Luke then traces the lineage backward, all the way to "Adam, the son of God"
(Luke 3:38). Through these genealogies the Bible presents Adam as the progenitor of the human race, Israel, and the Lord Jesus Christ.

Second, at a number of places Scripture presents Adam and Eve as historical persons, or Scripture speaks in a way that assumes their historicity. For
example, in Matthew 19 Jesus is asked for his views on divorce. He replies,
"Have you not read that he who created them from the beginning made them
male and female?" (v. 4) and then quotes Genesis 2:24. The text seems to indicate that our Lord understood Adam and Eve to be real persons.

Paul uses the events of Genesis 1–3 to make a point a number of times
(1 Cor. 11:7–12; 2 Cor. 11:3; 1 Tim. 2:13–14). In each instance it appears he
understood the Genesis account to be historical. The apostle clearly alluded to
Adam as a historical person when he spoke to the Athenians on Mars Hill, declaring that God "made from one man every nation of mankind to live on all
the face of the earth, having determined allotted periods and the boundaries

---

2. C. John Collins, *Did Adam and Eve Really Exist? Who They Were and Why You Should Care*
(Wheaton, Ill.: Crossway, 2011), 13–15.

of their dwelling place." (Acts 17:26). The New Testament views Adam and Eve as persons who really existed.

Theological Arguments Based on the Historicity of Adam and Eve *3. Federal Theology*

In two important New Testament passages, Romans 5:12–21 and 1 Corinthians 15:20–49, Paul builds theological arguments that seem to hinge on the historicity of Adam. In both passages Paul compares and contrasts Adam and Jesus. In Romans 5, the apostle explains that Adam is the source of sin and death and that Christ provided the remedy through his perfect life and vicarious atonement. Paul explains why we are dying sinners:

> Therefore, just as sin came into the world through one man, and death through sin, and so death spread to all men because all sinned—for sin indeed was in the world before the law was given, but sin is not counted where there is no law. Yet death reigned from Adam to Moses, even over those whose sinning was not like the transgression of Adam, who was a type of the one who was to come (Rom. 5:12–14)

However, because of Christ, Paul happily makes a contrast: "For as by the one man's disobedience the many were made sinners, so by the one man's obedience the many will be made righteous" (v. 19). In short, what Adam ruined, Christ has redeemed. Clearly Paul understood Adam to be a real person whose actions had real consequences for all.

In 1 Corinthians 15, Paul defends and explains the Christian understanding of the resurrection. He presents Adam and Christ as two federal heads over two realms. As representatives before God, Adam and Jesus stand in and over two different groups of humanity. Each group is said to be united, or "within" its respective, representative head. Each group, for better or for worse, experiences the same status as its respective head. Therefore, Adam and all those "in him" are united in a covenant of death. However, all those who are "in Christ" share in his life, and will one day share in his resurrection. The apostle declares, "For as by a man came death, by a man has come also the resurrection of the dead. For as in Adam all die, so also in Christ shall all be made alive" (1 Cor. 15:21–22). Again we see themes similar to those in Romans 5: Adam is the universal source of death; Christ is the universal source of life. What Adam lost through his disobedience, Christ has more than regained through his life, death, and resurrection. Paul continues his comparison and contrast of Adam and Jesus:

> Thus it is written, "The first man Adam became a living being"; the last Adam became a life-giving spirit. But it is not the spiritual that is first but the natural, and then the

spiritual. The first man was from the earth, a man of dust; the
second man is from heaven. As was the man of dust, so also
are those who are of the dust, and as is the man of heaven, so
also are those who are of heaven. Just as we have borne the
image of the man of dust, we shall also bear the image of the
man of heaven. (1 Cor. 15:45–49)

It should be noted that the apostle refers to Christ in this passage as "the
last Adam."

Virtually all New Testament scholars agree that Paul understood Adam
to be a historical person.[3] As we noted, in recent days some evangelicals have
questioned the historicity of the original couple and denied that the issue is
of any great importance. However, both Peter Enns and Denis Lamoureaux
admit that Jesus, Paul, and the other New Testament writers believed that
Adam and Eve were actual persons.[4] Enns and Lamoureaux conclude that the
New Testament authors simply were wrong on this matter. We believe this
conclusion is irreconcilable with a proper view of biblical inspiration.

The Challenge of Genetics

The American Scientific Affiliation is a society of evangelical scientists
and scholars with more than 1,500 members. A recent volume of its journal,
Perspectives on Science and Christian Faith, is entitled "Reading Genesis: The
Historicity of Adam and Eve, Genomics, and Evolutionary Science" with all
of its articles devoted to the question at hand. In the opening editorial, the
journal's editor, Arie Leegwater, warns that readers might find the volume
"a hard lesson to digest," as it surveys recent data in the field of comparative
genomics.[5] The mapping of the human genome and the subsequent mapping
of chimpanzees and gorillas has produced an explosion of research in genetic
origins. In one article, biologist Dennis Venema argues that recent findings
arrive at two conclusions that are irreconcilable with a historic Adam and
Eve: (1) humans descended from the same ancestors as did chimpanzees, and
(2) the population of original humans must have numbered around six thousand.[6] First, Venema contends that a comparison of human DNA with primate
DNA demonstrates that the two are not just similar, but nearly identical. The
respective genomes of humans and chimpanzees are nearly alike in sequence,

3. Collins, *Did Adam and Eve Really Exist?* 78–90.

4. Enns, *The Evolution of Adam*, 119–35; Lamoureux, *I Love Jesus and I Accept Evolution*,
80–84, 135–39.

5. Arie Leegwater, "A Hard Lesson: Interpretation, Genomic Data, and the Scriptures,"
Perspectives on Science and Christian Faith 62, no. 3 (September 2010): 145–46.

6. Dennis R. Venema, "Genesis and the Genome: Genomics Evidence for Human-Ape
Common Ancestry and Ancestral Hominid Population Sizes," *Perspectives on Science and
Christian Faith* 62, no. 3 (September 2010): 166–78.

redundancy, and organization. Even the "junk DNA" of both sequences are practically the same. Venema concludes, "Numerous independent lines of genomics evidence strongly support the hypothesis that our species shares a common ancestor with other primates."[7] – *or Comen design?*

Venema points to the second finding as being as problematic as the first: genetic evidence indicates that humans descended from an ancestral population of approximately six thousand individuals.[8] Even though it appears that all humans share a common female ancestor (often called "Mitochondrial Eve") who lived approximately 150,000 years ago, and a common male ancestor ("Y-Chromosomal Adam") from about 50,000 years ago, this does not mean they were the only progenitors. It simply means that they were the most successful ones. Venema declares, "As such, the hypothesis that humans are genetically derived from a single ancestral pair in the recent past has no support from a genomics perspective, and, indeed, is counter to a large body of evidence."[9]

Venema's article is followed by articles from Daniel Harlow and John Schneider, both faculty members of the religion department at Calvin College.[10] Both men argue strongly for understanding Adam and Eve strictly as literary characters. They recognize that this would necessitate a redefining of the doctrines of the fall, original sin, and even the inspiration of Scripture. They contend that the genomic evidence leaves no other option.

However, not all evolutionary creationists agree with Venema, Harlow, and Schneider. Surprisingly, a number of believing scientists who embrace evolution do not believe that it is necessary to jettison a historical Adam and Eve. Denis Alexander, Vernon Bauer, and Kenneth Kemp are evolutionary creationists who argue for continuing to affirm the historicity of an original couple.[11] We will look at their arguments in detail in Question 38 ("Can a Christian Hold to Theistic Evolution?").

Criteria for Integrating the Biblical Text and Scientific Findings

Collins asks, "Now then: how do we stay within the bounds of sound thinking?"[12] He then provides four criteria for evaluating our options. First,

7. Ibid., 166.
8. Ibid., 173–75.
9. Ibid., 175.
10. Daniel C. Harlow, "After Adam: Reading Genesis in an Age of Evolutionary Science," *Perspectives on Science and Christian Faith* 62, no. 3 (September 2010): 179–95; John Schneider, "Recent Genetic Science and Christian Theology on Human Origins: An 'Aesthetic Supralapsarianism,'" *Perspectives on Science and Christian Faith* 62, no. 3 (September 2010): 196–213.
11. Denis Alexander, *Creation or Evolution: Do We Have to Choose?* (Grand Rapids: Monarch, 2008), 234–43; Vernon W. Bauer, *Can a Christian Be an Evolutionist?* (North Charleston: CreateSpace, 2011), 309–14; Kenneth W. Kemp, "Science, Theology, and Monogenesis," *American Philosophical Catholic Quarterly* 85, no. 2 (Spring 2011): 217–36.
12. Collins, *Did Adam and Eve Really Exist?* 120–21.

the origin of the human race must be understood as something greater than merely the product of natural development. Humans possess the divine image, and it is difficult to see how this could emerge only from evolutionary processes. Second, Adam and Eve must be understood as "the headwaters of the human race."[13] Otherwise the unity of the human race is lost, along with humanity's collective and individual dignity and moral responsibility. Third, we must affirm the historicity of the fall, along with its corporate culpability.[14] In addition, the fall should be understood to have "occurred at the beginning of the human race."[15] And fourth, any attempt to merge evolutionary theory with a historical Adam and Eve must somehow preserve the notion of Adam's federal headship in such a way that preserves the full force of the New Testament teaching concerning original sin.

Conclusion

Clearly, an affirmation of the historicity of Adam and Eve must be maintained. Collins concludes his work by giving four reasons why this issue matters. First, the historicity of the original couple is essential for the grand narrative of redemption as given in the Bible. Collins states,

> If we abandon the conventional way of telling the Christian story, with its components of a good creation marred by the fall, redemption as God's ongoing work to restore the creatures to their proper functioning, and the consummation in which the restoration will be complete and confirmed, then we really give up all chance of understanding the world.[16]

Second, affirming the existence of a real original couple is necessary for affirming the reality of the original rebellion. Otherwise the biblical understanding of sin and Christ's atonement for sin are seriously undermined. Third, if we give up the biblical doctrine of humanity's common origin, then we also risk losing the doctrine of common human dignity and the possibility of a common salvation. And last, "sooner or later" we have to recognize that our answer on this question affects our stance on biblical authority.[17]

So is it possible to hold to evolution and a historical Adam and Eve? This is the challenge facing evangelicals who embrace evolutionary creationism. Question 38 focuses on that question.

---

13. Ibid.
14. See Question 27 for discussion on the effects of the fall.
15. Collins, *Did Adam and Eve Really Exist?* 120–21.
16. Ibid.,133–35.
17. Ibid.

REFLECTION QUESTIONS

1. What are the two lines of biblical evidence in favor of a historical Adam and Eve?

2. What theological arguments does the Apostle Paul make in which he assumes a historical Adam?

3. What two conclusions in the field of genetics are difficult to reconcile with a historical Adam?

4. What are Collins's four criteria for examining this question?

5. For what four reasons does the question of a historical Adam and Eve matter?

What Was the Nature of the Original Sin?

Many are generally familiar with the incident of the fall of Adam and Eve in the garden of Eden. There is not much agreement, however, about the nature of this first temptation and what led to the disobedience of the first command. We know that original sin stems from Adam and that his disobedience gave original sin a historical beginning, so that the present sinfulness of all can be traced back through the generations, to the first man, the progenitor of the race. John Calvin described the effects of this original sin as follows: "Original sin, therefore, seems to be a hereditary depravity and corruption of our nature, diffused into all parts of the soul, which first makes us liable to God's wrath, then also brings forth in us those works which Scripture calls 'works of the flesh'" (Gal. 5:19).[1] In recent years, interpreters have equated the nature of the original sin to such things as the desire to be God, envy, pride, depravation, and sexual temptation.[2]

To better understand the nature of the original sin, we must first look at the original command (Gen. 2:16–17), then the original temptation (Gen. 3:1–5), and finally the original violation (Gen. 3:6–7).

---

1. John Calvin, *Calvin: Institute of the Christian Religion*, trans. Ford Lewis Battles, 2 vols. (Philadelphia: Westminster, 1975), 1: 251. See Henri Blocher, *Original Sin: Illuminating the Riddle*, NSBT (Downers Grove: InterVarsity, 1997), 18. There is some indication from ancient Judaism that the fall included Eve's sexual defilement by the serpent. See *b. Shabbat* 146a; *b. Yebamot* 103b; *b. 'Abodah Zarah* 22b; Alan Cooper, "A Medieval Jewish Version of Original Sin: Ephraim of Luntshits on Leviticus 12," *HTR* 97, no. 4 (2004): 446, 450; Blocher, *Original Sin*, 112–13.
2. See Christian Duquoc, "New Approaches to Original Sin," *Cross Currents* 28, no. 2 (1978): 195; Leon O. Hynson, "Original Sin As Privation: An Inquiry into a Theology of Sin and Sanctification," *Wesleyan Theological Journal* 22, no. 2 (1987): 65–68. The early church fathers thought envy constituted the original sin. See Gustav Wingren, *Credo* (Minneapolis: Augsburg, 1981), 26.

The Original Command

After reading that God placed man in the garden (Gen. 2:15–17), we are immediately told that it was "not good" that the man was alone (Gen. 2:18). This circumstance was the only thing not good about God's creation. But before God began to correct the only thing that was "not good" with creation, God gave Adam a single command: "You may surely eat of every tree of the garden, but of the tree of the knowledge of good and evil you shall not eat, for in the day that you eat of it you shall surely die" (Gen. 2:16–17).

The stress of this original command was clearly on the goodness and generosity of God. Every tree would be available for man to eat, but one. The man had great freedom with only one prohibition, not to partake of the tree of the knowledge of good and evil. While the words "good and evil" occur in several Old Testament contexts, the exact Hebrew expression in Genesis 2–3 occurs elsewhere only in one passage, Deuteronomy 1:39. This passage applies the phrase "good and evil" to young children who do not as yet know the difference between "good and evil." Nahum Sarna comments on the implication of the use of this phrase from Deuteronomy 1:39 when he states, "There the context leaves no doubt that not to know good and bad means to be innocent, not to have attained the age of responsibility. In the present passage, then, it is best to understand 'knowledge of good and bad' as the capacity to make independent judgments concerning human welfare."[3]

The violation of the single prohibition not to partake of this tree would result in death—"you shall surely die" (Gen. 2:17). Physical death would occur (see Genesis 5) but also spiritual death is in view as disobedience would lead to a broken relationship with God (Gen. 3:7–10, 24). The prohibition was a test of trust and obedience, but they could still partake of the Tree of Life. As Gordon Wenham states, "Contrary to expectation, man is allowed to eat of the tree of life, but not of the tree of wisdom, for that leads to human autonomy and an independence of the creator incompatible with the trustful relationship between man and his maker which the story presupposes."[4]

The Original Temptation

Subsequent to God's command to Adam in Genesis 2:16–17, God formed the woman and instituted the marriage relationship in Genesis 2:18–24. The narrator then reports that the first man and woman were both naked but not ashamed (Gen. 2:25). Just as the phrase "knowledge of good and evil" alludes to the fact that the man and the woman were innocent in their pre-fall

---

3. Nahum M. Sarna, *Genesis*, JPSTC (Philadelphia: Jewish Publication Society, 1989), 19.
4. Gordon J. Wenham, *Genesis 1–15*, WBC 1 (Waco, Tex.: Word, 1987), 87. Thus, the first couple could not invoke deprivation if they were to disobey and eat the forbidden fruit. See Umberto Cassuto, *A Commentary on the Book of Genesis*, 2 vols. (vol. 1, *From Adam to Noah, Genesis I–VI:8*), trans. Israel Abrahams (Jerusalem: Magnes 1961–64), 1:125; Sarna, *Genesis*, 18.

condition, the same can be said with regard to the statement about their na-kedness. "So long as the harmony with God remained undisturbed, the pris-tine innocence and dignity of sexuality was not despoiled."[5]

Genesis 2:25 is a transitional verse in the narrative. It refers to the "two of them," who have been the focus of the narrative of Genesis 2:18–24, as well as the reference to the couple's nakedness (*arummim*), which relates to the next verse constituting a play on words—the serpent was more "crafty" (*arum*) than any beast of the field (Gen. 3:1).[6] The serpent's craftiness is on display in the dialogue in Genesis 3:1b–5.

The serpent began the conversation about God's command with the woman and, in doing so, exhibits his craftiness since she had not been created when God established the test in Genesis 2:16–17. She is approached because, unlike the man, she had not received the prohibition directly from God. Immediately, the serpent began to mislead as he softened God's instructions, changing what God had "commanded" (Gen. 2:16) to what God "said" (Gen. 3:1b). Then he misquoted God's command as he deliberately questioned what God had spoken: "Did God actually say, 'You shall not eat of any tree in the garden'?" In asking this question, the serpent's report of God's words has not been precise. In the original command in Genesis 2:16–17, the focus was on God's generosity as he magnanimously allowed the first couple to eat from "all" the trees of the garden but one. The serpent suggests just the opposite.[7] The serpent attempts to say that the restriction is not for only one tree but for all the trees of the garden. He exaggerates the prohibition whereas the original command focused on God's gracious provision. "By misrepresenting the orig-inal permission and overstating the conditions of the prohibition, the serpent seeks to plant the idea in the woman's mind that the prohibition is unfair."[8] As a consequence, the woman is drawn into a dialogue as she is compelled to correct the misquotation and perhaps senses a need to defend God.

Eve's response to the serpent's question occurs in Genesis 2:2–3. In Eve's response she gives a paraphrase of God's command, but in doing so utters three statements that are actually in conflict with the spirit of God's instruction. First, she minimizes God's provision. God had stated that they may "eat of every tree

5. Sarna, *Genesis*, 23.

6. The word "naked" also anticipates the change that occurs in Genesis 3:7. The word "crafty" (*arum*) occurs elsewhere in Job and Proverbs where it is used with a more positive conno-tation. It seems to be suggested that the snake possessed the "knowledge of good and evil," since otherwise the tempter could not have argued as he did in Genesis 3:1–5.

7. What the serpent has suggested could be interpreted to mean a total denial of food. The serpent also refers to God as simply God (Elohim) instead of LORD (Yahweh) God, which is used throughout Genesis 2–3. The name Yahweh is Israel's God's personal name and is associated with the covenant that exists between God and the nation, as well as the fulfill-ment of promises.

8. Kenneth M. Craig, Jr. "Misspeaking in Eden, or, Fielding Questions in the Garden (Genesis 2:16–3:13)," *Perspectives in Religions Studies*," 27, no. 3 (2000): 241.

of the garden" (Gen. 2:16). The woman minimizes this generous provision by omitting the word "every," stating, "we may eat of the fruit of the trees in the garden" (Gen. 3:2). This indicates a lack of gratitude for what God has provided.[9]

Secondly, she added to the initial command. Eve stated that the command included a prohibition regarding "touching the tree" (Gen. 3:3). This command is not part of the original command in Genesis 2:16–17.[10] By stating that not every tree is available for food and by adding the additional prohibition, there is the suggestion that Eve thinks God to be unreasonable.

Finally, the woman weakened the penalty for disobedience. God had stated in Genesis 2:17 that a violation of God's command would result in certain death—"you shall surely die." The construction of the verb is emphatic. Eve lessens the certainty of the penalty by announcing only "lest you die" (Gen. 3:3). She has in effect omitted a word that would lend emphasis to the statement. All these changes which lead to a watering down of the commandment function to increase the appeal to sin.[11]

As the serpent responded to Eve's explanation, it is clear that his wording is closer to the actual command (see Gen. 2:17). However, he contradicts God's statement by placing the negative particle "no"(Hb. *lo*) in front of God's words, when he stated, "You will not surely die" (Gen. 3:4). The serpent in effect denies that there will be a penalty for sin. Next, the serpent ascribes self-serving motives to God, undermining God's credibility in her eyes (Gen. 3:5). God is portrayed as keeping something from the couple because he knows that if they partake of the tree their eyes will be opened and they will "become like God, knowing good and evil." The serpent in effect lures the first couple with the hope of divinity. Sarna effectively summarized the serpent's adroitness in his dialogue with Eve: "The serpent's cunning reveals itself in the way it frames the question, in its knowledge of the divine proscription, in its claim to be able to probe God's mind and intent, and in the selection of its victim."[12]

The Original Violation

As Eve was convinced that God was trying to hold her and Adam back from being like God, the appeal of the forbidden fruit was sufficient to draw them into disobedience. After the somewhat lengthy discussion of the

---

9. She also does not refer to the tree by name, "the tree of the knowledge of good and evil." Richard S. Hess remarks that by not defining the tree, she has in effect removed the reason for not eating from it ("The Roles of the Woman and the Man in Genesis 3," *Themelios* 18 [1993]: 16).

10. The violation of adding to the Word of God comes to mind (Deut. 4:2; 12:32; Prov. 30:5–6; Rev. 22:18–19).

11. Following the serpent she also changes God's name from the LORD God (Gen. 2:16) to simply God (Gen. 3:3). See Wenham, *Genesis 1–15*, 73.

12. Sarna, *Genesis*, 24.

temptation in Genesis 3:1–5, the actual violation is now described in rapid and remarkable brevity: "So when the woman saw that the tree was good for food, and that it was a delight to the eyes, and that the tree was to be desired to make one wise, she took of its fruit and ate, and she also gave some to her husband who was with her, and he ate" (Gen. 3:6).[13]

The beginning of the violation begins with the phrase—"So when the woman saw that the tree was good" (Gen. 3:6a). This phrase echoes the seven times repeated phrase from the creation account—"God saw that it was good" (Gen. 1:3, 10, 12, 18, 21, 25, 31). By giving her own evaluation, it is as though she is putting herself in the place of God, assuming God's role, and is now independently determining what was good. As Wayne Grudem has stated, "Eve trusted her own evaluation of what was right and what would be good for her, rather than allowing God's words to define right and wrong" (Gen. 3:6).[14] The good has already been debased in her mind and its definition is now rooted in the appeal to the senses. Allen Ross comments, "Practicality for food, aesthetic beauty, and the potential for wisdom—the physical, emotional, and spiritual senses—all worked together to draw Eve into sin. The new possibilities of life enticed Eve to eat. This threefold description of what Eve perceived seems to be reflected in John's 'lust of the flesh, lust of the eyes, and the pride of life' (1 John 2:16). Natural desires for food, beauty, and knowledge are gifts from God but are to be used within his restrictions."[15]

It is at this point in the narrative that we learn that Adam, who received the original command from God, is now said "to be with her." The switch from the singular verbs in Genesis 2:16–17 to the plural in Genesis 3:1–6 indicates that Adam was in the garden all along and hence was privy to the whole discussion regarding God's original command.

As a result of the violation, we read in Genesis 3:7 that "their eyes were opened"—just as the serpent had foretold. The violation of the command had an immediate effect. The new insight they gained was only the consciousness of their own nakedness, resulting in shame which caused them to avoid fellowship with their Creator. They attempted to hide their shame by covering themselves with fig leaves (Gen. 3:8). Waltke comments on the significance of their nakedness when he states, "In the Bible, *arum* usually describes someone stripped of protective clothing and 'naked' in the sense of being defenseless, weak, or humiliated (Deut. 28:48; Job 1:21; Isa. 58:7). With an awareness of guilt and a loss of innocence, the couple now feels shame in their naked state. Their spiritual death is revealed by their alienation from one another,

---

13. The Hebrew narrative tense (the *waw*-consecutive with preterite, also called *wayyiqtol*) occurs no less than eleven times in Genesis 3:6–8.
14. Wayne Grudem, *Systematic Theology* (Grand Rapids: Zondervan, 1994), 493.
15. Allen P. Ross, *Creation and Blessing* (Grand Rapids: Baker, 1988), 136.

symbolized by sewing fig leaves together for barriers, and by their separation from God, symbolized by hiding among the trees."[16]

The innocent serenity of Genesis 2:25 has come to an end. In conversation with the serpent, the woman spoke as if she and the man were indeed bone of bone and flesh of flesh (Gen. 2:23). But now they are alienated. Notice that after the fall the original couple no longer refer to themselves as "we" but rather "I" or "me" (Gen. 3:10, 12–13).[17] And now because Adam and Eve have attained this sinful state, they must not eat of the Tree of Life.

They are prevented from eating of the Tree of Life so they cannot continue in this state forever (Gen. 3:22). Man, a creature, created by God is distinct from God and has a place as God's creature (Gen. 2:16–18, 21–22). A human desire to be like God on the part of man is an act of rebellion, transgressing the established limits.[18]

Search for Wisdom

The description of the serpent as "crafty" in the introduction to the fall account (Gen. 3:1) places a possible connection on the relationship between the fall and the human search for wisdom. God had made everything "good" for the first man and woman and yet they desired more—they wanted to expand their knowledge and be like God.[19] Martin Emmrich has noted man's limitations particularly with regard to the search for wisdom: "The acquisition of wisdom is seen as one of the highest goals of the godly according to the book of Proverbs. But the wisdom literature also makes it plain that there is a wisdom that is God's sole preserve, which man should not aspire to attain (e.g., Job 15:7–9, 40; Prov. 30:1–4), since a full understanding of God, the universe, and man's place in it is ultimately beyond human comprehension. To pursue it without reference to revelation is to assert human autonomy, and to neglect the fear of the LORD which is the beginning of knowledge (Prov. 1:7)."[20]

Conclusion

It is often asserted by many contemporary scholars that rabbinic thought does not have a clear concept of original sin or that there was not a consensus for understanding the origin of sin in first-century Judaism. This appears to

---

16. Bruce K. Waltke and Cathi J. Fredricks, *Genesis* (Grand Rapids: Zondervan, 2001), 92. See Sarna, *Genesis*, 25.
17. See Craig, "Misspeaking in Eden," 246. The singular forms in Genesis 3:9–13, apparently indicating their alienation, replace the plural verbal forms in Genesis 3:1–8.
18. See Alan Jon Hauser, "Genesis 2–3: The Theme of Intimacy and Alienation," in *I Studied Inscriptions from before the Flood*, ed. Richard S. Hess and David Toshio Tsumura (Winona Lake: Eisenbrauns, 1994), 390; Waltke and Fredricks, *Genesis*, 92.
19. See John H. Sailhamer, *The Pentateuch as Narrative* (Grand Rapids: Zondervan, 1992), 103.
20. Martin Emmrich, "The Temptation Narrative of Genesis 3:1–6: A Prelude to the Pentateuch and the History of Israel," *EvQ* 73, no. 1 (2001): 8.

be overstated. There is evidence in ancient Jewish interpretive tradition that the notion of original sin was a clear reality. For example, in the intertestamental work 2 Esdras 7:118, we read, "O Adam, what have you done? For though it was you who sinned, the fall was not yours alone, but ours also who are your descendants." The Apocryphal book Wisdom of Solomon states: "For God created us for incorruption, and made us in the image of his own eternity, but through the devil's envy death entered the world, and those who belong to his company experience it" (2:23–24).[21]

The "original sin," of course, was not foreign to the New Testament.[22] The New Testament says Eve was beguiled, but man sinned willfully (1 Tim. 2:14), while Romans 5:12–21 and 1 Corinthians 15:22 are Paul's classic analysis of the effects of the fall and the remedy in Christ.

As Genesis 3 gives us the historical understanding of how sin entered the world and affected all of Adam and Eve's descendants, it also gives us an example of what takes place, or what process is followed, when a person commits a sin.

We see from Genesis 3 that Satan is behind the temptation of our first parents, and he comes to them with a lie. The lie is that there is no punishment for disobedience "you will not surely die" (Gen. 3:4). Rightly did Jesus say that he was a liar from the beginning (John 8:44). The Bible is unequivocal. You cannot get away with sin. Disobedience and the commission of sin brings forth death. Dietrich Bonhoeffer perceptibly commented on the serpent's lie in Genesis 3: "That the lie portrays the truth as lie is the ultimate possible rebellion. It is the abyss of the lie that lives because it sets itself up as truth and condemns the truth as lie."[23]

Moreover, the deception is misleading. There is a certain truth that disobedience to God's commandment would make the first couple more "like God," but in a much more misleading way than they would have realized. With the knowledge of good there would also be the knowledge of evil, and what this would entail was not made clear to them. As Kenneth Mathews stated, "The serpent spoke only about what she would gain and avoided mentioning what she would lose in the process."[24] Their knowledge is expanded but it now creates a barrier in their relationship with God. In one sense it is true, they became more like God because their knowledge was expanded, knowing good and evil (see Gen. 3:22). But on the other hand, becoming like God,

21. Similarly, see Sirach 25:24; 2 Esdras 4:30; 2 Baruch 54:15, 19. See also E. P. Sanders, *Paul and Palestinian Judaism: A Comparison of Patterns of Religion* (London, SCM, 1977), 114; Charles A. Gieschen, "Original Sin in the New Testament," *Concordia Journal* 31, no. 4 (2005): 360–61; J. M. Moe, *Pharisaism and Christianity* (St. Louis: Concordia, 1964), 75.
22. For helpful discussions see Blocher, *Original Sin*, 34; Stanley E. Porter, "The Pauline Concept of Original Sin in Light of Rabbinic Background," *TynBul* 41, no. 1 (1990): 3–30.
23. Dietrich Bonhoeffer, *Creation and Fall: A Theological Interpretation of Genesis 1–3* (London: SCM Press, 1959), 70.
24. Kenneth Mathews, *Genesis 1–11:26*, NAC 1A (Nashville: B&H, 1996), 237.

knowing good and evil, only served to separate them from him. Wenham notes, "Becoming like God separates them from Him. . . . The snake's promises have come true but in a very different way from the way one might have expected, had they come from God. . . . In this sense they did die on the day they ate of the tree: they were no longer able to have daily conversation with God, enjoy his bounteous provision, and eat of the tree of life; instead they had to toil for food, suffer, and eventually return to the dust from which they were taken."[25] They experienced a spiritual death symbolized by their separation from God, as they tried to hide among the trees.[26]

It is also clear in Genesis 3 that temptation involves a misusing and a misunderstanding of God's Word. This is clearly seen in the temptation as God's original words are distorted. Furthermore, the woman presumes upon God's role of "knowing the good." She determines what is good on her own, and thus is not satisfied to live with God's provision. She seeks to determine her own morality and make her own moral judgments apart from God. The couple thus covet a better life situation than the one that God has so graciously provided.[27] Hence, the violation of the most comprehensive commandment, the tenth commandment, is possibly at the heart of the violation in Genesis 3.

Adam and Eve were surrounded by wonderful trees and provisions in the garden, including the Tree of Life, but all they could see was the one from which they could not partake. When Satan gets our eyes on what we cannot do, we are determined to do it. But by contrast, the focus of the Christian should be on all the good that God provides, not on the few restrictions that ultimately have our goodness and well-being in mind. The occurrence of the original sin from command, to temptation, to violation seems to follow the pattern of sin in James 1:14–15: "But each person is tempted when he is lured and enticed by his own desire. Then desire when it has conceived gives birth to sin, and sin when it is fully grown brings forth death." Genesis 3 not only explains the original sin and its effect, but at the same time is a paradigm for the process of temptation that has been repeated an almost infinite number of times in human history.

To enjoy God's good in creation, man must trust God and obey him. If man disobeys, he will have to decide for himself what is good and what is not good. Yet, there is hope in Genesis 3 as we learn that God did not create humans in their current condition. There is hope that God will reconstitute this fallen creation and creation will celebrate when the children of God are revealed (Rom. 8:19–23).

---

25. Wenham, *Genesis 1–15*, 74.
26. Waltke and Fredericks, *Genesis*, 103.
27. The use of two roots, "*delight* (root, *awah*) to the eyes," "*desired* (root, *khamad*) to make one wise," in Genesis 3:6 occur together elsewhere in Scripture only in the tenth commandment in Deuteronomy 5:21—the prohibition against coveting. See Mark F. Rooker, *The Ten Commandments: Ethics for the Twenty-first Century*, NACSBT (Nashville: B&H, 2010), 166, 168.

REFLECTION QUESTIONS

1. How did the serpent demonstrate his craftiness in Genesis 3?

2. Did Eve quote God's words accurately in Genesis 3? Explain.

3. What is the significance of the phrase, "the woman saw that the tree was good for food?" (Gen. 3:6)

4. What was Adam's role in the dialogue between Eve and the serpent?

5. Did Adam and Eve die when they ate from the forbidden tree? Explain.

Was There Animal Death Before the Fall?

The creation account of Genesis 1 ends with the declaration, "And God saw everything that he had made, and behold, it was very good" (Gen. 1:31). For this chapter and the next, the key issue boils down to what is meant by the expression "very good." On this matter, old-earth creationism (OEC) and young-earth creationism (YEC) proponents agree. More than the proper interpretation of Genesis 1–3, the age of the earth, or even the theory of evolution, this is the question that stands above all others: Did animals die before Adam and Eve fell in the garden?

The fossil record presents us with a troubling past. It reveals a history of predation, disease, and intrinsic selfishness. The rocks speak of a history in which, for every creature, nearly every moment was filled either with hunting prey or being hunted (or doing both at the same time). The past is filled with giant sea monsters and ancient diseases. The fossil remains of dinosaurs show evidence of tumors and other ailments. Natural history exhibits the intrinsic selfishness of natural selection—the survival of the fittest. The strong preyed upon the weak, and the weak were selected for extinction. Carnivorous behavior, suffering, and illnesses are typically labeled as "natural evils." What is troubling is that these evils appear to be present throughout natural history as presented in the fossil record.

The problem of immense suffering in the natural world was not lost on Darwin. He once observed, "What a book a Devil's chaplain might write on the clumsy, wasteful, blundering low & horridly cruel works of nature!"[1] Later Darwinists echo his opinion. Richard Dawkins states,

---

1. Charles Darwin, "Letter to J. D. Hooker," (July 13, 1856), http://www.darwinproject.ac.uk/entry-1924 (accessed 12/14/11).

The total amount of suffering per year in the natural world is beyond all decent contemplation. During the minute it takes me to compose this sentence, thousands of animals are being eaten alive; others are running for their lives, whimpering with fear; others are being slowly devoured from within by rasping parasites; thousands of all kinds are dying of starvation, thirst and disease.[2]

David Hull asks, "What kind of God [would create the] Galapagos Islands? . . . The God of the Galapagos is careless, wasteful, indifferent, almost diabolical. He is certainly not the sort of God to whom anyone would be inclined to pray."[3] They see the tragic history of the fossil record as difficult to reconcile with the Christian understanding of the benevolent nature of God.

So, was there animal death before the fall? Various groups of Christians hold to four different views: one that answers no and three that say yes. Arguing for the first view, Kurt Wise and Ken Ham contend that no creatures, including insects and bacteria, experienced death before Adam's fall. For them and other YEC proponents, the question of animal death goes to the very heart of the authority of Scripture and the nature of God.

William Demski presents a second view. He makes the interesting argument that, though animal death predated the events of Genesis 3, their deaths still are the outcome of Adam's sin. Adam's fall, like Jesus's atonement, was a cosmic event, and as such had retroactive effects. And still others, including C. S. Lewis and Charles Foster, give a third view. They suggest that natural evil came about with the arrival of the first evildoer—Lucifer. Satan committed the initial moral evil when he rebelled against God sometime in the primeval past and, in so doing, brought about natural evil. Therefore, suffering and death existed before Adam and Eve arrived on the scene. Finally, some, such as Hugh Ross, David Snoke, and Mark Whorton, say that animals died before Adam's fall, but they do not hesitate to attribute the cause of death to God. They argue that the nature and purpose of death changed when Adam and Eve rebelled.

This chapter and the next address the central issue of the creation-evolution controversy: the nature and effects of Adam's fall. The next chapter explores the general question of the effects of the fall, while this chapter specifically addresses the important question of animal death. We will briefly look at each of the four answers provided by evangelical Christians.

---

2. Richard Dawkins, *River Out of Eden* (New York: HarperCollins, 1996), 132. Cited in Michael J. Murray, *Nature Red in Tooth and Claw: Theism and the Problem of Animal Suffering* (Oxford: Oxford University Press: 2008), 4.

3. David L. Hull, "God of the Galapagos," *Nature* 392 (1992): 485–86. Cited in Charles Foster, *The Selfless Gene: Living with God and Darwin* (Nashville: Thomas Nelson, 2009), 152. Hunter has also documented the impact natural evil had on Darwin and later Darwinists (see Cornelius Hunter, *Darwin's God: Evolution and the Problem of Evil* [Grand Rapids: Brazos, 2001]).

No—There Was No Animal Death Prior to the Fall

YEC proponents universally agree that when God cursed Adam and Eve (Gen. 3) the effects resulted in death coming upon all creation. Five lines of argument can be noted. First, they contend that the Bible teaches that animals were originally vegetarian. On the sixth day of creation, God declares, "And to every beast of the earth and to every bird of the heavens and to everything that creeps on the earth, everything that has the breath of life, I have given every green plant for food" (Gen. 1:30). YEC advocates infer from this verse that, due to God's perfect design of the world, all creatures were intended to have strictly vegetarian diets.[4] In addition, when Christ returns this idyllic state will return also. Isaiah predicts that "the wolf and the lamb shall graze together; the lion shall eat straw like the ox" (Isa. 65:25). These verses indicate that the predator-prey relationship that is the norm in this present age is the result of Adam's fall. This relationship did not exist prior to the curse and will not continue in the *eschaton*.

Second, looking to the New Testament, YEC advocates argue that it points to Adam as the cause of all death in the world.[5] Paul declares that "just as sin came into the world through one man, *and death through sin* . . ." (Rom. 5:12, emphasis added). Similarly, he states "by a man came death" (1 Cor. 15:21). Therefore, physical death is only a temporary condition within creation due to Adam's sin. Prior to death being introduced into the world, all creatures were conditionally immortal—from the smallest bacteria to the largest dinosaurs. Third, YEC proponents suggest that prior to the fall, God's special providence was much more active in the natural order. They point to the experience of the Israelites in the wilderness.[6] Although they traveled through the desert for forty years, their clothes and sandals never wore out (Deut. 29:5). In like manner, God sustained all life in the pre-fall natural order.

Fourth, certain core theological commitments lead YEC proponents to hold to the no-death position. Kurt Wise argues that an old earth cannot be reconciled with a good God.[7] Some, such as Ken Ham, view the existence of death before the fall as contradictory to the doctrine of the atonement.[8] At the fall, God punished Adam and Eve with the curse. This curse introduced death

---

4. Tim Chaffey and Jason Lisle, *Old Creationism on Trial: The Verdict Is In* (Green Forest, Ark.: Master, 2008), 29.
5. Ken Ham, "Appendix One: Twenty Reasons Genesis and Evolution Do Not Mix," http://www.answersingenesis.org/articles/lie/genesis-evolution-not-mix (accessed 12/21/11).
6. Jonathan Sarfati, *Refuting Compromise: A Biblical and Scientific Refutation of "Progressive Creationism" (Billions of Years), As Popularized by Astronomer Hugh Ross* (Green Forest, Ark.: Master, 2004), 213–14.
7. Kurt Wise, *Faith, Form, and Time: What the Bible Teaches and Science Confirms About Creation and the Age of the Universe* (Nashville: B&H, 2002), 56–57.
8. Ken Ham, "Keeping at Arm's Length," http://www.answersingenesis.org/articles/2004/09/06/keeping-at-arms-length (accessed 12/20/11).

and bloodshed because of sin. The first animal death immediately followed as God skinned an animal to provide the first couple with clothing (Gen. 3:21). This sacrifice foreshadowed the future death of Christ, which would cover our sin. If death existed before the fall, then the doctrine of the atonement is stripped of its meaning and the gospel loses coherence.

Last (and this is an important point), YEC advocates do not hold to the no-death position due to their views concerning the age of the earth. Rather, it is their commitment to God introducing death during the fall that requires a young earth.[9] This commitment compels them to reinterpret the fossil record and its apparent account of death and disease throughout history. If one approaches the natural record with a prior commitment to death not being introduced until the advent of Adam, it is then impossible to accept the *prima facie* reading of the fossils.

Yes—But Animal Death Was Still Caused by Adam

In his work, *The End of Christianity*, William Dembski proposes that the earth is ancient and that death has reigned since the world's beginning.[10] However, even though death chronologically preceded Adam's fall by millions of years, it was still caused by Adam's rebellion. This is because Adam, like Christ, fulfilled the role of federal head over the cosmos. As the positional representative for all creation, Adam's decisions and actions (again like Christ) had an effect that transcends time.

Dembski argues primarily from analogy—comparing the transcendent, cosmic effects of Christ's death with the similarly cosmic impact of Adam's sin. When Jesus died, he not only paid for the sins of those who would come after him, but also for Old Testament believers. In the same way, it is possible that Adam's failure also transcended time causing death retroactively. This would mean that although death appears since creation, it was not caused by God. Instead, it is due to the future failing of Adam to disobedience. The next chapter deals with the effects of the fall, and Dembski's position will be given additional attention there.

Yes—Animal Death Was Caused by Satan

Proponents of a third view agree with Dembski that death predates Adam's fall, and they also agree that death is the result of rebellion against God. But instead of seeing Adam as the first morally responsible agent, they view Lucifer as the guilty party. Advocates such as Charles Foster argue that the other views do not adequately take into account that humans were not the first created beings to rebel. They also note that the creation accounts of

---

9. Ken Ham, "A Young Earth—It's Not the Issue!" www.answersingenesis.org/articles/1998/01/23/young-earth-not-issue (accessed 12/20/11).

10. William A. Dembski, *The End of Christianity* (Nashville: B&H, 2009).

Genesis 1–2 do not give any information about the timing of Satan's fall, but it is clear by Genesis 3 that it had already occurred.

So how might Lucifer's fall have affected the physical universe? Advocates of this position give two different answers. A few, such as G. H. Pember, argue that demonic beings actually created the killer animals.[11] Other proponents do not attribute such creative powers to Satan. R. A. Torrey and Donald Grey Barnhouse place a gap between the first two verses of Genesis 1.[12] At that time, they posit, Lucifer's war against God wreaked havoc on the created order and Satan corrupted what God created. Nor is there reason to assume that this supernatural twisting and perverting of creation has ceased. Gregory Boyd argues that all natural evils have a direct, supernatural catalyst.[13] Hurricanes, earthquakes, and floods are efficiently caused by the active evil forces within the supernatural realm.

Yes—Animal Death Was Caused by God

The answer given by most evangelical scholars who hold to an ancient earth is that God created animal death prior to the events of Genesis 3, but that humans (who were created in his image) were not intended to experience death. Five arguments can be noted. First, OEC proponents, such as Hugh Ross, David Snoke, and Mark Whorton, argue that the world was not originally created as a paradise—only Eden was.[14] They point to a number of aspects of the original creation to make their case. The Bible opens with an emphasis on the existence of the sea and the dark (Gen. 1:1–2). This demonstrates that the original creation was not a place of serene calm. For the Hebrew people (and the surrounding ancient Near Eastern cultures) both were a place of dread. Whorton notes that the Bible describes the original creation as "very good" but not "perfect." In fact, Scripture uses the same expression to describe certain features of this present, fallen state (e.g., Num. 14:7). Whorton argues that, rather than a "perfect paradise," the original creation fulfilled a "perfect purpose." He claims that the world of Genesis 1 "was very good because it was

11. G. H. Pember, *Earth's Earliest Ages* (Grand Rapids: Kregel, 1876 [1975]). See also David N. Livingstone, *The Preadamite Theory and the Marriage of Science and Religion* (Philadelphia: APA, 1992), 35. Livingstone notes that almost all who hold to a gap theory also argue for a pre-adamic race.

12. R. A. Torrey, *Difficulties in the Bible* (Chicago: Moody, n.d.), 37–43; Donald Grey Barnhouse, *The Invisible War* (Grand Rapids: Zondervan, 1965), 15–20. See also Hal Lindsey and Carole C. Carlson, *Satan Is Alive and Well on Planet Earth* (Grand Rapids: Zondervan, 1972), 51–58; Question 11 ("What Is the Gap Theory?").

13. Gregory Boyd, *God at War: The Bible and Spiritual Conflict* (Downers Grove: InterVarsity, 1997), 73–92.

14. Hugh Ross, *A Matter of Day: Resolving a Creation Controversy* (Colorado Springs: Navpress, 2004); David Snoke, *A Biblical Case for an Old Earth* (Grand Rapids: Baker, 2006); Mark S. Whorton, *Peril in Paradise,* (Waynesboro, Ga.: Authentic Media, 2005).

perfectly suited for the Creator's eternal purpose. The ultimate end for which this world was created is to glorify the Sovereign Creator."[15]

Proponents also point to several items in the mandates God gave to the original couple (Gen. 1:28–30; 2:15). Adam and Eve are commanded to "subdue" creation—an expression of conflict. This seems to indicate that nature was already experiencing travail. God instructed Adam to "keep" or "protect" the garden, which implies the existence of danger. OEC advocates argue that YEC proponents miss the point of Genesis 1:29–30 ("I have given every green plant for food"). Rather than commanding vegetarianism, the text highlights God's gracious provision to all life.[16] In addition, appealing to the conditions of the future kingdom works against the no-death position, since the Bible teaches that death will occur during the millennium (Isa. 65:20).[17] These items indicate that the living conditions within the garden of Eden were different from that of the rest of the world.

Second, Ross and Whorton argue that YEC proponents generalize the curse of Genesis 3 in a way that is not justified by Scripture.[18] They contend that Adam's sin affected only humans, and that the pertinent New Testament passages (Rom. 5 and 1 Cor. 15) refer only to human death ("Therefore, just as sin came into the world through one man, and death through sin, and so death spread *to all men*…." Rom. 5:12, emphasis added). Some YEC advocates point to Paul's description of creation groaning under the bondage of futility as further evidence that the curse upon Adam affected all creatures (Rom. 5:18–22). Snoke responds by pointing out that much of what the Bible describes as "futile" was that way from the beginning of creation.[19] For example, the actions of the sun, wind, and rivers are said to be futile (Eccl. 1:5–7), but these actions were established in Genesis 1–2.

Third, proponents point out that God takes credit for the fierce components of nature (Ps. 148) and that he specifically takes credit for the creation of predatory creatures (Job 38–41).[20] God glories in everything he has created, even carnivorous animals. Such animals play a good role in nature and should not be seen as a natural evil. The psalmist calls such behavior good (Ps. 104:24–28). In fact, God claims authorship for much of what is called "natural evil" (e.g., Isa. 45:6–7; Ps. 104:19–21). God reserves the right to be inscrutable, and we are to remember that he is dangerous and powerful (Rom. 1:20).

---

15. Whorton, *Peril in Paradise*, 26.
16. C. John Collins, *Genesis 1–4: A Linguistic, Literary, and Theological Commentary* (Phillipsburg: P&R, 2006), 165. See also Snoke, *A Biblical Case for an Old Earth*, 64–69.
17. Whorton, *Peril in Paradise*, 62. Whorton also points to Ezekiel 47:10–12, which teaches that fish will be caught for food in the age to come.
18. Ross, *A Matter of Days*, 100; Whorton, *Peril in Paradise*, 184.
19. Snoke, *A Biblical Case for an Old Earth*, 69–75.
20. David Snoke, "Why Were Dangerous Animals Created?" *Perspectives on Science and Christian Faith* 56, no. 2 (June 2004): 117–25.

The fourth point made by proponents of this view builds on the previous point. In contrast to YEC advocates who argue that before Adam's fall not even a single ant had died, Whorton argues that an animal kingdom without injury is not possible or credible.[21] We see animal death as bad due to the "Bambi effect" (i.e., we tend to anthropomorphize the animal kingdom). Because death is bad for us, we imagine that it must be the same for animals. Snoke contends that if Adam and Eve had not sinned then we would have observed animal mortality from a distance.[22]

Last, proponents of this view argue that YEC advocates confuse Eden with eschatology. Whorton argues that the expulsion from the garden was not paradise lost, nor will the second coming be merely paradise regained. As noted earlier, God pronounced the original creation "very good," but not "perfect." Revelation 21–22 presents a world far superior to the world of Genesis 1–2. The new heavens and the new earth will have many things that the first world did not, and vice versa (e.g., marriage).

Conclusion

The no-death position argued by YEC proponents seems to have biblical warrant, but that does not mean it is exegetically or theologically necessary. The three answers provided by OEC advocates are possible, but that is not the same as being likely. The divergent views espoused by those who hold to animal death before the fall shows that this is an issue that has not been settled within evangelicalism.

It may be helpful at this point to remember that there have been times in church history when an apologetic issue seemed to be crucial to certain Christians then, upon further reflection, turned out to not be so. Take, for example, when Galileo used his telescope to discover that the heavens were not perfect. Christians of his day believed this precipitated a theological crisis.[23] Today we do not give it a thought. Similarly, the notion of animal death existing prior to Adam's fall does not appear to be, theologically speaking, an insurmountable problem. Certainly this issue should not be the litmus test for biblical fidelity as some have made it. We look in the next chapter at the broader question of the fall's effects.

---

21. Ken Ham, "Zombie Parasites," http://www.answersingenesis.org/articles/kw/zombie-parasite (accessed 12/20/11); Whorton, *Peril in Paradise*, 108.
22. Snoke, "Why Were Dangerous Animals Created?" 125.
23. Whorton, *Peril in Paradise*, 98.

REFLECTION QUESTIONS

1. In what ways does the fossil record seem to present the problem of natural evil?

2. Why do many consider this question to be the central issue of the creation/evolution controversy?

3. How might Adam be the cause of animal death that predated his existence?

4. How might Satan be the cause of animal death?

5. How might God be the cause of animal death but not the Author of evil?

What Effect Did the Fall Have on Creation?

In the previous chapter we examined the question of whether or not animals died before the fall of Adam. Young-earth creationism (YEC) proponents consistently answer no, while old-earth creationism (OEC) and evolutionary creationism (EC) advocates answer yes in a variety of ways. The respective answers given lead naturally to the question of this chapter: What, then, were the effects of Adam's fall? As noted earlier, the issues covered in these two chapters provide the crux of the debate concerning creation and evolution.

We will briefly survey four representative answers. First, Paul Garner and Kurt Wise argue the YEC position that Adam's fall introduced death and corruption into the world. Second and third, we will look at two views presented by OEC proponents. In one view, David Snoke and Mark Whorton contend that Adam's fall changed the nature of death. That is, they argue that animal death existed before the garden events, but the fall extended the reach of death to now include humans. William Dembski provides another OEC view. On the one hand he agrees with YEC advocates that Adam's rebellion is the cause of all death. But on the other hand he argues, like other OEC proponents, that animals died prior to the time of Adam and Eve. He sees Adam's sin as a cosmic event with retroactive effects. Last, evolutionary creationist Denis Lamoureux argues that nature affected man, not the other way around. Lamoureux sees the account of the fall as a mythical retelling of a very real condition: humans are sinners, estranged from God. Though we may not know the details of how humanity came to be this way, our predicament is undeniable.

Adam's Fall Introduced Death and Corruption

When Adam was cursed, all creation was cursed with him. This is the position universally held by YEC proponents. Paul Garner and Kurt Wise perceive the original sin as producing three effects: all animals were placed under a curse, the environment became hostile, and humans were cursed with spiritual and physical death.[1]

First, Garner argues that the curse placed upon the serpent (Gen. 3:14–15) was applied to all animals.[2] Passages such as Romans 5, Romans 8, and 1 Corinthians 15 teach that Adam's sin affected all creation. This means that all creatures, prior to the fall, were vegetarian (Gen. 1:29–30). This would include animals that presently are predators or parasites. Garner points to a number of examples of animals generally considered predatory that actually are not: a vegetarian crocodile, nonstinging jellyfish, birds of prey that eats nuts, and a fruit-eating relative of the piranha.[3] He infers from these examples the possibility that all predators were originally intended to be vegetarian. Garner's argument contrasts with that of earlier YEC advocates, such as Henry Morris. Morris had suggested that God may have created predators after the fall.[4]

Along with predation, the fall introduced disease.[5] If there was no death prior to Adam's sin, then YEC proponents infer that there was no disease either. Malady producing parasites, viruses, and bacteria either did not exist prior to the fall, or more likely, were transformed by the fall into the malevolent entities that they are today. The curse also inaugurated the struggle for survival. Reproduction was accelerated and increased, which resulted in more offspring being produced than the earth can support. Now only the strong survive (i.e., the survival of the fittest).

Second, the environment became hostile, as illustrated by the biblical text with the introduction of thorns and thistles (Gen. 3:18). Earlier YEC proponents, such as Whitcomb and Morris, equated the second law of thermodynamics with the curse.[6] The second law, or entropy, is the principle that all things run down or tend to disorder. In practical terms, this means that things left to themselves fall apart. However, evidences of entropy—such as rivers (Gen. 2:10–14)—existed prior to the fall, so the view has few advocates today. Currently, Garner and Wise suggest a number of means by which the world became cruel and adversarial.[7] Perhaps certain natural laws were altered or removed. Some imperfections could be the result of changes in habitat or

1. Paul Garner, *The New Creationism: Building Scientific Theories on a Biblical Foundation* (Darlington: Evangelical, 2009); Kurt Wise, *Faith, Form, and Time: What the Bible Teaches and Science Confirms about Creation and the Age of the Universe* (Nashville: B&H, 2002).
2. Garner, *The New Creationism*, 156–57.
3. Ibid., 163.
4. Henry Morris, *The Twilight of Evolution* (Grand Rapids: Baker, 1963), 37–46; Henry Morris, "Adam and the Animals," http://www.icr.org/article/339/ (accessed 08/21/13).
5. Garner, 159.
6. John C. Whitcomb and Henry M. Morris, *The Genesis Flood: The Biblical Record and Its Scientific Implications* (Phillipsburg: P&R, 1961), 222–25.
7. Garner, *The New Creationism*, 161–63; Wise, *Faith, Form, and Time*, 150–66.

behavior. Biological effects could be the result of genetic alterations (which might be a significant contributor to the declining life spans recorded in Gen. 4). They also suggest that God created all life forms with latent mechanisms that kicked in when the fall occurred.

The third effect of the curse was that humans were subjected to death (Gen. 2:17; 3:19). Adam and Eve, and all their descendants, are condemned to physically die. The evils of "death, disease, struggle for survival, poison, thorns, and carnivory" were the consequence of the original sin.[8]

Adam's Fall Changed the Nature of Death

In their respective works, David Snoke and Mark Whorton devote a significant amount of space to critiquing the YEC position.[9] First, (as noted in the previous chapter) they argue that, concerning the Romans 5, Romans 8, and 1 Corinthians 15 passages, Paul teaches that Adam's sin affected all humanity—not all creation. They also note that when the apostle declares that all creation is subject to futility (Rom. 8:20–23) he does not say this is a result of the sin of Adam and Eve. Snoke argues that a close reading of Romans 8:22 indicates that creation was in its present condition (of futility) from the very beginning.[10] Solomon presents a number of things that are said to be futile from the moment of their origination—the sun, wind, and rivers (Eccl. 1:5–7). Futility does not entail evil or badness. Rather it highlights how a thing may be fleeting or temporary. For example, Genesis 1 includes the creation of grass, something the Bible often describes as futile (Isa. 40:6–8).

Second, Whorton contends that YEC advocates fail to appreciate the eternal nature of God's ultimate plan. Seen from the perspective of God's eternal decrees, the fall was not a detour.[11] Snoke concurs, pointing out that God glories in all his plans and actions, even those we might find disturbing. Specifically and relating to the matter at hand, God glories in creating carnivorous animals (Ps. 104:19–21).[12]

However, the main critique Snoke and Whorton make against the YEC position is that it seems to turn the fall into a second creation. A few YEC proponents, such as Henry Morris, suggest that God created the predatory

---

8. Wise, *Faith, Form, and Time,* 166.

9. David Snoke, *A Biblical Case for an Old Earth* (Grand Rapids: Baker, 2006); Mark Whorton, *Peril in Paradise* (Waynesboro: Authentic Media, 2005). This is not to say that YEC proponents do not also spend a great deal of effort denouncing the OEC position.

10. David Snoke, "Why Were Dangerous Animals Created?" *Perspectives on Science and Christian Faith* 56, no. 2 (June 2004): 122. "This verse [Rom. 8:22] says: 'We know that the whole creation has been groaning as in the pains of childbirth right up to the present time.' The phrase 'right up to the present time' is best translated as 'all the way up to the present time'; in other words, 'from the beginning up to now,' *not* 'from some intermediate time up till now'" (emphasis original).

11. Whorton, *Peril in Paradise,* 41–44.

12. Snoke, "Why Were Dangerous Animals Created?" 120.

animals after Adam's fall. Most YEC advocates posit that creatures experienced fundamental changes in their respective essences that turned them into savage beasts. Snoke and Whorton argue that such speculation introduces an event about which the Bible says nothing.

To say that creatures were twisted by the fall into vermin, pests, and predators is to fail to acknowledge just how specialized parasitical creatures really are. One finds highly specialized features in the present order of the animal kingdom: symbiotic relationships, sophisticated defense mechanisms, and immune systems—just to name a few. Discussing the specified digestive systems of carnivores, Whorton declares, "More important, the notion that herbivores could degenerate into carnivores is false. Carnivorous digestive systems are fundamentally distinct from herbivore systems."[13] Plant and animal species would have to have undergone such substantial changes that, in effect, "they would have become entirely new species."[14] In short, the YEC position requires a re-creation after the fall.

Instead, Scriptures teach that God created the ferocious animals in the very beginning. On day five God created the *tannin* ("great sea monsters" Gen. 1:21, NASB), a term which elsewhere in the Old Testament refers to dangerous beasts (Deut. 32:33; Job 7:12; Ps. 74:13–14; Isa. 27:1; Ezek. 29:3; Dan. 7:5; etc.). God takes credit for creating predatory animals and their cruel actions (Job 38–41).[15] There is little or no biblical evidence that the essences of animals were changed by the rebellion in the garden.

So, what effect did the fall have on creation? Snoke, Whorton, and most OEC proponents understand there to be three effects. The first person affected by the curse was Satan (Gen. 3:14–15). Though God addressed the serpent, he was directly speaking to the spirit who inhabited the snake—Lucifer. The language of humiliation is used: he would be forced to crawl, eat dust, and be crushed under foot. These are all signs of defeat and dishonor. The curse did not apply to the serpent or to animal life as a whole. Instead it applied to Satan. Nor does the biblical account teach that the snake lost it legs in the fall. The snake was already legless. Rather, like the rainbow (Gen. 9:12–16), a preexisting thing took on new significance.[16]

Second, the curse affected Eve. She would experience increased pain in childbirth ("I will surely multiply your pain in childbearing; in pain you shall bring forth children," Genesis 3:16a. Incidentally, that her pain is said to be increased indicates that pain was already present). In addition, her relationship to her husband would be distorted (Gen. 3:16b).

---

13. Whorton, *Peril in Paradise*, 124.
14. Ibid, 129.
15. Snoke, *A Biblical Case for an Old Earth*, 79–86.
16. Ibid., 50–56.

The third person affected was Adam. He had been given the task of managing the earth. Now the task becomes difficult (Gen. 3:17–19a). The text speaks of God cursing the ground. God does not address the ground directly, because it was not directly cursed. It was indirectly cursed in the sense that the man who was given stewardship over the earth had been cursed. Adam is sentenced to death (Gen. 3:19b). God had warned that the penalty for disobedience was death (Gen. 2:17); now the punishment was meted out upon him and his posterity (Rom. 5:12). Snoke argues, "Animals do not have eternity in their hearts. Is it therefore a great evil if they die? The Bible does not say it is evil if the animals die; it says it is a great evil if people die like animals."[17] Adam is expelled from the garden, and he no longer has it as his command center. The nature of the earth did not change, nor the task itself. What changed was Adam's ability to perform the task. The curse changed Adam.

Adam's Fall Was a Transcendent Federal Event

In his *The End of Christianity,* William Dembski presents a view of Genesis 3 that contains elements of both YEC and OEC positions.[18] On the one hand, like the YEC proponents, Dembski argues that the consequences of Adam's fall were universal. Death and disease find their origin in the original sin of Genesis 3. He criticizes Whorton and Snoke for failing to recognize the full implications of natural evil.[19] On the other hand, Dembski also agrees with OEC proponents that geologists and astronomers are basically correct in their estimation of the age of the cosmos. The earth is over 4 billion years old while the universe is more than 13 billion years old. In addition, paleontologists are right when they describe the ancient world as one of predation and suffering. He finds the typical YEC arguments as examples of special pleading.[20] So Dembski simultaneously affirms a suffering ancient earth and a literal Adamic fall, which occurred relatively recently. How does he reconcile the two affirmations?

First, Dembski contends that the Bible presents creation from two perspectives: the divine conception and the mundane realization.[21] He uses the terms *kairos* and *chronos* to distinguish the two ways of perception. Genesis 1 presents creation as God's perfect plan for the world (the *kairos* view). Genesis 2–3 present how God's plan unfolded in time and how sin impacted what God had created (the *chronos* view).

---

17. David Snoke, "Why Were the Dangerous Animals Created?" *Perspectives on Science and Christian Faith* 56, no. 2 (June 2004): 123.
18. William Dembski, *The End of Christianity: Finding a Good God in an Evil World* (Nashville: B&H, 2009).
19. Ibid., 78–81.
20. Ibid., 55–63.
21. Ibid., 124–26, 142–55.

Next, Dembski points to the federal relationship that Adam and Jesus, respectively, have with the human race. Adam, as the first head of the human race, plunged humanity to sin and ruin. Christ, as the last Adam, represents a new humanity saved by his atoning blood. Dembski argues that the impact of both men is cosmic and trans-historical. The saving effect of Christ's death went both forward and backward in time. Old Testament saints were saved by the blood of Christ, just like New Testament believers. Dembski argues that Adam's rebellion had the same transcendent (and hence retroactive) effects. He explains,

> By tacitly rejecting such backward causation, young-earth creationists insist that the corrupting effects of the Fall be understood *proactively* (in other words, the consequences of the Fall only act forward into the future). By contrast, I will argue that we should understand the corrupting effects of the Fall also *retroactively* (in other words, the consequences of the Fall can also act backward into the past). Accordingly, the Fall could take place *after* the natural evils for which it is responsible.[22]

Thus, Adam's sin retroactively produced the eons of natural evils evidenced in the fossil records.

Nature Affected Man, Not the Other Way Around

In his book, *I Love Jesus and I Accept Evolution*, Denis Lamoureux argues as the title indicates and presents the majority EC position concerning the fall. Lamoureux is an evangelical, charismatic Christian who affirms an orthodox Christology (Christ's virgin birth, vicarious death, and bodily resurrection) while at the same time arguing that evolution was the means by which Jesus created.[23] While he views EC's strongest point to be that it "embraces both biblical faith and modern science," he concedes that EC's weakest point is its denial of a literal or historical fall.[24] "In other words, evolutionary creation rejects the traditional Christian belief in the cosmic fall."[25] He argues that God used a fallible, errant account of origins to convey an infallible truth:

> To conclude, there is no sin-death problem. Adam never existed, and consequently, sin did not enter the world through

---

22. Ibid., 50 (emphasis original).
23. Denis O. Lamoureux, *I Love Jesus and I Accept Evolution* (Eugene, Ore.: Wipf and Stock, 2009), 32.
24. Ibid., 30.
25. Ibid., 31–32. However, there are some EC advocates who affirm a historical Adam and Eve. See Denis Alexander, *Creation or Evolution: Do We Have to Choose?* (Oxford: Monarch, 2008).

him. Nor then did physical death arise as a divine judgment
for his transgression, because once again, Adam never existed.
Indeed, sin did enter the world, but not through Adam.[26]

Lamoureux admits that his reading of Genesis 1–3 is "very unnatural and
counterintuitive" and "is not an easy position to accept."[27]

Lamoureux appeals to evangelicals not to dismiss theistic evolution too
quickly. The fall is a spiritual mystery, not unlike other mysteries affirmed by
Christian doctrine (i.e., the image of God and the age of accountability).[28]
Specifically, the fall is analogous to the age of accountability. Christians are not
in agreement regarding the spiritual state of children, whether a child is born
condemned or becomes morally accountable at a later date. For those who do
affirm an age of accountability, no one dogmatically holds to a certain time—
either for a particular child or for children in general. Though the doctrine of
the age of accountability is vague and mysterious, no orthodox Christian denies that all children possess an intrinsic, sinful propensity which eventually,
inevitably renders all guilty before God. Similarly, argues Lamoureux, we do
not understand the particulars of humanity's fall. There was no simple, single
original sin. Rather, "'original sin' was manifested gradually and mysteriously
over many generations during the evolutionary processes leading to men and
women."[29] Genesis 3 presents, in mythical terms, a present reality: humanity
is estranged from God.

The end result of Lamoureux's argument is the conclusion that man's
fallen state has had no impact on creation. Rather, it is the other way around.
Fellow EC proponent Daniel Harlow echoes Lamoureux's position when he
states, "Far from infecting the rest of the animal creation with selfish behaviors, we humans inherited these tendencies from our animal past."[30]

Conclusion

There is something wrong with creation—on this all parties agree. One
suspects more Darwinists would be open to the design argument if creation
did not seem to have so many flaws—disease, well-designed parasites, and
predators. In addition, at the present time scientists have found no clear empirical evidences of discontinuity in natural history (i.e., no clear evidences of
the universal effects of the fall).

YEC proponents seem to be dogmatic about a position which, upon closer
examination, appears to be more speculative than they have been willing to

---

26. Ibid., 148.
27. Ibid., 30–32.
28. Ibid., 29–30.
29. Ibid., 157.
30. Daniel C. Harlow, "After Adam: Reading Genesis in an Age of Evolutionary Science,"
    Perspectives on Science and Christian Faith 62, no. 3 (September 2010): 180.

admit. Dembski's argument is intriguing, but has very little biblical support. Tom Nettles has written a critique of the notion of Adam's fall producing natural evils via backward causation. He observes that in Dembski's theodicy, God is like the man who spanked his children on Sunday in anticipation of the things they would do the rest of the week.[31]

Lamoureux sees the origins account to be a fallible human text used by God to communicate an infallible message. He claims to hold to a version of inerrancy, but his view of Genesis 1–3 seems to be much closer to that of neo-Orthodoxy. Lamoureux's position runs the danger of revamping the fall beyond recognition. Finally, though Snoke's and Whorton's position is not without difficulties, it appears at present to have the least number of difficulties.

As we noted at the beginning of this chapter, the question of the fall and its effects is the most important issue concerning creation and evolution. How one answers this question determines, for the most part, how one approaches the remaining questions. As of yet, evangelicals have not reached a consensus.

REFLECTION QUESTIONS

1. What three effects do YEC proponents believe were produced by Adam's fall?

2. What do OEC proponents mean when they say that the YEC position seems to turn the fall into a second creation?

3. How does Dembski appeal to the federal headship of Christ to make his argument?

4. What do EC advocates concede to be the weakest point of their position?

5. What does Lamoureux mean when he says that the fall is analogous to the age of accountability?

---

31. Tom Nettles, review of *The End of Christianity: Finding a Good God in an Evil World,* by William A. Dembski, *SBJT* 13, no. 4 (2009): 80.

What Does Genesis 3:15 Say About God's Plan for Creation?

Through most of church history, Genesis 3:15 was understood as the *protoevangelium*, the first prophecy of the good news of the victory of Christ over evil. Only toward the end of the nineteenth century did scholars and interpreters begin to have doubts about the messianic interpretation of Genesis 3:15.

Recent critical scholarship has virtually rejected this messianic interpretation of Genesis 3:15.[1] Many of these scholars understand Genesis 3:15 to be an example of an etiology (the study of origins), explaining the hostility between human beings and snakes.[2] Many of these scholars argue that a messianic interpretation does not fit the context of Genesis 3:15. In Genesis 3:14–15, God announces the curse on the serpent as a result of the fall. It would be foreign to the context in the midst of an announcement of a curse for God to then give a promise or prophecy of a future victory of the Messiah. Moreover, the Hebrew term for "seed" (*zera*) has a collective sense, not referring to individuals, but rather descendants or offspring as a group.[3]

After the disobedience of the woman and the man in the garden, God addresses each of the participants by the order in which they appeared in the

---

1. See Gerhard Von Rad, *Genesis*, rev. ed. (Philadelphia: Westminster, 1972), 92–93; T. Desmond Alexander, "Messianic Ideology in the Book of Genesis," in *The Lord's Anointed*, ed. Philip E. Satterthwaite, Richard S. Hess, and Gordon J. Wenham (Grand Rapids: Baker, 1995), 28; Walter Wifall, "Gen. 3:15—A Protoevangelium?" *CBQ* 36 (1974): 361.
2. See Gordon J. Wenham, *Genesis 1–15*, WBC 1 (Waco, Tex: Word, 1987), 80; but also John Calvin, *The First Book of Moses Called Genesis*, trans. Rev. John King (Grand Rapids: Baker, repr. 1979), 167. This is also the view of the medieval Jewish commentator, Rashi (see Jack P. Lewis, "The Woman's Seed [Gen. 3:15]" *JETS* 34, no. 3 [1991]: 305).
3. See Claus Westermann, *Genesis 1–11*, trans. John J. Scullion S. J. (Minneapolis: Fortress, 1994), 260; Von Rad, *Genesis*, 92–93; Hans Peter Rüger, "On Some Versions of Genesis 3.15, Ancient and Modern," *BT* 27, no. 1 (1976): 107.

Genesis 3 account—the serpent, the woman, and then the man, who receives the longest address. Thus, the serpent who appears first in the passage (Gen. 3:1) is addressed first in the oracles of judgment. After announcing the initial curse upon the serpent in Genesis 3:14, God announced what will now be the future relationship between the serpent and the woman in Genesis 3:15. In addressing the issues regarding the question of the messianic interpretation of Genesis 3:15, we will focus on the two parts of the verse, the enmity between the serpent and the woman and the battle between the seed of the woman and the seed of the serpent.

The Enmity Between the Serpent and the Woman

As the serpent decided to initiate the dialogue with Eve and tempt her to sin (Gen. 3:1), God announced that the serpent's relationship with the woman will be forever altered. God announced in the curse of the serpent that he will place "enmity" (Hb. *evah*) between the woman and the serpent. The word enmity, related to the Hebrew word for "enemy," is used only rarely in the Bible. Besides its occurrence here, it occurs elsewhere only in Numbers 35:21–22 and Ezekiel 25:1; 35:5 in reference to murder as well as the hostility that exists during a time of war. While otherwise used to depict human hostilities, in Genesis 3:15 it is used to describe the future relationship between the serpent and the woman. From this time forward there will always be a hostile strife that will exist between the woman and the serpent. But this hostility will go beyond their existence and will extend into future generations.

The statement reveals the future aspect of this hostility between the woman and the serpent in that the enmity will continue between the woman's "offspring" (seed) and serpent's "offspring" (seed).[4] This collective use of the term seed is used here as it is in Genesis 12:7 when the Lord announced to Abraham: "To your offspring (seed) I will give this land." Similarly, in Genesis 28:14, Jacob is informed that his "offspring" (seed) "shall be like the dust of the earth" (see Gen. 13:15). The nation of Israel is also referred to as the "offspring" (seed) of Abraham (Isa. 41:8). But how are we to identify the offspring/descendants of the serpent and the woman (Eve)?

The Descendants of the Serpent and the Descendants of the Woman

It is possible that the seed of the serpent could generally refer to the forces of evil. Forces of evil emerge almost immediately after the fall as Cain, the first human being born into the world, kills his brother in cold blood. The idea would be that the forces of evil will always exist in the world. Thus, Cain should be viewed as from the seed of the serpent as he kills his brother Abel (Gen. 4:1–16).

---

4. The word "seed" is a key term in Genesis as it occurs in Genesis fifty-nine times out of the 231 total times in the Old Testament (see Alexander, "Messianic Ideology in the Book of Genesis," 22).

Immediately following the slaying of Abel by Cain, the narrative presents the wicked line of Cain (Gen. 4:17–24). The proclivity toward evil continues to emerge especially as seen in the actions of Lamech (Gen. 4:23–24). After Cain's descendants are traced, we are introduced to Seth who replaces Abel as part of the elect line, the seed of the woman (Gen. 4:25). Eve rejoices that God had provided another offspring (seed) in place of Abel. Seth illustrates that he is of the godly chosen line, the seed of the woman, as we find that in his days there were many who were worshippers of the true God. This righteous line of Seth is traced through the genealogy of Seth to Noah in Genesis 5:1–32 and then from Shem to Abram in Genesis 11:10–31. Sailhamer states, "In chapter 5, the list of ten patriarchs from Adam to Noah provided the necessary linkage between the 'seed' promised to the woman (3:15) and the seed of Noah, the survivor of the Flood (7:23). . . . The list in chapter 5, then, reveals a highly developed theological reflection on the promise, which had been made concerning the seed of the woman in 3:15. . . . There are two seeds, that of Cain and that of the woman. . . . Though the seed of Noah were scattered at Babylon, God had preserved a line of ten great men from Noah to the chosen seed of Abraham."[5] The promised line, the righteous seed of the woman, is then traced through Isaac, Jacob, and the twelve tribes of Israel.

The seed of the serpent can be identified in the activities of the Canaanites living in Sodom (Gen. 14:4–8), who resemble their ancestor Ham (Gen. 9:21–22).[6] As Bruce Waltke stated, "The seed of the serpent refers to a natural humanity whom he has led into rebellion against God. Humanity is now divided into two communities: the elect, who love God, and the reprobate, who love self (John 8:31–32, 44; 1 John 3:8). Each of the characters of Genesis will be either of the seed of the woman that reproduces her spiritual propensity, or of the seed of the serpent that reproduces his unbelief."[7] As noted above, this division emerges immediately in the hostility between Cain and Abel (Genesis 4). There is widespread evidence from early Jewish interpreters that Cain was considered to be a seed of the serpent.[8]

Support for this notion of the two lineages may be found in the fact that individuals within each line often resemble each other.[9] Lamech resembles Cain (4:19–24) while the immorality of the Canaanites in Sodom (19:4–8) is reminiscent of Ham, the father of Canaan (9:21–22). This is harmonious with the first occurrence of the word "seed" in reference to plants and trees, which likewise are to produce seeds according to their various kinds (Gen.

5. John H. Sailhamer, *The Pentateuch as Narrative* (Grand Rapids: Zondervan, 1992), 136–37.
6. See Michael Rydelnik, *The Messianic Hope: Is the Hebrew Bible Really Messianic?* NACSBT (Nashville: B&H, 2010), 142.
7. Bruce K. Waltke and Cathi J. Fredricks, *Genesis* (Grand Rapids: Zondervan, 2001), 93–94.
8. See James Hamilton, "The Seed of the Woman and the Blessing of Abraham," *TynBul* 58, no. 2 (2007): 257.
9. This meaning of *zera* ("seed"), "marked by moral quality," is noted in the BDB, 283.

1:11–12).[10] The establishment of the nature of the seed (offspring, posterity) of the serpent and the seed (offspring, posterity) of the woman sets the immediate context for the second half of Genesis 3:15.

The Battle Between the Seed of the Woman and the Serpent

After we are told that the enmity between the serpent and the woman will extend to further generations and will include their respective seeds, we are told in the second half of Genesis 3:15: "he shall bruise your head, and you shall bruise his heal." Right away, one notices that this statement does not refer specifically to the collective descendants of the serpent and the woman, but rather refers to a specific seed. First of all this should not surprise us as "seed" occurs in a number of places in Genesis with reference to an individual (Gen. 4:25; 15:3; 16:10; 21:13; 22:18; 24:60; 38:8–9). Secondly, the last half of Genesis 3:15 specifically refers to the serpent (not to his posterity); so it is appropriate to view this specific descendant of the woman as an individual. Waltke concurs as he states: "Like the English word, *zera* can refer to an immediate descendent (Gen. 4:25; 15:3), a distant offspring, or a large group of descendants. Here and throughout Scripture, all three senses are developed and merged. In this Genesis text we can infer both the single and collective senses. Since the woman's seed struggles against the serpent's seed, we infer that it has a collective sense. But since only the head of the serpent is represented as crushed, we expect an individual to deliver the fatal blow and to be struck uniquely on his heel."[11]

Also, since the "you" (the serpent) is contrasted with the "he" (woman's seed) and is thereby distinct from the seed of the serpent, we should expect in this final conflict an individual son arising out of the seed of the woman to deliver the blow to the serpent. Perhaps the clearest parallel to the individual nature of this seed is in 2 Samuel 7:13 where David is promised an offspring ("seed") that will build a house for God's name. The use of the independent pronoun "he" (Hb. *hu*) appears to make it clear that an individual is promised.

John Collins has observed in his study of the use of "seed" in the Old Testament that when an individual descendant ("seed") is referred to, the pronouns and suffixes are always singular, whereas when the pronouns and suffixes are plural, the reference is to a collective seed, offspring, or posterity in general.[12] This individual nature of the seed is abundantly clear from the Greek Septuagint, the oldest translation of the Old Testament.

---

10. See T. Desmond Alexander, "Genealogies, Seed and the Compositional Unity of Genesis," *TynBul* 44, no. 2 (1993): 260.
11. Waltke and Fredricks, *Genesis*, 93.
12. See John Collins, "A Syntactical Note (Genesis 3:15): Is the Woman's Seed Singular or Plural?" *TynBul* 48, no.1 (1997): 142–43.

In the Septuagint, at Genesis 3:15 the translator uses the independent masculine personal pronoun *autos* to translate the Hebrew pronoun *hu*, "he." This is unusual because the Greek word for "seed" is *sperma*, a neuter noun in Greek. Normally the translator in accordance with grammatical rules would use a neuter pronoun to refer to a noun that was neuter. By using the masculine pronoun, however, the translator understands the reference to be to an individual rather than a group (collective). This indicates that he had a messianic understanding of the verse. The Hebrew masculine personal pronoun occurs 103 times in Genesis, but this is the only time the Greek translators broke their own grammatical rules that requires a pronoun to agree in gender and number with its antecedent.[13]

This battle between the individual seed of the woman and the serpent is described as the "delivering of blows" or "striking at." The same Hebrew verb *shuf* occurs twice in the line to refer to the bruising of the head, as well as the bruising of the heal. The verb is rare outside this passage, occurring elsewhere only in Psalm 139:11 and Job 9:17, but the Psalm reference is somewhat problematic. The Job reference may indicate something like "crush or bruise" and this rendering is in harmony with the double use of the verb in Genesis 3:15b. The major ancient versions are also in agreement with this usage.

Yet, many interpreters like to distinguish the actions by noting that the first strike is "at the head" while the second strike is "at the heel." It is argued that the blow to the head would be a fatal blow as opposed to a strike at the heel.[14] Charles Aalders has argued that placing the phrase "you will strike at his heel" after the mention of "the striking the head" is of significance as it occupies a secondary place in the sentence. He thus understands the word order to indicate that the final triumph would be by the woman's seed while in the process of gaining the victory he would be wounded by the serpent.[15] Michael Rydelnik believes the use of the same verb twice in the same line has a significance that cannot be ignored and has argued that both blows, to the serpent and to the woman's seed, would be mortal. The woman's seed (the Messiah) will die, but through his death obtain victory over the serpent: "Most likely, therefore, the text is speaking of two comparable death blows:

---

13. See Lewis, "The Woman's Seed (Gen. 3:15)," 300; Walter C. Kaiser, *The Messiah in the Old Testament* (Grand Rapids: Zondervan, 1995), 40; Victor P. Hamilton, *The Book of Genesis Chapters 1–17*, NICOT (Grand Rapids: Eerdmans, 1990), 199.
14. See H. C. Leupold, *Exposition of Genesis*, 2 vols. (Grand Rapids: Baker, 1942) 1:166; Kaiser, *The Messiah in the Old Testament*, 41n.8; Kenneth Mathews, *Genesis 1–11:26*, NAC 1A (Nashville: B&H, 1996), 245; Hamilton, "The Skull Crushing Seed of the Woman," 42. No doubt because of the different objects of the strike, the Latin Vulgate translation translates the verb that occurs twice in the same line in two different ways. The first word, *conterere*, means "to crush," while the second word, *insidiari*, means to "lie in wait." See Marten H. Woudstra, "Recent Translations of Genesis 3:15," *CTJ* 6 (1971): 194–95.
15. See G. Charles Aalders, *Genesis*, 2 vols. (Grand Rapids: Zondervan, 1981), 1:106.

the future redeemer will strike the head of the tempter and thereby kill it, and at the same time the tempter will strike the heel of the redeemer and kill him. . . . the woman's seed will indeed have victory, but the victory will be achieved through suffering his own death."[16]

Conclusion

By way of conclusion, it should be pointed out that Westermann's original objection to Genesis 3:15 as a messianic prophecy—that it would be odd for a promise to be imbedded in the midst of an announcement of a curse—does not appear to be insurmountable. Collins is one who takes issue with Westermann's objection as he states, "The threat is spoken to the snake who has led the humans into disobedience and thus shown itself to be their enemy. In view of such enmity, the defeat of the snake is the rescue of the humans. Hence the idea that it is not possible for a pronouncement of punishment to have a promise contained in it (but what makes it 'impossible'?) overlooks both the fact that the 'promise' for the humans is an implicature of the punishment on the snake, and the relations between the participants."[17] God often offers hope in the midst of judgment throughout the contents of the Old Testament.

Understanding the text as an expression of an ancient conflict or fear of snakes does not seem to fit with the serious nature of God's oracle of judgment against humanity's first sin. The snake is more than a literal snake, and his seed more than a group of other snakes. The serpent possesses supernatural knowledge, with the power to speak. The serpent is motivated by a hostility to God and speaks as though he has access to the mind of God.[18] Mathews thus states that the snake is Satan's personal presence in the garden.[19] While there is no explicit attempt to equate Satan with the serpent in Genesis 3, Sailhamer skillfully summarizes the role of the snake and its significance in Genesis 3:15:

> As representative, the snake and the woman embody the fate of their seed. The fate of their seed is their fate as well. . . . In the second half of v. 15 the "seed" of the woman is one ("he") who will crush the head of the snake ("your head"), bringing to an end the curse it brought on humanity. The woman's "seed" is presented as one who lies in the distant future. Yet it is this same "seed" who is to crush the head of the snake. The crushing blow against the serpent will not be against the "seed" of the snake but against the snake itself. . . . In the

---

16. Rydelnik, *The Messianic Hope*, 141.
17. Collins, "A Syntactical Note (Genesis 3:15)," 147n.22.
18. See John Skinner, *Genesis*, ICC, 2nd ed. (Edinburgh: T&T Clark, 1930), 71–72; Kaiser, *The Messiah in the Old Testament*, 38.
19. See Mathews, *Genesis 1–11:26*, 234.

end, it is the snake, not his seed, whose head the seed of the woman must crush. The author views the snake in terms that extend beyond a particular snake of the garden. The snake is representative of someone or something else. . . . It is what the snake and his "seed" represent that lies at the center of the author's focus. With that "one" lies the "enmity" that must be crushed. No attempt is made to answer the question of the snake's role in the temptation over against the role of a higher being, e.g., Satan. That was, however, the nature of the drama later biblical writers saw in this story (cf. Rom. 16:20; Rev. 12:9). Judging from the details of the story, such a reading might not lie too far from that of the author. . . . it is a momentous moment in Genesis, and it is unlikely that at such a moment the author is interested in no more than humankind's proverbial fear of snakes. . . . They [God's words] are God's first statement to the first sinner. . . . Though wounded in the struggle, the woman's "seed" will prove victorious.[20]

It is thus in the New Testament where we more clearly understand that Satan is behind the serpent (Rom. 16:20; Rev. 12:9; 20:2). It is also in the New Testament that we more clearly see and understand the seed of the woman who gives the fatal blow to the head of the serpent. Like the use of the word seed in the Old Testament, the seed can be both collective, referring to the church (Rom. 16:20) and individual, referring to Christ (Gal. 3:16).

The most important connection of the line of the seed in Genesis and the rest of the Old Testament is the fulfillment of the line of the seed in Jesus Christ. He is called the seed of David (Rom. 1:3; 2 Tim. 2:8) who is born of a woman (Gal. 4:4). Jesus is also understood as the seed of the woman in Revelation 12 where, as in Genesis 3:15, he is in conflict with the ancient serpent.

The writer of Genesis conveys the promise that God's blessing to the world will be through the seed of Abraham (Gen. 12:3; 22:17–18). Abraham was promised to be the ancestor of kings (Gen. 17:6–7). This same promise was passed on to Jacob (Gen. 35:11). This promise was further narrowed to the line of Judah (Gen. 49:9–10). Thus, the seed of the woman is of a royal dynasty.[21] Christ, the Davidic Messiah, is king and the seed of Abraham (Gal. 3:16). John Davis comments on how this promise was first announced in the protoevangelium in Genesis 3:15 when he stated, "The traditional Christian interpretation, however, is that it is the first direct expression of the gospel. It recognizes the essential conflict between Satan and the Lord and indicates that this conflict also will involve the people of God and the followers of Satan

---

20. John H. Sailhamer, "Genesis," EBC, revised ed. (Grand Rapids: Zondervan, 2008), 91.
21. See Rydelnik, *The Messianic Hope*, 142.

(cf. John 8:44; Acts 13:10; 1 John 3:10). The seed of the woman is a clear reference to the Messiah, the Lord Jesus (cf. Rev. 12:1–5; Gal. 3:16, 19), who came 'to destroy the works of the devil' (Heb. 2:14; 1 John 3:8). The protoevangelium prophesied that Christ would deliver a death blow to Satan, but in so doing would suffer death Himself."[22] Genesis 3:15 should thus be viewed as the first announcement of the good news, the protoevangelium wherein God promised a remedy for our common sin problem through the atoning sacrifice of the seed of the woman (Gal. 4:4)!

REFLECTION QUESTIONS

1. What is the meaning of the word "seed"?

2. What does the seed of the serpent refer to?

3. What do we learn from the Septuagint's translation of Genesis 3:15?

4. How strong is the argument that the intention of Genesis 3:15 is to address the fear of snakes? Explain.

5. How does the New Testament interpret Genesis 3:15?

---

22. John J. Davis, *Paradise to Prison: Studies in Genesis* (Salem, WI: Sheffield, 1975, reissued 1998), 93.

Does the Flood Depict a Re-Creation?[1]

Even though the narrative of the flood account essentially describes the destruction of God's creation, it nevertheless alludes to and echoes the creation account in various ways. Even Noah's ark itself could be viewed as a microcosm of creation. As William Brown observed, the ark mirrors the three-tiered structure of the created cosmos with earth, sky, and firmament (Gen. 6:16; 1:6–10). He continued, "Noah's ark is a creation in miniature, designed to support the zoological diversity for which the cosmos was created."[2]

This interplay of the flood with the early chapters of Genesis continues even after the flood. There are clear parallels between the fall of man and life after the great deluge. As John Sailhamer noted, "Just as Adam and his family fell and brought on themselves a curse (3:17), so Noah and his family fell and brought on themselves a curse (9:25). It appears that the two stories are being cast as 'fall' narratives."[3]

But the parallels do not only correspond to the events of the postdiluvian world. The flood interacts with the creation narrative in the areas of the cause for the flood, the judgment of the flood, and the remedy for the flood.

The Cause for the Flood

In the prelude to the judgment of the flood, we come across a devastating assessment by God of the creation he had made, "The LORD saw that the wickedness of man was great in the earth, and that every intention of the thoughts of his heart was only evil continually" (Gen. 6:5). What is immediately striking in this assessment is the opening phrase "the LORD saw." This phrase immediately

---

1. For an additional analysis of this question along with a literary and theological assessment of the flood narrative, see Mark F. Rooker, *Studies in Hebrew Language, Intertextuality, and Theology*, Texts and Studies in Religion, vol. 98 (Lewiston, N.Y.: Edwin Mellen, 2003), 173–202.
2. William P. Brown, *The Ethos of the Cosmos: The Genesis of Moral Imagination in the Bible* (Grand Rapids: Eerdmans, 1999), 55.
3. John H. Sailhamer, "Genesis," EBC, rev. ed. (Grand Rapids: Zondervan, 2008), 134.

invokes the memory of God's assessment of creation when on seven occasions it is recorded that "God saw that it was good" (Gen. 1:4, 10, 12, 18, 21, 25, 31). Now the Lord saw what was not good. The pinnacle of God's creation, all of humankind, is now characterized by wickedness. Human beings have become utterly (after the fall, mankind was already "totally" depraved) depraved. In this prelude to the flood, the connection to creation cannot be missed as seen in God's determination to judge the earth in Genesis 6:6: "I will blot *man whom I have created* from the face of the land." More explicitly judgment must now come because "the earth was filled with violence" (Gen. 6:11). Whereas man's mandate in the creation account was to "fill" (*ml'*) the earth, now we find by contrast that the earth was "filled" (*ml'*), but with violence. "Violence and its accompanying effects make up the antithesis of creation's 'goodness.'"[4] The moral anarchy that has resulted from violence and corruption of the human race must lead to its logical and just consequence, the destruction of humans and land animals.[5] Just as the ground was cursed after man's first disobedience in Genesis 3:17, so must the earth be cursed because of the universal rebellion of mankind (Gen. 6:13; cf. Gen. 8:21). Moreover, the deliberate echo of Genesis 1:31 ("And God saw everything that he had made, and behold, it was very good") in Genesis 6:12 ("And God saw the earth, and behold, it was corrupt)," "heightens our sense of the tragedy that has overtaken the world since the creation. Then God was pleasantly surprised by his creation; here he is shocked by its corruption."[6]

The Judgment of the Flood

In contrast to the creation week where the waters were divided and the surface of the ground appeared (Gen. 1:6–13), the separated waters will now be rejoined for the purpose of destruction. The waters above and below the firmament are united again (Gen. 6:11) as if to reverse the work of creation of Genesis 1.[7]

When Noah entered the ark on the day the flood began (Gen. 6:13), we find another allusion to the creation account in Genesis 1. This connection has to do with Adam and Noah's relationship to the animal world. God brings the animals to Adam to be named, while he brings them to Noah to be protected (cf. Gen. 2:19 and Gen. 7:15).[8] However, this time it is creation in reverse. A reversal is observed in relation to the order of the groups that enter the ark. First, Noah's family enters, then the animals, and finally the birds (Gen. 7:13–14). In Genesis 1, however, the order of creation is birds, then the

---

4. See Brown, *The Ethos of the Cosmos*, 54.
5. The same word used to describe man's corruption (*shachath*; Gen. 6:11) is also used to describe his judgment (*shachath*; Gen. 6:13).
6. Gordon J. Wenham, *Genesis 1–15*, WBC 1 (Waco, Tex.: Word, 1987), 171.
7. See Derek Kidner, *Genesis: An Introduction and Commentary* (Downers Grove: InterVarsity, 1972), 91. The reference to the deep (Gen. 7:11; Hb. *tehom*) echoes the watery chaos of the primordial state mentioned in Genesis 1:2.
8. See Warren Austin Gage, *The Gospel of Genesis* (Winona Lake, Ind.: Carpenter, 1984), 11.

animals, and then finally the humans (Gen. 1:20–27). This indicates that the flood was a reversal of the good work God performed at creation. "The flood has the focused aim of bringing creation back to the drawing board by means of a controlled meltdown, or more accurately, dissolution."[9] Cassuto commented on the comprehensive judgment of life brought about by the flood and its effectual undoing of creation: "The paragraph (7:17–24) closes with an awe-inspiring picture of the mighty waters covering the entire earth. We see water everywhere, as though the world had reverted to its primeval state at the dawn of Creation, when the waters of the deep submerged everything. Nothing remained of the teeming life that had burst forth upon the earth."[10]

The Remedy for the Flood

The description of the emergence of the postdiluvian world reflects the original creation in many ways. We note at the outset that the initial state of the world, as with the flood, is a world covered by water (Gen. 1:2). And yet, the remedy for the uninhabitable world of Genesis 1:2 and of the flood is also immediately present as the renewal process begins. Just as the primordial state was descried as a watery chaos with the spirit of God hovering over the waters, so too in the flood account Noah's ark floating on the surface of the waters offers a glimmer of hope.[11] Moreover, as the flood waters began to abate, dry land appeared just as the dry land emerged from the waters in the creation week in Genesis 1:9–10 (see Gen. 8:5). Warren Gage has observed the parallels between Genesis 8 and Genesis 1:

> The ordering of the present heavens and earth out of the chaotic overthrow of the ancient world recorded in Genesis 8 parallels the original creation account of Genesis 1. In both chapters the theological narrative moves from the display of divine work to the account of divine rest. In Genesis 8:1 God brings about a wind to pass over the waters of the flood which, like the waters of original chaos (Gen. 1:2), cover the earth (Gen. 7:18–19). The emergence of the dry land and the bringing forth of vegetation (Gen. 1:12) find a mirror image in the olive leaf brought to Noah, which is taken as a token of the emergence of dry land (Gen. 8:11). . . . The sabbath rest of God at the conclusion of the original creation ("and He rested," *wayyisboth*, Gen. 2:2) finds correspondence in the sacrificial rest of God after the new creation is completed

---

9. Brown, *Ethos of the Cosmos*, 59; see John H. Sailhamer, *The Pentateuch as Narrative* (Grand Rapids: Zondervan, 1992), 123.

10. Umberto Cassuto, *A Commentary on the Book of Genesis*, 2 vols. (vol. 2, *From Noah to Abraham, Genesis VI:9–XI:32*), trans. Israel Abrahams (Jerusalem: Magnes 1961–64), 2:97.

11. William Brown has noted that the LXX uses the same Greek verb, *epipherō*, to describe both God's Spirit and Noah's ark in Genesis 1:2; 7:18 (*Ethos of the Cosmos*, 55n.61).

(and the Lord smelled the aroma of rest; *reach hannichoch* Gen. 8:21; cf. Ex. 20:11 in which the rest of God on the seventh day of creation is described by the verb *nuach*).[12]

In addition, at the beginning of Genesis 9 after Noah had offered a burnt offering to the Lord, God blessed Noah and his sons and commanded them to "be fruitful and multiply and fill the earth" (Gen. 9:1). This blessing also concluded the creation week after God had made man on the sixth day (Gen. 1:28).[13] One of the best ways to demonstrate that a recreation is depicted after the flood is to show how the key technical terms of the creation account are repeated in the renewing of the earth after the flood.[14]

	CREATION (GENESIS 1)	FLOOD / RECREATION (GENESIS 8–9)	
Gen. 1:2	earth, deep, spirit (*ruach*), water	wind (*ruach*), earth, waters, deep	Gen. 8:1b–2
Gen. 1:6–8	waters, sky	sky	Gen. 8:2b
Gen. 1:9	water, dry ground, appear	water, mountain tops, appear	Gen. 8:3–5
Gen. 1:20–23	birds, above ground	raven, dove, from … ground	Gen. 8:6–12
Gen. 1:24–25	Creatures, livestock Move on ground, wild animals	Creatures, birds, animals Move on ground	Gen. 8:17–19
Gen. 1:26–28	man, image of God male and female	man, image of God Noah and his wife	Gen. 9:6 Gen. 8:16, 18
Gen. 1:28	blessed, be fruitful, increase in number fill the earth, rule every creature	blessed, be fruitful, increase in number fill the earth, fear of you on every creature	Gen. 9:1–2

The connection between the flood and creation narratives is reinforced by the subsequent narratives that follow each account. The parallels to the flood continue immediately beyond the creation week and are reflected in the events in the garden of Eden narrative. This is best illustrated by the following layout.[15]

---

12. Gage, *The Gospel of Genesis*, 10–11.
13. God also blessed humans in Genesis 5:2 and commanded them to "be fruitful and multiply" in Genesis 8:17.
14. Adapted from Bruce K. Waltke and Cathi J. Fredricks, *Genesis* (Grand Rapids: Zondervan, 2001), 128–29.
15. See John H. Sailhamer, "Genesis," in *A Complete Literary Guide to the Bible*, ed. Leland Ryken and Tremper Longman III (Grand Rapids: Zondervan, 1993), 114. Walton likewise

GENESIS 2–3	GENESIS 9:18–29
Then God planted a garden (2:8)	Noah planted a vineyard (9:20)
And she took from the tree and ate (3:6)	And he drank from the wine and became drunk (9:21)
And they knew they were naked (3:7)	And he uncovered himself in the midst of the tent (9:21)
And they made clothing for themselves (3:7)	And they covered the nakedness of their father (9:23)
And their eyes were opened and they knew they were naked (3:7)	And Noah woke up from his sleep and knew what his young son had done (9:24)
"Cursed are you" (3:14)	"Cursed is Canaan" (9:25)
Cain, Abel, and Seth (4:1–2, 25	Shem, Ham, and Japheth (9:25–27)

Gage perceptively explains and elaborates on the connection between the fall and the flood:

> The structural and literary correspondence between the story of Noah's sin and the record of Adam's fall is striking. Noah's transgression begins with a vineyard (Gen. 9:20) while Adam's sin is set in a garden (3:1). Noah drank of the fruit of the vine while Adam ate of the fruit of the tree (Gen. 9:20; 3:2), both being acts of deliberate disobedience resulting in the sinner's awareness of shameful nakedness (Gen. 9:21; 3:7). While Noah's nakedness was covered by his eldest sons (Gen. 9:23), Adam's nakedness was covered by God (Gen. 3:32), and both the sin of Noah and the sin of Adam issued into a fearful curse and enduring division in their respective seed (Gen. 9:25; 3:15). In both accounts the narrative moves from the sin of the father to the genealogical development (Genesis 10 and 5). The authorial intention to relate the story of Noah's sin to Adam's Fall is literarily evident in the word-play in Genesis 9:20 (cf. *ish haadhamah* with *adham* in Gen. 2:7) and in the parallel of Genesis 9:24 (Noah awoke, i.e., by metonymy, his eyes were opened," cf. Gen. 3:7a).[16]

---

maintains that the parallel to the fall is in Ham's action, not in Noah's condition. Note how in the prelude to the fall Adam and Eve are unaware of their nakedness, as Noah is here. See John H. Walton, *Genesis* NIVAC (Grand Rapids: Zondervan, 2001), 346.

16. Gage, *The Gospel of Genesis*, 12.

Conclusion

In conclusion, it is clear that the narrative of the flood presents a re-creation theme and indicates that God is starting over again with humanity. The promise of the blessing of fruitfulness given to Adam and again to Noah with the same words in Genesis 1:28 and 9:1 signifies the role of fatherhood of Adam and Noah to the prediluvian and postdiluvian worlds respectively. Noah is the father of the new humanity just as Adam was head of the older order. The curse on the ground will not be increased, but neither will it be lifted (Gen. 8:21–22). And so while in many ways their roles are similar, the narrative makes it plain that the situation has changed in this new world.

The dominion of man over the animals has changed. Man's dominion over the animals is re-established, but now in the form of fear and dread (Gen. 9:2–3). Man must now bring the animals into subjection with greater effort by exerting himself, but because the relationship has changed he is now permitted to eat them (Gen. 9:3).

No matter what aspect of the flood we may be examining, we find that the flood account is saturated with creation language. The flood episode that enveloped the whole earth was God's way of starting again (2 Peter 3:6). The entire narrative of the flood is dominated by the uncreation/re-creation theme.[17]

REFLECTION QUESTIONS

1. What was the cause of the flood?

2. How does it appear that the flood undoes creation?

3. What are the parallels between Genesis 8 and Genesis 1?

4. What are the parallels between Noah's sin and Adam's fall?

5. How is man's dominion and relationship to the animal world changed since the flood?

17. See John Skinner, *Genesis*, ICC, 2nd ed. (Edinburgh: T&T Clark, 1930), 170; Walton, *Genesis*, 337; Gage, *The Gospel of Genesis*, 11; Wenham, *Genesis 1–15*, 207; Franz Delitzsch, *A New Commentary on Genesis*, trans. Sophia Taylor, 2 vols. (Edinburgh: T&T Clark, 1888, reprint. Minneapolis: Klock & Klock, 1978), 283; Allen P. Ross, *Creation & Blessing* (Grand Rapids: Baker, 1988), 190.

What Was the Extent of Noah's Flood? (Part 1: The Biblical Evidence)

The belief in a massive deluge of water is attested in many cultures. Evidence for a belief in a great deluge has been found in Greek, Mesopotamian, Australian, Indian, Malayan, Polynesian, Chinese, and Japanese cultures and cultures of the Western Hemisphere. In all, there are sixty-eight distinct legends of a massive flood.[1] No comparable event in biblical history has the same extra-biblical attestation as the flood in the history of religion and world history.

The flood stories that most closely resemble the biblical narrative are those which emanated from southern Mesopotamia. Three distinct legends of a flood have been discovered. The best known of these is the Gilgamesh Epic, which relates how a certain Utnapishtim[2] was arbitrarily chosen to be warned of a coming flood. There have been numerous attempts among those who adhere to the comparative religion school not only to link the Mesopotamian and biblical accounts but also to suggest that there was at least a literary dependency of the biblical flood on the Mesopotamian prototypes.

Indeed, the shared details between the Mesopotamian stories and the Genesis narrative are striking. The biblical flood and the Mesopotamian accounts share the following features: (1) only one man is warned of the coming deluge and instructed to build a vessel; (2) the insulation of the water vessels is lined with "pitch" (Heb. *kofer*; Akk. *kupru*); (3) the chosen

---

1. Jack P. Lewis, "Flood," *ABD*, 6 vols. ed. David Noel Freedman (New York: Doubleday, 1992), 2:798; Franz Delitzsch, *A New Commentary on Genesis*, trans. Sophia Taylor, 2 vols. (1888; repr., Minneapolis: Klock & Klock, 1978), 246; Derek Kidner, *Genesis: An Introduction and Commentary* (Downers Grove: InterVarsity, 1972), 96. See a helpful geographical layout of various traditions in James Boice, *Genesis: An Expositional Commentary*, vol. 1 (*Genesis 1:1–11:32*) (Grand Rapids: Zondervan, 1982), 285–87.
2. In other Mesopotamian accounts he is called Ziusudra or Atrahasis.

man is commanded what he is to bring into the boat; (4) specific mention is made of closing the door of the boat; (5) the deluge exterminated both man and beast; (6) mountains appear before the flood water begins to abate; (7) the boat lands on top of a mountain; (8) birds are released from the opening of a window; and (9) sacrifices are offered after the flood is over.[3] No consensus has ever emerged from this attempt to relate the different accounts, and in fact, claims of direct literary dependence have now largely been abandoned. As G. von Rad states: "Today, forty years after the height of the Babel-Bibel controversy, the dossier on the relation of the biblical tradition to the Babylonian story of the Flood as it is in the Gilgamesh Epic is more or less closed. A direct dependence of the biblical tradition on the Babylonian is no longer assumed."[4]

Each flood account has distinctive elements as well as differences that are often more significant than the similarities.[5] Particularly distinctive is the contrast between the ethical monotheism of the biblical account and the pagan polytheistic outlook of the Mesopotamian versions. The gods of the Babylonian accounts are often vindictive, capricious, and deceive not only humans but each other. Even the writers of these accounts display little reverence for these gods.[6] Consistent with the lack of ethics among the pagan gods is the lack of a moral worldview. This is seen, for example, in the Mesopotamian flood account. There are no ethical or moral reasons provided for the selection of the lone individual surviving the flood. Moreover, the gods are ultimately subservient to nature as they are somewhat startled by the conditions that resulted in the deluge.

How does one account for the specific terminological and literary connections between the Mesopotamian and biblical accounts? It is possible that some memories of Noah's flood were carried to different cultures where it was corrupted from the true and inspired description now faithfully recorded in the Genesis narrative. If so, the ancient Near Eastern account could contain elements of truth taken from the collective memory of Noah's descendants.[7]

---

3. See S. E. Loewenstamm, "מבול *mabbul*," *Encyclopaedia Biblica,* 9 vols. (Jerusalem: Bialik, 1950–1988), 4:601–2 [In Hb.]; Nahum Sarna, *Understanding Genesis: The Heritage of Biblical Israel* (New York: McGraw-Hill, 1966), 43–47.
4. G. von Rad, *Genesis,* rev. ed., OTL (Philadelphia: Westminster, 1972), 123. See also Nahum Sarna, *Genesis,* JPS Commentary (Philadelphia: Jewish Publication Society, 1989), 48.
5. Lewis, "Flood," 799.
6. John Skinner, *A Critical and Exegetical Commentary on Genesis,* 2nd ed., ICC (Edinburgh: T&T Clark, 1910), 178.
7. Todd S. Beall, "Contemporary Hermeneutical Approaches to Genesis 1–11," in *Coming to Grips with Genesis,* ed. Terry Mortenson and Thane H. Ury (Green Forest, Ark.: Master, 2008), 140; Kidner, *Genesis,* 96.

The interest in the flood and Noah's ark transcends the biblical narrative and has always been a subject of fascination. As early as the first century AD, Flavius Josephus, the Galilean general turned historian, cites a common belief that relics of the ark were preserved in Armenia. Similar testimony is found in rabbinic literature and from Berossus, a Babylonian priest who wrote in Greek, ca. 275 BC.[8] In the summer of 2000, an expedition sponsored by the National Geographic Society discovered under the Black Sea remnants of a human habitation that had apparently been suddenly inundated by a great flood several thousand years ago. Many believe this discovery is independent evidence for the biblical flood.[9]

Structure of the Flood Account

Assuming the literary cohesion of the account of the flood, Bernhard Anderson, emeritus professor of Princeton Theological Seminary maintains that the flood narrative was arranged according to a pattern of antithetical parallelism where the second half of the story reflects the sections of the first half but in reverse order. This parallelism, which is common in the Old Testament, accounts for the repetition. He analyzes the repetition in the following manner suggesting that God's graciousness to Noah is the central theme of the story:

Transitional introduction (6:9–10)
1. Violence in God's creation (6:11–12)
　　2. First divine address: resolution to destroy (6:13–22)
　　　3. Second divine address: command to enter the ark (7:1–10)
　　　　4. Beginning of the flood (7:11–16)
　　　　　5. The rising flood waters (7:17–24)
　　　　　GOD'S REMEMBRANCE OF NOAH (8:1)
　　　　　6. The receding flood waters (8:1–5)
　　　　7. The drying of the earth (8:6–14)
　　　8. Third divine address: command to leave the ark (8:15–19)
　　9. God's resolution to preserve order (8:20–22)
10. Fourth divine address: covenant blessing and peace (9:1–17)
Transitional conclusion (9:18–19)[10]

---

8. See L. Feldman, "Josephus' Portrait of Noah and Its Parallels in Philo, Pseudo-Philo's Biblical Antiquities, and Rabbinic Midrashim," *PAAJR* 55 (1988): 31–57; L. Ginzburg, *The Legends of the Jews: Notes to Volumes I and II From the Creation to the Exodus* (Philadelphia: Jewish Publication Society, 1968), 5:186n.48.

9. Tim Friend, "Evidence Possibly Tied to Biblical Flood Found in Sea," *USA Today*, September 13, 2000, 4A.

10. Bernhard Anderson, "From Analysis to Synthesis: The Interpretation of Genesis 1–11," *JBL* 97 (1978): 38. Similarly, a more detailed chiastic arrangement may be found in G. Wenham, "The Coherence of the Biblical Flood," *VT* 28 (1978): 336–48.

Umberto Cassuto breaks down the structure of the flood account into twelve paragraphs. Each paragraph deals with a given episode in the sequence of events, and they are all linked together by means of parallelisms of words and expressions. The series of paragraphs is composed of two groups, each comprising six paragraphs. The first six depicts, step by step, the acts of divine justice that bring destruction upon the earth, which had become filled with violence (Gen. 6:9–12, 13–22; 7:1–5, 6–9, 10–16, 17–24). The second group shows us consecutively the various stages of the act of divine compassion that renews life upon the earth (Gen. 8:1–14, 15–17, 18–22; 9:1–7, 8–11, 12–17).[11] As we now turn to the evidence for the universal flood, we will examine phrases and concepts from the biblical text that are proffered to defend the phenomenon of a global flood.

Support for Universal Flood[12]
Use of Land (erets)
According to universal flood proponents, the flood is said to cover the entire earth (*erets*). The Hebrew term for earth (*erets*), which occurs over forty times in the flood narrative, is frequently rendered as "earth," "(local) land," "ground," and even "underworld."[13] When *erets* refers to a particular piece of land, however, as Victor Hamilton notes, it is normally followed by a prepositional phrase that further identifies the land (e.g., the land of the Canaanites, land of the east, land of the fathers).[14] Furthermore, as Hamilton states, the reference in Genesis 7:3 to the animals of *kol-haarets*, "all the earth," argues for an understanding of *erets* elsewhere in the flood narrative as "earth" in that almost all uses of *kol-haarets* (outside Deuteronomy and Joshua-Samuel) are references to the earth (Gen. 1:26, 28; 11:1; Ex. 9:14, 16; 19:5).[15] And while inclusive language like "all the earth" may not always be universal in Genesis (e.g., 41:54–57), "the insistence of the narrative on the encompassing character of the flood favors the literal understanding of the universal view."[16]

---

11. Umberto Cassuto, *A Commentary on the Book of Genesis*, 2 vols. (vol. 2, *From Noah to Abraham, Genesis VI:9–XI:32*), trans. Israel Abrahams (Jerusalem: Magnes, 1984), 2:30–31.
12. For a helpful layout of the major issues of the local and universal flood accounts, see John H. Walton, *Chronological and Background Charts of the Old Testament* (Grand Rapids: Zondervan, 1994), 100–1.
13. For a fuller discussion of the use and meaning of *erets*, see Question 15 in this volume.
14. Victor P. Hamilton, *The Book of Genesis Chapters 1–17*, NICOT (Grand Rapids: Eerdmans, 1990), 273.
15. Ibid.
16. Kenneth A. Mathews, *Genesis 1–11:26*, NAC 1A (Nashville: B&H, 1996), 365.

Under All the Heavens

The universal nature of the phrase "all the earth" is seen too in the description of the flood taking place "under all the heavens," or alternatively translated "under the whole heaven" (Gen. 7:19). That the phrase suggests a universal understanding is supported by the previous phrase whose subject is "*all* the high mountains." Because it is possible that all mountains might be understood to comprise only local mountains, the Hebrew writer removes any possible ambiguity by attaching the phrase "under the whole heaven." The Hebrew phrase "under the whole heaven" appears only six other times in the Old Testament, but each conveys a universal sense.[17] The phrase is used to illustrate God's all-knowing omniscience: "For he looks to the ends of the earth and sees everything under the heavens" (Job 28:24). It also clearly illustrates God's sovereignty and ownership over his creation: "Who has first given to me, that I should repay him? Whatever is under the whole heaven is mine" (Job 41:11[Hb. 3]). "The God of the Old Testament does not see and own only what resides within the boundary of the nation Israel; he sees the whole earth and owns all of it. Because this same terminology is used to describe Noah's flood, it should not be geographically restricted but must be understood as universal."[18] Furthermore, the double use of "all" (*kol*) in Genesis 7:19, as well as the repetition of the emphatic adverb (*meodh meodh*) in the previous phrase, ("the waters prevailed *so mightily*"), cumulatively suggest an emphatic superlative.[19]

Annihilate All Life

The flood should not only be considered as universal because of its description; it should also be considered universal because of its result. The text repeatedly emphasizes the fact that the flood was extensive enough to annihilate all human and animal life on earth, apart from the water creatures (see Gen. 6:17; 7:4, 21–23).[20]

Final Judgment

The annihilation of life suggests a total judgment. The flood pictures and foreshadows the final judgment, a universal judgment upon man and the world. The reason the flood was coming upon *kol* "all" the earth and under *kol* "all" of heaven was because *kol* "all" human intention was

---

17. See Deuteronomy 2:25; 4:19; Job 37:3; Daniel 9:12.

18. Steven A. Austin, "Did Noah's Flood Cover the Entire World?" in *The Genesis Debate*, ed. Ronald Youngblood (Grand Rapids: Baker, 1990), 212.

19. H. C. Leupold, *Exposition of Genesis*, 2 vols. (Grand Rapids: Baker, 1942), 1:301–2. Genesis 7:19 records the first occurrence of the double occurrence of emphatic adverb, *meodh*. For the other occurrences which illustrate the emphatic nature of this repetition, see Genesis 30:43; Numbers 14:7; 1 Kings 7:47; 2 Kings 10:4; Ezekiel 37:10.

20. G. Charles Aalders, *Genesis*, 2 vols. (Grand Rapids: Zondervan, 1981), 1:193.

evil *kol* "all" continually (lit., *kol* "all" the day) (Gen. 6:5). As Mathews states, "The inclusive language, 'all,' 'every' and 'everything' (*kol*), imitates the universality and pervasiveness of humanity's wickedness (Gen. 6:5). By this linkage, the narrative shows the causal relationship between the sin of humanity and the consequent flood that came upon the perverse world."[21] The massive drowning was a form of purification of the wicked earth as it returned to the watery, chaotic, uninhabitable state of Genesis 1:2. This massive worldwide judgment is a forerunner of the final eschatological worldwide judgment. "It was a total judgment which made a division as deep and wide, and of as violent and universal a nature in the history of mankind, as the final judgment at the end of this world will alone produce."[22] Jesus referred to the flood as an analogy to the final eschatological judgment (Matt. 24:38–39). The Apostle Peter also made the connection between God's determination to judge the world in the judgment of the flood and the end of the world judgment (2 Peter 3:3–7).

Face Value of the Text

Taking the reading of the flood account at face value, it is difficult to deny that the reader of the passage will conclude that the judgment being described is a worldwide catastrophe. As Gerhard von Rad has stated, "According to the Priestly representation we must understand the flood as a catastrophe involving the entire cosmos. When the heavenly ocean breaks forth upon the earth below, and the primeval sea beneath the earth, which is restrained by God, now freed from its bonds, gushes up through yawning chasms onto the earth, then there is a destruction of the entire cosmic system according to biblical cosmogony."[23] Similarly Ken Mathews has pointed out that a face value reading of Genesis 8:19–23 overwhelming indicates that a worldwide destruction is in view. In this passage the word *kol* ("all," "every") appears eight times, indicating the comprehensive nature of the total destruction and the inundation of the earth even to the level of the high mountains. This clearly suggests a worldwide deluge.[24] The waters are everywhere as though the earth has returned to its "primeval state at the dawn of creation."[25]

Moreover, Jack Davis adds that the covenant established with Noah at the conclusion of the flood clearly indicates that the flood was universal. In this covenant God promises never to judge the world through a flood again, "The purpose of the flood was to judge the sinfulness of the entire

21. Mathews, *Genesis 1:1–11:26*, 380.
22. Franz Delitzsch, *A New Commentary on Genesis*, trans. Sophia Taylor, 2 vols. (Edinburgh: T&T Clark, 1888; repr.; Minneapolis: Klock & Klock, 1978), 1:235.
23. Von Rad, *Genesis*, 128.
24. Mathews, *Genesis 1:1–11:26*, 380.
25. Cassuto, *Genesis*, 2:97.

antediluvian population (Gen. 6:5–7, 11–13). Anything less than a universal flood would not have fulfilled this purpose. Furthermore, God covenanted with Noah that such a flood would never happen again. If the flood were local, God has broken His covenant because there have been many local floods since that one; if the flood was universal, then God has not broken His covenant."[26] Thus, Kidner reasons that if the passage is read in its own terms, it depicts a *total* judgment on the ungodly world—"not an event of debatable dimensions in a world we may try to reconstruct."[27]

Support for a Local Flood

Local flood advocates, of course, take issue with the interpretations presented by universal flood proponents. Even those who advocate or lean toward the universal flood view acknowledge alternative interpretations. Hamilton, a rather strong advocate for the universal flood position, in arguing for the understanding of *erets* as earth, acknowledges that the use of *erets* in Genesis 13:9, 15 shows that even in Genesis *kol-haarets* may refer to the whole land.[28] Similarly, Bruce Waltke concedes that while the language describing the flood suggests a worldwide flood (see Gen. 7:19–23; 8:21; 9:11, 15; 2 Peter 3:5–7), the same comprehensive language can be used for limited situations (see Gen. 41:56–57; Deut. 2:25; 1 Kings 4:34; 10:24; 2 Chron. 36:23; Dan. 2:38; 4:22; 5:19; Luke 2:1).[29] For example, the phrase, "under the whole heaven" in Deuteronomy 2:25 is qualified by the subsequent phrase "who shall hear the report of thee" and may have a limited rather than a universal nuance. Similarly, "all" is not always absolute in biblical language; it does not always indicate complete comprehensiveness. "All" may encompass only those of a more regionally delineated area.[30]

Local flood adherents, Mark Whorton and Hill Roberts, argue that "the world" can mean local areas in the Bible. They point to Genesis 41:56–57: "When the famine was spread over all (*kol*) the face of the earth (*erets*), . . . the people of all the earth (*kolerets*) came to Egypt to buy grain from Joseph" (NASB). Here clearly "all the earth" referred only to Egypt and the region surrounding it. Wharton and Hill observe, "Joseph clearly did not feed Pacific

26. John J. Davis, *Paradise to Prison: Studies in Genesis* (Salem, Wis.: Sheffield, 1975, reissued 1998), 126.
27. Kidner, *Genesis*, 95 (emphasis original). See also John Skinner, *Genesis*, ICC, 2nd ed. (Edinburgh: T&T Clark, 1930), 155; Warren Austin Gage, *The Gospel of Genesis* (Winona Lake, Ind.: Carpenter, 1984), 11n.14; Allen P. Ross, *Creation & Blessing* (Grand Rapids: Baker, 1988), 190; Hamilton, *Genesis 1–17*, 273; Bruce Waltke and Cathi J. Fredricks, *Genesis* (Grand Rapids: Zondervan, 2001), 127, 132–33n.34.
28. Hamilton, *Genesis 1–17*, 273.
29. Waltke and Fredricks, *Genesis*, 136.
30. John H. Walton, *Genesis*, NIVAC (Grand Rapids: Zondervan, 2001), 324–25.

Islanders or Native Americans from his storehouses in Egypt."[31] They make similar arguments about other universal language used to describe the flood:

> But how were "all the high mountains under the whole sky" covered by a local flood? The Hebrew phrase translated "high mountains" can refer to *any elevated landscape*, whether high hills or Mount Everest. Furthermore, since the text does not specify exactly what it was that covered the mountains, *The Theological Wordbook of the Old Testament* suggests that it may have been storm clouds rather than water that spread over the highest peaks. And as we saw above, "under the whole sky" often refers merely to a local patch of sky. Hence, from a language standpoint it is possible that Genesis only means to say there was enough water to thoroughly flood the local region.[32]

Wharton and Hill also note that the narrative says that after the flood the water "was dried up from the earth" (8:7, NASB) and that eventually "the earth was completely dry" (8:14, NIV). They argue, "To be consistent with a strictly literalistic interpretation of the language, a global flood implies a global desert after the flood."[33] But of course no one suggests such a thing, so they conclude that a local flood view is a reasonable, possible interpretation.

Conclusion

The face value reading of the narrative, even recognizing that terms and phrases may be understood in different ways in different contexts, is a strong argument in favor of a universal flood. John Walton, who is not an advocate of the universal view, concedes that the face value reading of Genesis 8:3–5 leads one to understand that the biblical flood was global.[34] Moreover, the fact that the flood functions as a biblical type of the coming eschatological judgment (along with the face value reading) may be among the strongest arguments in favor of a universal flood. In addition to the authors mentioned in the discussion, many other notable Old Testament scholars including Merrill Unger, Gleason Archer, Gerhard Hasel, and John Whitcomb have understood that the biblical flood was a universal, cosmic event.[35] Biblically, the local flood view is a possible interpretation, but the universal view seems to be a more natural reading of the text. Geologically, we will see that the situation appears to be reversed.

---

31. Mark Wharton and Hill Roberts, *Understanding Creation: A Biblical and Scientific Discovery* (Nashville: Holman Reference, 2008), 158–60.
32. Ibid. (emphasis original).
33. Ibid.
34. Walton, *Genesis*, 326.
35. See Austin, "Did Noah's Flood Cover the Entire World?" 227–28 for documentation.

REFLECTION QUESTIONS

1. What are the parallels between the Mesopotamian and Genesis accounts of the flood?

2. Did the flood account in Genesis borrow from the Babylonian account of the flood? Explain.

3. What is the antithetical parallelism pattern?

4. What is the support for a universal flood?

5. What is the support for a local flood?

What Was the Extent of Noah's Flood? (Part 2: The Geological Evidence)

In 1961, John Whitcomb and Henry Morris published *The Genesis Flood*. They intended the work to be a response to Bernard Ramm, who in 1954 had published a work arguing that Noah's deluge was a local catastrophe. Borrowing heavily from George McCready Price (1870–1963), a Seventh-Day Adventist author, Whitcomb and Morris contended that the flood of Noah's day accounts for practically all the geological record. By any standard, the book was a publishing success with over 300,000 copies sold. *The Genesis Flood* launched the modern young-earth creationism (YEC) movement.

In 2008, old-earth geologist Davis Young, along with co-author Ralph Stearley, published *The Bible, Rocks and Time*. Young and Stearley's book is a revision of Davis' earlier *Christianity and the Age of the Earth*. In 2009, young-earth geologist, Andrew Snelling, published *Earth's Catastrophic Past*, a two volume work intended to update Whitcomb and Morris' seminal work.

Reading Andrew Snelling's *Earth's Catastrophic Past* and Davis Young's *The Bible, Rocks and Time* side by side is a surreal experience. Both men are professional geologists, and both books exhibit the proficiency and expertise of their respective authors. Snelling's two volume set argues for young-earth creationism and that Noah's flood created the preponderance of the geological record. Young and his co-author, Ralph Stearley, present the case for an ancient earth and that Noah's flood was a local phenomenon. The two works together total over 1,500 pages. Reading them together can give a person cognitive whiplash.

Snelling is thorough in his presentation. He realizes that he is arguing against the consensus view of the geological community and therefore must meticulously make his case. Davis and Stearley give more attention to the historical development of the debate about the age of the earth, but they also give methodical attention to the evidences for their position. Both books attempt to make their respective cases via cumulative arguments—piling up one example after another. Snelling and Young often present the same geological data—the geological column of the Grand Canyon, the mid-Atlantic ridge, coral reefs, etc. But they almost always arrive at diametrically opposite conclusions.

What is going on here? There are at least four possible explanations: (1) The postmodernists and deconstructionists are right—all meaning is subjective and is created by the reader. In this case the text is the geological column and the readers are the geologists. (2) At least one side is engaged in deliberate deceit. (3) Spiritual forces are at work. One side is blinded by the evil one, while the other's mind is divinely illuminated. Or (4) at least one side has an almost pathological inability to see the truth. These blind spots render them unable to see what should be obvious.

None of the four above possibilities are very good. The postmodernist answer (1) is self-referentially contradictory. Deconstructionism may work as a descriptor but fails as a philosophy. As for explanation (2), there is nothing about Snelling or Davis that indicates either would be willing to deceive or be deliberately dishonest. As for (3), Christians have no doubt about spiritual warfare, and that spiritual battles occur in every avenue of human endeavor, and this includes the scientific realm. However, both Davis and Snelling (and the respective Christian communities they represent) affirm the Lordship of Jesus Christ over their vocations as geologists. Both are servants of Christ. The present authors are in no position to make a spiritual determination about either one. Of the four possible explanations, the phenomenon of blind spots (4) is the most likely.

Explanation (4) is also the most optimistic, even if one or both sides seem to be intransigent. Here the community of faith can play a crucial role. If Davis and Snelling, and others who hold to their respective views, will meet, talk, and pray together; if they will allow other godly, concerned, and informed brethren to speak truth into their lives; if they will be humble enough to acknowledge their respective blind spots, then it will be possible for progress to be made and for some type of consensus to be achieved. As it stands now, the dissonance between the two geologists and their respective books is so great that one has to wonder if they are looking at the same planet.

This chapter will first survey the global flood model presented by Whitcomb and Morris. Second, we will look at the updated version presented by Snelling and other adherents. Third, we will note some of the criticisms lodged by Young and other old-earth creationists and last, we will briefly recount the local flood interpretation.

The Classic Global Flood Theory of Whitcomb and Morris
Opposition to Uniformitarianism

Uniformitarianism is the principle that the processes of today should be used to interpret the past. Applied to geology, it implies that the geological formations were formed gradually over immense periods of time. Whitcomb and Morris argued the presupposition of uniformitarianism hopelessly biased modern geological theory so that geologists fail to see the clear evidences for the global catastrophe that occurred during Noah's day.[1] They further contended that this current blindness on the part of the geological profession is a fulfillment of the Apostle Peter's prophecy of apostasy during the latter days (2 Peter 3:3–7).[2] In this way, flood geology and young-earth creationism fit very well within the premillennial worldview of classic dispensationalism which dominated evangelical thinking for much of the twentieth century.

2nd Law of Thermodynamics as an Effect of the Curse

One of the most fundamental laws of nature is the second law of thermodynamics, otherwise known as entropy. It is the principle that nature has the tendency to move from a state of higher order to a lower state. In short, entropy is the phenomena of everything running down. Whitcomb and Morris interpreted the Genesis account to teach that the universe was originally created perfect: no death, decay, or deterioration. This, to them, does not seem to be compatible with entropy, so Whitcomb and Morris suggested that the second law came into effect when God cursed the earth for Adam's sake.[3]

The Canopy Theory

The creation account speaks of God separating the waters above the firmament from the waters below the firmament (Gen. 1:6). Whitcomb and Morris interpreted this to teach that God placed a vapor canopy above the atmosphere.[4] This canopy provided the waters that inundated the world during Noah's flood. Whitcomb and Morris argued that the vapor covering provided by the canopy created a very different environment for the pre-flood world from that of the present world.[5] The blanket of water produced a very favorable greenhouse effect that created a moderate climate worldwide. They interpreted Genesis 2:5–6 to teach that it in those days it did not rain and suggested that the vapor canopy provided the mist mentioned. In addition, the canopy acted as a protection from cosmic rays, which perhaps accounted for the remarkably long lives listed in the genealogies of Genesis 4–5.

Rejection of the Geological Column

Whitcomb and Morris argued that the geological column, with its strata and layers, was created by the flood waters of the deluge. Rather than giving evidence of great periods of time, the layers testify to different phases of the waters rising, cresting and receding. They pointed to "frequent flagrant contradictions to the

---

1. John Whitcomb and Henry Morris, *The Genesis Flood: The Biblical Record and Its Scientific Implications* (Phillipsburg: P&R, 1961), 130–42.
2. Ibid., 451–54.
3. Ibid., 225–27.
4. Ibid., 239–43.
5. Ibid., 243–58.

established geologic time sequences" and to inversions in the geological column in which the supposed ages are out of order. They concluded that the "geologic time scale is an extremely fragile foundation on which a tremendous and un-wieldy superstructure of interpretation has been erected."[6] The world underwent dramatic transformation during and immediately after Noah's flood, with the world's mountain ranges being formed as the waters receded.[7] In addition, the ice age, if it happened at all, occurred almost immediately after the deluge.[8]

Dinosaur and Human Fossils Together

A centerpiece to the cumulative case presented in *The Genesis Flood* was the finding of fossils in a limestone bed of the Paluxy River near Glen Rose, Texas. Whitcomb and Morris presented photographs of what appeared to be fossilized impressions of dinosaurs and human footprints side by side. This evidence, they argued, overturned the conventional interpretation of geological history that the era of dinosaurs and the time of humans were separated by millions of years. Under the photos they declared,

> These tracks were both cut from the Paluxy River Bed near Glen Rose, Texas, in supposedly Cretaceous strata, plainly disproving the evolutionist's contention that the dinosaurs were extinct some 70 million years before man "evolved." Geologists have rejected this evidence, however, preferring to believe that the human footprints were carved by some modern artist, while at the same time accepting the dino-saur footprints as genuine. If anything, the dinosaur prints look more "artificial" than the human, but the genuineness of neither would be questioned at all were it not for the geologi-cally sacrosanct evolutionary time-scale.[9]

This was a spectacular piece of evidence. The photos of the fossils played no small part in convincing many readers of the feasibility of Whitcomb and Morris' thesis. An article in *Scientific American* predicted that "all the geologists will resign their jobs and take up truck driving" if the prints were found to be genuine.[10] By providing a robust creationist model combined with exhibits such as the Paluxy River footprints, *The Genesis Flood* has had a powerful impact among conservative evangelicals. Unfortunately, as YEC proponent Paul Garner

---

6. Ibid., 209; cf. 169–211.
7. Ibid., 141–53.
8. Ibid., 288–303.
9. Ibid., 174–75.
10. Quoted in Ronald Numbers, *The Creationists* (New York: Alfred Knopf, 1992), 121–23.

acknowledges, "not all of the ideas of the book have stood the test of time"[11]—including, as we will see, the Paluxy footprints.

Current Global Flood Models

Whitcomb and Morris inspired a generation of young-earth creationists. One such YEC proponent is Australian geologist Andrew Snelling. Snelling wrote the two volume *Earth's Catastrophic Past: Geology, Creation, and the Flood* for the purpose of updating the flood model presented in *The Genesis Flood*. But in many ways Snelling's work is a total revamp. Snelling, along with other YEC researchers such as paleontologist Kurt Wise and astrophysicist Russell Humphreys, recognized that the case argued by Whitcomb and Morris needed significant retooling.

Omits the Canopy Theory

Significantly, Snelling abandons the canopy theory.[12] He and other current YEC advocates recognize that the biblical evidence for the canopy theory is tenuous at best. Some, such as Joseph Dillow, did extensive work to provide a viable model, but today most YEC proponents have given up on the theory.[13] Snelling points out there are simply too many scientific obstacles. Any such canopy would have created a runaway greenhouse effect that would have boiled the earth. He explains,

> One consideration is that much more than a few inches of liquid water equivalent in a vapor canopy appears to lead to a runaway greenhouse effect. A second is that the amount of latent heat released from the condensation of water vapor limits the amount of condensation that can occur during the Flood without boiling the oceans and killing all the life on earth because of the high temperatures required to radiate the latent heat to space at a sufficient rate. These considerations imply that even if a water vapor canopy did exist above the atmosphere, it could not have contained sufficient water vapor to have sustained forty days and nights of intense, global, torrential rainfall.[14]

Snelling accepts Humphrey's idiosyncratic interpretation that the "waters above the expanse" mentioned in Genesis 1:6–8 are located on the other side of the

---

11. Paul Garner, *The New Creationism: Building Scientific Theories on a Biblical Foundation* (Darlington: Evangelical, 2009), 183.
12. Andrew Snelling, *Earth's Catastrophic Past: Geology Creation, and the Flood*, 2 vols. (Dallas: ICR, 2009), 2:663–67.
13. Joseph Dillow, *The Waters Above* (Chicago: Moody, 1981).
14. Snelling, *Earth's Catastrophic Past*, 2:472–73.

universe.[15] So where did the floodwaters come from? Snelling, along with others, argue for "catastrophic plate tectonics" (CPT). They suggest that subterranean reservoirs were unleashed during a catastrophic shift in the tectonic plates.[16] The seismic activity exhibited today by plate tectonics is the residual effect of Noah's flood. In addition to dropping Whitcomb and Morris' canopy theory, Snelling also abandons the view that it did not rain prior to the flood (Gen. 2:4–7).[17]

Omits the 2nd Law of Thermodynamics as an Effect of the Curse
    Snelling, along with other global flood advocates, realized that Whitcomb and Morris' argument that entropy was a manifestation of the curse was extremely problematic.[18] Without the second law in force, no normal process would be able to function. For example, the second law is necessary for digestion. Whitcomb and Morris' theory also seemed to be contrary to certain biblical passages. The Bible states that Eden had four rivers (Gen. 2:10–14). Rivers are channels of water flowing from a higher level to a lower level. By definition they are examples of the second law in action.

Accepts the Geological Column
    Snelling departs from Whitcomb and Morris at another significant point in that Snelling accepts the validity of the geological column.[19] The column is real, and so is the sequence of the fossil record. Snelling, however, contends that the geological strata do not present a chronological record. Rather, they give evidence of geographical distinctions. The four broad geological divisions—the Precambrian, the Paleozoic, the Mesozoic, and the Cenozoic—give evidence of four distinct biogeographical regions. This forms the basis of the "ecological zonation theory," which we will examine next.
Drops the Paluxy River Fossils
    Snelling makes no mention of the fossils found in the riverbed of the Paluxy River. To their credit, most young-earth proponents (with a few notable exceptions) admit that the supposedly human footprints are in fact not human at all. Henry Morris' son, John Morris publicly acknowledges that none of the prints "can today be regarded as unquestionably of human origin."[20]

---

15. Ibid., 1:194–95, 212; 2:663–67; Russell Humphreys, *Starlight and Time: Solving the Puzzle of Distant Starlight in a Young Universe* (Green Forest, Ark.: Master, 1994), 53–80.
16. Snelling, *Earth's Catastrophic Past*, 2:683–706; Kurt Wise, *Faith, Form, and Time: What the Bible Teaches the Science Confirms about Creation and the Age of the Universe* (Nashville: B&H, 2002), 181–89.
17. Snelling, *Earth's Catastrophic Past*, 2:669–73.
18. Ibid., 2:620.
19. Ibid., 1:329–54.
20. John Morris, "The Paluxy River Mystery," http://www.icr.org/article/paluxy-river-mystery/ (accessed 11/05/12).

Humans and Dinosaurs Lived at the Same Time but in Different Regions

The current global flood model must account for the fact that the remains of dinosaurs and those of humans are never found in the same geological strata. Snelling and others posit the "ecological zonation theory."[21] YEC proponents argue that the pre-flood world was segregated into highly distinct zones. Garner explains, "According to the ecological zonation theory, the order of burial of adjacent ecological zones by the encroaching flood waters produced a vertical sequence of rock layers containing characteristic fossils."[22] Dinosaurs and humans ate different foods, so then they probably also lived in separate regions or "biomes."

Floating Continents

One serious challenge to the global flood model is the amount of coal and oil deposits located in the earth. Such deposits are the remnants of buried vegetation. There simply could not have been enough vegetation growing on the earth at one time to account for all the deposits that have been found. As a solution, Snelling, along with Wise and others, propose that during the pre-flood era there existed giant floating continents.[23] Upon these floating islands, which covered much of the world's oceans, grew immense forests.

> Based upon this, it has been proposed that the Primary plants actually formed the basis of a large floating forest biome. Based upon how much organic material made up the coals of the Primary, this floating forest may have been subcontinent-sized or even continent-sized. The basic structure was probably broadly similar to the "quaking bogs" found on a number of lakes in the upper Midwestern United States. Quaking bogs are floating vegetation mats whose outer edges are made up of aquatic plants.[24]

Thus Snelling, Wise, and other global flood proponents hope to account for the immense seams of coal and the oil fields that geologists find throughout the world.

Suspension of the Normal Laws of Nature

Snelling concedes that much of the geological evidence cannot be reconciled with any interpretation that uses the physical laws, properties and relationships

---

21. Wise, *Faith, Form, and Time*, 173–74; Snelling, *Earth's Catastrophic Past*, 727–63.
22. Garner, *The New Creationism*, 199–202.
23. Andrew Snelling, *Earth's Catastrophic Past*, 675–77.
24. Wise, *Faith, Form, and Time*, 171.

as they presently are. He postulates that God miraculously changed the laws of nature during the flood. Snelling explains,

> Coal beds were formed during the Flood year, approximately 4,500 years ago, as were many of the granites that contain uranium and polonium radio halos, because the granites intruded into Flood-deposited strata. Thus, it is concluded that hundreds of millions of years worth of radioisotope decay (at today's measured rates) must have occurred during the Flood year, only about 4,500 years ago.[25]

Appealing to a change in the laws of nature marks a remarkable change in YEC strategy, and in many ways it also makes a significant admission. As a strategy, it indicates an end to any real attempt to empirically establish the historicity of a global flood. Miracles, by definition, cannot be scientifically examined. The appeal also admits that the scientific evidence does not support the YEC model.

Compressed Ice Ages

Standard geological models hold that during earth's natural history there have been five distinct ice ages that cover hundreds of millions of years. In addition, mainstream geologists believe that over the last million years there have been several glacial periods where glacial ice has advanced and retreated. These models, of course, do not fit with a global flood model. Global flood adherents argue that at the very most, from beginning to end, the ice age was only seven hundred years long.[26] The ice surged out in a "couple of decades," and then receded within "a couple of decades."[27] The ice age lasted only a few centuries at the maximum. Therefore, rather than calling it the ice age, Snelling says a more accurate label would be "the ice advance."[28]

Accelerated Evolution

Global flood proponents recognize that the ark presents two problems related to speciation: (1) the number of species that were on the ark, and (2) the worldwide distribution of species after they disembarked. The number of species of life on earth is mind-boggling. James LeFanu points out that there are over forty species of parrots, seventy species of monkeys, tens of thousands of species

---

25. Snelling admits that "the strata assigned to the Flood even appear to record 500 to 700 million years worth (at today's measured rates) of accelerated radioisotope decay" (*Earth's Catastrophic Past*, 2:847–48).

26. Garner, *The New Creationism*, 209–21.

27. Wise, *Faith, Form, and Time*, 215–16.

28. Snelling, *Earth's Catastrophic Past*, 774–86.

of butterflies, 20,000 species of ants, 8,000 species of termites—this list goes on and on.[29] There are millions and millions of species.

How did Noah's ark contain so many different forms of life? And how did so many geographically specific species—such as kangaroos in Australia—disburse so quickly? The solution proposed by global flood advocates is one of the most controversial aspects of the model: a theory called AGEing process (where AGE stands for Altruistic Genetic Elements).[30] Snelling argues that instead of gathering the myriad of species, it was only necessary to gather progenitors who were specimens of each "created kind." For example, instead of loading dogs, wolves, hyenas, coyotes, and other canines onto the ark, it was necessary to have a male and female proto-canine (what he calls "baramin"). Then the number of required animals drop significantly. Snelling explains, "If, as the preponderance of evidence shows, the 'created kind' or *baramin* was possibly equivalent in most instances to the family (at least in the case of mammals and birds), then there would have only been about 2,000 animals on the Ark."[31]

The global flood model requires that a rapid diversification of species occurred immediately after the flood. So proponents posit that species proliferated and dispersed in a matter of decades. Garner suggests that the creatures were "front-loaded" with genetically recessive traits that expressed when needed. He admits that in this area, YEC has much more work to do, that there are "many as yet unanswered questions."[32] Wise argues that many of the vestigial organs are the result of the rapid evolution that occurred after the animals left the ark.[33]

Hugh Ross accuses proponents of the AGEing process of being "hyper-evolutionists" who out-Darwin the Darwinists. Ross considers it ironic that, in their attempt to rescue the global flood model, YEC adherents are embracing a version of "ultra-efficient biological evolution." He observes, "This efficiency of natural speciation exceeds by many orders of magnitude the most optimistic Darwinist estimate ever proposed.... If naturalistic evolutionary processes actually did proceed with such speed, the changes would be easily observable in real time—in our time."[34]

Criticisms of Global Flood Geology
The Preponderance of Geological Evidence

Critics of the global flood theory contend that the facts simply go against the model. In *The Bible, Rocks, and Time*, geologists Davis Young and Ralph Stearley,

29. Charles Le Fanu, *Why Us? How Science Rediscovered the Mystery of Ourselves* (New York: Vintage: 2009), 59–62.
30. Garner, *The New Creationism*, 140.
31. Snelling, *Earth's Catastrophic Past*, 136.
32. Garner, *The New Creationism*, 141.
33. Wise, *Faith, Form, and Time*, 219–21.
34. Hugh Ross, *A Matter of Days: Resolving a Creation Controversy* (Colorado Springs: NavPress, 2004), 121–30.

present a survey of the cumulative evidences for an ancient earth.[35] They contend that the multitude of data they present cannot be explained by a single catastrophic flood. Other old-earth advocates concur.

For example, consider the claim made by global flood adherents that the geological column presents different geographical regions rather than different chronological time periods. As we noted earlier, there are four broad geological divisions: the Precambrian, the Paleozoic, the Mesozoic, and the Cenozoic, with the oldest (Precambrian) located at the bottom and the youngest (Cenozoic) sitting on top. This sequence is found worldwide. The global flood model holds that these four systems were four contemporary, geographically distinct regions. Charles Foster contends that if the global flood model were correct, the fossil record would look different. He explains,

> If one looked at the fossils from a contemporary rain forest, a contemporary coral reef, and a contemporary city, one would see very different things. Well, true, but if they were contemporary but geographically separated, they would not lie neatly on top of one another, always in the same order wherever one looked in the world. If the creationists were right, you would find a mass of Paleozoic fossils in Europe, a mass of Mesozoic fossils in North America, and so on. But you do not. The problem is compounded for the creationist since the flood is supposed to have buried everything at the same time.[36]

After analyzing Snelling's argument that the geologic column was created during the flood, Timothy Helble concludes, "When one considers the math of lateral sediment transport necessary to form 4,000 feet of sedimentary strata in 150 days over hundreds of thousands of square miles, the implausibility of Flood geology becomes easier to comprehend."[37]

It Rejects the Field of Geology

A report by the National Academy of Sciences sums up in one sentence why mainstream geologists reject the global flood model: "The belief that Earth's sediments, with their fossils, were deposited in an orderly sequence in a year's time defies all geological observations and physical principles concerning sedimentation rates and possible quantities of suspended solid matter."[38]

---

35. We looked at those arguments in Question 20.
36. Charles Foster, *The Selfless Gene: Living with God and Darwin* (Nashville: Thomas Nelson, 2009), 55–56.
37. Timothy K. Helble, "Sediment Transport and the Conconino Sandstone: A Reality Check on Flood Geology," *Perspectives on Science and Christian Faith* 63, no. 1 (March 2011): 30.
38. Quoted by Helble, "Sediment Transport and the Conconino Sandstone," 26.

Mainstream geologists argue that flood geologists are forced to make ever more elaborate and unlikely scenarios (such as appeals to underground reservoirs of sediments and water for which there is little or no empirical evidence, selective use of mainstream research, appeals to the suspension of the laws of nature, and resorting often to special pleading). In short, proponents of a global flood are the geological equivalent to Ptolemaic astronomers. Pre-Copernican astronomers found it necessary to add ever more complicated epicycles to get the Ptolemaic model to resemble the empirical evidence. Copernicus recognized that Ockham's Razor required a paradigm shift (Ockham's Razor is the scientific principle that, all things being equal, the simplest solution is generally the correct one). So astronomers abandoned the Ptolemaic earth-centered model in favor of the Copernican sun-centered model. Critics contend that at some point flood geologists need to do the same thing.

The field of geology cannot be "tweaked" to accommodate a global understanding of Noah's flood. Geology, as currently understood, would have to be completely rejected and overthrown. As Francis Collins observes,

> In general, those who hold [YEC] views are sincere, well-meaning, God-fearing people, driven by deep concerns that naturalism is threatening to drive God out of human experience. But the claims of Young Earth Creationism simply cannot be accommodated by tinkering around the edges of scientific knowledge. If these claims were actually true, it would lead to a complete and irreversible collapse of the sciences of physics, chemistry, cosmology, geology, and biology.[39]

As Collins puts it, the global flood model cannot be incorporated into the field of geology simply by "tinkering around the edges."

It Embraces Outliers While Rejecting the Main Body of Evidence

Old-earth geologists accuse flood geologists of selectively choosing the data from mainstream sources. Helble states, "When YECs draw on material from the mainstream science community, other information that contradicts the young earth position can often be found in the same cited references."[40] Young and Stearley are more explicit in their criticism of the approach taken by global flood advocates:

> Because they have put on blinders, young-Earth creationists are unwilling to accept the totality of the available geologic

39. Francis Collins, *The Language of God: A Scientist Presents Evidence for Belief* (New York: Simon & Shuster, 2006), 173–74.
40. Ibid., 32.

evidence. They are unwilling to abandon their young-Earth, global-Flood hypothesis even when the evidence shows it to be untenable. They have ignored or distorted a vast body of evidence that is contrary to their preconceived notion of what Earth history must have been like. They have focused only on data that, taken in isolation from geologic contexts, might be seen as favorable to their own theory. They claim continually to argue from the evidence of nature, but they have repeatedly ignored what is inconvenient for them. Although some of the phenomena of the sedimentary rock record might be interpretable in terms of a great Flood, most of the phenomena to which they appeal are far more satisfactorily explicable in terms of much smaller scale processes than a global catastrophic Flood. More important, young-Earth creationists have refused to accept the abundant evidence of glacial deposits, lake deposits, desert deposits, delta deposits, shore deposits, reef deposits, and evaporate deposits in the rock record. Young-Earth creationists have refused to face the evidence from metamorphism, the kinetics of mineral formation and heat flow from cooling magmas. They have tried to make the evidence from radiometric dating say something opposite from what it does say. The attempt to find a way to have the decay constants of radioactive isotopes change in an unbelievably spectacular fashion is a desperate attempt to rescue their view of the world. To date, *all* physical evidence pertaining to decay constants indicates the virtual immutability of those constants. Although a tiny fraction of geologic evidence might suggest a global Flood if considered in complete isolation from the wealth of other evidence, the overwhelming totality of evidence argue mightily against a global deluge.[41]

Biblical scholars can understand the nature of this complaint. When someone uses an obscure passage of Scripture to come to a conclusion that is contrary to the clear teaching of the rest of the Bible, then that one is accused of mishandling the sacred text. Young and Stearley are making a similar accusation against the way global flood advocates interpret the geological evidence.

Presuppositional Bias?

Snelling repeats the assertion made by Whitcomb and Morris that the presuppositions held by mainstream geologists prevent them from considering the

---

41. Davis Young and Ralph Stearley, *The Bible, Rocks and Time: Geological Evidence for the Age of the Earth* (Downers Grove: InterVarsity, 2008), 472–73 (emphasis original).

global flood model. Those who decide to embrace assumptions that go against the young-earth model and flood geology reveal a decision to throw off the authority of Scripture. "The bias exhibited by one's choice of assumptions may not simply be a matter of objective science, but rather primarily of one's subconscious spiritual condition."[42] However, many, if not most, geologists of the early nineteenth century were Christians who held to a high view of the Bible. These geologists gave up flood geology only reluctantly, and then only after they were convinced that the empirical evidence left them with no choice. As early as 1834, long before Darwin published his theory, an article in the *Christian Observer* lamented that Christian geologists felt they were intellectually compelled to abandon flood geology:

> Buckland, Sedgwick, Faber, Chalmers, Conybeare, and many other Christian geologists, strove long with themselves to believe that they could: and they did not give up the hope, or seek for a new interpretation of the sacred text, till they considered themselves driven from their position by such facts as we have stated. If, *even now, a reasonable, or we might say* POSSIBLE *solution were offered, they would,* we feel persuaded, *gladly revert* to their original opinion.[43]

The Bible-believing geologists of the nineteenth century were driven by the geological findings to the conclusion that the earth is ancient and that Noah's flood cannot account for those findings. They resisted this conclusion, and did not come to it happily. They certainly were not motivated by an atheistic agenda nor were they blinded by naturalistic presuppositions.

The Accusation of Fideism Parading as Science
To account for evidence that goes against YEC in general and the global flood model in particular, Snelling suggests that God supernaturally intervened to change the laws of nature during the flood event. Young and Stearley, as fellow evangelicals, acknowledge that they, in principle, have no problem with an appeal to the miraculous. However, they contend that this puts the event beyond scientific investigation and defense.

The only recourse that flood catastrophists have to save their theory is to appeal to a pure miracle and thus eliminate entirely the possibility of historical geology. We think that would be a more honest course of action for young-earth advocates to take. Young-earth creationists should cease their efforts to convince the lay Christian public that geology supports a young earth when it does not

---

42. Snelling, *Earth's Catastrophic Past*, 1:295–97.
43. Quoted by Philip Henry Gosse, *Omphalos: An Attempt to Untie the Geological Knot* (London: John Van Voorst, 1857), 6n.2 (emphasis original).

do so. To continue that effort is misguided and detrimental to the health of the church and the cause of Christ.[44]

Davis and Stearley conclude that the entire "flood geology" enterprise is invalid as a scientific endeavor.

The Local Flood Model

The Local Flood Alternative

Geologist Carol Hill and her husband, physicist Alan Hill, propose a model in which "the land of the five seas"—the region encompassed by the Mediterranean Sea, the Caspian Sea, the Black Sea, the Red Sea, and the Arabian Sea—was flooded by a deluge that inundated the land for 150 days.[45] They point out that the region's unique features—a long, level plain surrounded by bodies of water—cause the area to have a history of intense storms that stall overland, producing what meteorologists and hydrologists call "the Noah effect." The Genesis account accurately describes the meteorological situation of Mesopotamia. The last Noah effect storm came in 1969, when it rained for twenty-four days and the region received seventy-five inches of rain.

The region is historically known for floods. Therefore, Noah's flood must have been unique for so many cultures to have recorded it. A forty-day downpour of rain would have flooded the entire alluvial plain. Because the Mesopotamian plain "is one of the flattest places on earth," the waters would have receded very slowly.[46] The wind spoken of in the biblical narrative would have created a storm surge, which kept the ark in the flooded plain. The Hills note five supernatural components of the flood of Noah: (1) God sent the flood to judge a corrupt world while showing grace to Noah. (2) God exercised sovereign control over the forces that caused the flood. (3) Noah built the ark in obedience to the direct command of God. It was God who shut them in. (4) God providentially restrained the waters and brought the Ark safely to Ararat. And (5) God established the covenant with Noah and made the rainbow its sign. They conclude, "If the actual meteorological and geographical conditions of the Iraq (Mesopotamia) area are taken into account, the Bible proves remarkably accurate in its record of the Flood account."[47]

The Genetic Evidence for Noah

Biochemist Fazale Rana and astrophysicist Hugh Ross argue for a local interpretation of Noah's flood and for old-earth creationism. They point to recent

---

44. Young and Stearley, *The Bible, Rocks and Time*, 474.
45. Carol Hill, "Qualitative Hydrology of Noah's Flood," *Perspectives on Science and Christian Faith* 58, no. 2 (June 2006): 120–29; Alan Hill, "Quantitative Hydrology of Noah's Flood," *Perspectives on Science and Christian Faith* 58, no. 2 (June 2006): 130–41.
46. Ibid.
47. Ibid., 128.

discoveries in molecular anthropology.[48] Geneticists believe that the mitochondrion within the human cell gives evidence that all humanity shares a common female ancestor who lived perhaps 50,000 years ago (hence she is often referred to as "mitochondrial Eve"). Similarly, molecular anthropologists believe that investigations of the Y-chromosome reveal that all humanity shares a common male ancestor, who lived perhaps as recently as 30,000 years ago. Rana and Ross argue that this is what the Bible predicts, in that all humanity originates from Eve (who evidently lived 50,000 years ago), and then the linage of the human race narrowed genetically to one man, Noah (evidently around 30,000 years ago). They explain:

> This explanation makes sense in light of the Flood account, because a single Y-chromosome sequence would be represented by Noah and his sons. The wives of Noah and his sons would have had up to four different mitochondrial-DNA sequences, making it appear as if the effective population size of the female linage was larger than the male lineage.[49]

Rana and Ross contend that, at the time of the flood, all humanity was located in the Fertile Crescent of the Mesopotamian plain. Hence, all humanity perished when the region was flooded. Humanly speaking, the impact of the flood was universal while its scope was local.

Conclusion

The modifications YEC adherents have made to their global flood models illustrate how creationism changes in a way that the doctrine of creation does not. The essential features of creation, as a doctrine, are derived from Scripture and as such are divinely revealed truths. Creationism, as an attempt by people of faith to understand the discoveries of modern science in the light of Scripture, is an ongoing, developing discipline that constantly needs amendment. We must remember the distinction between creation and creation*ism*.

Most geologists do not believe that the geological evidence indicates that a worldwide flood occurred approximately 4,500 years ago. Even geologists who advocate flood geology, such as Andrew Snelling, appeal to arguments beyond the empirical geological evidence. Flood geologists argue that the historical interpretation of Genesis 6–9 requires their position; they posit that the normal laws of nature were suspended during the flood; and finally they appeal to divine intervention.

---

48. Fazale Rana and Hugh Ross, *Who Was Adam? A Creation Model Approach to the Origin of Man* (Colorado Springs: NavPress, 2005), 64–67.
49. Ibid.

It appears that Young and Stearley have a point when they suggest that the best defense of a global flood is an appeal to the miraculous. In other words, if one is going to hold to a recent worldwide flood, then he should contend that God supernaturally caused the forty-day deluge and then supernaturally disposed of the flood waters afterwards. In this way Noah's flood is understood to be similar to the miracle of the sun standing still in Joshua 10:12–14. It was a direct, supernatural, miraculous act of God. This means that the flood is beyond empirical investigation and scientific explanation.

When flood geologists, such as Snelling, hold that God suspended or altered the normal laws of nature during the flood, they are taking the approach of appealing to the miraculous. For those of us who affirm the authority of Scripture, such appeals are perfectly legitimate. But we need to understand clearly what this tactic does to attempts by flood geologists to demonstrate the historicity of Noah's flood. This approach renders flood geology superfluous.

So after examining the biblical and geological evidences, what can be concluded? Biblically, the local flood model is a reasonable interpretation, though a natural reading seems to give more weight to the global model. Geologically, the evidence argues for the local flood interpretation. Global flood and local flood adherents do agree on one important point: Noah's flood happened—it is a historical fact. The flood in Genesis was a visitation of the judgment of God on the people of the earth. All humans, except for Noah and his family, perished. The event gives warning of the coming, final judgment (Luke 17:26–27) and Noah's deliverance serves as an example of the riches of God's saving grace (Gen. 6:8).

REFLECTION QUESTIONS

1. What are four possible reasons why YEC geologists and OEC geologists come to opposite conclusions about the extent of Noah's flood?

2. In what ways does Snelling's flood geology differ from that of Whitcomb and Morris?

3. What is the AGEing hypothesis proposed by some YEC advocates? Why do opponents criticize it as a form of "hyper-evolutionism"?

4. Each side warns against a presuppositional bias. What is it and why does it matter?

5. In what important points do both sides agree?

PART 6

QUESTIONS ABOUT EVOLUTION AND INTELLIGENT DESIGN

What Is the Theory of Evolution?

The word *evolution* has a number of distinct meanings, and this fact contributes to the confusion in the debates surrounding the concept.[1] In its most general and innocuous sense, evolution simply means change over time. Those in the biological sciences use the term in at least three ways: (1) as a descriptor of biological change (either change within a species or one species emerging from another species); (2) as a theory that all life descended from one common ancestor; and (3) as an overarching explanation of how biological change occurs.

- *First, evolution as a descriptor of the historical phenomenon of biological change over time.* The notion that species change, or "evolve," is uncontroversial. The mutation of viruses, finch's beaks adapting in response to environmental pressures, or the development of new breeds of domestic animals through selective breeding are all examples of evolutionary change. At this point, however, we need to make an additional distinction between *micro-evolution* and *macro-evolution*. Micro-evolution occurs within prescribed limits, and the examples just given would be instances of micro-evolution. Macro-evolution is understood to be significant innovations which produce new species.[2]

---

1. For discussions of the various meanings of the term *evolution*, see Jay W. Richards, "Squaring the Circle," in *God and Evolution*, ed. Jay W. Richards (Seattle: Discovery Institute, 2010), 18; Michael Murray and Jeffery Schloss, "Evolution" in *Routledge Companion to Theism*, ed. Charles Taliaferro, Victoria Harrison, and Stewart Goetz (New York: Routledge, 2013); Thomas Fowler and Daniel Kuebler, *The Evolution Controversy: A Survey of Competing Theories* (Grand Rapids: Baker, 2007); John Lennox, *God's Undertaker: Has Science Buried God?* (Oxford: Lion, 2007).
2. Michael Behe, *Darwin's Black Box: The Biochemical Challenge to Evolution* (New York: Free Press, 1996), 14: "The word *evolution* has been invoked to explain tiny changes in organisms as well as huge changes. These are often given separate names: Roughly speaking,

Scientists observe micro-evolution on a regular basis. Proponents of macro-evolutionary theory hypothesize that the same processes which cause micro-evolution are also sufficient to cause macro-evolution. The reality of micro-evolution is not debated. All parties consider it to be an observable, empirical fact of biology. By contrast, macro-evolution is much more controversial. If macro-evolution happens (i.e., one species evolves into another or emerges from another), it occurs over great spans of time—millions of years. So by definition macro-evolution cannot be observed and must be inferred from geological and biological data.

- *Second, evolution as a theory of common descent.* This component of evolutionary theory carries the implications of macro-evolution to their logical conclusion—the notion that the origin of all life on earth can be traced back to a common ancestor. Life began 3.8 billion years ago as a single cell. Eventually the "tree of life" branched out into the millions of species that live on earth today, with many earlier branches dying off as extinctions (though species generally went extinct gradually and in isolation, on rare occasions mass extinctions occurred). Closer relatives can be determined by their shared common characteristics. For example, humans are understood to have descended from earlier primates, as did other primates. Our closest relative is the chimpanzee, and the fact that 98 percent of the genetic code for humans and chimps is the same is seen as evidence of this relationship. According to the theory of common descent, humans are not unique, biologically speaking.

- *Third, evolution as explanation.* This aspect of evolutionary theory moves beyond the description of change over time to attempting to provide an account of how the change occurred. The leading explanation is that, given sufficient time, *random variation* and *natural selection* are able to produce macro-evolutionary change. Darwin's theory of evolution fits in this third category. It is a theory about *how* evolution occurred.

When Darwin wrote *On the Origin of Species* (1859) and *The Descent of Man* (1871), he could offer no mechanism to explain how random variation might occur or how advantageous variations might be preserved and reproduced. This problem, along with other shortcomings, nearly derailed Darwin's theory of evolution from becoming widely accepted among naturalists.

---

microevolution describes changes that can be made in one or a few small jumps, whereas macroevolution describes changes that appear to require large jumps."

However, around the start of the twentieth century, biologists became aware of Gregor Mendel's (1822–1884) earlier work on genetics. Mendel's discovery of genes and genetic mutation reasonably accounted for random variation and how those variations were retained from one generation to another.

Often called "survival of the fittest," natural selection simply means that creatures that are healthier, stronger, or for some reason more fitted to a particular environment are more likely to live long enough to reproduce than those who are less so. Long before Darwin, natural selection had been recognized by naturalists as a phenomenon occurring in nature. However, natural selection generally has the effect of weeding out innovation rather than producing it. Therefore, natural selection is more of a conserving process. Darwin made the novel argument that natural selection could also be a mechanism for change. In the early twentieth century, the discovery of genetic mutation was combined with Darwin's theory of natural selection and common descent, and this combination became known as the *Neo-Darwinian synthesis*. In paleontology, anthropology, and the biological sciences, this synthesis became the reigning paradigm for most of the twentieth century.

What is not easily recognized is that the notions of random variation, natural selection, and common descent are not necessarily connected, nor does one require the others. Rather, as Michael Behe points out, these concepts are "unrelated, entirely separate ideas."[3]

Evolution should not be equated with Darwinism. Rather, Darwinism is one particularly ambitious theory of biological evolution. In fact, Darwinism is more than just an evolutionary theory—it is an extrapolation of a biological hypothesis to a comprehensive worldview. It elevates evolution to an all-encompassing theory of everything. Darwinism is an ideology, and as such we examine it more closely in the next chapter.

The Evolutionary Speculations of the Early Greek and Roman Philosophers

Some of the ancient Greek philosophers, such as Aristotle (384–322 BC), argued for the immutability of species. Several others, however, held to various naturalistic, evolutionary theories. For example, Anaximander (ca. 610–546 BC) taught that life began in the oceans, "with simpler forms giving way to more complex forms."[4] But he suggested no mechanism for evolution. Empedocles (490–430 BC) appears to be the first to argue for a version of "the survival of the fittest" as an explanation for the origin of all living things.[5]

3. Michael Behe, *The Edge of Evolution* (New York: Free Press, 2007), 1–3.
4. Fowler and Kuebler, *The Evolution Controversy*, 43–45.
5. Edward Davis and Robin Collins, "Scientific Naturalism," in *Science and Religion*, ed. Gary B. Ferngren (Baltimore: John Hopkins University Press, 2002), 323–24.

The Epicurean Roman poet, Lucretius (ca. 99–55 BC), presented the first well-developed evolutionary theory in his *The Nature of Things*.[6] Like Empedocles, Lucretius argued for evolution, contending that the phenomenon of survival of the fittest acted as the driving force. "Lucretius's argument contained all the Darwinian essentials: a random set of variations that produced various life-forms coupled with the differential selection of these forms, such that those most fit to survive in their respective environments flourished."[7] These early theories also seemed to presuppose atheism. Anaximander, Empedocles, and Lucretius believed that nature exhibited no purpose or design, and none of the three appealed to any deity to account for the observed phenomena.

These early evolutionists recognized that the probability of living things occurring by random chance was remarkably low. However, they believed the cosmos was eternal and infinite. Given an infinite amount of time and an unlimited amount of working material, chance could and would produce anything and everything possible—no matter how improbable. Lucretius argued that the parts of animals would form by chance and then come together. Only those combinations of parts that fit into a viable pattern survived. Other ancient Greek philosophers, including Leucippus (fifth century BC) and Democritus (ca. 460–ca. 370 BC), contended that the cosmos was an infinite number of uncreated atoms moving eternally in an infinite, uncreated void.[8] These atoms collided by chance to form larger bodies, some of which became living things. Again the impact of eternalism on philosophical thought is evident.[9]

Enlightenment Precursors to Darwin's Theory of Evolution

Darwin's theory of evolution did not produce a culture of religious skepticism so much as the skeptical spirit of the age was receptive to an idea like Darwinism. In the seventeenth and eighteenth centuries, western culture experienced what became known as the Enlightenment. This worldview of the "age of reason" set scientific investigation against "religious superstition." During the two centuries prior to the *On the Origin of Species*, a virulent form of atheism came to dominant intellectual thinking, first in Europe and later in America. Philosophers, such as Julien la Mettrie (1709–1751) in his *Man a Machine* (1748) and Paul von Holbach (1723–1789) in his *System of Nature* (1770) argued for the eternality of the material universe, while Ludwig Feuerbach (1804–1872) in *The Essence of Christianity* (1841) diagnosed faith

---

6. Lucretius, *The Nature of Things,* trans. A. E. Stallings (New York: Penguin Classics, 2007).
7. Fowler and Kuebler, *The Evolution Controversy,* 43–45.
8. Edward Davis and Robin Collins, "Scientific Naturalism," 323–24.
9. See Question 18 for further discussion on eternalism.

in God as a form of mental illness.[10] Darwinism did not produce the materialism, naturalism, or atheism of the Enlightenment; these worldviews provided the metaphysical framework for Darwinism. Darwinism is an expression of the spirit of its time.

Prior to Darwin's theory, a number of naturalistic hypotheses were offered to account for the emergence of life from inanimate matter. There were several competing theories of evolution at the time *On the Origin of Species* was published. What made Darwin's account distinctive was his ability to merge an immense array of evidence with a naturalistic theory that seemed to provide a plausible explanation.

Spontaneous Generation

Noticing that maggots seem to instantaneously appear in dead flesh, certain materialist thinkers, such as Georges Leclerc, Comte de Buffon (1707–1788) and Denis Diderot (1713–1784) argued that living things spontaneously generated.[11] Sweaty underwear was believed to produce mice.[12] The notion was also called *abiogenesis*, and proponents argued that life regularly sprang up from nonliving things. It reinforced the opinion that the origin of life could be understood in entirely materialistic terms with no need to appeal to divine agency.

The theory would hold sway among many until it was disproven by Louis Pasteur (1822–1895) in 1862 (just three years after Darwin published *On the Origin of Species*). Even though Darwin himself wrote against spontaneous generation in his later years, his theory seems to require it. As Paul Davies (who is a self-described Darwinist) admits, "Darwin's theory of evolution and Pasteur's theory that only life begets life cannot both have been completely right."[13]

Zoonomia

In 1796, Charles Darwin's grandfather, Erasmus Darwin (1731–1802) published *Zoonomia or the Laws of Organic Life*. In it, the elder Darwin, a renowned poet and physician, suggests a theory of evolution. He states:

---

10. "Approximately 150 years before Haeckel, there emerged in France an atheism based on scientific and philosophical principles which soon had supporters in Germany and England and initially picked up on the atomism of antiquity" (Hans Schwarz, *Creation* [Grand Rapids: Eerdmans, 2002], 8–9). See also Colin Brown, *Christianity and Western Thought: From the Ancient World to the Age of Enlightenment* (Downers Grove: InterVarsity, 1990), 285–88.

11. Peter Bowler, "Evolution," *Science and Religion*, ed. Gary B. Ferngren (Baltimore: John Hopkins, 2002), 221.

12. Paul Davies, *The 5th Miracle: The Search for the Origin and Meaning of Life* (New York: Simon and Schuster, 1999), 82–83.

13. Ibid. 83.

> [P]erhaps millions of ages before the commencement of the history of mankind, would it be too bold to imagine, that all warm-blooded animals have arisen from one living filament, which THE GREAT FIRST CAUSE endued with animality, with the power of acquiring new parts, attended with new propensities, directed by irritations, sensations, volitions, and associations; and thus possessing the faculty of continuing to improve by its own inherent activity, and of delivering down those improvements by generation to its posterity, world without end![14]

When Erasmus Darwin postulated that all life arose from "one living filament," he was positing common descent. Remarkably, Charles Darwin never mentions his grandfather or his theories in his books, even though many believe that his grandfather explained evolutionary theory more clearly than he did.

Malthusianism

In 1798, Thomas Robert Malthus (1766–1834) published an influential book entitled *An Essay on the Principle of Population.* A British economist, Malthus argued that the population growth of the human race always tends to outrun the available food supply. By means of famine, pestilence, and war, nature steps in to reduce the population to sustainable levels. Though nature's methods are harsh and even cruel, they are necessary. Darwin credited Malthus's work with having a strong impact on his thinking.[15] Darwin applied Malthus's theory to animal populations as he developed his theory of natural selection and survival of the fittest.

Lamarckism

In 1809, the French naturalist Jean Baptiste Lamarck (1774–1829) published his *Zoological Philosophy.* Lamarck argued for a theory of evolution which hypothesized that creatures somehow inherited acquired characteristics. He attempted to explain evolution by pointing to the cumulative inheritance of modifications induced by environmental influence. For example, Lamarck contended that the short-necked ancestors of the giraffe in successive generations would have gradually developed longer necks by reaching for leaves. Lamarck's theory met significant resistance, due in no small part to the fact he was unable to provide a mechanism that would explain how

---

14. Erasmus Darwin, *Zoonomia: or the Laws of Organic Life,* vol. 1 (London: J. Johnson, 1796), 39.4.8.

15. Charles Darwin, *On the Origin of Species by Means of Natural Selection, or the Preservation of Favoured Races in the Struggle for Life,* 1st ed. (London: John Murray, 2003 [1859]), 63–64.

evolution occurred. The French, perhaps not surprisingly, view Lamarck—and not Darwin—as the true father of the modern theory of evolution.

Chamber's Vestiges

In 1844, Robert Chambers (1802–1871) anonymously published *Vestiges of the Natural History of Creation*. In an effort to make evolutionary thinking acceptable to the general public, Chambers argued that evolution should be understood as the march of progress through nature and human history. He contended that, rather than implying atheism, evolution was the manifestation of a divine plan programmed into nature from the beginning. Though Chambers distanced his position from Lamarckism, his theory suffered from the same problem as Lamarck's theory—he could provide no natural mechanism that could act as an engine for evolution. Still, the book was a sensation, and it helped to prepare the public for Darwin's work, which would be published fifteen years later. *Vestiges* proved to be so controversial that Chambers was not acknowledged as its author until after his death.

Paley's Natural Theology

Several Christians attempted to answer the various naturalistic theories by developing a *natural theology* (natural theology is the attempt to prove the existence of the Christian God by means of reason and evidence alone, without appealing to the Bible). William Paley produced the most famous work of this type, entitled appropriately *Natural Theology*.[16] Paley gives the watchmaker analogy, in which he argues that the world provides evidence similar to that of a well-designed timepiece. He describes the world as "contrived," by which he means that nature's intricate complexity exhibits God's benevolent purposes.[17] Critics contend that, brilliant as Paley's *Natural Theology* is, its emphasis on nature manifesting God's goodness and wisdom left it vulnerable to Darwinian-style attacks. Paley describes the world thusly:

> It is a happy world after all. The air, the earth, the water, teem with delighted existence. In a spring noon, or a summer evening, on whichever side I turn my eyes, myriads of happy beings crowd upon my view. "The insect youth are on the wing." Swarms of new-born flies are trying their pinions in the air.

---

16. John Hedley Brooke, "Natural Theology," in *Science and Religion: A Historical Introduction*, ed. Gary B. Ferngren (Baltimore: John Hopkins, 2002), 163–73. We will revisit Paley's watchmaker analogy in Question 39. A second, significant presentation of early 19th century natural theology is a series called the *Bridgewater Treatises*. Francis Edgerton, the 8th Earl of Bridgewater commissioned the series, which was published from 1833–1840. The eight books argued that nature manifested the care, wisdom, and goodness of God.
17. See Alister McGrath, *Darwinism and the Divine: Evolutionary Thought and Natural Theology* (Oxford: Wiley-Blackwell, 2011), 100–3.

Their sportive motions, their wanton mazes, their gratuitous activity, their continual change of place without use or purpose, testify their joy, and the exultation which they feel in their lately discovered faculties. A bee among the flowers in spring, is one of the most cheerful objects that can be looked upon. Its life appears to be all enjoyment; so busy, and so pleased: yet it is only a specimen of insect life with which, by reason of the animal being half domesticated, we happen to be better acquainted than we are with that of others. The whole-winged insect tribe, it is probable, are equally intent upon their proper employments, and, under every variety of constitution, gratified, and perhaps equally gratified, by the offices which the Author of their nature has assigned to them.[18]

Rather than Augustine's view of nature as being "red in tooth and claw," Paley sees the natural world as happy, delighted, and full of joy. When Darwin published *On the Origin of Species*, many immediately understood it to be a point-by-point refutation of Paley.[19]

Paley's approach conflated evidences of design with evidences of purpose. Paley used the word "contrivance" to describe his understanding of design. He left no room in nature for random occurrences and operated with the "undefended controlling presupposition that chance and design are mutually exclusive at every level."[20] In addition, Paley seemed to argue that every species was placed directly and supernaturally by God into its particular habitat. This claim goes beyond what Scripture itself declares and, in fact, seems to be contrary to the Bible's description of the distribution of species after Noah's flood. Most creationists today, both young earth and old earth proponents, understand that species migrate and adapt in response to environmental changes.

Some Victorian theologians and church leaders were concerned about the shortcomings of such an approach to natural theology.[21] John Henry Newman criticized the work of Paley and others for presenting a view of God that was more deist than Christian. Newman also warned that such an optimistic presentation of creation failed to account for the effects of sin upon creation. Natural theology, as developed by Paley and others, was particularly vulnerable to the Darwinian challenge. The paradigm they presented provided no room or any explanation for the reality of natural evil. They were at a loss to

---

18. William Paley, *Natural Theology: Or, Evidences of the Existence and Attributes of the Deity Collected from the Appearances of Nature* (New York: American Tract Society, 1881 [reprint]), 296.
19. Daniel Dennett, *Darwin's Dangerous Idea: Evolution and the Meanings of Life* (New York: Simon & Shuster, 1995), 29, 64–73.
20. Alister McGrath, *Darwinism and the Divine*, 191.
21. Ibid., 127–34.

account for the clear evidence of the mass extinctions of countless species and the vicious struggle for survival in nature. The Aristotelian natural theology of the pre-Darwinian Christian naturalists emphasized benevolent intent, hierarchy of being, and progressive development. The early church fathers saw nature as a fallen world rife with evidences of the fall. When Paley glosses over the travails of creation (Rom. 8:11–22), he reveals that he could have used more Augustine and less Aristotle. By contrast, Darwin repeatedly points out the dark side of nature—its uncaring cruelty and immense suffering.

Wallace's Theory of Natural Selection

Alfred Russel Wallace (1823–1913), a British naturalist and explorer, arrived at the theory of evolution by means of natural selection independently of Darwin. It appears that Wallace embraced the notion of common descent before Darwin, but that both men arrived at the idea of natural selection operating as the engine of evolution at approximately the same time.

In *Origin of Species,* Darwin reports that in 1858 Wallace sent to him a paper entitled "On the Tendency of Varieties to Depart Indefinitely from the Original Type."[22] Darwin realized that Wallace was positing the same theory as he was, and this fact spurred Darwin hurriedly to finish the manuscript upon which he had been working. Wallace and Darwin are generally credited as being the co-originators of modern evolutionary theory. Wallace will, in fact, apply the theory of evolution to humans in print before Darwin does.[23] Wallace rejected the notion that evolution entailed materialism. Instead, Wallace argued that evolution could not account for the mental and spiritual aspects of humans and spent the last years of his life advocating spiritualism (the attempt to communicate with the dead).[24]

Darwin's *On the Origin of Species*

Charles Darwin (1809–1882) was born into an upper class, prosperous English family which nominally belonged to the Anglican Church.[25] Darwin's father and grandfather were medical doctors, and he initially studied to be one also. But Darwin found the subject dull, and he intensely disliked performing surgery. So after dropping out of medical school, Darwin entered Christ College at Cambridge in order to study to be a minister. He hoped that by becoming a country parson he would have the time and opportunity to

---

22. Darwin, *On the Origin of Species,* 1–2.
23. Wallace published "The Origin of the Human Races and the Antiquity of Man Deduced from the Theory of 'Natural Selection'" in 1864 while Darwin did not publish *The Descent of Man* until 1871.
24. Denyse O'Leary, "Everything Old Is New Again: The Older Catholic Apologists' Response to Darwin," in *God and Evolution,* ed. Jay W. Richards (Seattle: Discovery, 2010), 173.
25. Adrian Desmond and James Moore, *Darwin: The Life of a Tormented Evolutionist* (New York: Warner, 1991), 21–100.

pursue what he really enjoyed, which was collecting and studying insects. At Cambridge, Darwin enjoyed attending geology classes, but his adherence to Christianity slowly gave way to more radical views.

Shortly after graduation, an opportunity opened for Darwin.[26] The HMS *Beagle* was going on a multiyear exploratory voyage, and it needed a naturalist. This five-year journey, which began in 1831, allowed Darwin to gather specimens from around the world (including the Galapagos Islands, which Darwin would make famous). Due to the publication of his findings, when the expedition ended in 1836, Darwin was a celebrity in scientific circles.

By the 1840s, Darwin was a respected naturalist and published authority in zoology. He worked steadily on his theory of evolution by natural selection, discussing it in correspondence with colleagues. Darwin realized from the beginning that his theory would be controversial. He confided in a letter to a friend that he had come to embrace evolution. Such an admission, Darwin said, felt like "confessing a murder."[27]

Darwin's theological moorings were always questionable at best, but evolutionary musings are not what did the most damage to his tenuous Christian faith. Rather, it was the problem of evil. Darwin could not reconcile the benevolent God of nature as presented by William Paley with the grotesque suffering he saw in the world. Darwin declared in a letter,

> There seems to me too much misery in the world. I cannot persuade myself that a beneficent and omnipotent God would have designedly created the Ichneumonidae [parasitic wasp] with the express intention of their feeding within the living bodies of caterpillars or that a cat should play with mice.[28]

In 1851, Darwin was devastated when his ten-year-old daughter, Annie, died from typhoid fever. He abandoned whatever Christian beliefs he had left. Darwin never allowed himself to be called an atheist, preferring the term agnostic instead.[29]

As mentioned earlier, Darwin's correspondence with Alfred Wallace will prod him into publishing his views on evolution. When *On the Origin of Species* was published in 1859, it instantly became a bestseller and a sensation. *Origin of Species* underwent six editions during Darwin's lifetime, with him making substantial changes with each edition in response to

---

26. Ibid., 101–94.
27. Charles Darwin, "Letter to J. D. Hooker," no. 729 (January 11, 1844). Online: http://www.darwinproject.ac.uk/letter/entry-729 (accessed 12/11/12).
28. Charles Darwin, "Letter to Asa Gray," no. 2814 (May 22, 1860). Online: http://www.darwinproject.ac.uk/letter/entry-2814 (accessed 12/05/12).
29. Desmond and Moore, *Darwin*, 375–90.

criticisms.[30] Though Darwin never mentions humans in *Origin of Species,* the implications of the book's thesis were clear to all who read it. Darwin published *Descent of Man* in 1871 and, at that time, openly argued that humans descended from primates.

In *Origin of Species*, Darwin had two goals. He wished to demonstrate, first, that all life was the product of evolution (i.e., macro-evolution) and, second, that natural selection is the engine that produced all evolution.[31] In making his first point, Darwin endeavored to demonstrate that the species were not the result of direct divine creation. Evolution produced all life through "descent with modification." On this point, Darwin expressed no real difference in evolutionary thinking from Lamarck and Chambers, who preceded him.

So what was so new about Darwin's theory? Why has his name come to be forever associated with the theory of evolution? The new aspect of Darwin's proposal was the argument that natural selection had the creative power necessary to account for all life. Natural selection was the primary, if not the sole, mechanism of evolution. As Darwinian enthusiast Daniel Dennett declares, "This was Darwin's great idea, not the idea of evolution, but the idea of evolution *by natural selection* [emphasis original] . . . ."[32] In two sentences (of which the first is incredibly convoluted but comprehensive), Darwin sums up his argument:

> If during the long course of ages and under varying conditions of life, organic beings vary at all in the several parts of their organization, and I think this cannot be disputed; if there be, owing to the high geometrical powers of increase of each species, at some age, season, or year, a severe struggle for life, and this certainly cannot be disputed; then considering the infinite complexity of the relations of all organic beings to each other and to their conditions of existence, causing an infinite diversity in structure, constitution, and habits, to be advantageous to them, I think it would be a most extraordinary fact if no variation ever had occurred useful to each being's own welfare, in the same way as so many variations useful to an organic being do occur, assuredly individuals thus characterized will have the best chance of being preserved in the struggle for life; and from the strong principle

---

30. Alister McGrath, *Darwinism and the Divine,* 150. By the time of his death, Darwin changed a full three-fourths of the sentences in *On the Origin of Species.*
31. Ronald Numbers, *The Creationists* (New York: Alfred Knopf, 1992), 4–5. See also Daniel Dennett, *Darwin's Dangerous Idea,* 39.
32. Dennett, *Darwin's Dangerous Idea,* 42.

of inheritance they will tend to produce offspring similarly characterized. This principle of preservation, I have called, for the sake of brevity, Natural Selection.[33]

With his proposal of natural selection, Darwin seemed to provide an account of all living things without having to appeal to any supernatural assistance or divine activity. Darwin's theory appeared to render God unnecessary by substituting intelligent design with the winnowing, "research and development" process of natural selection. Again Dennett explains,

> So Paley was right in saying not just that Design was a wonderful thing to explain, but also that Design took Intelligence. All he missed—and Darwin provided—was the idea that this Intelligence could be broken into bits so tiny and stupid that they didn't count as intelligence at all, and then distributed through space and time in a gigantic, connected network of algorithmic process.[34]

So atheists such as Daniel Dennett believe that Darwin's theory shows how evolution occurred: not merely by random chance (as critics often charge), but by an unguided process that effectively sifts all living things—natural selection. God the Creator is supposedly rendered superfluous.

Of his first goal—to convince the scientific community that evolution was a historical fact—Darwin succeeded almost immediately. Less than thirteen years after *Origin of Species*, the paleontologist Edward Drinker Cope (1840–1897) declared that "the modern theory of evolution has been spread everywhere with unexampled rapidity, thanks to our means of printing and transportation. It has met with remarkably rapid acceptance by those best qualified to judge of its merits, viz., the zoologists and botanists."[35] Even critics of Darwin's theory conceded that the idea of organic development had won "universal acceptance." The first leg of Darwin's theory—common descent—won an almost unanimous victory.[36]

---

33. Darwin, *On the Origin of Species,* 126–27.
34. Dennett, *Darwin's Dangerous Idea,* 133.
35. Quoted in Ronald Numbers, *The Creationists,* 6.
36. Stephen Jay Gould, "Darwinian Fundamentalism," *New York Review of Books* (June 12, 1997). Online: http://www.nybooks.com/articles/archives/1997/jun/12/darwinian-fundamentalism/ (accessed 01/12/13). Gould concurs, "Charles Darwin often remarked that his revolutionary work had two distinct aims: first, to demonstrate the fact of evolution (the genealogical connection of all organisms and a history of life regulated by "descent with modification"); second, to advance the theory of natural selection as the most important mechanism of evolution. Darwin triumphed in his first aim (American creationism of the Christian far right notwithstanding). Virtually all thinking people accept the factuality of evolution, and no conclusion in science enjoys better documentation."

The second part of Darwin's theory—that evolution can be explained by natural selection—did not fare so well. Natural selection, as a biological phenomenon, was relatively uncontroversial. Nineteenth century biologists and zoologists universally recognized that the "survival of the fittest" weeded out the weak and poorly adapted. However, this is a conserving process rather than a creative one. Darwin turned the consensus view about natural selection on its head. He argued that natural selection was also an agent of change—an agent sufficiently powerful to account for all the myriad forms of life on earth. This portion of Darwin's argument met stiff resistance from within the scientific community. By the beginning of the twentieth century, evolution as a biological phenomenon was generally accepted, while Darwin's theory of natural selection was in doubt. This changed, however, with the discovery of genetics.

The Neo-Darwinian Synthesis

One serious problem with Darwin's theory was that he could not suggest a mechanism that would explain how a species retained a particular acquired advantage. Then early in the twentieth century, the work of Gregor Mendel, a Catholic priest, in the field of genetics would become widely known. Mendel demonstrated that, via genes, living things pass their traits and characteristics to their offspring. Combining Darwin's theory of natural selection with Mendel's discoveries concerning genetic mutation came to be known as the Neo-Darwinian synthesis. Under the aggressive advocacy of proponents such as Thomas Huxley (who was known as "Darwin's Bulldog"), Neo-Darwinism became the reigning paradigm for most of the twentieth century.

Trouble in the Darwinian Paradise

The centennial year for *On the Origin of Species* arrived in 1959. At one commemoration, Julian Huxley (grandson of Thomas Huxley) declared, "In the evolutionary pattern of thought there is no longer either need or room for the supernatural. The earth was not created: it evolved. So did all the animals and plants that inhabit it, including our human selves, mind and soul as well as brain and body. So did religion."[37] However, the celebrations were premature. Challenges to Darwin's theory were coming from surprising quarters. By the 1970s, it had become apparent that some of the most significant predictions made by Neo-Darwinism were not being confirmed by the empirical evidence. Darwin predicted that the fossil record would produce an abundance of examples of transitional life forms, but the fossil evidence was conspicuously absent. The time frame required by the big bang hypothesis was not long enough for the supposed Darwinian forces to work. In addition,

---

37. Julian Huxley, quoted by Philip Johnson, "Bringing Balance to a Fiery Debate," in *Intelligent Design 101: Leading Experts Explain the Key Issues*, ed. H. Wayne House (Grand Rapids: Kregel, 2008), 25.

mathematical models seem to indicate that random, undirected processes could never produce the complexity necessary for life to begin, no matter how long the time frame.

As we noted, the second part of Darwin's hypothesis—that natural selection acted, for all intents and purposes, as the sole engine of evolution—was always controversial, even among evolutionists. This was not a small matter, because "descent through small, minute, incremental changes" was the centerpiece to Darwin's hypothesis. Darwin himself made this very clear:

> If it could be demonstrated that any complex organ existed, which could not possibly have been formed by numerous, successive, slight modifications, my theory would absolutely break down.[38]

Yet, as we will see over the next two chapters, the fossil and genetic records seemed to indicate a very different picture from what Darwin predicted.

Many evolutionists, including Stephen Jay Gould, admit that the problems for Neo-Darwinism are severe. Gould caused an uproar among his evolutionary colleagues when he declared that Neo-Darwinism was "effectively dead."

> I well remember how the synthetic theory beguiled me with its unifying power when I was a graduate student in the mid-1960s. Since then I have been watching it slowly unravel as a universal description of evolution. The molecular assault came first, followed quickly by renewed attention to unorthodox theories of speciation and by challenges at the level of macroevolution itself. I have been reluctant to admit it—since beguiling is often forever—but if Mayr's characterization of the synthetic theory is accurate, then that theory, as a general proposition, is effectively dead, despite its persistence as textbook orthodoxy.[39]

In 1972, Gould, along with Niles Eldridge, posited the theory of "punctuated equilibrium"—that evolution occurs during (relatively) brief periods of time, preceded and followed by long periods of stasis. This appears to fly in the face of the gradualism required by standard evolutionary theory and seems to be irreconcilable with the hypothesis that natural selection was the primary engine of evolution. We will look further at the notion of punctuated equilibrium in the next two chapters.

---

38. Darwin, *Origin of Species*, 189.
39. Stephen Jay Gould, "Is a New and General Theory of Evolution Emerging?" *Paleobiology* 6, no. 1 (January 1980): 120.

Conclusion

In popular thinking, Darwin's theory of evolution is considered to provide a satisfactory explanation for three basic questions: (1) How did life originate? (2) What process acted as the engine to produce the wide variety of species we find? And (3) what do the empirical evidences of geology and biology indicate? What many at the popular level do not realize is that today, even many evolutionists do not accept the Darwinist answer to these three questions.[40]

First, to the question of the origin of life, Darwinism provides no answer at all. Indeed, Darwinism cannot even speak to this issue, because natural selection operates only on living things. Therefore, evolutionists cannot appeal to natural selection to account for any type of pre-biotic evolution. Darwinism provides no answer concerning the beginning of life. Darwin himself avoided the question in *On the Origin of Species* (which is ironic, given the title of the book).[41] Suffice it at this point to say that evolutionary science has made little or no progress in this area.

As for the second question—providing a reasonable explanation of what acts as the engine of evolution—the appeal of Darwin's theory was that it seemed to give a simple, straightforward candidate: natural selection. Genetic mutations create variety and novelty in living things; natural selection chooses those rare changes that are advantageous. Starting with a single, common ancestor (assumed to be a single-celled life form), the process of "survival of the fittest" acting on random mutations has produced the plethora of species we see today. The problem with this explanation, to put it bluntly, is that is does not fit the evidence it is supposed to explain. As evolutionist James Shapiro explains,

> As to the actual nature of evolutionary change processes [the empirical evidences] tell us that the simplifying assumptions made in the 19th and early 20th Centuries are plainly wrong. They fail to account for the variety of cellular and genomic events we now know to have occurred.[42]

Natural selection simply does not do all that Darwinists claim that it can.[43]

Third, concerning the question of the empirical evidences, a straightforward examination of the empirical data (geological evidence, genetic evidence, etc.) does seem to indicate some type of progression over time of simpler life forms to those that are more complex. But the progression found in the natural record is not what Darwin predicted, nor is it what his theory

---

40. James Shapiro, *Evolution: A View from the 21st Century* (Upper Saddle River: FT Press, 2011), 127–28.
41. We address this matter further in Question 40.
42. Shapiro, *Evolution*, 128.
43. We will look further at the limitations of natural selection in Questions 34 and 36.

seems to require. Darwinism predicts a record of slow, random, gradual change. Geology and genetics present a very non-Darwinian picture of natural history. The geological record presents changes in life forms occurring in leaps and jumps, with new species (geologically speaking) appearing suddenly. Rather than supporting the standard neo-Darwinian paradigm, the empirical evidence seems to be much more compatible with some version of intelligent design.

These serious shortcomings have not stopped many evolutionists from continuing to embrace the Darwinian paradigm. In fact, many view Darwinism as something much more expansive than a biological theory. They understand Darwinism in ideological terms and hold to the theory as a worldview and even as a religion. This may help to explain why such proponents have been so unwilling to re-examine Darwinism's tenets. Darwinism as an all-encompassing explanation is the subject of our next chapter.

REFLECTION QUESTIONS

1. What are the three primary ways the term "evolution" is used in the biological sciences?

2. What is Lamarkism and how is it different from Darwinism?

3. For what other careers did Darwin study before departing aboard the *Beagle*? What event in Darwin's life more than any other thing caused him to abandon his religious faith?

4. What are the two main arguments of *On the Origin of Species*?

5. What was added to the Darwinian theory to produce the Neo-Darwinian synthesis?

What Is Darwinism?

Darwinism began as a theory about biological evolution but quickly jumped out of its scientific framework into the broader arena of western culture. In short, Darwinism reigns. It is the predominant worldview in modern intellectual thought. In his book, *Darwin's Dangerous Idea*, philosopher Daniel Dennett (atheist and Darwinian devotee) explains the effect that Darwinism has had on modern thinking: it is a "universal acid."

> Did you ever hear of universal acid? This fantasy used to amuse me and some of my schoolboy friends. . . . Universal acid is a liquid so corrosive that it will eat through *anything*! The problem is: what do you keep it in? It dissolves glass bottles and stainless-steel canisters as readily as paper bags. What would happen if you somehow came upon or created a dollop of universal acid? Would the whole planet eventually be destroyed? What would it leave in its wake? After everything had been transformed by its encounter with universal acid, what would the world look like? Little did I realize that in a few years I would encounter an idea—Darwin's idea—bearing an unmistakable likeness to universal acid: it eats through just about every traditional concept, and leaves in its wake a revolutionized world-view, with most of the old landmarks still recognizable, but transformed in fundamental ways.[1]

As Dennett's enthusiasm illustrates, Darwinism operates as much more than merely a scientific theory. It is a scientific theory elevated to a metanarrative

---

1. Daniel Dennett, *Darwin's Dangerous Idea: Evolution and the Meanings of Life* (New York: Simon & Shuster, 1995), 63 (emphasis original).

or ideology. As such, Darwinism operates as an intellectual assault (i.e., as a "universal acid") on the Christian doctrines of creation and divine providence.

Darwinism is a belief system. Cardinal Schonborn asks, "How has this strange 'sacralization' of a scientific theory come about? How is it that this theory is the only one, so far as I know, that has become an '-ism'? There is no 'Einsteinism' corresponding to Einstein's theory of relativity, nor is there any 'Newtonism' or 'Heisenbergism.' Why is there a 'Darwinism?'"[2] The very label—Darwin*ism*—indicates we are dealing with a worldview. As we will see, many of its most enthusiastic proponents are happy to own Darwinism as their religion.[3]

Components of Darwin's Theory

As we saw in the previous chapter, Darwinism, as a scientific theory, has three parts: common descent, random variation, and natural selection.[4]

- *Common descent*: Life began on earth approximately 3.8 billion years ago as a single-cell life form. From this original ancestor there developed an untold myriad of single-cell species. Eventually some single-cell species cooperated together to the point they became a multi-cellular species. Over time, multi-cellular life developed and diverged into the plethora of plant and animal life that we see today.

- *Random variation*: All life reproduces, either by sexual or asexual means. By chance, genetic mutations introduce variety and modifications into a population. Most of these mutations are bad, and they have detrimental effects. However, occasionally a variation gives a creature an advantage.

- *Natural selection*: The mechanism that chooses the advantageous changes over the detrimental ones is the process of natural selection. In this way, natural selection acts as a sieve or a winnowing process. As noted in the previous chapter, naturalists recognized natural selection as a naturally occurring process long before Darwin. Darwin's innovation was to propose that natural selection was a transformative engine sufficient to cause new species to evolve from older ones.

---

2. Christoph Cardinal Schonborn, *Chance or Purpose? Creation, Evolution, and a Rational Faith* (San Francisco: Ignatius, 2007), 77.
3. See Michael Shermer, "Science Is My Savior," *Science and Spirit* 16, no. 4 (July-August 2005): 48–50. He embraces what he calls *sciencuality*—"the sensuality of discovery." It is worth noting that Shermer is a former evangelical.
4. James Shapiro, *Evolution: A View from the 21st Century* (Upper Saddle River: FT Press, 2011), 127–28. See also Thomas Fowler and Daniel Kuebler, *The Evolution Controversy: A Survey of Competing Theories* (Grand Rapids: Baker, 2007), 142–48.

Darwinists acknowledge that random variation (i.e., random chance), by itself, could not produce life as we see it on earth. They claim that random chance *plus natural selection* is indeed up to the task. They argue that adding natural selection to random chance makes all the difference in the world—literally. Given enough time, evolution uses incremental adaptations to make significant changes. Richard Dawkins illustrates this incremental, counterintuitive hypothesis with a story he calls "Climbing Mount Improbable."[5] Imagine a tall, sheer, steep-faced mountain that clearly cannot be climbed. Yet the backside of this imposing mount consists of a gentle, sloping ridge. What appears to be impossible from one side is revealed to be entirely accessible from another. As paleobiologist Simon Conway Morris explains, "Part of the explanation, as is so often the case in evolution, may be to look for a step-like arrangement: once one stage is achieved, other things then become so much more likely."[6]

Darwinism's Challenge to the Traditional Doctrine of Creation

For many, the attraction of Darwin's theory is that it seems to give an explanation for life on earth that does not have to appeal to any supernatural cause. Darwinism's challenge to the doctrine of creation occurs on three successively deeper levels: (1) a rejection of direct creation, (2) a rejection of design, and finally (3) a rejection of teleology.

- *A rejection of direct creation*: Traditionally, Christians have understood the creation account of Genesis (Genesis 1–2) to teach that God created the various "kinds" in an immediate, supernatural manner so that each kind is essentially distinct. Darwinism, like most other theories of evolution, argues that all life descended from a common ancestor. Species are seen as mutable with one species segueing into another.

- *A rejection of design*: Old-earth creationists and intelligent-design proponents are willing to acknowledge that different species appear on earth in different, successive stages spanning many millions of years. And since the creation account speaks of God "calling forth" certain things from elements he had already created (namely, the earth and the sea), then it is reasonable to think that God mediated his creative activity through secondary causes. Yet, these stages are so distinct and so improbable to occur naturally that they are recognizable as evidences of miraculous design. Darwinism explicitly rejects this design scenario, arguing that all can be explained by natural means. Richard Dawkins dismisses evidences of

5. Richard Dawkins, *Climbing Mount Improbable* (New York: W. W. Norton, 1996), 73.
6. Simon Conway Morris, *Life's Solution: Inevitable Humans in a Lonely Universe* (New York: Cambridge University Press, 2003), 18.

design in nature as "designoid objects"—objects which give the appearance of being produced by design, but in fact, were not.[7]

- *A rejection of teleology*: While the argument of design points to those evidences that cannot be explained merely by the laws and properties of nature, the teleological argument makes the more modest claim that God guides and governs by means of natural processes. In other words (at the risk of oversimplification), the design argument makes a claim about God's miraculous activity while the teleological argument points to signs of God's providence.[8] Design arguments, like those generally made by intelligent-design proponents, point to evidences of God's activity as the efficient cause in creation, while teleological arguments, like those generally made by evolutionary creationists, argue for God's plan and purposes as the final cause.

  Searching for evidences of design and recognizing evidences of teleology are two very different approaches to the scientific data. For instance, an archeologist may find an artifact that shows clear signs of design and artistry, even if he may not be able to determine the specific purpose of the artifact. But a person may use a rock for a paperweight. The rock shows no evidence of design (i.e., to keep paper in place), but it is being used for a purpose.[9] Design is evidence of intelligent contrivance; teleology simply evidences purpose or intent.

But teleology is explicitly rejected by Darwinism. Darwinists emphasize that their model disallows any notion of a plan. They adamantly deny that nature exhibits any sign of purpose or intent. When Karl Marx read Darwin's theory, he declared, "Not only is a death blow dealt here for the first time to 'Teleology' in the natural sciences but their rational meaning is empirically explained."[10] Paleontologist George Gaylord Simpson expressed the Darwinist viewpoint when he stated, "Man is the result of a purposeless and natural process that did not have him in mind."[11]

So Darwinism explicitly rejects divine activity on three levels: direct creation, design, and teleology. Different Christian groups have responded to these challenges at each of the three levels. Young-earth creationists defend the notion

---

7. "Designoid objects are living bodies and their products. Designoid objects look designed, so much that some people—probably, alas, most people—think they are designed. These people are wrong" (Dawkins, *Climbing Mount Improbable*, 6–7).
8. Alister McGrath, *Darwinism and the Divine: Evolutionary Thought and Natural Theology* (Oxford: Wiley-Blackwell, 2011), 185–216.
9. We wish to thank Jeff Schloss for this illustration.
10. Quoted in Dennett, *Darwin's Dangerous Idea*, 62.
11. Quoted by Ann Gauger, Douglas Axe, and Casey Luskin, *Science and Human Origins* (Seattle: Discovery Institute, 2012), 9.

of direct creation, old-earth creationists argue for evidences of intelligent design, and evolutionary creationists contend evolution does not prohibit teleology. Darwinism, as presented by leading Darwinists, supports a materialistic or naturalistic view of the world that rules out any notion of divine plan, activity, or purpose. It is easy to see why atheists such as Richard Dawkins, Daniel Dennett, and John Dupre are so adamant in their support of Darwinism.[12]

Conclusion

Clearly, Darwinism (as defined by its most ardent supporters) is not compatible with the Christian faith in general and the doctrine of creation in particular. The rejection of direct creation, design, and teleology cannot be reconciled with biblical theism. Darwinism as a worldview promotes the antithesis of the Christian ethic of being guided by love for God and neighbor. As we will see in the next two chapters, even many evolutionists are disturbed at the religious zeal exhibited by "ultra-Darwinists." The expression "theistic Darwinism" is an oxymoron.

REFLECTION QUESTIONS

1. Why do some refer to Darwinism as "a universal acid"?

2. What are the three components of Darwinism?

3. What is the point of Richard Dawkins's illustration of "climbing Mount Improbable"?

4. Why is natural selection such a crucial feature to Darwin's theory?

5. In what three ways does Darwinism attack the biblical doctrine of creation?

---

12. Take for example, John Dupre's declaration, "[T]he point that I have stressed . . . is that science, especially in the guise of Darwinism, has undermined any plausible grounds for believing that there are any gods or other supernatural beings" (John Dupre, *Darwin's Legacy: What Evolution Means Today* [Oxford: Oxford University Press, 2003], 57).

How Is Darwinism an Ideology?

We can see that Darwinism is a statement about the nature of nature—a declaration about reality. Furthermore, that declaration is that the universe has no plan, no goals, no direction, and no purpose. Philosophers and scientists do not hesitate to add an adjective to make the point clearer by referring to this version as "orthodox Darwinism."[1] There is no way to integrate orthodox Christianity and orthodox Darwinism. They are competing religions that make diametrically opposite faith claims. At the centennial celebration of the publication of *On the Origins of Species*, Julian Huxley (grandson of Thomas Huxley), made the religious implications clear:

> [A]ll aspects of reality are subject to evolution, from atoms and stars to fish and flowers, from fish and flowers to human societies and values—indeed, that all reality is a single process of evolution. . . . In the evolutionary pattern of thought, there is no longer either need or room for the supernatural. The earth was not created; it evolved. So did all the animals and plants that inhabit it, including our human selves, mind and soul as well as brain and body. So did religion. . . . Finally, the evolutionary vision is enabling us to discern, however incompletely, the lineaments of the new religion that we can be sure will arise to serve the needs of the coming era.[2]

---

1. Michael Chorost, "Where Thomas Nagel Went Wrong," *The Chronicle Review* 59, no. 36, May 17, 2013, B13.
2. Julian Huxley, quoted by Eddie Colanter, "Philosophical Implications of Neo-Darwinism and Intelligent Design: Theism, Personhood, and Bioethics" in *Intelligent Design 101: Leading Experts Explain the Key Issues*, H. ed. Wayne House (Grand Rapids: Kregel, 2008), 155.

Richard Dawkins concurs, arguing that Darwinism is more than a scientific theory. In an essay entitled exultantly, "Darwin Triumphant: Darwinism as a Universal Truth," he presented the theory as an overarching understanding of reality—Darwinism as ultimate truth.[3] For orthodox Darwinists, Darwinism offers more than a description of reality; it provides an explanation of all things. For these "ultra-Darwinists" or "Darwinian fundamentalists," as they are sometimes called, Darwinism "is a world view, a *grand recit*, a metanarrative—that is to say, a totalizing framework, by which the great questions of life are to be evaluated and answered."[4]

Since *On the Origins of Species* was published, the social implications of Darwinism have been promoted by advocates during two distinct times with two distinct agendas—first *social Darwinism* during the late nineteenth and early twentieth centuries, then *sociobiology* from the 1970s to the current day.

Social Darwinism

Almost immediately after Darwin's theory became public, enthusiasts viewed evolution with religious awe.[5] Promoters, such as Herbert Spencer in Great Britain and Ernst Haeckel in Germany, argued for social Darwinism. Social Darwinists reasoned that if natural selection is the ultimate reality, then society should be guided by the dictum of survival of the fittest. Darwinian evolution became the justification for an amoral approach to ethics, economics, and government—often with horrific results.

Totalitarian governments in both the Soviet Union and Nazi Germany explicitly claimed to base their respective political philosophies on the Darwinian principle that "might makes right." In Great Britain and America, social Darwinism became the basis for a predatory form of capitalism. No one more exemplified this ruthless approach to business than did steel tycoon Andrew Carnegie. Upon reading Darwin and Spencer, Carnegie declared,

> I remember that light came as in a flood and all was clear. Not only had I got rid of theology and the supernatural, but I had found the truth of evolution. "All is well since all grows better" became my motto, my true source of comfort. Man was not created with an instinct for his own degradation, but from the lower he had risen to the higher

---

3. Richard Dawkins, "Darwin Triumphant: Darwinism as a Universal Truth," in *Man and Beast Revisited,* ed. Michael Robinson and Lionel Tiger (Washington, DC: Smithsonian, 1991); cf. Richard Dawkins, *The Devil's Chaplain: Reflections on Hope, Lies, Science, and Love* (New York: Houghton, Mifflin, Harcourt, 2004), 61.

4. Alister McGrath, *Darwinism and the Divine: Evolutionary Thought and Natural Theology* (Oxford: Wiley-Blackwell, 2011), 34.

5. Robert Wright, *The Moral Animal: Why We Are, the Way We Are: The New Science of Evolutionary Psychology* (New York: Vintage, 1994), 329.

> forms. Nor is there any conceivable end to his march to
> perfection. His face is turned to the light; he stands in the
> sun and looks upward.[6]

For proponents of cutthroat capitalism, social Darwinism instilled the attitude that helping the disadvantaged harms society as a whole because such
charity hinders the natural process of weeding out the weak.[7]

Social Darwinism manifested itself in the even more sinister theory of
eugenics. Eugenics is the selective breeding of humans. It is the application
of animal husbandry to people. Francis Dalton, Darwin's cousin, was the first
advocate of eugenics. In the early part of the twentieth century, various governments and institutions promoted and practiced compulsory sterilizations
and forced abortions. Even in the United States, sterilizations of the mentally
ill and handicapped were conducted in the name of eugenics.[8] In a chapter
entitled "The Smoking Gun of Eugenics," Stephen Jay Gould points out that
when Sir Ronald Fisher in 1930 proposed merging Darwinism with genetics
to be the first to argue for the neo-Darwinian synthesis, Fisher devoted the
last third of his book to the advocacy of eugenics.[9]

Nowhere was eugenics more embraced and practiced methodically than
in Nazi Germany. In a damning article, "Darwinism and Death: Devaluing
Human Life in Germany 1859–1920," Richard Weikart documents how social Darwinism played a central role in the acceptance in Nazi Germany
of infanticide, abortion, euthanasia, and eventually genocide.[10] Declaring
that "Evolution is henceforth the magic word by which we shall solve all
the riddles that surround us," German biologist and social Darwinist Ernst
Haeckel advocated the practice of "racial hygiene."[11] Today's Darwinists

---

6. Andrew Carnegie, *Autobiography of Andrew Carnegie* (London: Constable and Company, 1920), 339. Available online: http://www.gutenberg.org/files/17976/17976-h/17976-h.htm (accessed 4/2/13).

7. See William Graham Sumner, *What the Social Classes Owe Each Other* (New York: Harper and Bros., 1881). In a chapter entitled, "On a New Philosophy: Poverty Is the Best Policy," Sumner, who was a professor at Yale, argued that the privileged owed the destitute nothing, and that few things are as evil as programs designed "to help the poor" (13–15).

8. Denyse O'Leary, "Everything Old Is New Again: The Older Catholic Apologists' Response to Darwin," in *God and Evolution: Protestants, Catholics, and Jews Explore Darwin's Challenge to Faith*, ed. Jay Richards (Seattle: Discovery Press, 2010), 169; James Le Fanu, *Why Us? How Science Rediscovered the Mystery of Ourselves* (New York: Vintage, 2009), 159–63.

9. Stephen Jay Gould, *Dinosaur in a Haystack* (New York: Random House, 1995), 296–308.

10. Richard Weikart, "Darwinism and Death: Devaluing Human Life in Germany 1859–1920," *Journal of the History of Ideas* 63, no. 2 (2002): 323–44.

11. Ernst Haeckel, *The Riddle of the Universe at the Close of the Nineteenth Century* (New York: Harper and Brothers, 1901), 233–34. For Haeckel, Darwinism entailed that human life has little value, and some humans are less valuable than others. "I share essentially your view of life, dear father, only I value human life and humans themselves much less than you. . . . The individual with his personal existence appears to me only a temporary

attempt to distance Darwin from the racism of social Darwinism, but even they will generally admit that there is at least a historical link.[12] Some overlook the subtitle Darwin provided for *On the Origin of Species*. He subtitled it *The Preservation of Favored Races in the Struggle for Life*. Darwin was convinced that the superior races (i.e., those from northern Europe) would eventually eliminate the weaker races (he mentions the Turks by name).[13]

Sociobiology

After World War II, the horrors of the Holocaust revealed the full implications of eugenics, and social Darwinism became an intellectual pariah. By the 1960s, however, a number of sociologists began to advocate a retooled version of Darwinian ethics, labeling it sociobiology. On a popular level, biologist (and former Southern Baptist) E. O. Wilson published *Sociobiology* in 1975, and one year later biologist Richard Dawkins published *The Selfish Gene*. The label "sociobiology" reminds too many of social Darwinism, so often the term "evolutionary psychology" is used instead.

Rather than presenting natural selection as a process to emulate, evolutionary psychologists make the (slightly) more modest claim that Darwinism provides an overarching explanation of aspects of life. Robert Wright, a Darwinian advocate (and who, like Wilson, is a former Southern Baptist) spells out the implications of evolutionary psychology in his *The Moral Animal: Why We Are, the Way We Are: The New Science of Evolutionary Psychology*. Wright explains, "Slowly but unmistakably, a new worldview is emerging. Here 'worldview' is meant quite literally. The new Darwinian synthesis is, like quantum physics or molecular biology, a body of scientific theory and fact; but, unlike them, it is also a way of seeing everyday life. Once truly grasped (and it is much easier to grasp than either of them), it can entirely alter one's perception of social reality."[14]

First, explains Wright, *one must understand that selfishness is the fundamental basis of all that we do*. Natural selection has one goal and one goal only: the propagation of one's genetic code. Everything is about reproduction. Natural selection is not concerned with an individual's happiness.

---

member in this large chain, as a rapidly vanishing vapor. . . . Personal individual existence appears to me so horribly miserable, petty, and worthless, that I see it intended for nothing but for destruction" (quoted by Weikart, "Darwinism and Death," 329).

12. Dennett, *Darwin's Dangerous Idea*, 264; Wright, *The Moral Animal*, 329–32.
13. Charles Darwin, "Letter to William Graham," (July 3, 1881). Available online: www.darwinproject.ac.uk/letter/entry-13230 (accessed 03/23/13). "Lastly I could show fight on natural selection having done and doing more for the progress of civilization than you seem inclined to admit. . . . The more civilized so-called Caucasian races have beaten the Turkish hollow in the struggle for existence. Looking to the world at not very distant date, what an endless number of the lower races will have been eliminated by the higher civilized races throughout the world."
14. Wright, *The Moral Animal*, 4–5.

In fact, the unhappy strife of struggle and competition promotes natural selection, so misery is guaranteed. This is why Dawkins describes our DNA as a "selfish gene." Dominic Johnson and Jesse Bering concur, explaining, "To put it bluntly, all life on Earth is based on Selfishness. Genes that replicate fastest spread at the expense of others. Any that incur costs by sacrificing self-interest disappear from the gene pool, gobbled up by the inexorable mill of natural selection."[15] Selfishness is not the main characteristic of living beings; it is the *only* characteristic.

But many actions taken by humans do not appear to be driven by selfishness. In fact, many charitable and kind deeds seemed to be motivated by love.

This brings up Wright's *second point: the main tool of natural selection is deception.* According to the "cynical logic of natural selection," morality, ethics, and codes of conduct are all mechanisms of deception. But we are not really to blame for this state of affairs—we deceive ourselves most of all. Wright explains, "Natural selection appears to have hidden our true selves from ourselves."[16] A mother's love is just "kinship selection." Charity, sacrifice, and gratitude are examples of mercenary "reciprocal altruism." Wright declares, "Exquisitely sensitive sympathy is just highly nuanced investment advice. Our deepest compassion is our best bargain hunting."[17] Unselfish acts are simply selfish acts that are well disguised. Evolutionary biologist Michael Ghiselin explains, "Scratch an 'altruist' and watch a 'hypocrite' bleed."[18] We deceive ourselves in order to deceive others better.

Wright's *third point* follows naturally from the first two: *natural selection explains everything—literally everything.* Everything reduces down to genetics. "Altruism, compassion, empathy, love, conscience, the sense of justice—all of these things, the things that hold society together, the things that allow our species to think so highly of itself, can now confidently be said to have a firm genetic basis."[19] Wright and other sociobiologists take the same reductionistic approach to all human endeavors. Ethics, morals, music, art, and religion are all the products of our selfish genes. Francis Crick, codiscoverer of the DNA molecule, explains the "nothing but" approach of reductionism: "You, your joys and your sorrows, your memories and ambitions, your sense of personal identity and free will, are in fact no more than the behavior of a vast assembly of nerve cells and their associated molecules."[20]

---

15. Dominic Johnson and Jesse Bering, "Hand of God, Mind of Man: Punishment and Cognition in the Evolution of Cooperation," in *The Believing Primate*, ed. Jeffrey Schloss and Michael Murray (Oxford: Oxford University Press, 2009), 26.
16. Wright, *The Moral Animal,* 10.
17. Ibid., 205.
18. Quoted by Le Fanu, *Why Us?* 170.
19. Wright, *The Moral Animal,* 12.
20. Francis Crick, *The Astonishing Hypothesis: The Scientific Search for the Soul* (New York: Scribner: 1995), 3.

To make sure we understand the implications of evolutionary psychology, Wright spells them out. Morality is a genetic contract: "Thus a moral code is an informal compromise among competing spheres of genetic self-interest, each acting to mold the code to its own ends, using any levers at its disposal."[21] If a child dies, we grieve because of the loss of "reproductive potential."[22] If a couple is having marital trouble, it is because "emotions are simply evolution's executioners. Beneath all the thoughts and feelings and temperamental differences that marriage counselors spend their time sensitively assessing are the stratagems of the genes— cold, hard equations composed of simple variables: social status, age of spouse, number of children, their ages, outside opportunities, and so on." He concludes, "Once you start seeing everyday feelings and thoughts as genetic weapons, marital spats take on new meaning."[23] That's for sure.

If Wright seems to be indicating that he does not believe in free will, he removes all doubt when he writes that we are "puppets":

> Understanding the often unconscious nature of genetic control is the first step toward understanding that—in many realms, not just sex—we're all puppets, and our best hope for even partial liberation is to try to decipher the logic of the puppeteer. The full scope of the logic will take some time to explain, but I don't think I'm spoiling the end of the movie by noting here that the puppeteer seems to have exactly zero regard for the happiness of the puppets.[24]

Free will is an illusion for one simple reason: the very notion of the "self" is an illusion.[25] The very notions of good and evil and moral accountability are dismantled. Humans are "robots responsible for their malfunctions."[26] Darwin recognized the terrible implications of his theory, but he comforted himself with the belief that these implications would never become common knowledge.[27] He was wrong.

Sociobiology and evolutionary psychology could be dismissed as absurdities were it not that so many are taking them seriously. They certainly are ripe for satire. Denyse O'Leary lampoons the way natural selection supposedly

21. Wright, *The Moral Animal*, 146.
22. Ibid., 178.
23. Ibid., 88–89.
24. Ibid., 37.
25. This is a point made repeatedly by evolutionary psychologists. See Jan Westerhoff, "The Self: The Greatest Trick Your Mind Ever Played," *New Scientist* 217, no. 2905 (February 23, 2013): 32–42.
26. Wright, *The Moral Animal*, 355.
27. Ibid., 353.

explains how anything "from ample bosoms to gay lifestyles is somehow se-lected by Darwinian means." She spells out what the comprehensive Darwinist vision looks like. Evolution explains all the following:

> Why children don't like vegetables (nothing to do with young 'uns preference for sweet things); why hungry men prefer plump women (not just because those women prob-ably know where the kitchen is); why we have color vision (mainly to detect blushing); why we are sexually jealous (not fear of abandonment, but "sperm competition"); why toddlers are Neanderthals (not just immature); why we don't stick to our goals (evolution gave us a kludge brain); why women prefer men with stubble (except for those who don't); why gossip is good for you (despite wrecked relationships due to slander); why moral behavior is based on primitive disgust (not rational evaluation); why music exists (to "spot the savannah with little Pavarottis"); why art exists (to recapture that lost savannah); why art exists (to spread selfish genes); why altruism is really a form of sexual display; why altruism is really just selfishness; why a child must have a selfish motive for saving her sister's life; why right and wrong don't really make sense; why we don't eat Grandma (because she might baby sit the kids); why we don't (usually) hurt ourselves to hurt others; why we can't help behaving badly (it is programmed into our genes); oh, and religion is a sort of replicator or "meme" in our brains; and why we believe in God (because he is a supernatural cheat detector); or else why we believe in God (because belief is and is not adaptive at the same time); or, finally why we believe in God (because we have a genetic predis-position to communicate unverifiable information). There is a dark side too. Our Stone Age ancestors are deputized to explain, as Sharon Begley observes in *Newsweek*, why we rape, kill and sleep around.[28]

In the end, sociobiology is the glorification of selfishness. Selfishness lies at the root of all choices, decisions, and actions. Even altruistic ones—they are merely well-concealed selfish actions. In this way, Darwinian forces are understood to be playing a trick. By disguising all such selfish behavior as sacrificial love, we are fooled into commending these actions. Dawkins, Dennett, Wright, and other Darwinian enthusiasts view selfishness as

---

28. O'Leary, "Everything Old Is New Again," 178–79.

the core, primary motive of all living things. They believe that genetic forces have managed to disguise selfish acts as charitable, altruistic deeds. Evolutionary psychologists view this as the supreme ruse. What Christians see as the ultimate sin—the idolizing of the self—Darwinists see as the ultimate virtue.

Wright makes clear that for him and other evolutionists like him, Darwinism is a faith position. He professes:

> The theory of natural selection is so elegant and powerful as to inspire a kind of faith in it—not blind faith, really, since the faith rests on the theory's demonstrated ability to explain so much about life. But faith nonetheless; there is a point after which one no longer entertains the possibility of encountering some fact that would call the whole theory into question. I must admit to having reached this point.[29]

This is a version of scientism, which is the belief that the scientific method is the only valid source of knowledge. Scientism and Darwinism entail atheism. Though sociobiologists reject faith in God, their affirmation of Darwinism is in itself a profession of faith. As Darwinist Michael Ruse admits, "Evolution is promoted by its practitioners as more than mere science. Evolution is promulgated as an ideology, a secular religion—a full-fledged alternative to Christianity, with meaning and morality."[30]

Alvin Plantinga points out that scientism in general, and Darwinism in particular, contains a logical inconsistency.[31] Darwinists place faith in the capacity of the human brain to discern the ultimate truth of Darwinism. But Darwinism teaches that the brain evolved by irrational processes, and that it certainly did not evolve for the purpose of discovering truth. So why should a Darwinist trust his own brain when he comes to the Darwinian conclusion that everything is the result of purposeless, meaningless, irrational chance? It seems that Darwinism is self-referentially contradictory.

---

29. Robert Wright, *The Moral Animal*, 383. In that same section Wright notes, "In 1859, after Darwin sent his brother Erasmus a copy of *On the Origin of Species*, Erasmus replied with a letter of praise. . . . 'In fact the *a priori* reasoning is so entirely satisfactory to me that if the facts won't fit in, why so much the worse for the facts is my feeling.' This sentiment is more widely shared by evolutionists than some of them would admit."

30. Quoted by Thomas Fowler and Daniel Kuebler, *The Evolution Controversy: A Survey of Competing Theories* (Grand Rapids: Baker, 2007), 40–41.

31. Alvin Plantinga, *Where the Conflict Really Lies: Science, Religion, and Naturalism* (New York: Oxford University Press, 2011), 309–15.

Conclusion

What are we to think of evolutionary psychology and the application of Darwinism to every aspect of life? First, the recognition that selfishness and self-interests are primary motivators in human relationships is hardly a new or novel discovery. Nor is it a news flash that humanity in general is blinded by self-deception as to the true, unsavory motives of our actions. In fact, one could argue that evolutionary psychologists are simply catching up to the biblical doctrine of original sin.

Second, evolutionary psychologists go beyond contending that self-interests operate as a central creative power in human relationships and activities. They assert that natural selection works as the unseen force lurking underneath these selfish interactions. Here, sociobiologists have not made their case and are assuming what they hope to prove.

Third, many of the "predictions" made by evolutionary psychology are nothing of the kind. Sociobiologists observe certain behaviors, and subsequently search for Darwinian explanations. These explanations are then presented as predictions and touted as further evidences of the scientific fruitfulness of Darwinism.[32] Critics of evolutionary psychology, such as Stephen Jay Gould, rightly dismissed these predictions as pseudo-scientific "just-so" stories.

Fourth and finally, it is more than a little ironic that just as evolutionary psychologists are demanding that all intellectual disciplines—science, humanities, and religion—be understood in Darwinian terms, many evolutionists are raising red flags about the viability of Darwinism as an explanation of evolution. These concerns range from expressions of doubt to outright rejection. The last couple of decades have seen the phenomenon of evolutionists who are opposed to Darwinism, a topic that will be discussed in the next chapter.

REFLECTION QUESTIONS

1. Why are some evolutionists called "ultra-Darwinists" or "Darwinian fundamentalists"?

2. What social engineering and policies were justified by social Darwinism?

3. What are the three main tenets of sociobiology?

---

32. Daniel Dennett as much as admits this when he describes Darwinists explanations as "evolutionary reverse engineering" (*Darwin's Dangerous Idea*, 249–50).

4. What is a "just-so" story and why is sociobiology accused of taking this approach?

5. What do sociobiologists mean when they claim that altruism is simply well-disguised selfishness?

Why Are Some Evolutionists Opposed to Darwinism?

In terms of intellectual progress, things are not going entirely well for Darwinists. One of the more interesting developments in evolutionary studies is the serious discontent among evolutionists themselves about Darwinism.[1] Many share the growing conviction that Darwinism as a scientific theory is problematic and that Darwinism as a sociological approach is misguided. We examine Darwinism's shortcomings in greater detail in the remaining chapters, but for now we want to highlight five major challenges to the Darwinian paradigm. What makes these objections so intriguing is that they are not coming from creationists or even proponents of intelligent design. Rather, these challenges are coming from evolutionists—many of whom are hostile to creationism and who are self-described atheists. The objections can be grouped under five headings and can be associated with five prominent evolutionists—Stephen Jay Gould, Jerry Fodor, Paul Davies, James Shapiro, and Thomas Nagel.

Inability to Account for the Fossil Record

Before his death in 2002, Stephen Jay Gould, paleontologist at Harvard, was considered one of the foremost proponents of evolutionary theory. As we discussed in a previous chapter, as early as the 1970s Gould, along with Niles Eldridge, acknowledged that research of the geological column does not reveal findings that Darwin's theory expected. Darwinism predicts fossil evidence of gradual accumulations produced by constant transitions and adaptations. Rather, there is little or no evidence of evolution occurring through successive tiny changes over generation after generation. Gould explains, "The absence of fossil evidence for intermediary stages between major

---

1. Peter Williams, "Atheists Against Darwinism," *Evangelical Philosophical Society.* Available online: http://epsociety.org/library/articles.asp?pid=66 (accessed 12/23/09).

transitions in organic design, indeed our inability, even in our imagination, to construct functional intermediates in many cases, has been a persistent and nagging problem for gradualistic accounts of evolution."[2] The lack of transitional forms in the fossil record is not a problem with the record. The notion of gradual transitional forms is simply wrong.

Instead of gradualism, the fossil record indicates "punctuated equilibrium." By punctuated equilibrium, Gould and Eldridge mean that the data indicates almost all species remain constant throughout their existence (i.e., equilibrium) with new species appearing suddenly (i.e., punctuated). They attempt to amend Darwin's theory by positing that the history of evolution is immense periods of stasis, with change occurring rapidly in isolated populations. This goes against Darwin's theory of gradual adaptation and seems to abandon natural selection as the engine of evolution. This is why in the early 1980s, Gould described Darwinism, as a scientific theory, as being "effectively dead."[3]

Gould argued that his views are compatible with those of Darwin himself, and that Darwin understood natural selection only as the *primary* engine of evolution rather than the *exclusive* engine. However, Gould's theory is opposed most vehemently by many within the evolutionary community. Gould lamented the rise of "ultra-Darwinists"—and he reserved special scorn for Richard Dawkins and Daniel Dennett.[4] He accused Dawkins and Dennett (whom Gould described as "Dawkins's lapdog") of hijacking Darwin's theory to promote what he called "Darwinian fundamentalism." Because of their virulent opposition to teleology, these Darwinian purists are not able to recognize (or at least not able to admit to recognizing) that much of the recent findings in genetics, microbiology, and paleontology point away from natural selection.

Gould explained why the new atheists hold to natural selection with a radical zeal: it overthrows the Christian worldview.

> The radicalism of natural selection lies in its power to dethrone some of the deepest and most traditional comforts of Western thought, particularly the notion that nature's benevolence, order and good design, with humans at a sensible summit of power and excellence, proves the existence of an omnipotent and benevolent creator who loves us most of all (the old-style theological version) or at least that nature has meaningful directions, and that humans fit into a sensible

2. Stephen Jay Gould, "Is a New and General Theory of Evolution Emerging?" *Paleobiology* 6, no. 1 (1980): 119–30.
3. Ibid, 120.
4. Stephen Jay Gould, "Darwinian Fundamentalism," *The New York Review of Books* 44, no. 10, June 12, 1997, 34–38. Available online http://www.nybooks.com/articles/archives/1997/jun/12/darwinian-fundamentalism/?pagination=false (accessed 4/29/11).

and predictable pattern regulating the totality (the modern and more secular version).[5]

In other words, Darwin's understanding of natural selection deposes the notion of a good creation which exhibits evidences of the handiwork and plans of a loving God.

Gould reserved special scorn for Darwinian sociobiology as promoted by Dawkins, Dennett, and Wright. Gould lamented that these ultra-Darwinists "are now engaged in an almost mordantly self-conscious effort to 'revolutionize' the study of human behavior along a Darwinian straight and narrow under the name of 'evolutionary psychology.'"[6] He assessed Dawkins's "selfish gene theory" as a "hyper-Darwinian idea that I regard as a logically flawed and basically foolish caricature of Darwin's genuinely radical intent." To Gould, proponents of evolutionary psychology are presenting "just-so" stories in the guise of scientific respectability. He used Wright's explanation of our affection for sugar as an illustration of a just-so story:

> The task of evolutionary psychology then turns into a specu-
> lative search for reasons why a behavior that may harm us
> now must once have originated for adaptive purposes. To
> take an illustration proposed seriously by Robert Wright
> in *The Moral Animal*, a sweet tooth leads to unhealthy obesity
> today but must have arisen as an adaptation. Wright there-
> fore states: "The classic example of an adaptation that has
> outlived its logic is the sweet tooth. Our fondness for sweet-
> ness was designed for an environment in which fruit existed
> but candy didn't." This ranks as pure guesswork in the cock-
> tail party mode; Wright presents no neurological evidence of
> a brain module for sweetness, and no paleontological data
> about ancestral feeding. This "just-so story" therefore cannot
> stand as a "classic example of an adaptation" in any sense de-
> serving the name of science.[7]

Gould accuses sociobiology of committing the greatest of scientific crimes: it does not deal with the facts.

Paleobiologist Simon Conway Morris of Cambridge echoes Gould's denunciation of ultra-Darwinists when he accuses them of hubris ("their

5. Ibid.
6. Ibid.
7. Stephen Jay Gould, "Evolution: The Pleasures of Pluralism," *New York Review of Books* 44, no. 11 (June 26, 1997): 47–53. Available online: http://www.nybooks.com/articles/archives/1997/jun/26/evolution-the-pleasures-of-pluralism/ (accessed 01/12/13).

almost unbelievable self-assurance, their breezy self-confidence"), dishonesty ("sophistry and sleight of hand in the misuse of metaphor, and more importantly a distortion of metaphysics in support of an evolutionary program"), and fanaticism ("the pronouncements of ultra-Darwinists can shake with a religious fervor"). Morris's criticism is all the more telling since he, like Gould, embraces evolution.[8]

Noting that "the modern ultras push their line with an almost theological fervor," Gould speculated about the motives of Dawkins, Dennett, and company:

> Why then should Darwinian fundamentalism be expressing itself so stridently when most evolutionary biologists have become more pluralistic in the light of these new discoveries and theories? I am no psychologist, but I suppose that the devotees of any superficially attractive cult must dig in when a general threat arises. "That old time religion; it's good enough for me."[9]

According to Gould, the ultra-Darwinists are driven by a theological and ideological agenda rather than scientific concerns.

However, many consider Gould's proposal of punctuated equilibrium to be a case of making a virtue out of necessity. It seems to require too much genetic change in too little time. Darwinists appear to have good reason for opposing punctuated equilibrium. Gradualism is the hinge component of Darwinian evolution, and the theory is wounded (perhaps mortally) without it.

Inability to Account for a Creative Power

Recently, cognitive scientists Jerry Fodor and Massimo Piattelli-Palmarini published a critique of Darwinism provocatively named *What Darwin Got Wrong*. They begin by declaring that they are atheists, not just run-of-the-mill atheists, but "outright, card-carrying, signed-up, dyed-in-the-wool, no-holds-barred atheists."[10] The authors make this point so it will be clear that their opposition is not religiously motivated. They contend that Darwin's theory of natural selection is "fatally wrong." Unfortunately, because allegiance to Darwinism has become a litmus test for deciding who does, and who does

---

8. Simon Conway Morris, *Life's Solution: Inevitable Humans in a Lonely Universe*, (New York: Cambridge University Press, 2003), 314–16.
9. Gould, "Darwinian Fundamentalism," 50.
10. Jerry Fodor and Massimo Piattelli-Palmarini, *What Darwin Got Wrong* (New York: Farrar, Straus, and Giroux, 2010), xiii.

not, hold a "'properly scientific' world view," most strident neo-Darwinists are "distressingly uncritical" in embracing natural selection.

Fodor and Piattelli-Palmarini have no problem accepting evolution in the macro sense of the word, but they are convinced that Darwin's theory of natural selection is "irredeemably flawed." They make no attempt to provide an alternative theory. Rather, they admit, "In fact, we don't know very well how evolution works. Nor did Darwin, and nor (as far as we can tell) does anybody else."[11] No straightforward, single-level theory, similar to Newton's law of gravity, is going to be able to explain what is observed in natural history. Rather, they contend, a multi-level explanation is necessary (multi-level explanations are like historical theories which attempt to explain why Napoleon did what he did at Waterloo). Therefore, a simplistic theory such as natural selection cannot be an adequate solution.[12]

Fodor and Piattelli-Palmarini explain that four attitudes about natural selection exist among evolutionists.[13] First, neo-Darwinists (those Gould labeled Darwinian fundamentalists) believe that natural selection explains all. The second attitude is manifested by Darwin himself. He believed that natural selection was the primary force in evolution (but not the only mechanism). A growing number of current biologists exhibit the third attitude when they view natural selection as one force among many (and probably not primary). Fodor and Piattelli-Palmarini go the final step and contend that natural selection plays no role in evolution at all. They argue that Darwinism is an ideological cadaver. "One thing that happens to theories that hang around past their time is that they're nibbled to death by 'routine findings.'"[14] They conclude with a confession of evolutionary agnosticism: "'Ok, so if Darwin got it wrong, what do you guys think is the mechanism for evolution? Short answer: we don't know what the mechanism of evolution is. As far as we can make out, nobody knows exactly how phenotypes evolve."[15] This is quite a conclusion to come from authors who admit that their presuppositions forbid them from considering creationism.

Inability to Account for the Origin of Life

This issue will be discussed further in Question 39, so only a few words are sufficient here. Astrophysicist Paul Davies has a remarkable ability to communicate dense scientific theory in a way that is accessible to a broader public, which is a major reason why his more than twenty books have sold so well. Davies is an evolutionist and describes himself as a Darwinist. Yet, in his

---

11. Ibid., xiv.
12. Ibid., 153–63.
13. Ibid., 43.
14. Ibid., 55.
15. Ibid., 153.

The 5th Miracle: The Search for the Origin and Meaning of Life, Davies admits that all attempts at formulating a materialistic theory for the origin of life have failed—and not from a lack of trying.[16]

Davies recognizes that Darwinism provides no explanation for the arrival of life on earth. Since natural selection, as a mechanism, works only on living, reproducing creatures, then evolutionists cannot appeal to natural selection when formulating prebiotic hypotheses.[17] He concedes that the materialist claim that reality is "Darwinism all the way down" does not fit the evidence.[18]

Tentatively, Davies argues that the path forward requires a "radical" approach that "many scientists are extremely reluctant to contemplate."[19] He contends that progress will be made only when scientists recognize that no merely chemical answer will suffice. Information theory, with its notions of embedded information, offers more promise. However, the idea of information "planted" within nature seems to imply teleology, and it also seems to require an intelligent source.

Inability to Account for the Complexity of Living Cells

James Shapiro is a molecular biologist at the University of Chicago and is a recognized expert in genetics. Shapiro rejects the foundational neo-Darwinian tenet that evolutionary change comes about by "randomness and accident." He sees the commitment to "accidental, stochastic mutations" as a "determination in the 19th and 20th Centuries by biologists to reject the role of a supernatural agent in the religious accounts of how diverse living organisms originated."[20]

 "Living cells do not operate blindly," Shapiro explains.[21] They continually acquire information, make adjustments, self-regulate, and self-correct. They constantly monitor their environment, their situation, and their health. Molecular biologists increasingly realize that the number of regulatory and control processes in cells outnumbers the functions which actually accomplish a task. There are layers upon layers of interconnected networks that constantly process information. This recognition has given rise to the discipline of *systems biology*—the study of how groups of molecules coordinate to work cooperatively.[22]

Shapiro specifically rejects the notion that random variations are introduced through accidental mutations in DNA. The standard neo-Darwinian

16. Paul Davies, *The 5th Miracle: The Search for the Origin and Meaning of Life* (New York: Simon and Shuster, 1999), 123–33.
17. Ibid., 137–38.
18. Ibid., 260.
19. Ibid., 258.
20. James Shapiro, *Evolution: A View from the 21st Century* (Upper Saddle River, N.J.: FT Press, 2011), 1–2.
21. Ibid., 7.
22. Ibid., 4–7.

model fails to take into consideration that the cell auto-corrects the errors in its DNA.[23] Replication of the DNA strand, explains Shapiro, occurs with extreme precision and speed, and then a multistage process of proofreading takes place. This proofreading happens both during replication and afterward. "The efficiency of the mismatch repair system is about 99%, increasing replication accuracy by a further 100-fold to its amazing final precision of less than one mistake per billion incorporations."[24] In processes reminiscent of quality control systems in human manufacturing, cells identify errors, remove the injured portions, and then repair the damage—and this includes damage caused by external factors.[25] Some proteins function within cells as checkpoints: they make sure that certain processes (some of which are incredibly complex) do not proceed until all the prior processes have been completed. It is not mechanical precision that ensures success in cellular tasks and reproduction. Rather, it is the layer upon layer of proofreading, auto-correcting, and quality control.[26]

Shapiro presents cells almost as if they are *thinking*. The proteins within cells work as "microprocessors" with "regulatory circuits."[27] These proteins assess their environments and react differently to different situations. Shapiro argues that the phenomena of cell cognition—sensing, information transfer, and decision making—challenges the notion that cells simply carry out the commands given by DNA. He contends that current discoveries have caused "the intellectual foundations of molecular biology" to "have indeed been shaken—and shaken hard."[28]

But the notion of auto-correcting is not Shapiro's main point. His main contention is that DNA does not operate simply as a "read-only memory" which is changed only occasionally and accidentally. Rather DNA deliberately changes—in a nonrandom and nonaccidental way—in response to changing environments and contexts. In this way, DNA operates as a "read-write memory system."[29]

Shapiro has a name for this ability of living cells to react malleably to circumstances and situations. He calls this mechanism "natural genetic engineering."[30] Cells have the capacity to restructure themselves. Why is this view of cellular function not more widespread among biologists? Shapiro provides an answer:

---

23. Ibid., 12.
24. Ibid., 13.
25. Ibid., 14.
26. Ibid., 19–20.
27. Ibid., 11.
28. Ibid., 24–25.
29. Ibid., 28.
30. Ibid., 43.

> A major assertion of many traditional thinkers about evolu-
> tion and mutation is that living cells cannot make specific,
> adaptive use of their natural genetic engineering capacities.
> They make this assertion to protect their view of evolution
> as the product of random, undirected, genome changes. But
> their position is philosophical, not scientific, nor is it based
> on empirical observations.[31]

In other words, a presuppositional bias prevents many from seeing the "purposeful manipulations" of the genome.

Make no mistake: Shapiro is an evolutionist. But he is not a Darwinist.
Rather than evolution occurring gradually through "numerous, successive,
slight variations" (as Darwin predicted and the neo-Darwinian model requires), the data overwhelmingly indicates that change occurs in "large steps"
and "leaps."[32] Shapiro declares, "As to the actual nature of evolutionary change
processes . . . the simplifying assumptions made in the 19th and early 20th
Centuries are plainly wrong. They fail to account for the variety of cellular
and genomic events we now know to have occurred."[33] The evidence points to
rapid, nonrandom, non-Darwinian change.

> However, little evidence fits unequivocally with the theory
> that evolution occurs through the gradual accumulation of
> "numerous, successive, slight modifications." On the con-
> trary, clear evidence exists for abrupt events of specific kinds
> at all levels of genome organization. These sudden changes
> range from horizontal transfers and the movement of trans-
> posable elements through chromosome rearrangements to
> whole genome duplications and cell fusions.[34]

Shapiro affirms evolution as a historical event. Yet he firmly believes that
Darwin's prediction that the fossil record would indicate gradual change has
failed. Whatever occurred happened in leaps and jumps, with species (geologically speaking) suddenly appearing.

The implications of "natural genetic engineering" are obvious, and
these implications are the reason many evolutionists are resistive. "There is
a convincing (perhaps overwhelming) case for the role of basic engineering
principles in genome evolution. . . . Nevertheless, the phrase *natural genetic
engineering* has proven troublesome to many scientists because they believe it

---

31. Ibid., 56.
32. Ibid., 89–90.
33. Ibid., 128.
34. Ibid.

supports the Intelligent Design argument."[35] Engineering implies an engineer. Shapiro laments that biologists have been taught to avoid teleology, because teleology is where the evidence leads.

> From the foregoing, then, it should be evident that the concept of cell-guided natural genetic engineering fits well inside the boundaries of 21st Century biological science. Despite widespread philosophical prejudices, cells are now reasonably seen to operate teleologically: their goals are survival, growth, and reproduction. In multicellular organisms, cells have elaborate control regimes to ensure that they fit into the overall morphology and physiology.[36]

Provocatively, Shapiro concludes that cells "are built to evolve."[37] He argues for a return of teleology to biological studies, and he contends that the opposition to teleology is philosophical, not scientific.

> If the ideas of cell cognition, decision-making, and goal-oriented function are within contemporary biological perspectives—and if the natural genetic engineering concept is subject to empirical investigation—we can legitimately ask why the idea has been so fiercely resisted by mainstream biologists, and evolutionists in particular. My personal opinion is that the opposition is deeply philosophical in nature and dates back to late 19th Century disputes over evolution and also to the early 20th Century "mechanism-vitalism" debate.[38]

In Shapiro's opinion, many biologists and geneticists are too biased to accept the clear empirical evidences. He expresses the hope that those entering the field from outside disciplines will bring an influx of "new blood" which will remedy the situation.[39]

Inability to Account for the Existence of Consciousness and Mind

Thomas Nagel is one of the premier philosophers living today.[40] This is one reason why his recent book, *Mind and Cosmos: Why the Materialist*

---

35. Ibid., 134 (emphasis original).
36. Ibid., 137.
37. Ibid., 143.
38. Ibid., 138.
39. Ibid., 146.
40. Andrew Ferguson, "The Heretic: Who Is Thomas Nagel and Why Are So Many of His Fellow Academics Condemning Him?" *The Weekly Standard* 18, no. 27 (March 25,

Neo-Darwinian Conception of Nature Is Almost Certainly False, caused such a stir. Another reason is Nagel's religious convictions (or lack thereof). He is a militant atheist. In a chapter entitled "Evolutionary Naturalism and the Fear of Religion," Nagel makes a candid admission about why he and most atheists are so committed to evolution:

> I am talking about something much deeper—namely, the fear of religion itself. I speak from experience, being strongly subject to this fear myself: I want atheism to be true and am made uneasy by the fact that some of the most intelligent and well-informed people I know are religious believers. It isn't just that I don't believe in God and, naturally, hope that I'm right in my belief. It's that I hope there is no God! I don't want there to be a God; I don't want the universe to be like that.[41]

Nagel explains that at the root of his (and other atheists') visceral revulsion to theism is what he calls "the cosmic authority problem"—the rejection of any accountability to God. He continues, "Darwin enabled modern secular culture to heave a great collective sigh of relief, by apparently providing a way to eliminate purpose, meaning, and design as fundamental features of the world."[42] Because many materialists recognize that acknowledging the evidence that points to purpose and design is tantamount to admitting to the reasonableness of theism, they would rather welcome what Nagel calls "Darwinist imperialism." One is reminded again of Dawkins's observation that "Darwin made it possible to be an intellectually fulfilled atheist."[43] Like Fodor and Piattelli-Palmarini, Nagel's rejection of Darwinism is all the more intriguing because of his adamant allegiance to atheism.

Darwinism, as we noted earlier, is fundamentally reductionistic. Nagel argues that consciousness, as experienced by sentient creatures, cannot be reduced merely to physical states; therefore the fact that minds exist cannot be explained by evolutionary processes. We "do not just *happen* to be conscious."[44] If Darwinism cannot explain the existence of consciousness in higher order animals, then it is even more incapable of providing a naturalistic explanation for the cognitive abilities of human beings. Why

---

2013). Online: http://www.weeklystandard.com/articles/heretic_707692.html (accessed 03/25/201).

41. Thomas Nagel, "Evolutionary Naturalism and the Fear of Religion," in *The Last Word* (Oxford: Oxford University Press, 2003), 130–31.

42. Ibid.

43. Richard Dawkins, *The Blind Watchmaker: Why the Evidence of Evolution Reveals a Universe without Design* (New York: W. W. Norton, 1986), 6.

44. Thomas Nagel, *Mind and Cosmos: Why the Materialist Neo-Darwinian Conception of Nature Is Almost Certainly False* (New York: Oxford Press, 2012), 44–45 (emphasis original).

does mathematics work, and how is it that human brains (which supposedly evolved simply so that their owners could gather food and reproduce) are able to comprehend math? Evolution via natural selection does not and cannot supply an answer.

Nagel agrees with Christian philosophers, such as Alvin Plantinga, when they argue that Darwinism cannot supply sufficient reason to have confidence in rationality.[45] If beliefs are simply states of the brain, and natural selection chooses such states according to their contribution to survival rather than any relationship to truth, then there is no reason to trust our beliefs as actually adhering to something that is true. Then what does this say about the evolutionist's belief in Darwinism? Confidence in the truthfulness of Darwinism is completely undermined. Dennett's imagery of Darwinism as a universal acid has returned with a vengeance. The acid has consumed itself. Even though Nagel (tragically) refuses to consider theism as a viable option, he recognizes that theism has a much stronger rational footing than does Darwinism and the materialism underlying it.

Evolutionary biologists have savaged Nagel and his views about Darwinism to the point that several secular journals have published articles about their vitriolic reactions (the London *Guardian* labeled his book the "most despised science book of 2012").[46] As one article explains:

> Joan Roughgarden, an ecologist and evolutionary biologist at the Hawaii Institute of Marine Biology, agrees that evolutionary biologists can be nasty when crossed. "I mean, these guys are impervious to contrary evidence and alternative formulations," she says. "What we see in evolution is stasis— conceptual stasis, in my view—where people are ardently defending their formulations from the early 70s."[47]

Roughgarden describes her fellow evolutionary biologists, on this issue, as being obnoxious and close-minded. This is quite a rebuke to come from a fellow evolutionary biologist. However, a significant number of evolutionists are concluding that Darwinism is counterproductive to progress in the

---

45. Ibid., 24–28, 31–32.

46. In addition to Chorost's article ("Where Thomas Nagel Went Wrong," *The Chronicle of Higher Education*, May 13, 2013), see also Leon Wieseltier, "A Darwinist Mob Goes After a Serious Philosopher," *The New Republic* (March 8, 2013), Online: http://www.newrepublic.com//article/112481/darwinist-mob-goes-after-serious-philosopher (accessed 04/12/13); Ferguson, "The Heretic."

47. Chorost, "Where Thomas Nagel Went Wrong," B14.

biological sciences. Perhaps the title of one recent *The New York Times* article sums up their attitude: "Darwinism Must Die So That Evolution May Live."[48]

Conclusion

The website "Dissent from Darwin" contains a document entitled "A Scientific Dissent from Darwinism." The document makes a simple two-statement declaration: "We are skeptical of the claims of random mutation and natural selection to account for the complexity of life. Careful examination of the evidence for Darwinian theory should be encouraged." Then the site provides twenty pages of names of scientists in the fields of biology, genetics, chemistry, and the other natural sciences who have signed the document—over 800 signatories in all.[49] Clearly within the relevant fields there is significant suspicion about the validity of Darwinism.

The question of whether other, non-Darwinian, evolutionary theories are compatible is, at this point, left unanswered. Many evolutionary creationists take pains to distance themselves from Darwinism. The conviction of these two authors is that "theistic Darwinism" is not an option for evangelicals. Question 38 will look at the question of whether or not a Christian can hold theistic evolution.

REFLECTION QUESTIONS

1. What is it about the fossil record that compelled Gould and Eldridge to posit the punctuated equilibrium hypothesis?

2. According to Jerry Fodor and Massimo Piattelli-Palmarini, what did Darwin get wrong?

3. According to James Shapiro, why are evolutionists hesitant to recognize evidence of teleology in living cells?

4. According to Thomas Nagel, what cannot be explained by Darwinism?

5. Why is it significant that most of the evolutionists cited in this chapter described themselves as atheists?

---

48. Carl Safina, "Darwinism Must Die So That Evolution May Live," *The New York Times*, April 30, 2010. Online: http://www.nytimes.com/2009/02/10/science/10essa.html (accessed 01/20/13).

49. http://www.dissentfromdarwin.org/ (accessed 01/19/2011).

What Are the Arguments for Evolution?

Since this is a work by evangelicals written mainly to evangelicals, we have chosen to give special attention to the arguments for (this chapter) and against (next chapter) evolution that evangelicals have been provided. Though we note arguments provided by Darwinists such as Richard Dawkins and Daniel Dennett, we focus primarily on those provided by evolutionary creationists such as Denis Lamoureaux, Denis Alexander, and Darrel Falk. In Question 37 we will address the question of whether or not evolution is biblically and theologically viable for a Christian who holds to the inerrancy of Scripture. In Question 32 we looked at the distinctions between micro- and macro-evolution. Micro-evolution—the phenomenon of a species adapting to an environment—is observed regularly in nature and is uncontroversial. Macro-evolution—the thesis that species evolve into other species and that all species share a common ancestor—is another matter. "Evolution" in this chapter and the next refers to macro-evolution—the theory that large scale innovation occurs in nature, primarily by means of natural selection, which results in new genetic material, new organs, and then in turn results in new species. Arguments for the theory of evolution can be grouped under two headings: *scientific fruitfulness* and the *empirical evidences*. Proponents contend that these two aspects of the hypothesis make a strong cumulative case for the viability of evolutionary theory.

Scientific Fruitfulness

Advocates for evolution argue that the theory possesses two components that scientists consider key to a robust scientific hypothesis—*explanatory power* and *predictive ability*. A theory that provides a plausible explanation for all or most of the relevant empirical evidence is said to have strong explanatory power. Fowler and Kuebler explain that a primary reason why so many scientists accept the notion of evolution is "the simple fact that it works."[1] The ability of bacteria to develop resistance to antibiotics and the mutations of viruses all indicate that natural selection does work, at least at the micro-evolutionary level. Even young-earth creationist Kurt Wise acknowledges the explanatory power of the theory of evolution. He states:

> It is claimed and it is true: biological evolution is powerfully ev-
> idenced. Similar trees of similarity are derived from a study of
> adult organisms, organismal development, and biochemistry
> as if they evolved in the branching pattern suggested by those
> trees. Organisms can be arranged in a hierarchy of increas-
> ingly large groups as if they were all derived from a common
> ancestor. Organisms develop along trajectories similar to the
> path of evolution they are thought to have traveled, and the bi-
> ological world is near perfect. Evolutionary theory provides a
> simple explanation for each of these major features of biology
> and as such is powerfully evidenced by these same features.[2]

In addition to explanatory power, advocates argue that evolutionary theory exhibits strong predictive ability. Predictive ability refers to a theory's ability to generate testable predictions. For example, recent discoveries by the Human Genome Project seem to be what the theory predicted. Charles Foster points out that the differences in human and chimp DNA are less than 2 percent.[3]

Further, the geological column appears to be what evolution predicts. The lower layers, which are interpreted to have been deposited earlier, contain the fossils of simpler and more primitive life forms.[4] And, though rare, the fossils of transitional life forms can be found.[5] Foster argues that there is a very simple way to kill the theory of evolution—find a fossil that is out of order in the geological column. He states,

> Haldane, asked what would disprove Darwinism, replied,
> "A rabbit in the Ordovician." He was right. If tomorrow's

---

1. Thomas Fowler and Daniel Kuebler, *The Evolution Controversy: A Survey of Competing Theories* (Grand Rapids: Baker, 2007), 149–53.
2. Kurt Wise, *Faith, Form, and Time: What the Bible Teaches and Science Confirms about Creation and the Age of the Universe* (Nashville: B&H, 2002), 137–38.
3. Charles Foster, *The Selfless Gene: Living with God and Darwin* (Nashville: Thomas Nelson, 2009), 70.
4. Darrel Falk, *Coming to Peace with Science: Bridging the Worlds between Faith and Biology* (Downers Grove: InterVarsity Press, 2004), 83–134; Vernon W. Bauer, *Can a Christian Be an Evolutionist?* (North Charleston: CreateSpace, 2011), 169–77.
5. Denis Lamoureux, *I Love Jesus and I Accept Evolution* (Eugene, Ore.: Wipf and Stock, 2009), 105, 108–19.

newspapers reveal that a fossil rabbit has been discovered from the Ordovician era, before the first land plants, insects, amphibians or reptiles, Darwinism will be dead, biology will have no ruling paradigm, and everyone will go baffled back to the drawing board.[6]

According to Foster and other evolutionary creationists, the compatibility of the geological column with evolutionary theory is another argument in the theory's favor. Denis Lamoureaux contends that both young-earth creationists and old-earth creationists have difficulty explaining the fossil record in a way that does not make God appear to be deceptive.

Empirical Evidences

Proponents of evolutionary theory marshal data from a range of scientific disciplines. They contend that these empirical evidences, taken together, provide strong support for the theory of common descent. These evidences can be grouped together under five headings.

Similar Features

Evolutionary advocates point to commonalities exhibited by all living things—at the anatomical level, at the cellular level, and at the molecular level. Homology is the science of comparative anatomy. Primates share remarkably similar anatomical features.[7] And though the forelimbs of different mammals do different things—bat wings, whale fins, horse legs, and human hands—"they all share the same basic structure."[8]

In addition to anatomical similarity, evolutionists point to similarities at the cellular level. Paul Davies explains, "There are several good reasons to believe in a universal ancestor. For a start, every known organism shares a common physical and chemical system. The metabolic pathways of the cell—how it grows, which molecules do what and when, how energy gets stored and liberated, where proteins get made and what they do—are basically the same throughout."[9]

But the similarities go even deeper than the cellular level. At the genetic level, all living things have DNA at the core of their respective cellular structure. Davies again explains, "Perhaps the most convincing evidence for a common origin is that genetic instructions are implemented using a universal code. . . . It is too much to believe that all these complex and highly specific

---

6. Foster, *The Selfless Gene*, 40.

7. Lamoureux, *I Love Jesus and I Accept Evolution*, 124.

8. Foster, *The Selfless Gene*, 64. See also Fowler and Kuebler, *The Evolution Controversy*, 97–100; Bauer, *Can a Christian Be an Evolutionist?* 179–83.

9. Paul Davies, *The 5th Miracle: The Search for the Origin and Meaning of Life* (New York: Simon and Schuster, 1999), 71.

features arose independently many times. More likely, they reflect properties already present in a universal ancestor, and inherited by its descendants."[10] Evolutionists highlight the fact that the basic structure of DNA is the same for all living things—flies, bacteria, oak trees, or humans—all use the same four chemicals to spell out their respective codes.

Inefficiently Designed Traits

A second argument made by evolutionary advocates points to what appears to be suboptimal improvisations. This is known as the "panda's thumb" argument, made famous by Stephen Jay Gould.[11] Gould contends that the panda's thumb, which is merely a bone spur, is at best adequate. If it was the product of design, then it exhibits poor craftsmanship. A better way to understand the creature's thumb is to see it as an evolutionary example of clumsy adaption. Advocates point to a number of similar creaturely features which appear to be opportunistic adaptations rather than the products of exquisite design.[12]

Leftover Parts

Evolutionary proponents point to what appear to be leftover parts, or vestigial organs.[13] Vestigial structures are those "anatomical features that no longer perform their original purpose in a species."[14] Examples of leftover features would be the remnants of leg bones found in whales, and tailbones found in humans.

The Distribution of Species

This is the phenomenon known as biogeography, and it was first noted by Darwin in his investigations of the Galapagos Islands.[15] Rather than all species being distributed rather evenly (as one might expect if all living things were created directly), species are similar primarily to those in neighboring regions. Commonalities decrease the greater the geographical distance. Isolated animals, such as the marsupials found in Australia, exhibit unique features found nowhere else. Advocates argue that these geographical traits support an evolutionary hypothesis.[16]

---

10. Ibid.
11. Stephen Jay Gould, *The Panda's Thumb: More Reflections in Natural History* (New York: W. W. Norton, 1980), 22–24.
12. Fowler and Kuebler, *The Evolution Controversy*, 80–83.
13. Ibid. See also Foster, *The Selfless Gene*, 64.
14. Bauer, *Can a Christian Be an Evolutionist?* 183.
15. Charles Darwin, *On the Origin of Species by Means of Natural Selection, or the Preservation of Favoured Races in the Struggle for Life*, 1st ed. (London: John Murray, 2003 [1859]), 388–406.
16. Falk, *Coming to Peace with Science*, 135–68; Bauer, *Can a Christian Be an Evolutionist?* 177–79.

Genetic Evidence

Christian adherents of evolution, such as Darrel Falk and Denis Lamoureaux, argue that the recent decoding of the human genome has provided incontrovertible evidence of common descent.[17] They point to three lines of genetic discoveries: genetic similarity, similar defective genes, and evidence that small changes in genes can produce dramatic changes in a species.

As noted earlier, the DNA of humans and primates are very similar. Humans share 93 percent of the same genetic code with monkeys. The similarity with humans and chimpanzees rises to almost 99 percent. From this, evolutionary creationists conclude that chimpanzees are our closest relatives.[18] The genetic code is remarkably similar across a wide range of species—this is true regardless if the species in question is a mammal, insect, or whatever. The similarity is so close that some human genes can be inserted into houseflies and those genes will function correctly. Lamoureux explains, "These genetic similarities are so striking that in some cases genes from one organism can be used to rescue defects in other organisms."[19] Not only do species possess similar genes, but often two different species will use the same gene to perform different functions.

Evolutionary proponents also point to the phenomena of similar defective genes. DNA molecules contains large quantities of *pseudogenes* and other "junk DNA." Pseudogenes were believed to be genes that have degenerated to the point they no longer have a function, and now simply are highly repetitive sequences devoid of purpose. When the results of the Human Genome Project were first published, it was reported that nearly 97 percent of human genetic code was pseudogenes (or "ancient repetitive elements" as they are sometimes called).[20] Primates seem to contain nearly the same junk DNA as people do. Denis Lamoureux points to one example in particular:

Just like a bad trait that is passed down through a family, genetic errors have descended along related evolutionary lines. For example, a gene required to produce vitamin C does not function in either chimpanzees or humans, and consequently a diet including this essential nutrient is needed for survival. Notably, it is functional in nearly all other animals. The existence of this same genetic error in chimps and people indicates that it was passed down from their last common ancestor about 6 million years ago.[21]

In addition to genetic similarity and similar genetic defects, advocates of evolutionary theory point out how small changes in genes can produce dramatic changes in an organism. Denis Lamoureaux and Vernon Bauer give

---

17. Falk, *Coming to Peace with Science*, 169–202; Lamoureux, *I Love Jesus and I Accept Evolution*, 126–28.
18. Lamoureux, *I Love Jesus and I Accept Evolution*, 126.
19. Fowler and Kuebler, *The Evolution Controversy*, 101–3.
20. Ibid., 106–7. See also Jonathan Wells, *The Myth of Junk DNA* (Seattle: Discovery, 2011).
21. Lamoureux, *I Love Jesus and I Accept Evolution*, 127.

the apparent fusion of the second chromosome in humans. Primates have 48 chromosomes, while humans have 46. "[T]he reason for this difference is that human chromosome 2 is made up of two previously independent chromosomes. A comparison of this chromosome with chimpanzee chromosomes 12 and 13 reveals essentially the same genes, arranged in a similar sequence along the chromosome."[22] Lamoureaux states that the fact that small genetic changes could result in significant changes in a species was the key notion that led him to accept evolution.[23]

Conclusion

One has to admit that evolutionary creationists present an impressive cumulative case. However, before we come to any conclusions we need to examine the arguments made by opponents. Those arguments are the focus of the next chapter.

REFLECTION QUESTIONS

1. What are the two traits that demonstrate that a theory has scientific fruitfulness?

2. Why would "a rabbit in the Ordovician" disprove the theory of evolution? What point was Haldane making when he made this statement?

3. What are vestigial organs, and why are they considered important to the debate?

4. What is the argument from "junk DNA"?

5. What is the "panda's thumb argument"?

---

22. Ibid., 128. See also Bauer, *Can a Christian Be an Evolutionist?* 192–96.
23. Lamoureux, *I Love Jesus and I Accept Evolution*, 107.

What Are the Arguments Against Evolution?

In the previous chapter we surveyed the arguments for evolution. Those arguments can be grouped under two headings: the claim of scientific fruitfulness and the empirical evidences. In this chapter, we look at the responses of the opponents of evolution using the same two headings.

Reply to the Claim of Scientific Fruitfulness

Scientific fruitfulness is indeed important, but fruitfulness alone is not proof that a theory is correct. Mark Discher points to Newtonian physics as an example of a scientific paradigm that had great fruitfulness but was eventually overturned by Einstein's theory of relativity.[1] The fruitfulness that gives scientists great confidence about a theory often also makes it psychologically difficult for them to see a theory's shortcomings.

Many critics are not willing to concede that evolutionary theory exhibits sufficient scientific fruitfulness in the areas of explanatory power and the ability to make scientifically verifiable predictions. Opponents contend that evolution does not have the explanatory power that its adherents claim that it does, and these opponents also contend that many Darwinian predictions have turned out to be wrong.

Evolution's Explanatory Power Is Limited

Oxford mathematician John Lennox argues that evolution has limited explanatory power, and at many crucial junctures in natural history, it has failed to provide any explanation at all. There is general agreement that evolution has explanatory power at a micro level. But the extrapolation from micro- to

---

1. Mark Discher, "Van Till and Intelligent Design," *Perspectives on Science and Christian Faith* 54, no. 4 (December 2002): 224.

macro-evolution is a risky endeavor, and the legitimacy of such a logical jump is the very question at hand.[2] In other words, those who appeal to examples of micro-evolution to argue for macro-evolution are assuming what they hope to prove. Charles Foster admits that, at this point, the inference to macro-evolution "remains just that—an inference."[3] Evolutionists argue that the reality of macro-evolution is a reasonable and warranted assumption, but they admit that they are, indeed, assuming what they hope to prove.

Not only is the explanatory power of evolution limited, but at crucial junctures it has been found to be positively lacking. The last chapter of this book is devoted to questions concerning the origin of life (which is sometimes called abiogenesis), the presence of irreducible complexity found within living organisms, and the information content of the DNA molecule. A growing segment of those engaged in biological, molecular, and evolutionary studies recognizes that standard evolutionary models do not provide a satisfactory explanation for these phenomena. Only the "ultra-Darwinists" seem to be willing to live by faith at this point, while other researchers have decided to look for different solutions.[4]

In 1996, biochemist Michael Behe published *Darwin's Black Box*. He points out that, for all the many thousands of articles on evolution in peer review journals such as *Journal of Molecular Evolution*, one would be hard pressed to find a single article that described the step-by-step process by which any evolutionary change had occurred. Instead, the authors uniformly appeal uncritically to Darwinian theory as if it functioned like a black box which mysteriously caused evolution to happen (hence the title of the book). Behe declares, "If a theory claims to be able to explain some phenomenon but does not generate even an attempt at an explanation, then it should be banished. Despite comparing sequences and mathematical modeling, molecular evolution has never addressed the question of how complex structures came to be."[5] Behe's observation is that, at the point where it really matters, evolutionists appeal to mystery.

---

2. John Lennox, *God's Undertaker: Has Science Buried God?* (Oxford: Lion, 2007), 107. Lennox quotes the verdict of geneticist Richard Goldschmidt: "the facts of microevolution do not suffice for an understanding of macroevolution."

3. Charles Foster, *The Selfless Gene: Living with God and Darwin* (Nashville: Thomas Nelson, 2009), 80. Jay Gould concurs. While trying to minimize the shortcomings of inferences, Gould admits the inferential nature of the evolutionary paradigm: "Since evolution, in any substantial sense, takes so much time (more than the entire potential history of human observing!), we cannot, except in special circumstances, watch the process in action, and must therefore try to infer causes from results—the standard procedure in any historical science, by the way, and not a special impediment facing evolutionists" (Stephen Jay Gould, "Darwinian Fundamentalism," *New York Review of Books*, June 12, 1997. Online: http://www.nybooks.com/articles/archives/1997/jun/12/darwinian-fundamentalism/ [accessed 01/12/13]).

4. James Shapiro, *Evolution: A View from the 21st Century* (Upper Saddle River, N.J.: FT Press, 2011), 127–47.

5. Michael Behe, *Darwin's Black Box: The Biochemical Challenge to Evolution* (New York: Free Press, 1996), 186. Behe repeats and expands this claim in his follow-up book, *The Edge of*

Evolution's Predictive Power Is Questionable at Best

As we noted in Question 34 and Question 35, what often passes for evolutionary predictions turn out to be just-so stories and examples of "evolutionary reverse engineering." In other words, often a characteristic is noted and then an evolutionary explanation is sought. The explanation is then presented as something Darwinian evolution predicted. The simplicity of many Darwinian explanations make them initially attractive and helps to obscure that the explanation has little or no empirical support.[6]

Yes!.

Some evolutionary creationists, such as Alister McGrath, acknowledge the weakness of Darwinism's predictive ability. He admits that if some definitions of a scientific theory were applied to Darwinism, then we would be required to reject "Darwin's work as unscientific and even unethical." However McGrath contends that Darwinism is "sufficiently robust" as a "working hypothesis" to more than compensate for its lack of predictive power.[7]

However, opponents of evolution contend that Darwinism is anything but robust. They argue that a close examination of the empirical evidences discloses results that, in at least three important areas, evolutionary theory failed to make correct predictions. Darwin erred in his predictions concerning the geological column; he was wrong in his understanding of the complexity of livings cells; and he incorrectly ascribed creative powers to natural selection that it does not have. Opponents of evolutionary theory argue that in these three areas, not only did Darwin's predictions fail, but in many ways the empirical evidence indicates the exact opposite.

First, the geological column is not the way Darwin predicted it to be. In *On the Origin of Species*, he acknowledged the lack of transitional forms in the fossil evidence. Darwin attributed the problem to "the extreme imperfection of the geological record." He reasoned:

> But just in proportion as this process of extermination has acted on an enormous scale, so must the number of intermediate varieties, which have formerly existed on the earth, be truly enormous. Why then is not every geological formation and every stratum full of such intermediate links? Geology assuredly does not reveal any such finely graduated organic chain; and this, perhaps, is the most obvious and gravest objection which can

Evolution: The Search for the Limits of Darwinism (New York: Free Press, 2007). Fodor and Piattelli-Palmarini present a similar critique (Jerry Fodor and Massimo Piattelli-Palmarini, *What Darwin Got Wrong* [New York: Farrar, Straus, and Giroux, 2010], 3–5).

6. Keith Ward, *God, Chance, and Necessity* (Oxford: Oneworld, 1996), 69–72.
7. Alister McGrath, *Darwinism and the Divine: Evolutionary Thought and Natural Theology* (Oxford: Wiley-Blackwell, 2011), 153–54.

be urged against my theory. The explanation lies, as I believe, in the extreme imperfection of the geological record.[8]

In Darwin's day, paleontology was a young science, and he expressed the hope that as the discipline developed and matured the missing transitional species would be discovered. Darwin posited that the number of transitional links must be "inconceivably great":

> By the theory of natural selection all living species have been connected with the parent-species of each genus, by differences not greater than we see between the varieties of the same species at the present day; and these parent-species, now generally extinct, have in their turn been similarly connected with more ancient species; and so on backwards, always converging to the common ancestor of each great class. So that the number of intermediate and transitional links, between all living and extinct species, must have been inconceivably great. But assuredly, if this theory be true, such have lived upon this earth.[9]

Darwin recognized that, not only should there be intermediates, but they should make up the overwhelming majority of fossils.

But despite claims to the contrary, opponents of evolutionary theory argue that transitional forms are few and far between. David Raup, curator of geology at the Field Museum of Natural History, explains:

> The evidence we find in the geologic record is not nearly as compatible with Darwinian natural selection as we would like it to be. . . . There were several problems, but the principal one was that the geologic record did not then and still does not yield a finely graduated chain of slow and progressive evolution. In other words, there are not enough intermediates. There are very few cases where one can find a gradual transition from one species to another and very few cases where one can look at a part of the fossil record and actually see that organisms were improving in the sense of becoming better adapted.[10]

---

8. Charles Darwin, *On the Origin of Species by Means of Natural Selection, or the Preservation of Favoured Races in the Struggle for Life*, 1st ed. (London: John Murray, 2003 [1859]), 280.

9. Ibid., 281–82.

10. David Raup, "Conflicts between Darwin and Paleontology," *Field Museum of Natural History Bulletin* 50, no. 1 (January 1979): 22–29. Available online: http://archive.org/stream/fieldmuseumofnat50chic/fieldmuseumofnat50chic_djvu.txt (accessed 03/13/13).

To understand Raup's point, consider shallow-water marine invertebrates. These invertebrates provide the most thorough record of fossils that paleontologists have found (in fact, they make up 95 percent of the fossils discovered). Yet, no transitional fossils have been found "even though these are the best represented animals in the fossil record."[11] According to neo-Darwinian theory, gradual species change should fill the fossil record with innumerable transitional forms. Darwin said that the lack of transitional species was "the most obvious and gravest objection" against his theory. Many modern day evolutionists acknowledge the problem; others do not.[12]

But the problem with the geological record is more severe than merely the absence of transitional fossils. Anomalies, such as the "Cambrian explosion," provide positive evidence that goes against gradualistic theories. The rocks representing the Cambrian era, according to the standard model, were deposited approximately 530 million years ago. The strata underlying the Cambrian rocks contain only the fossils of single-cell life. Then, in the Cambrian strata, a plethora of fossils appear. In the blink of an (evolutionary) eye, thirty phyla appear.[13] Some evolutionists respond by claiming that some transitional forms must have actually existed in the Precambrian rocks. But most admit they are hard pressed to explain how so much evolutionary change happened in such a (geologically) brief period of time. In addition, there appears to have been three "morphogenetic explosions," of which the Cambrian was just the first. The most recent was 1.5 to 2 million years ago.[14] Opponents of Darwinian evolution suggest that taking the fossil record at face value does not lend itself easily to any gradualistic theory of evolution. Instead, they argue in favor of a version of progressive creationism.[15]

**Second, cellular complexity is not what Darwin predicted.** Opponents of evolutionary theory posit that nineteenth century evolutionists were completely wrong about the elaborate nature of the cell. Jay Richards explains, "Biologists believed that the cell was a simple homogenous globule of protoplasm—like a simple glob of green gelatin."[16] Early Darwinist Ernst Haeckel spoke of the ease in which he believed cellular life could randomly come about, and he characterized single-cell creatures thusly:

---

11. Kurt Wise, *Faith, Form, and Time: What the Bible Teaches and Science Confirms about Creation and the Age of the Universe* (Nashville: B&H, 2002), 125.
12. Thomas Fowler and Daniel Kuebler, *The Evolution Controversy: A Survey of Competing Theories* (Grand Rapids: Baker, 2007), 166–73.
13. Stephen Meyer, *Darwin's Doubt: The Explosive Origin of Animal Life and the Case for Intelligent Design* (New York: HarperOne, 2013), 6–14.
14. Fodor and Piattelli-Palmarini, *What Darwin Got Wrong*, 50.
15. Casey Luskin, "Finding Intelligent Design in Nature," in *Intelligent Design 101: Leading Experts Explain the Key Issues*, ed. H. Wayne House (Grand Rapids: Kregel, 2008), 95.
16. Jay Richards, "Why Are We Here? Accident or Purpose?" in *Intelligent Design 101: Leading Experts Explain the Key Issues*, ed. H. Wayne House (Grand Rapids: Kregel, 2008), 135.

[O]rganisms which are, in fact, not composed of any organs at all, but consist entirely of shapeless, simple, homogeneous matter. The entire body of one of these Monera, during life, is nothing more than a shapeless, mobile, little lump of mucus or slime, consisting of an albuminous combination of carbon. Simpler or more imperfect organisms we cannot possibly conceive.[17]

In other words, Haeckel, like other biologists of the late nineteenth century, believed that cells were simple compositions ("just a tiny sac of gray, biological goo"[18]) which could spontaneously generate with very little effort.

But cells are anything but simple. It would be difficult to exaggerate how much, on this point, Haeckel and other early evolutionists were completely wrong. We know of no structures more complex than living cells. The complexity of major cities and of supercomputers pales in comparison to that of cellular life. The cell's origin, complexity, and information content cannot be explained by any known process, including natural selection. As we will see further in chapter 39, questions about the nature of living cells figure prominently in the debates about evolution and design.

The genetic code does not exhibit the malleability required by neo-Darwinism. There are limits to genetic variations. Fowler and Kuebler note, "For centuries, breeders have selectively bred livestock and plants to enrich them for various desirable traits such as size, milk production, or hardiness. Although the results have been impressive, there appears to be a limit to the amount of change that a population can undergo."[19] Evolutionary creationist Charles Foster admits that the "problem of speciation" has not yet been solved, and that there are limits to variations within species. He concedes that artificial selection has failed to produce any new species. He notes, "You can make rabbits bigger, but you cannot make them as big as cows."[20]

Third, natural selection does not operate as Darwin predicted. As noted earlier, early naturalists recognized the effects of natural selection, but they believed that natural selection's abilities are limited.[21] Darwin theorized that

---

17. Ernst Haeckel, *The History of Creation: or The Development of the Earth and Its Inhabitants by the Actions of Natural Causes* (New York: Appleton, 1880), 184. Available online: http://www.gutenberg.org/files/40472/40472-h/40472-h.htm (accessed 06/12/13).

18. Thomas Woodward and James Gills, *The Mysterious Epigenome: What Lies Beyond DNA* (Kregel: Grand Rapids, 2012), 24.

19. Fowler and Kuebler, *The Evolution Controversy*, 92–97.

20. Charles Foster, *The Selfless Gene: Living With God and Darwin* (Nashville: Thomas Nelson, 2009), 81.

21. Meyer, *Darwin's Doubt*, 18–25. Meyer presents Louis Agassiz and Adam Sedgwick as naturalists who were contemporaries of Darwin that disagreed strongly with him about natural selection's creative abilities.

natural selection has great creative power—power sufficient to produce all life on earth. Darwinist Richard Dawkins uses the analogy of an "arms race" between cheetahs and gazelles to describe how he understands natural selection to operate.[22] The slow cheetahs starve; the sluggish gazelles are eaten. The fast cheetah survives and reproduces; ditto the speedy gazelles. Thus cheetahs become faster and faster; and gazelles acquire ever more darting and dodging capabilities—and vice versa. Thus natural selection drives an ever-escalating process (hence the analogy of an "arms race.").

Michael Behe responds to Dawkins' arms race analogy by describing it as yet another just-so story. Behe explains, "The Just-So story seems plausible at first only because it doggedly focuses its gaze on just one trait—speed—ignoring the rest of the universe of possibilities. But in the real world Darwinian evolution has no gaze to focus; it is blind."[23] The struggle between cheetahs and gazelles is indeed an example of natural selection at work. But it is an example of natural selection weeding out the weak and infirm of the respective creatures, not changing them into different species. Behe argues that, rather than an arms race, natural selection operates more like trench warfare. There is dreadful attrition, but no real progress is made in one direction or the other. The innovative capacity evolutionists ascribe to natural selection has yet to be demonstrated.

Current critics of the Darwinian view of natural selection argue that the early naturalists were right and that Darwin was wrong. Natural selection tinkers with living things but it does not engineer them. Fodor and Piattelli-Palmarini use a musical metaphor to describe natural selection's limited impact on nature: it is a piano tuner, not a composer.[24]

James Shapiro points out that there is significant empirical evidence that is applicable to the question of natural selection's innovative capabilities. He notes that for nearly seventy-five years, we have been conducting a real-world, worldwide experiment in evolution in the areas of antibiotics and animal husbandry. Certain bacteria (sometimes referred to as "superbugs") have developed resistance to all known antibiotics. The standard model says that, through random mutations, a small percentage of disease-causing bacteria are able to survive. Those that survive, reproduce, passing on the antibiotic-resistant mutations. Shapiro says that there was "only one problem with this experimentally confirmed theory: It was wrong."[25] Random mutations cannot account for the speed and efficiency with which bacteria have adapted to the threat of antibiotics. Rather, the bacteria *horizontally transferred DNA*

22. Richard Dawkins, *The Blind Watchmaker: What the Evidence of Evolution Reveals a Universe without Design* (New York: W. W. Norton, 1986), 178–81.
23. Behe, *The Edge of Evolution*, 41.
24. Fodor and Piattelli-Palmarini, *What Darwin Got Wrong*, 21.
25. Shapiro, *Evolution: A View from the 21st Century*, 90.

from other organisms that enabled them to overcome or neutralize the anti-biotics in a number of ingenious ways.[26] The bacteria are not just inheriting favorable characteristics—they are borrowing these traits from other living things. Whatever is going on that enables such a response, one thing is for sure: it's not Darwinian natural selection. Shapiro concludes, "The systems view of proteins implies that they evolve by natural genetic engineering rather than by localized mutation."[27] In other words, bacteria adapt the way they do because they were engineered (or designed) to do so.

The second type of evolutionary experiment Shapiro says we have been conducting is one we noted earlier—animal husbandry. Husbandry is the selective breeding of animals in order to produce new breeds. Here the limitations of selection become apparent. Shapiro explains, "It is important to note that selection has never led to formation of a new species, as Darwin postulated. No matter how morphologically and behaviorally different they become, all dogs remain members of the same species, are capable of interbreeding with other dogs, and will revert in a few generations to a common feral dog phenotype if allowed to go wild."[28] John Lennox concurs, noting that we have bred thousands of generations of fruit flies and 25,000 generations of the E. coli bacterium. Throughout all this research "no real innovative changes were observed."[29]

Darwin called certain parts of the fossil record "an abominable mystery," because the record indicated that—rather than after slow, gradual, step-by-step change—species arrive quickly and fully formed.[30] Shapiro concludes that 150 years of research and exploration have exacerbated the mystery rather than lessened it.[31] Three significant predictions made by Darwinian theory concerning the fossil evidence, cellular complexity, and natural selection's capabilities have turned out to be wrong.

Reply to Empirical Evidences

Opponents of evolutionary theories have provided alternative interpretations to each of the empirical evidences presented by evolutionists.

Similar Features

To the argument based on similar features ("homologous structures"), Norman Nevin responds with three points. First, he notes that the argument

---

26. Ibid., 91–95.
27. Ibid., 97.
28. Ibid., 121.
29. Lennox, *God's Undertaker*, 107–8.
30. Charles Darwin, "Letter to J. D. Hooker," No. 12167 (July 22, 1879), http://www.darwin-project.ac.uk/entry-12167.
31. Shapiro, *Evolution: A View from the 21st Century*, 122.

is circular.[32] Evolutionists define homology as "similarity due to a common descent" and then they argue that homology provides evidence for common descent. Second, some creatures possess similar features even though, according to evolutionary theory, they are not closely related. For example, the octopus eye and the human eye share some similar features, but no one thinks they have a close common ancestor.[33] Third, it appears that many similar features are produced by different genes in different species. Nevin concludes, "The facts of comparative anatomy provide no support for evolution in the way conceived by Darwin and research at the molecular level has not demonstrated a correspondence between the structure of the gene and the structural and physical homology."[34] Similar features could be the result of similar environment, an economy of design, and that they originated from a common Creator.[35]

Molecular biologist Ann Gauger argues that the evidences for common ancestry could just as easily be interpreted as evidences for common design. The assumption that similarity indicates common ancestry, she contends, is simply that—an assumption. Similarity in structure, in features, or in sequences, by itself does not confirm common descent. Gauger explains, "'Mustang' and 'Taurus' cars have strong similarities, too, and you could argue that they evolved from a common ancestor, 'Ford.' But the similarities between these cars are the result of common design, not common ancestry."[36] Both inferences—common descent and common design—are compatible with the evidence (and some intelligent design proponents do not consider the two inferences to be mutually exclusive).

The power of the argument from similarity is its simplicity. Molecular biologist Douglas Axe contends that what gets lost in this logical simplicity is the enormous gulf—in terms of random mutation and genetic drift—that exists between two species such as humans and chimps. Research done by Gauger and Axe indicates that similarity of structure is not enough to demonstrate that there exists an adaptive path. Axe observes, "It's one thing to say that chimps and humans are similar enough that their likeness calls for careful explanation (few would argue with that), but as we've now seen it's quite another that they're similar enough for Darwin's engine to have traversed the gap between

---

32. Norman Nevin, "Interpretation of Scientific Evidence: Homology" in *Should Christians Embrace Evolution? Biblical and Scientific Responses,* ed. Norman Nevin (Phillipsburg, N.J.: P&R, 2009), 137–42. See also, Michael Denton, *Evolution: A Theory in Crisis* (Chevy Chase, Md.: Adler & Adler, 1985), 142–56.

33. Nevin, "Interpretation of Scientific Evidence: Homology," 137–42.

34. Ibid.

35. Paul Garner, *The New Creationism: Building Scientific Theories on a Biblical Foundation* (Darlington: Evangelical, 2009), 152–53.

36. Ann Gauger, Douglas Axe, and Casey Luskin, *Science and Human Origins* (Seattle: Discovery Institute Press, 2012), 12.

them."[37] They conclude that, even if humans and apes were determined to have a common ancestor, the steps required are so extraordinary, unnatural, and unknown that the process would have to be labeled (literally) as a miracle.

Inefficiently Designed Traits

Many "suboptimal improvisations" turn out to be pretty good. Kurt Wise notes that evolutionists provide very few examples of suboptimal improvisations. He points out that the most famous example—the panda's thumb—supposedly (according to the conventional model) has been doing fine for millions of years.[38] In fact, the evidence is the opposite of what Darwinism predicts. Darwinism predicts that rarely, if ever, will optimal adaptations be found. Yet, as many evolutionists note, species regularly exhibit "optimal or near-optimal solutions."[39]

In addition, the argument that God would not use a "suboptimal" design is not a scientific objection so much as it is a theological one. One prominent theme of Scripture is that God is able to perfectly accomplish his will through imperfect creatures. In addition, many truly suboptimal characteristics could have been acquired after the fall.

Genetic Evidences

One repeated piece of evidence is the nearly 99 percent similarity between the genetic code of humans and that of chimpanzees. However, Vern Poythress argues that the figure is misleading. It refers only to the regions of DNA "where an alignment or partially matching sequence can be found."[40] A full 28 percent of the total human DNA code is excluded because no alignment or similarity can be detected at all. Luskin contends that recent data contradicts the standard evolution model concerning humans and apes, and that "some parts of the genome tell one evolutionary story while others tell a different, contradictory story. Our genome is not painting a consistent picture of common descent."[41]

As noted earlier, a significant argument set forth by evolutionists over the last decade has been the discovery of defective genes and "pseudogenes"—the junk DNA argument. However, it appears that the non-coding DNA is not junk after all. In *The Myth of Junk DNA*, Jonathan Wells demonstrates that

---

37. Ibid., 27–28, 41.
38. Kurt Wise, *Faith, Form, and Time: What The Bible Teaches and Science Confirms about Creation and the Age of the Universe* (Nashville: B&H, 2002), 125.
39. Fodor and Piattelli-Palmarini, *What Darwin Got Wrong* (New York: Farrar, Straus, and Giroux, 2010), 81–92.
40. Vern Poythress, "Adam Versus Claims from Genetics," *WTJ* 75 (2013): 67.
41. Casey Luskin, "Study Reports a Whopping '23% of Our Genome' Contradicts Standard Human-Ape Evolutionary Phylogeny," *Evolution News and Views* (June 3, 2011) Online: http://www.evolutionnews.org/2011/06/study_reports_a_whopping_23_of047041.html (accessed 04/12/13).

the view that most of our DNA is junk is not just wrong—it is "spectacularly wrong."[42] After the Human Genome Project was completed, the ENCODE project began. ENCODE (which stands for Encyclopedia of DNA Elements) is a consortium dedicated to determining the specific functions of the DNA code. Researchers have shown that what was originally thought to be defective, repetitive genes turns out to be multilayered programming. The so-called pseudogenes accomplish tasks ranging from proofreading to auto-correcting. Originally it was reported that only 3 percent of the human DNA molecule contained recognizable genes, and that over 90 percent of our DNA "was flawed or useless." The ENCODE project completely reversed that perception when it demonstrated that at least 74 percent to 93 percent of human DNA routinely carried out functions within the cell.[43]

As for the argument that the apparent chromosomal fusion in the human genome indicates a common ancestor for humans and apes, Casey Luskin contends that the evidence is as compatible with common design as it is with common descent. He argues, "But—and this is the key point—even if human chromosome #2 is the result of two other chromosomes which became fused, this is not evidence for human/ape common ancestry. At most, it shows our human lineage experienced a chromosomal fusion event, but it does not tell us whether our lineage leads back to a common ancestor with apes."[44]

In sum, opponents of evolutionary theory reply that the genetic arguments are not as strong as evolutionists contend, and that some of the arguments evolutionists have made (i.e., the junk DNA argument) have been shown to be wrong.

Conclusion: Does Evolution Require God in Order to Work?

There does seem to be evidence for species employing significant adaptations. This notion is not particularly controversial, even among young-earth creationists. As we noted earlier, YEC proponent Kurt Wise acknowledged that evolution is "powerfully evidenced." In addition, as we saw in Question 31, geologist and fellow YEC advocate Andrew Snelling argues that Noah's ark carried only about 2,000 species in the deluge. He contends that those 2,000 species then developed into the millions of species we see on earth today. Evidences, such as the progression of fossils in the geological record and the genetic similarities between species cannot, and should not, be denied.

However, the case for evolution, at significant crucial junctures, depends much more on inferences than it does on solid empirical evidences. Common descent remains merely an inference. The adaptive paths between species are

---

42. Wells, *The Myth of Junk DNA*, 9.
43. Woodward and Gills, *The Mysterious Epigenome*, 20–21.
44. Casey Luskin, "Francis Collins, Junk DNA, and Chromosomal Fusion," in *Science and Human Origins*, (Seattle: Discovery Institute Press, 2012), 97.

assumed rather than demonstrated. The fossil record and the genetic evidences both give little or no support to the idea that gradualistic, unguided processes produced the plethora of life on earth. Natural selection simply does not have the creative capacity that evolutionists ascribe to it. In the words of Douglas Axe, natural selection is "Darwin's little engine that couldn't."[45]

Often the question arises, "Is there room for God in the theory of evolution?" Christian philosopher Alvin Plantinga argues that it is the other way around. Evolution requires God in order to work. If evolution is true, then naturalism must be false.[46] Theologian Kirk MacGregor agrees. In a section entitled, "Evolution as Evidence for God's Existence," MacGregor contends that evolution is so improbable, inexplicable, and unexplainable by natural processes that its very existence in nature is evidence of the divine. He gives the following syllogism:

1. If biological evolution occurred, it would undoubtedly have been extraordinarily improbable, beyond scientific ability to explain *why* it happened (although science certainly has the ability to show *that* it happened).

2. By definition, events beyond scientific ability to explain why they happened constitute miracles, whose reality demand the existence of God.

3. If biological evolution occurred, it would have been a miracle requiring the existence of God.

4. Beyond reasonable doubt genetic evidence primarily, and fossil evidence secondarily, establishes the reality of biological evolution *(that* evolution happened).

5. Beyond reasonable doubt, God exists.[47]

In other words, evolution is a miracle. The only way evolution could work is if God worked through it. One does not have to accept that evolution has happened (4) in order to agree with the force of MacGregor's argument. But one wonders if such a model should be labeled "evolution." Many would identify Plantinga's and MacGregor's proposal as a type of progressive creationism.

With such fundamental disagreements existing among leaders in the fields of science, philosophy, theology, and biblical studies, one can excuse

45. Douglas Axe, "Darwin's Little Engine that Couldn't," in *Science and Human Origins,* 31–43.
46. Alvin Plantinga, "Evolution Versus Naturalism," in *The Nature of Nature: Examining the Role of Naturalism in Science,* ed. Bruce Gordon and William Dembski (Wilmington, Del.: ISI Books, 2011), 137–51.
47. Kirk MacGregor, *A Molinist-Anabaptist Systematic Theology* (Lanham, Md.: University Press of America, 2007), 183–87 (emphasis original).

laypersons for being bewildered. New genetic discoveries are happening at an ever-increasing pace. There is *some* empirical support for the notion of *some* variation of species in natural history, but there is little or no support for the Darwinian model which claims to provide an all-encompassing naturalistic explanation. But what about theistic versions of evolutionary theory (i.e., evolutionary creationism)? Specifically, what do these theories say about the origin of Adam and Eve? We give our attention to these questions in the next chapter.

REFLECTION QUESTIONS

1. What three predictions did Darwin make that turned out to be wrong? Why are these failures significant?

2. Why do some contend that it is misleading to claim that nearly 99 percent of the genetic code of humans and that of chimpanzees is similar?

3. What has been the impact of the ENCODE project on our understanding of "junk DNA"?

4. Why do some philosophers and theologians argue that evolution is evidence of the existence of God?

5. Why is natural selection sometimes described as "Darwin's little engine that couldn't"?

Can a Christian Hold to Theistic Evolution?

Is it possible to be a Christian evolutionist? Henry Morris famously answered yes and then concluded, "Just as one can be a Christian thief, or a Christian adulterer, or a Christian liar. It is absolutely impossible for those who profess to believe the Bible and to follow Christ to embrace evolutionism."[1] For good reason, evolutionary creationists generally take offense at Morris's answer. And they point to a number of significant Christian leaders who embraced theistic evolution or at least expressed openness to it. B. B. Warfield, the great nineteenth century Reformed theologian and defender of the inerrancy of Scripture, seems to have accepted a version of evolution.[2] So did C. S. Lewis, though it is important to note that both Warfield and Lewis carefully distinguished between theistic evolution and Darwinism.[3] On more than one occasion, Billy Graham has tentatively acknowledged his acceptance of common descent.[4] Still, most evangelicals—including (and perhaps especially) leaders, pastors, and scholars—have strongly rejected any concession to evolutionary theory.

---

1. Quoted by Charles Foster, *The Selfless Gene: Living with God and Darwin* (Nashville: Thomas Nelson, 2009), 23–24.
2. B. B. Warfield, "On the Antiquity and Unity of the Human Race," *The Works of Benjamin B. Warfield*, vol. 9 (Grand Rapids: Baker, 2003 [1932]), 235–58; idem, "Creation, Evolution, and Mediate Creation," in *Evolution, Science, and Scripture: Selected Writings*, ed. Mark Noll and David Livingstone (Grand Rapids: Baker, 2000 [1901]), 197–210.
3. C. S. Lewis, *The Problem of Pain* (New York: Harper Collins, 2009 [1940]), 72–84; idem, *Miracles: A Preliminary Study* (New York: Harper Collins, 2009 [1960]), 18–23.
4. Both Denis Lamoureux and Vernon Bauer provide quotes of Graham affirming evolutionary theory. See Denis Lamoureux, *I Love Jesus and I Accept Evolution* (Eugene, Ore.: Wipf and Stock, 2009), vi; Vernon Bauer, *Can a Christian Be an Evolutionist?* (N Charleston: CreateSpace, 2011), 299.

As we saw in Question 27 ("What Effect Did the Fall Have on Creation?"), many evolutionary creationists (such as Denis Lamoureux and Karl Giberson) hold that Adam and Eve are nonhistorical symbols that express the human condition.[5] We do not question the devotion and commitment to Christ of Lamoureux, Giberson, and other evolutionary creationists who take a similar position, but we believe that there are serious and detrimental theological consequences to their model.

By contrast, other evolutionary creationists recognize the importance of affirming the historicity of the original couple and their subsequent rebellion. Tim Keller, who affirms a version of theistic evolution, explains:

> I am not arguing something so crude as "if you don't believe in a literal Adam and Eve, then you don't believe in the authority of the Bible!" I [accept] that we cannot take every text in the Bible literally. But the key for interpretation is the Bible itself. I don't believe Genesis 1 can be taken literally because I don't think the author expected us to. But Paul is different. He most definitely wanted to teach us that Adam and Eve were real historical figures. When you refuse to take a biblical author literally when he clearly wants you to do so, you have moved away from the traditional understanding of the biblical authority. As I said above, that doesn't mean you can't have a strong, vital faith yourself, but I believe such a move can be bad for the church as a whole, and it certainly can lead to confusion on the part of laypeople.[6]

We argued in chapter 24 that the historicity of Adam and Eve should serve as a litmus test for any model. Any viable theory at a minimum must be able to affirm the following:

- The uniqueness of the human race to possess and reflect the divine image.

- The unity of the human race.

- The historicity of the original couple and their disobedience.

In this chapter we survey the positions taken by evolutionary creationists who join Keller in his ~~ cern and who try to present models that retain Adam and hese proposals can be grouped under three headings: (1)

us and I Accept Evolution, 80–84, 135–39.

Evolution, and Christian Laypeople," 9. Online: www.biologos.org/
_white_paper.pdf (accessed 02/02/11).

Adam was a recent hominid[7] (about 8,000 to 10,000 years ago) whom God chose to be both the biological origin and federal head of the human race, (2) Adam was an ancient hominid (about 100,000 to 150,000 years ago) whom God chose to be the biological origin and federal head of humanity, and (3) Adam was a recent hominid (about 8,000 to 10,000 years ago) whom God chose to be the federal head but not the biological ancestor of all humanity.

The Current Understanding of the Paleontological and Genetic Evidence

According to standard scientific models, the evidence indicates that *Homo sapiens* appeared on earth approximately 200,000 years ago, first in Africa and then eventually throughout the inhabitable world. A small population (perhaps as few as fifty to sixty or as many as a thousand) of these *Homo sapiens* left Africa about 70,000 years ago. Their descendants spread throughout the rest of the world, finally arriving at the American continents about 15,000 years ago. Earliest evidences of tool making, weapons, and art date from 30,000 to 50,000 years ago, and there are indications of religious practices (such as burying the dead) as early as 25,000 years ago.[8]

A little over 10,000 years ago the Neolithic era began. Around Mesopotamia, the region surrounding the Tigris and Euphrates rivers in what is parts of modern Iraq and Iran, *Homo sapiens* began farming. They created stone tools and domesticated certain animals. Permanent settlements grew into towns and cities. In the area where the Bible locates the garden of Eden, civilization began.

The DNA evidence indicates that the entire human race has both a common female ancestor and a common male ancestor. There were a "mitochondrial Eve" and a "Y-chromosome Adam" in our past, though it is unclear if these two were a couple. Using mitochondrial evidence (which is passed down only through the mother) and evidence from the Y-chromosome (which is provided only by the father), researchers conclude that the entire human race has a common female ancestor who lived about 150,000 years ago and that we have a common male ancestor who dates back approximately from 100,000 to 150,000 years ago.

Evolutionary creationists lament that this evidence has been interpreted to mean that all humanity descended from a solitary original pair. Alexander corrects this interpretation: "It does not mean at all that this woman was the only female human alive at the time; it just means that female transmission with a large enough number of generations will

---

7. "Hominid" is the classification of all two-legged primates and is considered to include humans.
8. See Denis Alexander, *Creation or Evolution: Do We Have to Choose?* (Oxford: Monarch, 2008), 221; Bauer, *Can a Christian Be an Evolutionist?* 298–300.

ad back to only one woman, by definition, who can be the
mitochondria."[9] In other words, the evidence indicates we all
᠆ common ancestor, but it does not indicate that she was our *original*
ancestor. The same goes for "Y-chromosome Adam." Alexander explains,
"Again remember that this does not mean that this was the only male alive
at the time, only that the male descendents of the other males then alive led
to lineages that eventually lacked further descendents, in much the same
way . . . for female mitochondrial DNA transmission."[10] Current interpretation of the genetic evidence is that we originate from a small community of hundreds or a few thousand.[11] So how, according to evolutionary
creationism, does the Genesis account relate to the standard scientific
models? As we mentioned earlier, the evolutionary creationists who affirm
a real Adam and Eve take three approaches.

Adam as Recent Hominid Who Was the Seminal and Federal Head of Humanity

John Stott and Derek Kidner present an older, more conservative version of theistic evolution.[12] They propose that Adam was a Neolithic farmer
who lived 8,000 to 10,000 years ago in the Fertile Crescent region. God
chose Adam to impart his divine image upon him. Genesis 2:7 speaks of
God breathing into Adam's nostrils "the breath of life," and this is interpreted to signify the moment of impartation. At that moment, Adam was
transformed from being merely a *Homo sapien* into being a *Homo divinus*.[13]
Adam reflected the *imago dei* (the image of God), so he enjoyed a conscious,
loving relationship with God (some argue that this new relationship with
God was the essence of the divine image). With this new privilege came
responsibility and accountability.

Kidner argues that, though God chose an existing hominid to create
Adam, he created Eve directly. Kidner interprets literally the account of
Eve being taken from Adam's side.[14] As Tim Keller points out, in many ways
this model is a hybrid position, blending some elements of evolutionary

---

9. Alexander, *Creation or Evolution*, 222.
10. Ibid., 224.
11. It is worth noting that geneticist Ann Gauger challenges this interpretation. She contends
   that the genetic evidence can reasonably be interpreted to indicate that the human race
   originated from one couple. See Ann Gauger, "The Science of Adam and Eve," in *Science
   and Human Origins* (Seattle: Discovery Institute, 2012), 105–22.
12. Their views are older in the sense that Stott and Kidner published their proposals prior
   to the completion of the Human Genome Project in 2000. See John Stott, *The Message
   of Romans* (Downers Grove: InterVarsity, 1994), 162–66; Derek Kidner, *Genesis: An
   Introduction and Commentary* (Downers Grove: InterVarsity, 1967), 26–31.
13. Stott, *The Message of Romans*, 164.
14. Kidner, *Genesis: An Introduction and Commentary*, 29. Kidner speaks of "the special creation of Eve."

yes!

creationism with old-earth creationism.[15] God used evolutionary means to create Adam, but he created Eve directly and immediately. This couple, who have a special relationship with God and a special mandate from him, are placed in the garden, where they fail the temptation presented by the serpent.

Stott seems to contend that Adam and Eve were the biological ancestors of all humanity. He declares,

> All humans share the same anatomy, physiology, and chemistry, and the same genes. Although we belong to different so-called 'races' . . . we nevertheless constitute a single species, and people of different races can intermarry and interbreed. This homogeneity of the human species is best explained by positing our descent from a common ancestor.[16]

Adam was not intended for death. Had he not rebelled, Stott suggests, perhaps Adam (and his descendants) would have been translated (like Elijah and Enoch), transformed (like believers will be when Christ returns), or maybe even transfigured (like Christ on the Mount of Transfiguration). At any rate, when Adam fell his sin was federally imputed to all his contemporaries, and death passed to all his descendants.

Other evolutionary creationists generally make one main criticism against Stott's and Kidner's model. They point out that it does not square with the current genetic evidence that indicates that our common ancestors lived much earlier than 10,000 years ago. The genetic data seems to point toward a common origin in Africa over 100,000 years ago.[17]

Adam as Ancient Hominid Who Was the Seminal and Federal Head of Humanity

Michael Murray and Jeffrey Schloss present a model that is in many ways similar to Stott's and Kidner's, with the main difference being that they move the time of Adam from 10,000 years ago to over 100,000 years ago. Many evolutionary creationists who accept the older dates assign Adam and Eve a nonliteral or mythical status.[18] However, Murray and Schloss wish to affirm the historicity of the biblical couple.

---

15. Keller, "Creation, Evolution, and Christian Laypeople," 12.
16. Stott, *The Message of Romans*, 163.
17. See Allan J. Day, "Adam, Anthropology and the Genesis Record—Taking Genesis Seriously in the Light of Contemporary Science," *Science and Christian Belief* 10, no. 2 (1998): 136.
18. See Denis Alexander, "How Does a BioLogos Model Need to Address the Theological Issues Associated with an Adam Who Was Not the Sole Genetic Progenitor of Humankind?" 5–6. Available online: www.BioLogos.org/projects/scholar-essays (accessed 12/11/11).

They, like Stott, posit that God chose a hominid and gave him the divine image. Thus, Adam became the first *Homo divinus*. Also in agreement with Stott, they argue that Adam and Eve are the common ancestors of all humanity. They explain:

> Some of the very studies that point to a common origin for humanity also affirm that the current human population is descended from a large group of individuals in the ancestral population and not a unique pair. Nevertheless, to say that humanity did not arise from a single pair is not the same thing as saying we do not all share an ancestor in our genealogies. That is, we can (and demonstrably do) all share one or more individuals in ancestry even though we are not descended from an initial human pair. . . . Given this, at least some interpretations of a historical Adam as a common ancestor but not single progenitor are reconcilable with contemporary evolutionary data.[19]

So Murray and Schloss posit that Adam and Eve were our *common* progenitors, not our *only* progenitors. They accept the standard view that the common male and female progenitors lived perhaps as early as 200,000 years ago.

The main critique made by other evolutionary creationists against this model is that it moves Adam and Eve out of a Near East setting.[20] According to the standard paleontological model, our common ancestors were in Africa. If the biblical couple lived as early as Murray and Schloss suggest, then the garden of Eden would not have been in the Fertile Crescent region. This would be difficult to square with the geographical indicators presented in the Genesis account.

Adam as Recent Hominid Who Was the Federal Head of Humanity Only

Evolutionary theory has *Homo sapiens* appearing around 200,000 years ago, but the biblical evidence seems to indicate that Adam and Eve lived about 10,000 years ago. The problem facing the first two models is that they create a discrepancy of approximately 190,000 years. Denis Alexander and Vernon Bauer separately offer a solution by proposing that Adam is the federal head of humanity only, not the biological progenitor of all.[21] Whoever "Mitochondrial

---

19. Michael Murray and Jeffry Schloss, "Evolution" in *Routledge Companion to Theism*, ed. Charles Taliaferro, Victoria Harrison, and Stewart Goetz (London: Routledge, 2012),

Creation or Evolution, 240.

tion or Evolution, 236–43; Bauer, *Can a Christian Be an Evolutionist?*

Eve" and "Y-Chromosome Adam" were, they should not be understood as the couple God chose to represent humanity when he impressed upon them the divine imprint.

Like Stott and Kidner, Alexander and Bauer affirm Adam's federal headship. One big difference from Stott and Kidner is that they interpret the creation of Eve in nonliteral terms. The biblical text states:

> So the LORD God caused a deep sleep to fall upon the man, and while he slept took one of his ribs and closed up its place with flesh. And the rib that the LORD God had taken from the man he made into a woman and brought her to the man." (Gen. 2:21–22)

Alexander and Bauer suggest that the point of these verses is that God gave a female hominid the same awareness of the divine that he gave to a male hominid. Still, they wish to hold to a historical couple who, when tested, failed to obey God. Among evolutionary creationists who wish to hold to the historicity of Adam and Eve, the federal headship model of Alexander and Bauer is probably the majority position.

Alexander concedes that the model he proposes is not found in the biblical text. He presents his proposal as a working model for understanding a possible "narrative behind the narrative." But he does believe that his model is compatible with the narrative and the theological content of the Genesis account. He argues that it is consistent on four counts.[22] First, the cultural context of Genesis 1–5 fits well with that of Neolithic farmers. The mentioning of certain metals and precious stones (Gen. 2:11–12; 4:22), the tilling and tending of a garden (Gen. 2:15; 4:12), and musical instruments (4:21) are all consistent with the established farming communities that existed 6,000 to 8,000 years ago. Second, the model is consistent with the fact that other individuals and communities seem already to be present. The evolutionary creationism hypothesis provides a plausible explanation as to where Cain got his wife, why he was concerned about others killing him, and how he was able to found a city (Gen. 4:17). Third, the model fits well with the genealogical lineages given in Genesis 4–5 and in other places in Scripture. And last, Alexander points out that his proposal fits with a historical, albeit local, flood in Noah's day, in which the godly line is saved.

Evolutionary creationists generally admit that they leave certain questions unanswered. For example, what about the eternal destiny of those who lived before Adam and Eve? Bauer contends since these *Homo sapiens* were not yet *Homo divinus,* then they were not yet truly human beings, at least in the biblical sense of possessing the image of God. Alexander leaves the question

---

22. See Alexander, *Creation or Evolution*, 241.

open. In addition, Alexander does not assert that his model is correct, merely that it is tenable, and that he is willing to discard it if a better model comes along.[23] But for the time being, he presents his proposal as a working hypothesis. He contends that it fits the biblical motif of God choosing individuals to accomplish his will and his plan. This pattern is repeated in the calling of Abram, of Israel, and ultimately in the calling of the last Adam (1 Cor. 15:45).

Conclusion

Evolutionary creationists such as Bauer are to be commended for affirming the Bible's inspiration, inerrancy, and authority, and for recognizing that the matter of the first historical couple is not a trivial issue. Bauer affirms Adam and Eve as "real, historical individuals" and considers the issue of their existence as a "non-negotiable."[24] Regarding the "litmus test" items listed at the beginning of this chapter—humanity's uniqueness, unity, and fallen condition—the models presented in this chapter meet that criteria.

Many remain unconvinced that evolutionary creationism is a viable option for evangelicals. In his forward to a book entitled *Should Christians Embrace Evolution?*, Wayne Grudem gives eight objections:

> (1) Adam and Eve were not the first human beings, but they were just two Neolithic farmers among about ten million other human beings on earth at that time, and God just chose to reveal himself to them in a personal way. (2) Those other human beings had already been seeking to worship and serve God or gods in their own ways. (3) Adam was not specially formed by God of 'dust from the ground' (Gen. 2:7) but had two human parents. (4) Eve was not directly made by God out of a 'rib that the Lord God had taken from the man' (Gen. 2:22), but she also had two human parents. (5) Many human beings both then and now are not descended from Adam and Eve. (6) Adam and Eve's sin was not the first sin. (7) Human physical death had occurred for thousands of years before Adam and Eve's sin—it was part of the way living things had always existed. (8) God did not impose any alteration in the natural world when he cursed the ground because of Adam's sin.[25]

Grudem expresses the concerns of a significant portion of evangelicals, perhaps even a majority.

---

23. Ibid., 234, 243.
24. Bauer, *Can a Christian Be an Evolutionist?* 297.
25. Wayne Grudem, "Foreword," in *Should Christians Embrace Evolution? Biblical and Scientific Responses*, ed. Norman Nevin (Phillipsburg, N.J.: P&R, 2011), 9.

One gets the impression that evolutionary creationism is a theory in search of theological justification. It is easy to see why believing scientists who hold to evolution would want to find ways that evolution could be compatible with orthodox Christian doctrine. They are followers of Christ who desire to be faithful to the gospel by working with integrity within their scientific vocations. Theologically speaking, however, the danger of the tail wagging the dog is quite clear. Evolutionary creationists appear to be starting with a scientific conclusion and then looking for a biblical sanction. Most scientists would not want to do science the way evolutionary creationists seem to be asking theologians to do theology.

In addition to theological concerns, the evolutionary creationist models presented in this chapter face hermeneutical challenges. This seems to be particularly true in the account of Eve's creation from Adam's side (Gen. 2:21–25). Kidner's hybrid proposal seems to be the only interpretive approach that takes seriously what the biblical text says. Proponents of evolutionary creationism seem to recognize that their argument is weak on this point.[26] The versions of evolutionary creationism presented in this chapter may be within the theological boundaries of orthodoxy, but advocates have yet to formulate a model that fits well with the biblical text.

REFLECTION QUESTIONS

1. What must be the bare-minimum elements of any viable evangelical theory of human origins?

2. Why does Keller describe the hypothesis put forth by Stott and Kidner as a "hybrid model"?

3. What do some evolutionary creationists mean when they make a distinction between *Homo sapiens* and *Homo divinus*?

4. What is the difference between Adam's seminal headship and his federal headship?

---

26. After surveying the approaches taken by evolutionary creationists regarding the question of the historical Adam and Eve, Deborah Haarsma and Loren Haarsma ask, "Not satisfied with any of these scenarios?" They then answer their own question: "Neither are we! All of the Adam and Eve scenarios discussed in this chapter seem to have significant scientific or theological challenges or both." Their candor and commitment to Scripture is refreshing. See Deborah Haarsma and Loren Haarsma, *Origins: Christian Perspectives on Creation, Evolution, and Intelligent Design* (Grand Rapids: Faith Alive, 2011), 270. Deborah Haarsma is President of the BioLogos Foundation.

What Is Intelligent Design?

Beginning in the 1980s, the argument from design has made a remarkable resurgence. More precisely, intelligent design (ID) proponents argue for the "design inference." Rather than trying to prove God's existence by appealing to design, ID intends to scientifically show that the design inference constitutes an "inference to the best explanation."[1] This approach is considered to be more promising than most young-earth models because the ID inference is more cautious and scientifically precise.

Arguments from design for the existence of God are as old as the ancient Greek philosophers. Four centuries before Christ, Socrates and Plato both argued that the evidence of design in nature requires a Designer.[2] In the thirteenth century, the medieval scholastic Thomas Aquinas presented the teleological argument as one of his "five ways" of knowing that there is a God.[3] *Teleological* refers to that which shows evidence of purpose and intention. For example, if Neil Armstrong had found a soda can when he visited the moon, he reasonably could have inferred that another intelligent being had been there before him. Unlike a jumble of rocks or moon dust, an aluminum can, by its very nature, gives evidence of being created for a *telos*—a purpose.

Perhaps the best known argument from design is William Paley's famous "watchmaker" analogy. In the early nineteenth century, Paley argued:

1. Stephen Meyer, "The Explanatory Power of Design," in *Mere Creation: Science, Faith, and Intelligent Design,* ed. William Dembski (Downers Grove: InterVarsity Press, 1998), 138–39.
2. Norman Geisler, "Teleological Argument," in *Baker Encyclopedia of Christian Apologetics* (Grand Rapids: Baker, 1999), 714. As we noted in Question 33, evidences of design and evidences of teleology are not exactly the same. Evidence of design is a sign of deliberate contrivance, while evidence of teleology merely shows intention. These two concepts are so similar that they are often used interchangeably.
3. Thomas Aquinas, *Summa Theologica,* 1.2.3 (Lander, Wyo.: The Aquinas Institute, 2012).

In crossing a heath, suppose I pitched my foot against a **stone**, and were asked how the stone came to be there; I might possibly answer, that, for anything I knew to the contrary it had lain there forever; nor would it perhaps be very easy to show the absurdity of this answer. But suppose I had found a **watch** upon the ground, and it should be inquired how the watch happened to be in that place; I should hardly think of the answer which I had before given, that, for anything I knew, the watch might have always been there. Yet why should not this answer serve for the watch as well as for the stone? . . . [Because] a watch must have a maker. . . . There cannot be design without a designer; contrivance without a contriver; order without choice; arrangement without anything capable of arranging; subserviency and relation to a purpose without that which could intend a purpose; means suitable to an end, without the end ever having been contemplated or the means accommodated to it. Arrangement, disposition of parts, subserviency of means to an end, relation of instruments to a use implies the presence of intelligence and mind.[4]

However, Darwin's theory of evolution by natural selection was believed to have answered Paley's argument. Darwin was considered to have shown that natural processes alone can bring about things that have the mere appearance of design. Darwinism, because it argues that all life is the product of blind, purposeless forces, is diametrically opposed to any teleological understanding of nature.[5] Yet the design argument did not go away. By the latter part of the twentieth century, it was evident to many that the Darwinian model simply did not have the explanatory power sufficient to account for the sophisticated mechanisms, intricate structures, and integrated functions found in living things.

The Beginnings of the Intelligent Design Movement

Tom Woodward identifies four principle figures in the beginning of the ID movement: biochemist Michael Denton, law professor Phillip Johnson,

---

4. William Paley, quoted in Ed Miller, *God and Reason: An Invitation to Philosophical Theology* (Englewood Cliffs, N.J.: Prentice Hall, 1995), 70–71 (emphasis original).
5. Ronald Nash, *Faith and Reason: Searching for a Rational Faith* (Grand Rapids: Zondervan, 1988), 137–38. Almost 100 years before Darwin, David Hume was considered to have provided a substantial logical rebuttal of design arguments based on analogy. However, Darwin's theory was viewed as giving a credible alternative. This is the thesis of Richard Dawkins, *The Blind Watchmaker: Why the Evidence of Evolution Reveals a Universe without Design* (New York: W. W. Norton, 1986). See Questions 32–34 for further discussion about evolution and Darwinism.

biologist Michael Behe, and mathematician William Dembski.[6] In 1985, Denton published *Evolution: A Theory in Crisis*. Though he accepted evolution as a biological phenomenon, Denton argued that many biochemical and genetic discoveries were not compatible with the reigning neo-Darwinian theory. So many anomalous discoveries had accumulated that a new paradigm was necessary. In his critique of the Darwinian model, Denton concluded that "the problems are too severe and too intractable to offer any hope of resolution in terms of the orthodox Darwinian framework."[7]

During a sabbatical, Phillip Johnson read Denton's book side-by-side with Richard Dawkin's *The Blind Watchmaker*. Johnson, a professor of logic, found Denton's arguments persuasive. But Johnson believed that Dawkin's rhetorical flair covered up the holes in his arguments. In 1991, Johnson presented his critique in his book, *Darwin on Trial*. The book sold over 250,000 copies, and the intelligent design movement began in earnest. In 1996, Michael Behe published *Darwin's Black Box*. Behe, a tenured biology professor who, like Denton, accepts evolution, gave a blistering attack on Darwinism which "firmly lodged the 'design inference' as a *plausible scientific notion* in the American consciousness."[8] In 1998, William Dembski followed up with *The Design Inference*, which provides a mathematical process (which he calls the "explanatory filter") for detecting evidences of design in nature. Today, the Discovery Institute, headquartered in Seattle, acts as the primary advocate for intelligent design. Unlike the creationist movement, the ID movement began within the academy. For the most part, its principal proponents are academics with expertise in fields related to the issues at hand. ID, observes Woodward, enjoys a credibility young-earth creationism has never had.[9]

ID is characterized by two strategies. First, ID proponents avoid creationism and, second, they focus almost entirely on providing a critique of Darwinism. ID deliberately chooses not to address issues on which there is little agreement among creationists. Therefore ID has nothing to say about the age of the earth, the nature of the fall, the extent of Noah's flood, or many of the other issues covered in books like this one.[10] Phillip Johnson notes how advocates of young-earth creationism (YEC), such as Henry Morris and Ken Ham, continually fight with advocates of old-earth creationism (OEC), such as Hugh Ross. Johnson observes:

---

6. Thomas Woodward, *Doubts about Darwin: A History of Intelligent Design* (Grand Rapids: Baker, 2003), 20–27.
7. Michael Denton, *Evolution: A Theory in Crisis* (Chevy Chase, Md.: Adler & Adler, 1986), 16.
8. Woodward, *Doubts about Darwin*, 25 (emphasis original).
9. Ibid., 18–19. However, by the same token, evolutionary creationism probably enjoys an academic credibility which in similar fashion trumps that of intelligent design.
10. Thomas Fowler and Daniel Kuebler, *The Evolution Controversy: A Survey of Competing Theories* (Grand Rapids: Baker, 2007), 240.

Two camps developed—young earth and old earth creationism. Sadly, they fought one another bitterly. Various
books were fired back and forth, leveling all sorts of charges
on both sides, from heresy to ignorance to deception.
Needless to say, the Darwinists looked upon this debate with
glee, realizing that the general public—who largely didn't
care if Noah rode a dinosaur or a camel onto the ark—was
theirs for the taking.[11]

Because of such infighting, creationists have not been able to provide a united
front against Darwinism.

Johnson calls on the warring factions to focus instead on the major
common opponent: Darwinian evolution and the philosophical naturalism
(materialism and atheism) that underlies it.[12] As a result, ID proponents
represent a spectrum of positions: young-earth creationism, old-earth creationism, and even some versions of evolutionary creationism (as evidenced
by Denton and Behe).

The Arguments for the Design Inference
The case for intelligent design as currently argued by ID proponents focuses on five arguments. We will briefly summarize them here and give some
of these arguments more attention in the final chapter.

Arguments from the Big Bang Theory
The big bang theory implies that the universe has had a beginning. ID
proponents point out that this aspect of the theory, as presently understood,
lends itself well to a theistic worldview.[13] As we saw in Question 18, during the
twentieth century many within the scientific community strongly resisted the
big bang hypothesis. For a while some entertained notions of an oscillating
universe, eternally expanding and contracting. But most recognize now that
an oscillating model is unworkable.

Those who opposed the big bang hypothesis did so because they realized
the implications of a universe that is not eternal. And ID advocates call attention to these implications.[14] First, it means that there has not been enough
time for evolution to occur (or, more precisely, not enough time for blind,

---

11. Phillip Johnson, "Bringing Balance to a Fiery Debate," in *Intelligent Design 101: Leading
    Experts Explain the Key Issues,* ed. H. Wayne House (Grand Rapids: Kregel, 2008), 27.
12. Fowler and Kuebler, *The Evolution Controversy,* 241–43.
13. William Lane Craig and Quentin Smith, *Theism, Atheism, and Big Bang Cosmology* (New
    York: Oxford University Press, 1993).
14. Robert Jastrow, *God and the Astronomers* (New York: Warner, 1978); Stanley L. Jaki, *God
    and the Cosmologists* (Washington, DC: Regnery Gateway, 1989); Neil Manson, ed. *God
    and Design: The Teleological Argument and Modern Science* (New York: Routledge, 2003).

random evolution of the Darwinian type to occur). The current theory holds that the cosmos is 13.7 billion years old and the earth is about 4.5 billion years old. But this does not provide near enough time for random processes to generate the complex features of living cells. Second, the big bang hypothesis is an acknowledgement that there are limits to the scientific enterprise. What was happening "before" the big bang is inaccessible to scientific inquiry. Some posit that our universe is part of a multiverse; that is, our universe is but one part of an infinite number of universes. But this theory, by definition, is beyond our abilities to test. The multiverse hypothesis truly belongs to the realm of metaphysics. Third, the big bang hypothesis requires that we admit that the universe is not the sum total of reality.

For the reasons given above, ID proponents point out that the big bang theory presents a serious challenge to philosophical naturalism or materialism. The evidence and arguments for the big bang theory are discussed more fully in Question 18.

The Fine-Tuning Argument

Along with the acceptance of the big bang hypothesis came the realization among the scientific community that the initial conditions of the universe must have been calibrated to a level that is humanly incomprehensible. Numerous physicists and astronomers have expressed amazement at the level of precision exhibited by the fundamental constants of nature. We live in a "Goldilocks universe."[15] The conditions of our universe are beyond being "just right." They cannot be described as merely on a razor's edge. It is as if a million razors—edge upon edge—are balanced one upon another. ID advocates argue that the extremely precise calibration of the universe gives evidence that an Intelligence planned it with purpose and care—hence the name, "the fine-tuning argument." Because the universe appears to be precisely designed for human life, the fine-tuning argument is also often called the "anthropic principle."[16]

The science behind the fine-tuning argument is well established. Leading scientists such as Stephen Hawking and several Nobel Prize winners have acknowledged the salient points of the argument. For this reason, it is also widely used by both OEC proponents, such as Hugh Ross, and EC adherents, such as Francis Collins.[17] We devote Question 40 to a fuller discussion of the fine-tuning argument.

---

15. Paul Davies, *The Goldilocks Enigma: Why Is the Universe Just Right for Life?* (New York: Houghton Mifflin, 2006).

16. John Barrow and Frank Tipler, *The Anthropic Cosmological Principle* (New York: Oxford University Press, 1986).

17. Hugh Ross, *The Creator and the Cosmos* (Colorado Springs: NavPress, 1993); Francis Collins, *The Language of God: A Scientist Presents Evidence for Belief* (New York: Free Press, 2006).

The Mystery of the First Living Cell

Darwin theorized that all living things descended from one common ancestor—the theory of common descent. This primitive common ancestor is believed to have been a single-cell organism. But despite the best attempts of Darwinian biologists and geneticists, little or no progress has been made in formulating a plausible hypothesis which can account for the origin of that first living cell.[18]

The better we understand living cells, the more we realize the immense complexity they contain. Each cell is a veritable city, much more complex and intricate than an urban metropolis. It is difficult to devise a scenario in which such a complicated thing could come about by unguided processes. In addition, it seems that only living organisms are capable of making many of the essential components of cells. No known inorganic processes have the ability to produce many of the organic molecules vital for life. Scientists have been working for over one hundred years to formulate a plausible Darwinian account of the first living cell, and they appear to be no closer today than they have ever been. Evolutionist Simon Conway-Morris observes, "It is certainly not my intention to suggest that the origin of life is a scientifically intractable problem, but at this stage of the proceedings simply to register mild surprise at the relative lack of experimental success."[19] After giving a history of origin of life experiments, Conway-Morris describes the results as a "catalogue of disasters." He concludes, "It appears that the field has now reached a stage of stalemate."[20] ID proponents argue that the mystery of the first living cell demonstrates the reasonableness of the intelligent design hypothesis.[21]

The Argument from Irreducible Complexity

In *Darwin's Black Box*, Michael Behe argues that the principle of irreducible complexity demonstrates that the Darwinian theory of evolution is inadequate at best, if not outright wrong. He defined irreducible complexity in this way, "By *irreducibly complex*, I mean a single system which is composed of several interacting parts that contribute to the basic function, and where the removal of any one of the parts causes the system to effectively cease

---

18. Charles Thaxton, Walter Bradley, and Roger Olsen, *The Mystery of Life's Origin: Reassessing Current Theories* (New York: Philosophical Library, 1984); Fazale Rana and Hugh Ross, *Origins of Life: Biblical and Evolutionary Models Square Off* (Colorado Springs: NavPress, 2004).

19. Simon Conway-Morris, *Life's Solution: Inevitable Humans in a Lonely Universe* (New York: Cambridge University Press, 2003), 44–49.

20. Ibid., 48.

21. Fazale Rana, *The Cell's Design: How Chemistry Reveals the Creator's Artistry* (Grand Rapids: Baker, 2008); Stephen Meyer, *Signature in the Cell: DNA and Evidence for Intelligent Design* (New York: Harper One, 2009).

functioning."[22] Behe provides the famous example of a mousetrap. A typical mousetrap can be reduced to six essential components. If the mousetrap lacks any of these six parts, then it will not merely work poorly—the trap will not work at all. Behe proceeds to apply the concept of irreducible complexity to a number of biological phenomena such as the eyeball, blood clotting, and bacterial flagellum. He argues that each example exhibits an irreducible complexity on a level many magnitudes greater than that of a simple mousetrap.

The Argument from Specified Complexity

The fifth type of evidence used by ID advocates utilizes the new field of information theory. Information theory was developed by communication engineers in order to determine the principles underlying the transmission of data. Information theorists came to realize that matter and energy do not make up the sum of the observable universe. Information "rides upon" the medium that transmits it and is not dependent on the medium. Thus information cannot be reduced to mere matter. Information theorists now recognize that the universe is filled with information. And nowhere is information more concentrated than it is in the DNA molecule of every living cell.

There are three levels of information, with the highest level being "specified complexity." The page you are presently reading is an example of specified complexity. The alphabetic letters are arranged in a specific manner, agreed upon by both sender and receiver, so as to communicate information. ID adherents point out that the human DNA molecule contains enough third-tier information—specified complexity—to fill hundreds of volumes of books. ID advocates note that the only known source of specified complexity is an intelligent agent.[23] Obviously, this implies that life originated from an Intelligent Designer (God).

The Criticisms Directed at the Intelligent Design Movement

One measure of ID's impact is the amount of opposition the movement has generated. In addition to the expected unfriendliness of Darwinists, ID has also received a remarkable amount of criticism from representatives of the respective YEC, OEC, and EC camps. Darwinists dismiss ID as "creationism in a cheap suit," but creationists such as Ken Ham and Kurt Wise also oppose ID for what they perceive as dangerous compromises.[24] Seven criticisms are noteworthy.

---

22. Michael Behe, *Darwin's Black Box: The Biochemical Challenge to Evolution* (New York: Free Press, 1996), 39 (emphasis original).
23. Meyer, *Signature in the Cell*, 349–72.
24. Rob Moll, "The Other ID Opponents: Traditional Creationists See Intelligent Design as an Attack on the Bible," *Christianity Today*, April 25, 2006. http://www.ctlibrary.com/ct/2006/Aprilweb-only/117-22.0.html.

The Lack of Focus

As noted earlier, Johnson and other pioneers of the ID movement made the conscious decision to avoid questions that divided the various creationist camps. This strategy cuts both ways. Critics point out that ID proponents sometimes write as if highlighting the problems in Darwinism equates to disproving evolution. In addition, many of the supporters of the ID movement hold to young-earth creationism, but many of the arguments presented assume an ancient earth.[25] This lack of internal coherence causes the ID message to sometimes seem confused.

The Lack of a Positive Agenda

As Johnson makes clear, the primary goal of the ID project is to discredit Darwinism and philosophical naturalism. However, cursing the darkness takes one only so far. Eventually one must light a candle. Critics challenge ID proponents to present a viable alternative model. However, such a model would require ID advocates to take positions on matters such as the age of the earth and the extent of Noah's flood—positions which they (so far) have steadfastly abstained from doing. Philip Kitcher asks, "What's the non-evolutionary explanation? Johnson doesn't tell us. . . . Johnson's attempt to dispute the 'fact of evolution' is an exercise in evasion."[26]

Not Truly Science

Darwinian critics often argue that ID is an exercise in metaphysics. Therefore it is a philosophical construct rather than a scientific project. J. P. Moreland responds thusly:

> [I]ntelligent design theory really is science because (1) it generates positive and negative test results; (2) it actually explains facts in scientifically standard ways; (3) it can be confirmed by facts; and (4) it solves internal conceptual problems that evolution doesn't solve. These are four things that a scientific theory ought to do, and intelligent design does all four.[27]

According to the principles given by Moreland, ID appears to meet the definition of science.

---

25. Hugh Ross, *More than a Theory: Revealing a Testable Model for Creation* (Grand Rapids: Baker, 2009), 40–43.

26. Kitcher, quoted by Ross, ibid.

27. J. P. Moreland, "Intelligent Design and the Nature of Science," in *Intelligent Design 101: Leading Experts Explain the Key Issues,* ed. H. Wayne House (Grand Rapids: Kregel, 2008), 60–61.

Return of "God-of-the-gaps"

Critics contend that the ID venture represents a return to the misguided "god-of-the-gaps" approach of earlier creationists. In the past, whenever a ready answer could not be provided to a scientific problem, some would posit divine agency to explain this "gap" in the current knowledge. The most famous example is when Sir Isaac Newton took this approach. He could not explain the consistency of the planetary orbits, so he suggested that perhaps God intervened at times to provide regularity. When Pierre LaPlace provided the mathematical explanation which filled in that "gap" of scientific knowledge, divine agency seemed to be displaced. Opponents argue that ID is making the same mistake.

However, John Lennox argues that when the data itself indicates evidence of intelligent agency, then accepting the evidence is not a "god-of-the-gaps" error. There is a difference between appealing to God's action whenever we do not have an answer to a scientific question and recognizing when scientific evidence points to intelligent agency.[28] In addition, Jonathan Wells argues that this accusation is an example of the pot calling the kettle black. Many evolutionists, he contends, are guilty of practicing a "Darwinism-of-the-gaps."[29]

Susceptibility to the Problem of Evil

Critics of ID point out that often nature provides evidence of inefficient design. The cruelty, wastefulness, and inefficiency found in nature seems to indicate that if "the world is indeed the work of a genius, it is the work of an evil genius."[30] ID proponents respond by pointing out that this objection is not a scientific objection, but a theological one. Behe dismisses such arguments as squeamishness. He concludes, "Revulsion is not a scientific argument."[31]

Conclusion

The complaint that ID eventually must present a positive, testable model appears to have merit. However, despite the criticisms listed above, it is clear that ID is making a powerful impact. The ID movement has elevated the discussion and has rightly highlighted the serious shortcomings of the reigning Darwinian orthodoxy. In the next chapter we will look at what is generally agreed to be ID's strongest argument—the fine-tuning argument.

---

28. John Lennox, *God's Undertaker: Has Science Buried God?* (Oxford: Lion, 2007), 71.
29. Jonathan Wells, "Darwin of the Gaps" in *God and Evolution*, ed. Jay W. Richards (Seattle: Discovery Institute: 2010), 117–28.
30. Charles Foster, *The Selfless Gene: Living with God and Darwin* (Nashville: Thomas Nelson, 2009), 84–87.
31. Michael Behe, *The Edge of Evolution: The Search for the Limits of Darwinism* (New York: Free Press, 2007), 238–39.

REFLECTION QUESTIONS

1. What two strategies characterize the ID movement?

2. How do ID proponents appeal to the mystery of the first cell as evidence for their case?

3. What is the argument from irreducible complexity?

4. How has information theory impacted the debate about origins?

5. The ID movement is often accused of taking a "God-of-the-gaps" approach. How do ID proponents respond?

What Is the Fine-Tuning Argument?

Most arguments for intelligent design (ID) have been focused on biology and genetics. Though recent findings in cosmology have not received as much attention, they may present an even more powerful case for ID.[1] This is because these discoveries lend themselves more readily to precise mathematical formulation and verification than does much of the biological evidence. In addition, one finds broad agreement among physicists, astronomers, and cosmologists—regardless of religious affiliation—about the findings. The gist of these discoveries is that the universe has been formulated with a level of precision that is quite literally astronomical. For this reason, these findings are often called "the fine-tuning argument." The evidence overwhelmingly indicates that Someone has balanced the physical constants of this universe on a razor's edge and has orchestrated things in such a way that intelligent life—human life—could thrive on Earth. This chapter intends to highlight the basic features of the fine-tuning argument (or the anthropic principle, as it is otherwise known).

The "fine-tuning" perspective is a far cry from what has been the standard understanding of the universe during much of the modern era. For at least a century and half, the principle of mediocrity (otherwise known as the Copernican principle) has reigned as the prevailing zeitgeist within the academic and scientific community. The principle of mediocrity states that there is nothing special or privileged about our place in the universe. There is nothing special about humans or the home we inhabit. Before he died in 1996, well-known astronomer and atheist Carl Sagan wrote *The Pale Blue Dot* (1994). The title for the book came from a famous picture taken of Earth in 1990 by the Voyager 1 satellite. As Voyager 1 was leaving our solar system, NASA scientists had the satellite turn its camera back toward Earth. From

---

1. Ira M. Schnall, "Anthropic Observation Selection Effects and the Design Argument," *Faith and Philosophy* 26, no. 4 (October 2009): 361–62.

a distance of nearly four billion miles, Earth appeared as a faint, bluish dot against a backdrop of darkness. However, because of the way sunlight struck the camera's lens, earth also seemed to be bathed in a narrow band of light. To Sagan, the photo highlighted our misguided tendency to see ourselves as somehow important, when the reality is that we are cosmically insignificant. He expressed his conviction by stating:

> Because of the reflection of sunlight off the spacecraft, the Earth seems to be sitting in a beam of light, as if there were some special significance to this small world. But it is just an accident of geometry and optics. . . . Our posturings, our imagined self-importance, the delusion that we have some privileged position in the Universe, are challenged by this point of pale light. Our planet is a lonely speck in the great enveloping cosmic dark. In our obscurity, in all this vastness, there is no hint that help will come from elsewhere to save us from ourselves.[2]

For Sagan, Earth's loneliness was exceeded only by its insignificance.

In marked contrast to Sagan, many other scientists are coming to a very different conclusion. In the 1960s and 70s, some astronomers and physicists began to note that the cosmos seemed to exhibit an "anthropic principle"— that a number of independent physical constants were precisely calibrated to allow intelligent life to exist somewhere in the universe.[3] As Schnall puts it, "It is not merely that the constants are right; it is that the constants are *just right*."[4] Some who marvel at our "Goldilocks universe" have not or will not face the implications of such a world. Several will acknowledge that the most reasonable conclusion is to infer design, but because of a prior commitment to philosophical naturalism, they will not take the next logical step.

---

2. Carl Sagan, *Pale Blue Dot: A Vision of the Human Future in Space* (New York: Random House, 1994), 8–9. My attention was drawn to this quote by William Dembski's book, *The End of Christianity* (Nashville: B&H, 2009), 41.

3. See Neil A Manson, "Introduction," in *God and Design: The Teleological Argument and Modern Science*, ed. Neil Manson (New York: Routledge, 2003), 4. Manson calls the phenomena "anthropic coincidences."

4. Schnall, "Anthropic Observation Selection Effects and the Design Argument," 369. Over the last quarter century, a plethora of books have come out highlighting this phenomenon. The first work to significantly bring the observations about fine-tuning into the broader popular market was John Barrow and Frank Tipler's *The Anthropic Cosmological Principle* (1986). Other books have followed: Hugh Ross, *The Creator and the Cosmos* (1993); Peter Ward and Donald Brownlee, *Rare Earth* (2000); Guillermo Gonzalez and Jay Richards, *The Privileged Planet* (2004); Paul Davies, *The Goldilocks Enigma* (2008); Alister McGrath, *A Fine-Tuned Universe* (2009).

ID advocates often discern two levels of fine-tuning: local and universal. As noted earlier, examples of local evidences of design are such things as the complexity of living cells or the information contained within cells. But fine-tuning proponents generally point to local evidences of a cosmological sort, namely the remarkable characteristics of Earth and its place in our solar system. Gonzalez and Richards' book, *The Privileged Planet*, is a good example of an argument based on localized fine-tuning. At the universal level, ID proponents point to the precise calibration of the fundamental constants of nature necessary for life to exist anywhere in the cosmos. Ross, in *The Creator and the Cosmos*, lists no less than twenty-five such constants as he makes the case for universal fine-tuning.[5] Local and universal approaches show that ID proponents can make arguments from both the trees and the forest. We will first look at a few of the local arguments and then examine some of the universal ones.

Evidences of Local Fine-Tuning

In their book, *Rare Earth*, geologist Peter Ward and astronomer Donald Brownlee have bad news for Star Trek fans. Even though Ward and Brownlee are Darwinian evolutionists, they are convinced that it is highly likely that Earth is the only place in the galaxy, and perhaps even the universe, where intelligent life resides.[6] They suspect that single-cell organisms probably are not uncommon throughout the cosmos. But they conclude that the necessary prerequisites for complex life—and specifically intelligent life—are so extraordinary that not only is the Earth exceptional, it is reasonable to conclude that our home is one of a kind.[7] Astronomer Guillermo Gonzalez and philosopher Jay Richards come to a similar conclusion in their work, *The Privileged Planet*, although Gonzalez and Richards write from an overtly theistic perspective.[8] They contend that our world is special, not only because it is uniquely habitable, but also because it is exceptionally situated for the scientific enterprise. Both sets of authors present impressive cumulative cases that earth is an extraordinary example of localized fine-tuning. From their extensive compilations of evidence, let us highlight just a few notable examples.

5. Hugh Ross, *The Creator and the Cosmos: How the Greatest Scientific Discoveries of the Century Reveal God* (Colorado Springs: NavPress, 1993), 111–14.
6. Peter D. Ward and Donald Brownlee, *Rare Earth: Why Complex Life Is So Uncommon in the Universe* (New York: Copernicus, 2000), xvii.
7. "In this book we will argue that not only intelligent life, but even the simplest of animal life, is exceedingly rare in our galaxy and in the Universe" (ibid., xviii). According to Ward and Brownlee, the Rare Earth Hypothesis postulates "the paradox that life may be nearly everywhere but complex life almost nowhere . . ." (xxv).
8. Guillermo Gonzalez and Jay Wesley Richards, *The Privileged Planet: How Our Place in the Cosmos Is Designed for Discovery* (Washington, DC: Regnery, 2004). "Simply stated, the conditions allowing for intelligent life on Earth also make our planet strangely well suited for viewing and analyzing the universe" (p. x).

First, *the location of Earth's orbit in the solar system turns out to be just right.* Given the Sun's size and energy output, there is only a relatively narrow band in which Earth could orbit and still be habitable by life. The distance from the Earth to the Sun turns out to be optimal. Initial studies indicated that if our planet were just one percent closer to the Sun, the additional heat would cause the oceans to evaporate. However, if the Earth's orbit were just 5 percent farther away from the Sun, all the world's oceans would be frozen solid. As Hugh Ross puts it, Earth's biosphere is "poised between a runaway freeze-up and a runaway evaporation."[9] In addition, the average temperature had to be such that water would be retained while other greenhouse molecules such as methane and ammonia would largely dissipate. Though recent studies show that the parameters may be broader than originally believed, the range of the habitable zone still is "quite narrow."[10]

Second, *our planet exhibits characteristics that are uniquely suitable for life.* For example, Earth is the only planet in the solar system found to have plate tectonics.[11] Plate tectonics cause earthquakes, but they also play a surprisingly important role in sustaining life. As it turns out, plate tectonics play a key role in such things as maintaining stable global temperatures and a stable ocean environment. Another example of Earth's unique status is its lunar partner. Our Moon is remarkably large for a planet the size of Earth. It is one-fourth the size of its host planet. All the other planets of our solar system have moons that are much smaller in relation to their respective sizes. Along with factors such as plate tectonics, the Moon's influence on the Earth's attitude and rotation acts to stabilize the Earth's temperature. Our moon maintains the Earth's tilt of 23 degrees. Without the presence of the Moon, the Earth's rotation would be wobbly.

The examples given in the previous paragraph are just a few of what could be cited. In his book, *The Creator and the Cosmos,* Hugh Ross lists thirty-three parameters that must be met in order for a planet to support life. He calculates that the probability of all thirty-three parameters occurring in one planet is one in 10^{-42}. However, astronomers estimate that the maximum possible number of planets is 10^{22}. Ross concludes that the odds of a planet such as Earth existing by chance are "much less than one in a quintillion."[12] Our terrestrial ball really is a special place.

Third, *our Sun itself is just right for habitable life on Earth.* One would get the impression from many astronomy textbooks that the Sun is a rather ordinary and undistinguished star. Ward and Brownlee point out that actually our Sun is not typical at all. Rather, 95 percent of all stars are smaller than the Sun.

---

9. Ross, *The Creator and the Cosmos,* 127.
10. Ward and Brownlee, *Rare Earth,* 18.
11. Ibid., 220.
12. Ross, *The Creator and the Cosmos,* 134.

In fact, the majority of stars are M-class luminaries that are only 10 percent of the size of the Sun.[13]

If the Sun were smaller than it is presently, then its habitable zone would also be much smaller, which would require the Earth to orbit closer than it does now. However, the closer orbit would mean that the Sun's gravity would have a much greater effect on the Earth's rotation upon its axis. In short, rather than rotating every twenty-four hours, our planet's rotation would slow to the point it would turn only once per year. Then Earth's rotary motion would resemble that of Mercury (the closet planet to the Sun) which rotates only one and a half times per revolution around the Sun. Think of the similar effect Earth's gravity has on the Moon. The Moon rotates only once per orbit around the Earth (i.e., once per month), and so we see only one side of the Moon (the other side faces the Earth only during the dark phase of the lunar cycle). So the end result of the Earth orbiting closer to the Sun would be that the same side of the planet would face the brunt of solar heat for extended periods of time. That side would be hundreds of degrees hot while the dark side would be hundreds of degrees below zero (which in fact are the conditions on Mercury). Life on Earth would not be able to exist.[14]

However, if the Sun were much larger than it is, that too would prove catastrophic for life. A larger Sun would put out much higher levels of ultraviolet light—too much ultraviolet light, in fact, for life to survive.[15] Life on Earth is sustained by a "Goldilocks star."

The Sun provides the Earth with more unique properties than just its size. Most stars in the Milky Way (two-thirds, in fact) are binary stars or are grouped in clusters of three or more stars. Any planet that belongs to binary stars has an orbit too erratic to provide the stable and temperate environment necessary to sustain life, and the energy that planet receives would vary too much. The solitary status of our Sun is an essential quality for life.[16]

Fourth, *our neighboring planets are just right.* As it turns out, Earth benefits greatly from having large sibling planets such as Jupiter and Saturn patrolling the outer regions of the solar system. And both planets are needed. Saturn and Jupiter are the right size and distance to keep each other in a stable orbit. If either planet were substantially different, Jupiter would sling Saturn out of the solar system, and Jupiter would go into an elliptical orbit, which could eventually crash into us.[17] As it is, Jupiter acts as a cosmic vacuum sweeper for Earth. If Jupiter did not exist, Earth would be struck by space debris at a rate 10,000 times greater than it is. As it is, "extinction-causing

---

13. Ward and Brownlee, *Rare Earth*, 23. "It is often said that the sun is a typical star, but this is entirely untrue."
14. Ibid., 23–24.
15. Ibid., 22.
16. Ibid., 25.
17. Ibid., 21–22.

projectiles" strike our planet at the rate of once every 100 million years. Without Jupiter the rate would be once every 10,000 years, which would not give life enough time to recover.[18]

Fifth, *our location in the Milky Way is just right.* Our galaxy, the Milky Way, is 85,000 light years across. We are located about 25,000 lights years from the center. This turns out to be ideal for life. Just as our solar system has a habitable zone, so does our galaxy.[19] On the one hand, if we were closer to the center of the Milky Way, then we would be irradiated by cosmic rays and the particles emanating from exploding supernovae. On the other hand, if we were farther from the center, then there would be no heavy elements available. The outer bands are made up almost entirely of hydrogen and helium. The heavier, essential building blocks of life—oxygen, nitrogen, carbon, iron, etc.—are absent. Earth is located in the optimal region of the Milky Way: far enough from the center to escape most of the radiation yet near enough for all the major elements to be available.

There are basically three of types of galaxies in the universe: spiral, elliptical, and irregular.[20] The Milky Way is a large, spiral galaxy that has major spiral arms composed of stars and dust. We are located in a relatively open part of the Milky Way (our nearest star is four light-years away), between two spiral arms. Most stars are in globular clusters—tens of thousands of stars grouped within a small region—and these clusters are generally contained within the spiral arms of the Milky Way. Whatever planets might be located in these clusters are constantly bombarded with radiation and particles that would make life impossible.[21] Since our solar system resides in an open region between the spiral arms, Earth is spared from this high-intensity barrage.

In addition, Gonzalez and Richards point out that if our planet was situated within one of the spiral arms, then our night sky would be dramatically different from what we see now.[22] The cosmic dust would obscure everything. Rather than a canopy of stars, every evening would be shrouded in a dull fog. We would have had no reason to investigate beyond our planet since nothing else would be visible. Gonzalez and Richards contend that, in such a dreary setting, the scientific revolution more than likely would never have gotten off the ground. Our actual location is felicitous for astronomical investigations. Situated in "our highly accommodating perch," we enjoy "the best seating in the galaxy" for viewing the starry sky.[23]

18. Ibid., 238–39.
19. Ibid., 27.
20. Gonzalez and Richards, *Privileged Planet*, 144.
21. Ward and Brownlee, *Rare Earth*, 25–27.
22. Gonzalez and Richards, *Privileged Planet*, 146–51.
23. Ibid., 146.

Evidences of Universal Fine-Tuning

Beyond the local characteristics of our planet and its surrounding environment, the universe as a whole displays a number of remarkable examples of fine-tuning. The cosmos contains a long list of universal initial conditions and constants, each independent from the other, each essential for life to occur, which exhibit a level of calibration that is astounding. Our universe is poised on a razor's edge.

A dilemma faces writers who hope to communicate the full scope of these evidences to a popular audience. The subject matter at hand is by definition rather esoteric. In the typical discussion on universal fine-tuning, proponents present a plethora of scientific facts in a barrage that seems intended to overwhelm the reader—and they often succeed. Barrow and Tipler devote four-hundred pages of their book to example after example of fine-tuning taken from the fields of physics, astrophysics, biochemistry, quantum mechanics, and more.[24] Others, such as Hugh Ross, list dozens of the "cosmic coincidences" in brief bullet points that cover only about fifteen pages.[25] Either way, the presentations are both impressive and intimidating for those for whom science is not their home turf. We intend to offer a few of the more salient examples in everyday language so that (hopefully) the reader can get the gist of the universal fine-tuning argument.

First, *the relationships between the constants of nature must be exactly what they are to an amazing level of precision.* There are four fundamental forces: the strong-nuclear force, the weak-nuclear force, the electromagnetic force, and gravity. John Lennox explains that if the ratio of the nuclear strong force to the electromagnetic force were different by one part in 10^{16}, then the stars would not be able to form. This, of course, would mean there would be no Sun. Or if the ratio of the electromagnetic force to gravitational force were different by one part in 10^{40}, then only very small or very large stars would be able to form. Again, this would mean a star like our Sun could not exist.[26]

Second, *the rate of the expansion of the universe is calibrated with remarkable exactitude.* Stephen Hawking notes that, on the one hand, if the expansion of the universe had been less by one part in 10^{10}, standard big bang models show that the universe would quickly have collapsed. On the other hand, if the expansion had been more by one part in 10^{10}, then the universe today would be essentially empty.[27]

Third, Paul Davies and Hugh Ross give a great deal of attention to *the precise relationship between protons, electrons, and neutrons.* These, of course,

---

24. John D. Barrow and Frank J. Tipler, *The Anthropic Cosmological Principle* (Oxford: Oxford University Press, 1986), 122–576.

25. Hugh Ross, *The Fingerprint of God* (Orange, Calif.: Promise, 1991), 119–32.

26. John C. Lennox, *God's Undertaker: Has Science Buried God?* (Oxford: Lion, 2007), 69.

27. Cited by Alister E. McGrath, *A Fine-Tuned Universe: The Quest for God in Science and Theology* (Louisville: Westminster John Knox, 2009), 85.

are the building blocks of molecules, and physicists have discovered that an amazing accuracy was required in the ratio of one to the other in order for stars and planets to exist. For example, if the number of electrons were slightly different from the number of protons, then the electromagnetic forces would have overpowered the gravitational forces to the point stars and planets would not be able to form. How slight a difference are we talking about? In other words, what level of exactness was required? The answer is astounding. Davies and Ross report that it has been determined that the number of electrons must equal the number of protons to an accuracy of one part in 10^{37}.[28]

At this point it is helpful to consider how large a number 10^{37} really is. Simply put, 10^{37} is unimaginable. A number of this magnitude is beyond everyday human experience, so it risks losing any true significance to us. So Paul Davies came up with an illustration that helps to put things into a little better perspective. Imagine a marksman who is so skilled that he is able to shoot a coin with a pistol from a distance of 100 yards away. The odds of the typical person managing to pull off such a stunt are small, but there are sharpshooters who can make this type of shot with regularity. But what if the distance was not 100 yards, but on the other side of the universe? Now we are talking about odds so absurdly high that we dismiss them as impossible. But as Davies explains, that is the odds of 1 in 10^{37}.[29] Incredibly, the ratio of electrons to protons exhibit a level of calibration, that, if random, were as if a person using a pistol managed to shoot a coin located at the opposite side of the known universe.

Hugh Ross gives another illustration designed to show just how amazing the odds of 1 in 10^{37} really are. Imagine the United States covered in dimes. And this pile of dimes is so high it reaches to the moon. Now imagine one billion piles of the same size and magnitude. Suppose, out of that immense number of mounds of coins, a single dime is painted red. Now envision the challenge, while blindfolded, of having to pick out that red coin from all those coins and having only one chance to get it right. That is the odds of 1 in 10^{37}.[30] Sir Fred Hoyle, who coined the phrase "Big Bang," admitted that discoveries of such astronomical precision shook his atheism "to the core." He observed that the universe appeared as if a "super intellect has monkeyed with physics, as well as chemistry and biology."[31] Indeed.

Yet, the cosmos exhibits a level of precision that makes the previous examples pale into insignificance. Stephen Hawking has discovered that the rate of the expansion of the universe cannot be different from what it is by one part in 10^{55}. If it were any faster, there would be no stars, galaxies, or planets. If the

28. Ross, *The Creator and the Cosmos*, 109.
29. Cited by Lennox, *God's Undertaker*, 69.
30. Ross, *The Creator and the Cosmos*, 109.
31. Lennox, *God's Undertaker*, 69.

rate were any slower, the universe would be simply a giant black hole.[32] Roger Penrose, who was Hawking's collaborator in his initial work on black holes, has demonstrated that the entropy of the universe exhibits a precision of one part in $10^{(10)123}$. Keep in mind the number $10^{(10)123}$ far exceeds the number of atoms in the universe. Penrose states, "I cannot even recall seeing anything else in physics whose accuracy is known to approach, even remotely, a figure like one part in $10^{(10)123}$."[33]

The above instances are just a sampling from the long list of examples that could be provided. After surveying the evidence of the universe's precise calibration, Paul Davies concludes, "It seems as though someone has fine-tuned nature's numbers to make the Universe. . . . The impression of design is overwhelming."[34] Arno Penzias, winner of the Nobel Prize in physics, concurs: "Astronomy leads us to a unique event, a Universe which was created out of nothing, one with the very delicate balance needed to provide exactly the right conditions required to permit life, and one which has an underlying (one might say 'supernatural') plan)."[35] Either we "hit the cosmic jackpot" (Davies's phrase), or we are the recipients of extraordinary providential care. At the end of their discussion covering much of the same evidences just given, Ward and Brownlee quote a Clint Eastwood line from the movie *Dirty Harry*. "Do you feel lucky? Well do ya?"[36] Lucky? No. Blest? Definitely.

Objections to the Fine-Tuning Argument

Objections to the fine-tuning argument can be grouped into two categories: (1) those that argue that the discovery of fine-tuning is attributable to "the observation selection effect" and (2) those that appeal to the anthropic principle itself (and for that reason are often called "the anthropic principle objection").[37] The first objection is fairly easy to answer and, as for the second objection, more than one Christian philosopher has expressed his surprise that the argument gets much traction.[38]

The "observation selection effect" objection claims that the fine-tuning argument is based on the tendency to notice remarkable coincidences while ignoring other mundane yet pertinent data. Opponents claim that advocates of

---

32. Ross, *The Creator and the Cosmos*, 110.
33. Cited by William Lane Craig, "Design and the Anthropic Fine-Tuning of the Universe," in *God and Design: The Teleological Argument and Modern Science*, ed. Neil A. Manson (New York: Routledge, 2003), 157.
34. Cited by Lennox, *God's Undertaker*, 70.
35. Ibid., 57.
36. Ward and Brownlee, *Rare Earth*, 257.
37. Schnall, "Anthropic Observation Selection Effects and the Design Argument," 361–77.
38. Ibid. "I must admit that I still find the AP objection somewhat puzzling. I only hope that my analysis will prompt others to respond in a way that will allay the puzzlement" (362). William Lane Craig makes a similar statement (see "Design and the Anthropic Fine-Tuning of the Universe," 168–71).

the fine-tuning argument are like the fisherman who, after fishing in a lake using a net with three-inch holes, concludes that the lake contains no fish smaller than three inches.[39] In other words, the "observation selection effect" contends that the theist sees evidence of fine-tuning because his biases have colored his perspective.

In response, it must be admitted that the tendency to see evidence through jaundiced eyes is always a very real possibility. However, that does not appear to be what is happening in this case. The first discoverers of the universe's fine-tuned characteristics were not looking for any such evidence. Many, in fact, initially were skeptical of their own findings. Only after example after example of the fine-tuned constants accumulated independently did scientists call attention to the phenomena.

Richard Swinburne answers the "fishing net analogy" with the "firing squad analogy"—an illustration repeated by William Lane Craig.[40] Imagine standing before a firing squad of one hundred marksmen. They fire simultaneously on command, but you find that you are still standing. How did this happen? Though it is possible that all one hundred trained sharpshooters unintentionally missed, it is highly improbable. Ockham's razor (the principle that states, all things being equal, the simplest solution should be preferred) points to a more likely explanation: someone orchestrated a fake execution. The "observation selection effect" objection argues that we are amazed about something that may be merely fortuitous, but the objection seems to suffer a similar slashing by Ockham's blade. Craig likens the objection's reasoning to be similar to that of a silk merchant whose thumb just happened to have covered the moth hole of the cloth he just sold you. "My thumb had to be somewhere," he explains, and each place on the garment was equally improbable.[41] The "observation selection effect" objection does not apply to the fine-tuning argument.

The second argument, the "anthropic principle objection," is more subtle, and is even more unconvincing. It states that, given the fact we exist, we should not be surprised that the conditions necessary for our existence also exist. In other words, proponents of the argument are pointing out that our existence logically entails that the conditions for our existence also must exist. We are here, so the constants necessary for our existence must also be here. In his presentation of the "anthropic principle objection," Sober concludes that since we exist, "the constants must be right, regardless of whether the Universe was produced by intelligent design or by chance."[42] The conditions

39. The fishnet analogy comes from Elliott Sober, "The Design Argument," in *God and Design: The Teleological Argument and Modern Science*, ed. Neil A Manson (New York: Routledge, 2003), 43–44.

40. Craig, "Fine-Tuning of the Universe," 170.

41. Craig, "Design and the Anthropic Fine-Tuning of the Universe," 161.

42. Sober, "The Design Argument," 44–45.

for our existence are logically required by the fact we are here. Therefore, he concludes, the initial fine-tuned conditions were logically necessary.

In response, it must be pointed out that the "anthropic principle objection" confuses logical necessity with causality. Yes, the fact that we are here necessitates that the conditions for our existence also exists. But it does not follow that those conditions were necessary. For example, if a car accident occurs, then obviously the conditions for the accident to happen also existed. But those conditions did not necessarily exist. The problem with Sober's presentation of the anthropic objection is that he has the arrow of causality pointing the wrong way. Our existence logically necessitates that the constants be what they are, but our existence does not cause them to exist. In his response to Sober, Schnall makes an additional important point: the fact we exist entails that the conditions necessary for our existence also exist, but it does not entail that those conditions are fine-tuned.[43]

Conclusion

If a turtle is atop a fence post, then we can assume that someone put him there. And if the universe is poised upon a razor's edge, then we can believe it is because Someone willed it so. At this time the fine-tuning argument appears to provide one of the strongest empirical cases for intelligent design.[44]

REFLECTION QUESTIONS

1. How does the fine-tuning argument challenge the "Copernican principle of mediocrity"?

2. What is meant by the expression "local fine-tuning"?

3. What are the three types of "universal fine-tuning" given?

4. Why do authors such as Davies and Ross find it necessary to resort to outlandish illustrations to make the fine-tuning argument accessible?

5. What is the "observation selection effect" objection and how do fine-tuning proponents respond?

43. Schnall, "Anthropic Observation Selection Effects and the Design Argument," 370–71.
44. An expanded version of this chapter can be found in Kenneth D. Keathley, "Detecting the Invisible Gardner: The Fine-Tuning Argument," in *Defending the Faith: Engaging the Culture*, ed. Bruce A. Little and Mark D. Liederbach, 157–78 (Nashville: B&H, 2011).

Select Bibliography

Alexander, Denis. *Creation or Evolution: Do We Have to Choose?* Oxford: Monarch Books, 2008.

Alexander, T. D. *From Paradise to the Promised Land.* Grand Rapids: Baker Books, 1995.

Barr, James. "The Image of God in the Book of Genesis—A Study of Terminology." *BJRL* 51 (1968–69) 11–26.

Beale, G. K. *The Temple and the Church's Mission: A Biblical Theology of the Dwelling Place of God.* New Studies in Biblical Theology 17. Downers Grove: InterVarsity Press, 2004.

Behe, Michael J. *Darwin's Black Box: The Biochemical Challenge to Evolution.* New York: The Free Press, 1996.

Berry, R. J. and T.A. Noble, eds. *Darwin, Creation, and the Fall: Theological Challenges.* Nottingham: Apollos, 2009.

Bonhoeffer, Dietrich. *Creation and Fall: A Theological Interpretation of Genesis 1–3.* London: SCM Press Ltd, 1959.

Brown, William P. *Structure, Role and Ideology in the Hebrew and Greek Texts of Genesis 1:1–2:3.* SBL Dissertation Series 132. Atlanta: Scholars Press, 1993.

Cassuto, Umberto. *A Commentary on the Book of Genesis,* 2 vols. Vol. 1, *From Adam to Noah, Genesis I–VI:8.* Translated by Israel Abrahams. Jerusalem: Magnes 1961–64.

Clines, D. J. A. "The Image of God in Man." *TynBul* 19 (1968) 53–103.

Collins, C. John. *Did Adam and Eve Really Exist? Who They Were and Why You Should Care.* Wheaton, IL: Crossway, 2011.

Collins, Francis S. *The Language of God: A Scientist Presents Evidence for Belief*. New York: Free Press, 2006.

Collins, Jack. "A Syntactical Note (Genesis 3:15): Is the Woman's Seed Singular or Plural?" *TynB* 48.1 (1997) 139–48.

Conway Morris, Simon. *Life's Solution: Inevitable Humans in a Lonely Universe*. New York: Cambridge University Press, 2003.

Dembski, William A. *The End of Christianity: Finding a Good God in an Evil World*. Advance Reader's Copy. Nashville: B&H Academic, 2009.

Desmond, Adrian and James Moore. *Darwin: The Life of a Tormented Evolutionist*. New York: Warner Books, 1991.

Diere, S. D. *A New Glimpse of Day One: Intertextuality, History of Interpretation, and Genesis 1.1–5*. Berlin: Walter de Gruyter, 2009.

Falk, Darrel R. *Coming to Peace with Science: Bridging the Worlds Between Faith and Biology*. Downers Grove: InterVarsity Press, 2004.

Fields, Weston W. *Unformed and Unfilled*. Nutley, NJ: Presbyterian and Reformed Publishing Company, 1976.

Fishbane, Michael. *Text and Texture*. New York: Schocken Books, 1979.

Fodor, Jerry and Massimo Piattelli-Palmarini. *What Darwin Got Wrong*. New York: Farrar, Straus, and Giroux, 2010.

Foster, Charles. *The Selfless Gene: Living with God and Darwin*. Nashville: Thomas Nelson, 2009.

Fowler, Thomas B. and Daniel Kuebler. *The Evolution Controversy: A Survey of Competing Theories*. Grand Rapids: Baker Academic, 2007.

Gage, Warren Austin. *The Gospel of Genesis*. Winona Lake, IN: Carpenter Books, 1984.

Garner, Paul A. *The New Creationism: Building Scientific Theories on a Biblical Foundation*. England: Evangelical Press, 2009.

Gentry, Kenneth L. and Michael R. Butler. *Yea, Hath God Said?: The Framework Hypothesis/Six Day Creation Debate*. Eugene OR: Wipf and Stock Publishers, 2002.

Gonzalez, Guillermo and Jay W. Richards. *The Privileged Planet: How Our Place in the Cosmos is Designed for Discovery*. Washington, DC: Regnery Publishing, Inc., 2004.

Gunton, Colin E. *The Triune Creator: A Historical and Systematic Study*. Grand Rapids: WM. B. Eerdmans Publishing Company, 1998.

Haarsma, Deborah B. and Loren D. Haarsma. *Origins: A Reformed Look at Creation, Design, and Evolution*. Grand Rapids: Faith Alive Christian Resources, 2007.

Hamilton, James. "The Skull Crushing Seed of the Woman: Inner-Biblical Interpretation of Genesis 3:15." *SBJT* 10,2 (2006): 30–54.

Hamilton, Victor P. *The Book of Genesis Chapters 1–17*, NICOT (Grand Rapids: Eerdmans, 1990)

Hart, Ian. "Genesis 1:1–2:3 As a Prologue to the Book of Genesis." *TynBul* 46.2 (1995) 315–36.

Hasel, Gerhard F. "The Meaning of 'Let Us' in Gn 1:26." *Andrews University Seminary Studies* 13 (1975): 58–66.

Heidel, Alexander. *The Babylonian Genesis*. Chicago: The University of Chicago Press, 1942.

Humphreys, D. Russell. *Starlight and Time: Solving the Puzzle of Distant Starlight in a Young Universe*. Green Forest, AR: Master Books, 1994.

Laansma, Jon. *I Will Give You Rest*. Tübingen: Moher Siebeck, 1997.

Lamoureux, Denis O. *I Love Jesus and I Accept Evolution*. Eugene, OR: Wipf & Stock Publishers. 2009.

Jackson, Patrick Wyse. *The Chronologers' Quest: The Search for the Age of the Earth*. New York: Cambridge University Press, 2006.

Jónsson, Grunnlaugur A. *The Image of God: Genesis 1:26–28 in a Century of Old Testament Research*. Old Testament Series 26. Uppsala: Almqvist & Wiksell International 1988.

Kulikovsky, Andrew S. *Creation, Fall, Restoration: A Biblical Theology of Creation*. Scotland: Mentor, 2009.

Külling, Samuel R. *Are the Genealogies in Genesis 5 and 11 Historical and Complete, that is, Without Gaps?* Riehen, Switzerland: Immanuel-Verlag, 1996.

Lennox, John C. *Seven Days That Divide the World: The Beginnings According to Genesis and Science*. Grand Rapids: Zondervan, 2011.

May, Gerhard. *Creatio Ex Nihilo: The Doctrine of Creation out of Nothing in Early Christian Thought*. Translated by A. S. Worrall. Edinburg: T & T Clark, 1994.

McGrath, Alister E. *Darwinism and the Divine: Evolutionary Thought and Natural Theology*. United Kingdom: Wiley-Blackwell, 2011.

Meyer, Stephen C. *Darwin's Doubt: The Explosive Origin of Animal Life and the Case for Intelligent Design*. New York: HarperOne, 2013.

———. *Signature in the Cell: DNA and the Evidence for Intelligent Design*. New York: HarperOne, 2009.

Murray, Michael J. *Nature Red in Tooth and Claw: Theism and the Problem of Animal Suffering*. New York: Oxford University Press Inc., 2008.

Nevin, Norman C., ed. *Should Christians Embrace Evolution?: Biblical and Scientific Responses*. Phillipsburg, NJ: P&R Publishing, 2011.

Niels-Erik A. Andreasen, *The Old Testament Sabbath: A Tradition-Historical Investigation*. Vol. 7. Society of Biblical Literature. Missoula, MT: SBL, 1972.

Numbers, Ronald L. *The Creationists: The Evolution of Scientific Creationism*. New York: Alfred A. Knopf, Inc., 1992.

Oswalt, John N. *The Bible Among the Myths*. Grand Rapids: Zondervan, 2009.

Ross, Allen P. *Creation & Blessing*. Grand Rapids: Baker Publishing, 1988.

Ross, Hugh. *The Fingerprint of God*. Orange, CA: Promise Publishing, 1991.

_____. *A Matter of Days: Resolving a Creation Controversy*. Colorado Springs: NavPress, 2004.

Sailhamer, John H. *Genesis Unbound*. Sisters OR: Multnomah Books, 1996.

Sarna, Nahum M. *Genesis*. JPSTC. Philadelphia: Jewish Publication Society, 1989.

_____. *Understanding Genesis*. New York: Schocken Books, 1966.

Shapiro, James A. *Evolution: A View From the 21st Century*. Upper Saddle River, NJ: FT Press Science, 2011.

Snelling, Andrew A. *Earth's Catastrophic Past: Geology, Creation, and the Flood*. Vols. 1 and 2. Dallas: Institute for Creation Research, 2009.

Snoke, David. *A Biblical Case for an Old Earth*. Grand Rapids: BakerBooks, 2006.

Tsumura, David Toshio. *The Earth and the Waters in Genesis 1 and 2*. JSOTSS 83. Sheffield: JSOT Press, 1989.

Waltke, Bruce and Cathi J. Fredricks. *Genesis*. Grand Rapids: Zondervan, 2001.

Walton, John H. *The Lost World of Genesis One*. Downers Grove: IVP Academic, 2009),

Wenham, Gordon J. *Genesis 1–15*. WBC. Vol. 1. Waco, TX: Word Books, 1987.

_____. "Sanctuary Symbolism in the Garden of Eden Story." In *Preceedings of the Ninth World Congress of Jewish Studies*, 1986.

Whitcomb, John C. and Henry M. Morris. *The Genesis Flood*. Grand Rapids: Baker Book House, 1961.

Whorton, Mark S. *Peril in Paradise: Theology, Science, and the Age of the Earth*. Waynesboro, GA: Authentic Media, 2005.

Wilson, Robert R. *Genealogy and History in the Biblical World.* New Haven and London: Yale University Press, 1977.

Wise, Kurt P. *Faith, Form, and Time: What the Bible Teaches and Science Confirms About Creation and the Age of the Universe.* Nashville: B&H Publishers, 2002.

Young, Davis A. and Ralph F. Stearley. *The Bible, Rocks and Time: Geological Evidence for the Age of the Earth.* Downers Grove: IVP Academic, 2008.

Young, Edward J. *Studies in Genesis One.* Philadelphia: Presbyterian and Reformed Publishing, 1964.

Scripture Index

Genesis

1 . . . . 32, 58,
    59, 60, 61, 62, 63, 64, 65, 66, 71,
    73, 74, 77, 78, 79, 81, 83, 87, 88,
    89, 90, 113, 119, 120, 121, 123,
    124, 127, 129, 130, 132, 133, 134,
    135, 138, 139, 141, 144, 145, 147,
    148, 149, 150, 151, 152, 153, 157,
    158, 159, 162, 164, 165, 210, 231,
    259, 267, 280, 281, 282, 284, 378
1:1 . . . .27, 33, 45, 61, 65, 66, 68, 69, 70,
    71, 73, 74, 75, 76, 77, 78, 79, 80,
    81, 83, 88, 89, 91, 111, 113, 114,
    117, 138, 147, 148, 149, 151, 152,
    153, 154, 155, 161, 181, 228, 230
1:1–2 . . . . 73, 74, 78, 80, 118, 259
1:1–2:2 114
1:1–2:3 . . . . 68, 74, 80, 83, 84,
                87, 88, 89, 92, 99,
                117, 124, 126, 127,
                131, 132, 134, 137,
                149, 153, 154, 160,
              162, 228, 229, 231, 233
1:1–2:4 . . . . 140, 231
1:1–3 79
1:1–5 . . . . 69, 78, 80
1:1–11:26 290
1:1–11:32 285
1:1, 21, 27 68
1:1–23 130
1:1–31 86
1:2 . . . . 59, 60, 64, 65, 69, 73, 74,
    77, 78, 79, 80, 88, 89, 111,
    112, 114, 115, 116, 117, 118,
    140, 144, 148, 149, 150, 151, 153,
    154, 155, 228, 280, 281, 282, 290
1–2 . . . . 22, 43, 46, 57, 60, 66,
           138, 204, 218, 219, 233,
           234, 259, 260, 261
1:2–2:3 . . . . 65, 78, 154
1:2–31 . . . . 74, 77, 79, 148,
              149, 150, 153
1:3 . . . . . 62, 65, 73, 79, 80, 89, 111, 132
1–3 . . . . 15, 22, 23, 45, 189, 237,
           238, 255, 269, 270
1:3–2:3 80
1:3, 10, 12, 18, 21, 25, 31 249
1:3–31 73
1:4 128
1–4 260
1:4, 10, 12, 18, 21, 25, 31 . . . . . . 32, 280
1:5 165
1–5 383
1:5, 8, 13, 19, 23, 31 157
1:5, 8, 13, 23, 31 157
1:5, 14–16 159
1:6 297
1:6–7 89
1:6–8 . . . . .214, 282, 299
1:6–10 279
1:6–13 280
1:7 . . . . .66, 113
1:7, 16, 25, 26, 31 113
1:7, 16, 25, 26, 31 66
1:9 282
1:9–10 . . . . 90, 281
1:10 148

1:11. 74
1–11 . . . . .20, 74, 76, 77, 170, 171, 201,
                228, 229, 234, 276, 286, 287
1:11–12. . . . . .27, 113, 273
1–11:26. . . . . .251, 288
1:12. 281
1:14. . . . . .128, 161
1:14–18. 162
1:14–19. . . . . .62, 161
1–15 . . . . 74, 75, 229, 246, 248, 252
1:16. . . . . .66, 113, 204
1–17 .233, 235
1:18. 128
1:20–21. 68
1:20–23. 282
1:20–27. 281
1:21. . . . . .62, 266
1:21–22. 68
1:21, 24–25 230
1:21, 25. 113
1:21, 25, 27. 66
1:21, 27. . . . . .68, 149
1:22. 230
1:22, 28. 93
1:24–25. . . . . .122, 282
1:25. . . . . .62, 66, 113
1:26. . . . . . . 99, 228, 229, 230, 232, 234
1:26–27. . . 39, 66, 68, 88, 113, 228, 232
1:26, 28. . . . . .89, 154, 288
1:26–28. . . . . . . 172, 228, 232, 234, 282
1:26–31. . . . . .227, 233
1:27. . . . . .88, 228, 229, 230
1:27–28. 68
1:28. . . . . .46, 230, 282, 284
1:28–29. 235
1:28–30. . . . . .227, 260
1:29–30. . . . . .83, 260, 264
1:30. 257
1:31. . . . . 66, 113, 117, 143, 255, 280
2 . . . . . . .46, 83, 86, 87, 88, 89, 90, 103,
                104, 121, 129, 132, 141, 144,
            147, 149, 150, 162, 165, 231, 233
2:1. . . . . .91, 92, 143, 154

2:1–3. . . . . 91, 94, 98, 99, 139, 140, 163
2:1, 4. 77
2:1–17. . . . . 85, 103, 138, 144, 163
2:2. . . . . 92, 97, 133, 134, 143, 164, 281
2:2, 3. 66
2:2–3. . . . . .163, 164, 247
2:2–4. 113
2:3. . . . . 66, 68, 91, 93, 95, 113, 143
2–3 . . . . . . 98, 105, 246, 247, 267, 283
2:4. . . . . .46, 83, 88, 89, 113, 121,
                    122, 124, 159, 160, 170
2:4–3:24 102
2:4–7. . . . . .83, 101, 300
2:4–24. 89
2:4–25. . . . . .83, 88, 89, 149
2:5. . . . . 83, 84, 85, 86, 88,
                        89, 102, 104, 105
2:5–6. . . . . .89, 297
2:5, 15. 85
2:6. . . . . .84, 89
2:7. . . . . .27, 39, 66, 84, 85, 88, 89,
                    90, 122, 283, 380, 384
2:8. . . . . 84, 85, 86, 101, 283
2:8–9. 84
2:8–14. 46
2:8–17. .85, 101
2:9. . . . . .85, 89
2:9–14. . . . . .85, 86
2:9–17. 85
2:9–25. 89
2:10. 85
2:10–14. . . . . 84, 101, 150, 264, 300
2:11. 141
2:11–12. 383
2:11–13. 86
2:12. 141
2:13–14. 150
2:14. 86
2:15. . . . . .86, 101, 102, 103, 104,
                    105, 106, 142, 260, 383
2:15–17. . . . . .85, 162, 246
2:15–23. 122
2:15–25. 227

2:16. . . . . .103, 247, 248
2:16–3:13 247
2:16–17. . . . . 235, 245, 246,
247, 248, 249
2:16–18, 21–22 250
2:17. . . . . 86, 159, 246,
248, 265, 267
2:18. . . . . .86, 122, 129, 246
2:18–20. 162
2:18–23. . . . . 87, 88
2:18–24. . . . . .246, 247
2:18–25. 86
2:19. . . . . 46, 90, 122, 129, 132, 280
2:19–20. . . . . .231, 233
2:20. . . . . .86, 122, 125, 162
2:20, 23. 233
2:21. . . . . 87, 122
2:21–22. 383
2:21–25. 385
2:22. . . . . 90, 384
2:22–25. 123
2:23. . . . . .87, 162, 250
2:23–24. 87
2:24. . . . . 87, 238
2:25. . . . . .88, 246, 247, 250
3 . . . . 30, 65, 88, 89, 248,
251, 252, 253, 257,
259, 260, 267, 269, 276
3:1. . . . . 247, 250, 272, 283
3:1–5. . . . . .245, 247, 249
3:1–6. .249, 250
3:1–8. 250
3:2. . . . . .248, 283
3:3. . . . . .235, 248
3:4. . . . . .248, 251
3:5. 248
3:6. . . . . 249, 252, 253, 283
3:6–7. 245
3:6–8. 249
3:7. . . . . .247, 249, 283
3:7–10, 24. 246
3:8. . . . . 49, 106, 143, 145, 249
3:8–24. 84

3:9–13. 250
3:10, 12–13 250
3:14. . . . . .272, 283
3:14–15. . . . . .264, 266, 271
3:15. . . . . 46, 271, 272, 273, 274,
275, 276, 277, 278, 283
3:16. 266
3:17. . . . . .279, 280
3:17–19. 267
3:18. . . . . .83, 264
3:19. . . . . .85, 265, 267
3:21. . . . . .133, 142, 258
3:22. . . . . .74, 250, 251
3:22–24. 141
3:23. . . . . .102, 104, 105
3:24. . . . . .85, 150
3:32. 283
4 . . . . .265, 273
4:1–2, 25. 283
4:1–16. 272
4:2, 12. 105
4–5 . . . . .189, 297, 383
4:12. 383
4:17. 383
4:17–24. 273
4:19–24. 273
4:21. 383
4:22. 383
4:23–24. . . . . .172, 273
4:24. 95
4:25. . . . . .273, 274
5 . . . . 169, 171, 172, 174,
176, 238, 246, 283
5:1. 170
5:1–2. . . . . .68, 171, 172
5:1–32. 273
5:2. 282
5:3. . . . . .229, 234
5:3–31. 171
5:24. 172
5:29. 171
5:32. 171
6:1–10. 287

6:3–4. 74
6:5. . . . . .279, 290
6:5–7, 11–13 291
6:6. 280
6:8. 310
6:9. 170
6–9 . . . . 189, 192, 207, 309
6:9–12, 13–22 288
6:11. 280
6:11–12. 287
6:12. 280
6:13. 280
6:13–22. 287
6:16. 279
6:17. 289
7:1–5, 6–9, 10–16, 17–24. 288
7:1–10. 287
7:3. . . . . .153, 288
7:4, 21–23. .289
7:11. 280
7:11–16. 287
7:13–14. 280
7:15. 280
7:17–24. . . . . .281, 287
7:18. 281
7:18–19. 281
7:19. 289
7:19–23. 291
7:23. 273
8 . . . . .281, 284
8:1. . . . . .281, 287
8:1–2. 282
8:1–5. 287
8:1–14, 15–17, 18–22. 288
8:2. 282
8:3–5. . . . . .282, 292
8:5. 281
8:6–12. 282
8:6–14. 287
8:7. 292
8, 9 282
8:9. 153
8:11. 281

8:14. 292
8:15–19. 287
8:16, 18. 282
8:17. 282
8:17–19. 282
8:19–23. 290
8:20–22. 287
8:21. . . . . .280, 282, 291
8:21–22. 284
8:22. . . . . .92, 133
9 282
9:1. . . . . .282, 284
9:1–2. 282
9:1–7, 8–11, 12–17 288
9:1–17. 287
9:2–3. 284
9:3. 284
9:6. . . . . 227, 228, 234, 235, 282
9:11. . . . . .153, 175
9:11, 15. 291
9:12–16. 266
9:18–19. 287
9:18–29. 283
9:20. 283
9:21. 283
9:21–22. 273
9:23. 283
9:24. 283
9:24–27. 171
9:25. . . . . .279, 283
9:25–27. 283
10 . . . . 169, 171, 172, 173, 283
10:1. 170
10:2, 6, 21. .171
10:5, 20, 31. 171
10:10. 147
10:19. 172
10:21, 24. 172
10:21–31. 172
10:22. 172
10:25. 172
11 . . . . 169, 171, 172, 174, 238
11:1. 288

11:10 170
11:10–26 172
11:10–31 273
11:14–26 172
11:27 170
12:1–3 47
12:3 277
12:7 272
13:9, 15 291
13:10 85
13:15 272
14:4–8 273
14:13 173
15 150
15:3 274
15:18 150
16:10 274
17:6–7 277
18:18, 25 152
18:25 148
19:4–8 273
19:5 288
21:13 274
21:15 83
21:22 91
22:17–18 277
22:18 . . . . 152, 274
24:60 274
25:12 170
25:12–18 169
25:19 170
26:5 102
28:14 272
29:14 159
30:43 289
31:1–2, 22–32 150
35:11 277
35:23–26 173
36:1, 9 170
36:1–43 169
36:9 85
37:2 170
38:8–9 274

39:11 92
41:54–57 288
41:56–57 291
45:8 149
46:10 75
46:18 173
46:27 173
49:1 75
49:9–10 277

Exodus

1:1 79
2:2–3 113
3:12 142
6:12 173
6:14–25 173
6:16–20 173
6:26 173
9:14, 16 288
12:16 96
12:40 176
15:17 66
16:23–30 96
20 . . . . 145, 153, 158
20:1–2 229
20:8 94
20:8–11 . . . . 91, 95, 99, 126, 158
20:9–11 164
20:10 98
20:11 . . . . 66, 80, 93, 94, 113,
                     117, 125, 130, 133, 139,
                     149, 153, 158, 164, 282
23:12 . . . . 93, 96
23:34 95
25:1 141
25:7 141
25:31–39 95
26:31 141
28:4, 29 142
28:9 141
29:37 94
30:11 141
30:17 141

30:22. 141
30:29. 94
30:34. 141
31 153
31:1. 141
31:3. 140
31:12. 141
31:12–17. 140
31:17. . . . . 130, 133, 153, 164
34:6. 98
34:10. . . . . 67, 113
34:21. . . . . 93, 96
35:2. 98
35:2–3. 140
35:3. 96
35:35. 98
39:6–7. 141
39:32. 143
39–40 140
39:43. . . . . 142, 143
40:2, 27. 140
40:9–11. 143
40:33. 92
40:33–34. 143
40:34–38. 142

Leviticus

3:8, 28. 96
12 245
16:4. 142
16:29. 96
18:5. 105
19:3–4. 96
23 96
23:2. 96
23:32. 93
23:34. 95
24:5–9. 95
24:8. 95
25 95
25:10. 94
26:1–2. 96
26:12. 106, 143

Numbers

1:53. 105
3:7–8. . . . . .103, 105, 142
4:23–24, 26 105
8:25–26. . . . . 103, 142
8:26. . . . . 103, 142
14:7. . . . . .32, 259, 289
15:32–36. 96
16:30. 67
17:9. 105
18:5–6. . . . . 103, 142
28:2. 142
28:9–10. 95
33:52. 228
34:1–12. 172
35:21–22. 272

Deuteronomy

1:39. 246
2:25. 289, 291
3:24. 77
4:2. 248
4:16. 229
4:19. . . . . .91, 105, 289
4:32. 67
5:21. 252
11:12. 75, 152
12:9–10. 97
12:32. 248
17:3. 91
23:15. 143
28:48. 249
29:5. 257
32:8. 173
32:10. 151
32:33. 266

Joshua

5:12. 92
5:13–15. 150
6:3–4. 95
10:12–14. 310

Judges

14:4 159

Ruth

4:18–22 173

1 Samuel

2:6–8 26
6:5 228

2 Samuel

7:6–7 143
7:13 274

1 Kings

4:34 291
6:1 176
6:23–28 141
6:29 141
7:47 289
8 140
10:24 291
22:19 91

2 Kings

4:23 95
5:14 95
10:4 289
11:18 228
16:18 95
17:16 91
19:15 153
19:15, 19 152

1 Chronicles

7:13 173
7:23–27 173
23:31 95
23:32 . . . . 103, 142

2 Chronicles

2:12 153

8:13 95
31:3 95
35:23 138
36:23 291

Ezra

3:4 76
6:1–6 76
6:38 76
6:49–52 61

Nehemiah

6:3 . . . . 92, 93
9:6 . . . . 26, 33, 66, 71, 91, 113
13:15–21 96

Job

1:21 249
3:8 61
4:17 71
4:19 84
7:12 . . . . 61, 266
8:7 147
9:8 214
9:13 . . . . 61, 62
9:17 275
10:8–12 71
10:9 84
15:7–9, 40 250
26:12–13 62
27:16 84
28:24 289
30:4, 7 83
30:19 84
31:15 71
32:22 71
33 69
33:4 71
35:10 71
36:3 71
36:27 84
36:32 69
36–41 123

37:3 289
37:6 69
37:7 71
38:7 33
38:8–11 69
38:19 162
38:19–20 132
38–41 . . . . 260, 266
40:15 71
40:25–41:34 61
41:11 289
41:25 113
42:12 75

Psalms

1:3 81
2 148
2:2 148
8 . . . . 32, 123, 235
8:1–9 32
8:5 39
8:5–8 39
19 123
19:1 31
19:1–6 21
19:7–11 22
33 123
33:6 81
33:6, 9 . . . . 31, 69
40:4–5 61
44:19–20 61
51:10 66
51:12 66
74:12–19 61
74:13–14 . . . . 62, 266
87:4 61
89:9–12 62
89:9–15 61
90:1 96
90:2 . . . . 27, 81
90:3 84
90:4 . . . . 122, 125, 159, 160, 165
92 95

95 123
95:11 . . . . .97, 144, 145
96:5 26
102:25–27 28
104:2 . . . . 162, 214
104:9 69
104:19–21 . . . . 260, 265
104:24–28 260
104:25–26 . . . . 61, 62
104:29 84
104:30 67
107 34
115:15 26
119:73 71
119:90 33
132 . . . . 139, 145
132:7–8, 13–14 139
132:8 139
132:14 . . . . 144, 145
136:5–9 29
139:11 275
139:13–16 71
147:15–18 69
148 . . . . 32, 123, 260
148:1–5 113
148:1–6 32
148:2 91
148:5–6 69
148:7–14 32

Proverbs

1:7 250
3:19–20 32
6:6–11 98
6:31 95
8:22 76
8:22–23 79
8:22–36 32
8:23 75
8:27 66
8:29 69
8:30–31 32
21:25 98

22:2 71
24:16 95
30:5–6 248

Ecclesiastes

1 53
1:5–7 . . . . 260, 265
7:8 75
12:1 71

Song of Songs

4:16 103

Isaiah

1:13 95
2:4 105
14:4 92
14:12–15 111
17:1 266
17:7 71
24:1 49
24:8 92
24:12 116
27:1 61
27:1–2 62
29:16 84
30:7 61
34:4 49
34:11 . . . . 115, 116, 117, 118
37:16 153
37:16, 20 152
40:6–8 265
40:21 74
40:22 214
41:4, 26 74
41:8 272
41:20 . . . . 67, 113
42:5 26
42:24 75
43:7 113
44:2, 24 71
44:9–10 85
44:24 81

45:5 26
45:6–7 260
45:7–8, 18–19 26
45:12 69
45:18 . . . . 115, 116
46 75
46:10 . . . . 74, 75, 81, 152
48:6–7 67
48:12–15 75
48:13 69
49:5 71
51:3 . . . . 86, 150
51:9–10 61
51:9–11 62
54:1–10 47
57:16 113
57:19 66
58:7 249
58:13 95
60:19–20 . . . . 161, 162
65:17 77
65:17–18 . . . . 48, 67
65:20 260
65:21–25 105
65:25 257
66:1 144
66:1–2 . . . . 138, 139

Jeremiah

1:5 . . . . 71, 94
4:23 . . . . 115, 117, 118
4:23–26 151
4:27 116
5:22 69
10:12 . . . . 32, 214
10:16 81
17:19–27 95
17:21–22 96
18:2 122
23:24 77
25:26, 29–30 152
26:1 151
26:6 152

27:1 151
27:5–6 149
28:1 . . . . 147, 151
31:16 113
31:31–34 47
31:32 67
31:35–36 69
31:36 92
33:25 69
49:34 151
51:15 . . . . 26, 32

Lamentations

1:10 95
2:6 95

Ezekiel

11:17–21 47
20:16–24 96
25:1 272
28:11–19 111
29:3 266
29:3–6 61
32:2–8 61
35:5 272
36:9 105
36:26–27 47
36:33–36 145
36:35 . . . . 85, 150
37 85
37:9 85
37:10 289
44:14 . . . . 103, 142
47:10–12 260

Daniel

2:38 291
4:22 291
5:19 291
7:5 266
8:17–19 75
9:12 289

Hosea

1:2 76
9:9 159
10:9 159

Joel

2:3 . . . . 86, 150

Amos

5:8 69
8:5 96
9:2–3 61
9:6 69
9:7 173
9:13–14 105

Jonah

1:9 39

Micah

4:3 105
5:1 74

Habakkuk

1:12 74
3:8–11, 14–15 62

Zechariah

4:10, 14 152
12:1 214
14:8 . . . . 86, 150

Matthew

1 174
1:8 173
1:11 174
11 174
19 238
19:4 . . . . 45, 76
24:21 76
24:38–39 290

Mark

1:5 132
1:21, 29 97
3:1 97
10:6 76
13:19 76
15:38 145

Luke

2:1 291
3:23–38 173
3:38 238
4:16 97
4:44 97
13:10 97
17:26–27 310

John

1:1 76
1:1–3 51
1:3 . . . . 38, 70
1:14 . . . . 106, 145
2:1–11 219
2:10 219
2:11 220
5:17 133
8:31–32, 44 273
8:44 . . . . 111, 251, 278

Acts

4:24 . . . . 26, 32
13:10 278
13:14, 42, 44 97
17:2 97
17:24–26 30
17:25, 28 71
17:25–28 34
17:26 . . . . 45, 173, 239
18:4 97

Romans

1:3 277
1:18–21 50
1:20 260
1:22–31 50
3:25–26 47
4:17 . . . . 26, 70
5 . . . . 189, 239, 260, 264, 265
5:12 . . . . 257, 260, 267
5:12–14 239
5:12–21 251
5:21–21 239
8 . . . . 264, 265
8:11–22 321
8:19 50
8:19–22 50
8:19–23 . . . . 53, 252
8:20 53
8:20–23 265
8:21 50
8:22 265
11:36 34
14:5 99
14:5–23 97
15:20 277
16:20 277

1 Corinthians

8:6 . . . . 38, 51
11:7–12 238
15 . . . . 189, 239, 260, 264, 265
15:20–49 239
15:21 257
15:21–22 239
15:22 251
15:28 . . . . 34, 52
15:45 384
15:45–49 240

2 Corinthians

11:3 238

Galatians

3:16 277
3:16, 19 278
4:4 . . . . . 277, 278
5:19 245

Ephesians

1:10 . . . . . 50, 52
4:24 235
5:28–31 85

Colossians

01:16 33
1:17 . . . . . 34, 51
1:17–18 52
1:20 50
2:14–15 47
2:16–17 97
3:10 235

1 Thessalonians

5:11 98

2 Thessalonians

3:10 98

1 Timothy

2:13–14 238
2:14 251
4:4–5 32

2 Timothy

2:8 277

Hebrews

1:1–3 . . . . . 38, 51
1:3 . . . . . 34, 51
1:10 76
2 235
2:14 278
2:14–15 47
3 289

3:7, 13 130
4 . . . . . 123, 133, 134, 164
4:1–11 97
4:3 45
4:3–11 163
4:4 133
4:4, 9–10 130
4:9 97
4:9–11 163
7 133
10:19–20 145
11:3 . . . . . 70, 81
11:13 26

James

1:14–15 252
3:9 . . . . . 227, 235
3:17–18 209

1-Peter

3:8 122

2 Peter

3:1–13 49
3:3–7 . . . . . 199, 290, 297
3:4 76
3:5–7 291
3:6 284
3:8 . . . . . 125, 159, 160, 180
3:12 50
3:13 51

1 John

1:5 161
2:2 47
2:16 249
3:8 . . . . . 273, 278
3:10 278

Revelation

3:14 76
4:11 30
12 277

12:1–5 278
12:9 277
20:2 277
20:11 50
21:1 50
21:1–2 51
21:3 49

21:18 145
21–22 . . . . 48, 145, 261
22 45
22:1–2 . . . . 49, 86, 150
22:1–3 49
22:5 . . . . 161, 162
22:18–19 248

Ancient Sources Index

2 Baruch

21:4 . . . . 69, 77
54:15, 19 251

2 Enoch

24:2 . . . . 69, 76, 77

2 Esdras

4:30 251
7:118 251

2 Maccabees

7:22–29 69
7:28 69

4 Esdras

6:38 80

4 Ezra

3:4 . . . . 69, 77
6:6 76
6:38 . . . . 69, 77

Abodah Zarah

22b 245

Abot

3:15 235

Enuma Elish

IV:14–48, 96–100 62
IV:41, 95, 112 62

Exodus Rabbah

25:12 96

Irenaeus, *Against the Heresies*

4.20.1 38

Josephus, *Against Apion*

2:175 97

Josephus, *Antiquitates judaicae*

16:43 97

Josephus, *The Jewish War*

3, 7:7 139

Jubilees

2:2 . . . . 69, 80
22, 4 76

Midrash Genesis Rabbah

1.9.1 69
16:5 142

Shabbat

146a 245

Sirach

15:14 77
24:9 76
25:24 251
39:25 76

Targum Pseudo-Jonathan: Genesis

2:15 103

The Gospel of Philip

  75:2 42

Wisdom of Solomon

  2:23–24 251

Yebamot

  103b 245

Yoma

  54b 139, 150